NATIONALISM AND REFORM IN INDIA

BY

WILLIAM ROY SMITH

NEW HAVEN
YALE UNIVERSITY PRESS
LONDON · HUMPHREY MILFORD · OXFORD UNIVERSITY PRESS
1938

CONTENTS

FOREWORD

This book is the result of eighteen years of study, travel, and interest in the people and problems of India. We spent the winter of 1919–20 in India, when feeling was running high over the events of the previous spring. We visited the Jallianwala Bagh a few months after the "massacre" of Amritsar, and reached London in the early summer, in time to attend all the debates in Parliament on the conduct of General Dyer.

In 1929–30 we visited all the British dominions and protectorates in Africa and every town where there is a considerable Indian community. In 1934 we were in Fiji, Australia, and New Zealand. These journeys made possible innumerable conversations and conferences with British officials, with nonofficial British residents and travelers, and with Indians of all classes and castes.

Much of the research was done in many summers spent in London. Grateful recognition should be given to the librarians of the India Office, and of the British Museum, especially those in the Newspaper Room. A deep debt of gratitude is also due to Professor John C. Archer of Yale University, whose careful reading of the manuscript made early publication possible.

All the chapters, except the last, were subject to continual revision and rewriting as events in India changed or modified the political outlook. Thus, the last chapter lacks a conclusion as the author postponed writing any summary until he knew the reactions of the people of India to the new Constitution. The Bibliographical Note, complete as far as it goes, was left unfinished.

Had the author written a dedication, I feel sure it would have been addressed to the four hundred and eighty students, who, since 1912, have attended his lectures on "British Imperialism"; whose interest and enthusiasm were a never-failing encouragement, and whose letters and postcards—literally from the ends of the earth—were a constant delight. They seemed to prove that two of the author's ruling passions are communicable—a love of study and a love of travel.

M. P. S.

September, 1938

NATIONALISM AND REFORM IN INDIA

CHAPTER I

HISTORICAL SURVEY (1600–1917)

INDIA has never attained political unity. It includes within its limits at the present time British, French, and Portuguese possessions and the independent principalities of Nepal and Bhutan. There is a lack of uniformity even in the British area, although efforts are now being made to narrow the gap between British India and the Indian States which are subject to the paramount authority of the Crown in all external affairs. The centrifugal forces that destroyed the Mogul (Mughal) Empire are still active and it is probable that they will wreck the modern Empire if it is brought prematurely under Indian control. A large measure of Home Rule has been granted, but it is to be hoped that independence and the withdrawal of the small British army will be postponed until the people have learned to govern their country and to protect it from anarchy and invasion.

The Indian Empire of Great Britain is not coterminous with India as a geographical unit. It does not include the whole peninsula and it does include Baluchistan and a few other territories that lie beyond the physical limits of India. Excluding Burma, it has an area of 1,575,187 square miles and a population (1931) of 338,170,632 people. There are two chief race stocks and several smaller ones blended together in every conceivable proportion. These chief stocks are the Dravidian in the south and the Indo-Aryan in the north. Corresponding in a general way to this distribution of races, there are two main linguistic groups, the Dravidian, spoken by 71,642,000 people and the Indo-European (Aryan) spoken by 257,488,000. There are wide dialectical variations and many vernaculars that do not belong to either of the major groups.

These facts are important, but their significance can easily be exaggerated. The majority of the books written about India take it for granted that because racial and linguistic homogeneity is more or less essential to the growth of nationalism in the West it is equally essential in the East. As a matter of fact there is no race problem in India, as "race" is ordinarily understood. It is true that racial differences were in some measure responsible for the origin of the caste system and it is also true that there is a certain amount of race prejudice between Indians and Europeans. There is, however, no conscious connection between race and caste at the present time and there is every reason to believe that if the political element were eliminated the feeling against Europeans would disappear. The language problem is more difficult, but it is by no means insuperable. India will always be governed by a small minority of its people and they will be able to communicate with one another either in English or in Hindustani (Hindi-Urdu). The federal system of government will be used in any case and the large polyglot provinces of the present day will undoubtedly be broken up into smaller administrative units corresponding more closely with the linguistic grouping of the population.

Another common mistake in dealing with India is the tendency to underestimate the influence of religion. This is especially true of Indian writers themselves. Educated according to Western tradition and imbued with Western ideas of nationalism, they are apt to forget that while patriotism is a very modern concept in India the feud between Hindus and Moslems has lasted for nearly a thousand years. In 1931, Hindus constituted 68.24 per cent of the population, Moslems 22.16, Buddhists (chiefly in Burma) 3.65, tribal groups 2.36, Christians 1.79, Sikhs 1.24, Jains .35, Parsees .03, Jews .01, and minor religions .16. With Burma excluded, the Buddhist percentage would be negligible, and the others slightly higher.

There are two main administrative areas, British India and the Indian States. British India, as defined by act of Parliament in 1889, includes "all territories and places within Her [His] Majesty's dominions which are for the time being governed by Her [His] Majesty through the Governor-General of India, or through any Governor or other officer subordinate to the Governor-General of India." It covers about 55 per cent of the territory of the Indian Empire and contains 76 per cent of the population. It consists of eleven major provinces—Bengal, Bombay, Madras, Bihar and Orissa, the United Provinces of Agra and Oudh, the Punjab, the Central Provinces and Berar, Sind, Assam, and the North-West Frontier Province—with a population of 256,000,000; and six minor provinces—British Baluchistan, Delhi, Ajmer-Merwara, Coorg, the Andaman and Nicobar Islands, and Panth Piploda—with a population of about 2,000,000. The system of dyarchy, the most essential feature of the Montagu-Chelmsford plan of government, was put into operation only in the major provinces, the minor provinces being excepted either because they are small or backward or because they occupy strategic positions.

The Indian States may be defined as territories governed by rulers under the suzerainty of His Majesty exercised through the Governor-General or through any governor or other officer subordinate to the Governor-General. They occupy about 45 per cent of the area of India and contain 24 per cent of the population. According to the usual reckoning, there are 562 of them in all, varying in size from Hyderabad with 14,555,000 inhabitants to tiny districts which consist of only a few small villages. More than half of the total population of the State area live in the ten largest states—Hyderabad, Mysore, Travancore, Kashmir and Jammu, Gwalior, Jaipur, Baroda, Jodhpur, Udaipur, and Rewa.

The Paramount Power controls the external affairs of the states, including their relations with one another. It also exercises a certain amount of supervision over internal affairs, which varies from state to state and is regulated partly by usage and partly by sanads, i.e., charters, treaties, and other agreements. It may, for example, intervene in any state to settle a dispute over the right of succession, to prevent gross misrule, to protect religious minorities, to acquire land for military purposes, or to determine the size of the chief's army. The majority of the states deal directly with the government of India or its agents, but a few small ones in Assam, Bengal, the Punjab, and the United Provinces are still under the supervision of the provincial governments.

The administrative history of India since the beginning of

British intervention may be divided into two main periods: I. The Period of Company Rule from 1600 to 1858; II. The Period of Crown Rule from 1858 to the Present Time. The first period may in turn be further divided into two sub-periods. From the founding of the East India Company in 1600 until about the time of the Battle of Plassey in 1757, in Bengal, the Company was primarily a trading corporation. It laid down regulations for its own employees, but it made no general effort to establish territorial sovereignty or to bring the Indians under its control. After the victory at Plassey, however, it was compelled gradually to assert complete administrative jurisdiction over Bengal and other parts, and to legislate for Indians as well as for its European employees. From that time onward there were two main tendencies at work. In the first place, by war, intrigue, and disregard of the Indian laws of inheritance and adoption, the Company gradually extended its authority over other parts of the country or, to use the modern terminology, British India grew larger and the area of the states became more restricted. The discontent aroused by this ruthless policy of territorial expansion was the fundamental cause of the Great Mutiny of 1857. The second tendency of the period was the steady growth of parliamentary interference in Indian affairs which culminated in 1858 in the final transfer of the government from the Company to the Crown.

"The Governor and Company of Merchants of London trading into the East Indies" was chartered by Queen Elizabeth, December 31, 1600, and was rechartered several times during the next century. It had some trouble with Courteen's Association (1635–57), but the first serious attack upon its monopoly was made in 1698 when "The English Company trading to the East Indies" was established. The rivalry with this organization, though bitter while it lasted, was of short duration. There was a temporary union of the two corporations in 1702 and a final amalgamation in 1708 under the title of "The United Company of Merchants of England trading to the East Indies."

Under the original charter of 1600 the machinery of government in England, the so-called home administration of Indian affairs, was composed of a General Court of stockholders, a Governor, and twenty-four committees. Sir Thomas Smith, an alderman of London and governor of the Levant Company, was the first Governor. The committees were not really committees in the modern sense of the word, but were twenty-four individuals who constituted a Board or Court of Directors. Specific qualifications for membership in the courts were gradually adopted. At the beginning of the eighteenth century every holder of £500 worth of stock was a member of the General Court, now called the Court of Proprietors, and every holder of £2,000 worth of stock was eligible for election to the Court of Directors. No member of the Court of Proprietors could cast more than five votes. The Proprietors elected the Directors and also had the power to overrule their proceedings. The classic example of the exercise of this power occurred during the latter part of the administration of Warren Hastings when Hastings was kept in office by the Proprietors against the opposition of the Directors.

A permanent trading post was established by the Company at Surat in 1612. The Island of Bombay was acquired by Charles II in 1661 as a part of the marriage dowry of Catherine of Braganza. It was transferred to the Company in 1668, and in 1687 the seat of administration of the west coast factories was removed from Surat to the town of Bombay. Fort St. George at Madras was founded in 1640 and it soon became the headquarters for the factories on the east coast.[1] The settlements near the mouth of the Hugli were detached from Madras and formed into a separate district in 1707 with Calcutta (founded in 1690) as its headquarters. In other words, the local administration of the Company in India was decentralized. There were three presidencies or groups of factories, centering about Bombay, Madras, and Calcutta (Fort William). Each presidency had its own President (or Governor) and a Council of from twelve to sixteen members who were usually appointed in accordance with the rule of seniority. The President was on a par with the Councilors, all matters

1. The factory at Masulipatan was founded in 1611 and two or three other factories were established on the east coast before 1640.

being decided by a majority vote. Each presidency was independent of the other two, but they were all subordinate to the Court of Directors in England.

This system worked fairly well so long as the business to be attended to was purely mercantile in character. It betrayed its weakness, however, in the course of the long struggle with the French from 1744 to 1763 and it proved hopelessly incompetent after the grant of the Diwani, "administration," of Bengal in 1765, when the Company was called upon to govern an oriental empire. Partly for this reason and partly because of the disordered condition of the Company's finances, a series of parliamentary inquiries were held which resulted in some ineffective legislation in 1767 and finally culminated in the passage of Lord North's Regulating Act of 1773.

There was no essential change made by this act in the government of the Company in England, but the sections relating to the administrative machinery in India were epoch-making. The first step in the centralization of authority was taken when provision was made for a Governor-General and four Councilors in the presidency of Bengal with power to exercise a general supervision over the other two presidencies. The presidencies of Bombay and Madras were forbidden to wage war or to conclude treaties without the previous consent of the Governor-General in Council. Their Governors were also required to obey the orders of the Governor-General in Council and to keep him informed on all important matters. The first Governor-General and Council were chosen by Parliament for a period of five years[2] and it was provided that nominations in the future, though made by the Directors, should be subject to the approval of the Crown. This part of the bill, which was strongly opposed by Burke as an unwarrantable attack upon a private corporation, was the real beginning of the transfer of the government of India from the Company to the Crown.

The act also authorized the establishment of a Supreme Court of Judicature at Calcutta, consisting of a chief justice

2. This is probably the origin of the custom that limits the tenure of office of the Governor-General and all other high officials in India to five years, although there is no limitation imposed by statute or by the commissions of appointment.

and three puisne judges appointed by the Crown. This court, which was to have jurisdiction over the inhabitants of Calcutta and British subjects and persons employed by the Company in all parts of Bengal, and Bihar and Orissa, was formally organized by a royal charter of March 26, 1774, with Sir Elijah Impey as the first chief justice.

There were two serious defects in this legislation: the Governor-General could be overruled by a majority of the Council, and the Governor-General and the Council together might be overruled by the Supreme Court. The quarrel between Warren Hastings and Philip Francis and his clique in the Council is one of the best-known episodes in Indian history. The friction between the Governor-General in Council and the Supreme Court was more fundamental and its results were more enduring. The Governor-General in Council was vested with supreme administrative authority, the Supreme Court with supreme judicial authority. No serious effort was made to delimit their respective fields of activity and neither was specifically given the right to say the final word in cases of conflicting jurisdiction. The Governor-General in Council represented the Company and the Supreme Court represented the Crown. Although the Company ultimately derived all of its authority from the Crown, the territory which it governed was not at that time a British possession. The rights of sovereignty were still vested in the Grand Mogul at Delhi. As the local agent of an oriental despot, the Company was naturally unwilling to have its work subjected to review by a British court.

Of the many issues involved in the conflict, one of the most important was the vigorous effort of the Supreme Court to protect the people of the country against official oppression. This, together with the fact that Indians have always been more freely admitted to the bench than they have to administrative positions, helps to explain the popularity of the judiciary in India at the present time. There is also a survival of the old feeling in the popular demand that district magistrates and collectors, who are primarily administrative officials, should be deprived of their judicial functions.

Indian affairs were kept prominently before the English public during the next few years, in spite of the distractions of the American Revolution, partly because of the strenuous character of Warren Hastings' administration and partly because of the attack made by Adam Smith on the Company in the *Wealth of Nations*, which was published in 1776. The quarrel between the executive and the judiciary was practically brought to a close in 1781 by an act of Parliament which settled all outstanding disputes in favor of the executive and deprived the judiciary of the power to make any serious trouble in the future.

Two parliamentary committees on Indian affairs were appointed in 1781 with Burke and Dundas as chairmen. Their reports were unfavorable to the Company and, in 1783, Fox introduced his famous East India Bill, which passed the House of Commons, but was defeated in the House of Lords by the direct intervention of the King. The subsequent events are well known to all students of British parliamentary history. It has, however, been too generally assumed that Pitt's success in the general election of 1784 was due to his "courage, skill, and determination and the blunders of his opponents." As a matter of fact, his victory was primarily a triumph of corruption. He won because the stockholders of the East India Company contributed a huge campaign fund to defeat the coalition and to save their business from destruction.

The victory of the Company was incomplete. Although it escaped the drastic provisions of the Fox Bill, its stockholders soon realized that it would have to submit to some form of governmental control. Pitt's India Act of 1784 marks the first step in the interference of Parliament with the home administration of Indian affairs. Provision was made for a Board of Control of not more than six members to be appointed by the Crown "with authority to direct all operations relating to the civil and military government and revenues of India." The membership of the board was gradually reduced and its powers were almost entirely exercised by its president, an official who may properly be regarded as the forerunner of the present Secretary of State for India. The board had access to the correspondence and records of the Company, and was given copies of all dispatches sent to or received from India. No order dealing with noncommercial matters could be sent to

India without its approval and it had the power to make any alterations it pleased. The board also exercised positive functions. It could compel the Directors of the Company to send to India dispatches on any subject that it saw fit or even dispatches that the board itself had drafted. The board had practically complete control over all questions affecting war or peace, negotiations with foreign countries, and relations with Indian States. Communications in regard to these subjects passed through the hands of a small Secret Committee of the Court of Directors and were not seen by the other Directors at all.

The extent of governmental control under this system was not fully appreciated at the time, partly because the Company was allowed to exercise its initiative in all ordinary matters of administration and partly because orders that really originated with the Board of Control were always issued in the name of the Court of Directors or their Secret Committee. The Company also had a large amount of patronage at its disposal, although its nominations of Governor-General, Commander in Chief, and Governors had to be approved by the Crown.[3] Finally, so long as the Company had any commercial powers, it exercised them independently of the Board of Control.

The membership of the Governor-General's Council was reduced from four to three, one of whom was to be the Commander in Chief of the Company's forces in India. The presidencies of Bombay and Madras were each to have a Governor and three Councilors, including the Commander in Chief of the presidency army. The control of the Governor-General in Council over Bombay and Madras was extended, so far as questions of war, revenue, and diplomacy were concerned, although, in actual practice, those presidencies were never very completely subordinated to the authorities at Calcutta until they were brought into closer physical relations with Bengal through the annexation of intervening territory and through improvements in the system of transportation.

3. From the point of view of the Company this was a great improvement over Fox's Bill which had provided for the transfer of practically all patronage to the government.

With a few modifications, the government of India was based upon Pitt's Act of 1784 until the Company was superseded by the Crown in 1858. In 1786, at the beginning of Lord Cornwallis' administration, the Governor-General was empowered in special cases to overrule a majority in the Council and to act on his own responsibility. By another statute passed in the same year the power of the Crown to veto the nomination of a Governor-General was revoked, but the right of recall was retained and the veto itself was restored in 1813.

The most significant changes made during this period were embodied in a series of acts passed every twenty years for the renewal of the charter (1793, 1813, 1833, 1853). The Company was gradually deprived of its mercantile privileges. In 1813 it lost its monopoly except with regard to tea and the trade with China, and in 1833 it was compelled to give up its commercial business entirely and to become a purely political and administrative body acting as a trustee for the Crown.

The Act of 1813 was epoch-making in its social and political results. It legalized the entrance of Christian missionaries into India and it also threw open the doors, under certain restrictions, to a general invasion of traders, planters, and other European adventurers. Both of these movements were deplored by the adherents of the Company, who prophesied all sorts of dire consequences. So far as the missionaries are concerned these prophecies have not been fulfilled. Their connection with India is ephemeral in the sense that very few of them remain in the country after the term of their service has expired. Their theological propaganda has been a failure, but they have justified their existence by spreading the knowledge of Christian ethics and by performing educational and medical services of a very high character.

With the business community the conditions are different. Many of its members in the early days brought their families with them and settled down as permanent residents. Their descendants, together with the descendants of British soldiers in India, now constitute the major portion of what is called the European domiciled community. They are a people without a country. They have lost all connection with Europe, but have not been assimilated by India. They are often distrusted by the British official class and hated by the real natives of the country. Their attitude toward the Indians is usually arrogant and they are responsible in many cases for the stories of brutality which have aroused so much bitterness among Indian Nationalists. Their unpopularity is further intensified by the fact that they hold a large proportion of the secondary government jobs, especially in the Police, Railway, and Public Works Departments.

The businessmen and the soldiers were also responsible, along with the civil employees of the Company, for the creation of the Anglo-Indian or Eurasian element of the population. Although these people have much in common with the domiciled Europeans, they are regarded as a separate community entitled to elect their own legislative representatives and to hold a certain proportion of the posts in the Railway and other government services.

The Charter Renewal Act of 1833 made several fundamental changes in the machinery of Indian government. It deprived Bombay and Madras of their local powers of legislation and completed the process of centralization at Calcutta. As a logical result of this change, the chief executive, who had previously been called the Governor-General of Fort William in Bengal, was given the full title of Governor-General of India. He still retained direct control of the government of Bengal until 1854 when a special Lieutenant-Governor was appointed for that presidency. As a matter of fact, although Bengal was the largest and richest province in India, its provincial administration continued to be overshadowed by the central government until the federal capital was removed from Calcutta to Delhi in 1912. It was then for the first time allowed to have a Governor and an Executive Council.

No attempt was made before 1833 to differentiate between executive and legislative bodies. Laws were made and enforced by the same set of men, the Governor-General in Council, in Bengal, and the Governors in Council, in Bombay and Madras. The Act of 1833 retained the Councils in Bombay and Madras, but as indicated above they were deprived of their legislative functions, the Governor-General in Council being authorized to legislate for all the presidencies. The Governor-General's Council was at the same time increased by the appointment of a Law Member, who played an active part in the legislative sessions, but did not have the power to vote when the Council met in its executive capacity. Although the Charter Act of 1853 gave the Law Member a regular seat on the Executive Council, the principle of differentiation was strengthened by the appointment of six so-called additional members who attended only the legislative sessions.

The Act of 1833 also provided for the appointment of an Indian Law Commission to inquire into the jurisdiction, powers, and rules of the existing courts of justice, into the forms of existing judicial procedure, and into the nature and operation of all civil and criminal laws, whether written or customary, that were then in force in India. This was the origin of the famous commission which prepared the Indian Penal Code (1860) and took the initial steps in the preparation of the more recently enacted Codes of Civil and Criminal Procedure. Its most active member was Lord Macaulay, the historian, who also did excellent work as the first Law Member of the Governor-General's Council.

Before leaving the Act of 1833 mention should be made of one provision, more honored in the breach than in the observance, which has recently been given a great deal of prominence. Section 87 declared that "no native of the said territories, nor any natural-born subject of His Majesty resident therein, shall by reason only of his religion, place of birth, descent, colour, or any of them, be disabled from holding any place, office or employment under the Company."

The dual administration of Indian affairs under Pitt's Act worked very badly. There were constant friction and division of responsibility between the Board of Control and the Court of Directors and a corresponding lack of efficiency. It is not at all surprising, therefore, that the charter was renewed in 1853, not for the usual period of twenty years, but only "until Parliament shall otherwise provide." The Mutiny brought matters to a crisis. By the Government of India Act of 1858 the government, territories, and revenues were transferred from the Company to the Crown and the foundation was laid for the system of the present day.

From 1858 until 1915 the organic law of British India was contained in a series of parliamentary statutes, of which the most important were the Government of India Acts of 1858, 1865, 1869, 1870, and 1912; the Indian Councils Acts of 1861, 1892, and 1909; and the Indian High Courts Acts of 1861 and 1911. The essential provisions of these statutes and of various other measures dealing with the subject were consolidated in the Government of India Act of 1915. This act was in turn slightly amended by the Government of India (Amendment) Act, 1916, and very considerably modified by the Government of India Act, 1919, which embodied the Montagu-Chelmsford Reforms. In accordance with Section 45 of the Act of 1919, the Acts of 1915, 1916, and 1919 were incorporated into one document which was cited as the Government of India Act. This document, however, was only an outline, the details being filled in by rules made by the Governor-General in Council with the sanction of the Secretary of State in Council. Their work had to be laid before Parliament but usually no positive action was required, the rules remaining in force if neither house expressed its disapproval within thirty days. The Act of 1919 will gradually be superseded by the new Government of India Act of 1935, first in the provinces and later in the central government.

The constitutional history of India since 1858 may be divided into three parts. The first deals with the period before 1921, the second with the Montagu-Chelmsford Reforms, and the third with the history of the new Constitution of 1935. Under the old system as it existed before 1921, British control was absolute and unquestioned in every important branch of the government—central, provincial, and local. The administrative machinery was dominated by the Indian Civil Service, generally known as the I.C.S. The history of this Service will be considered more in detail in a later chapter. Here it will be sufficient to say that it was at that time recruited entirely in Great Britain and, while a few Indians occasionally entered its ranks, it was almost exclusively a British organization. Its members have always maintained a high standard of honesty, justice, efficiency, and clean living, but they have developed a bureaucratic tradition and a strong feeling of racial superiority. Their government is efficient, but not sympathetic. Most of them are convinced that an Indian is incapable of exercising administrative responsibility and are unwilling to give him a chance to prove the contrary.

Opinions differ in regard to the effects of the Montagu-Chelmsford Reforms upon this system. The general feeling in India was that the Indian Civil Service was still in an impregnable position and that it still blocked every effort to give the people a real share in the government. The members of the Service, on the other hand, were also despondent. They felt that the Reforms were revolutionary, that their own careers were ruined, and that India was likely to drift into a state of anarchy. The truth lies somewhere between these two extremes, but the changes introduced by the Montagu-Chelmsford plan were certainly radical enough to mark the beginning of a new era. This is also true of the Government of India Act of 1935. The attempt to create a federal system which includes the states as well as the provinces is a very decided innovation.

The transfer of authority from the Company to the Crown and the reorganization of the machinery of government—administrative, legislative, and judicial—were brought about by the enactment of three parliamentary statutes, the Government of India Act of 1858, the Indian Councils Act of 1861, and the Indian High Courts Act of 1861. The Government of India Act provided that the Crown was to administer the affairs of India through a Secretary of State in Council who was to have all the powers formerly exercised by the Company or by the Board of Control. The Council was a body of experts consisting of fifteen members, of whom at least nine must have had ten years of Indian experience. This arrangement was in the nature of a compromise. It continued, with some modification, the old system of divided responsibility. The Secretary of State was supposed to inherit the powers and traditions of the Board of Control and the Council to inherit those of the Court of Directors. The majority of the Council have usually been retired members of the Indian Civil Service and it is the common belief in India that their chief function has been to block the adoption of measures which are supposed to be inimical to the interests of the Service.

The terms of the Act of 1858 were of course soon made known in India. At a grand Durbar, held at Allahabad on November 1, Lord Canning published a Royal Proclamation announcing that the Crown had taken over the government. This document referred to Canning as the Viceroy and thus originated that title as applied to the Governor-General of India. The actual framework of government in India was not affected by this proclamation or by the Government of India Act. The first step in that field was taken two years later when Parliament, after hearing the views of Lord Canning, Mr. J. P. Grant, Lieutenant-Governor of Bengal, Mr. Barnes Peacock, Chief Justice of Bengal and others,[4] passed the Indian Councils Act (1861). The chief features of this measure were the effort to bring about legislative decentralization, the introduction of a nonofficial Indian element into the Legislative Councils, the definite subordination of the legislature to the executive, and the definition of the jurisdiction of the government of India.

Legislative Councils were restored in Bombay and Madras and provision was made for the establishment of similar bodies in Bengal, the North-West Provinces and the Punjab.[5] In spite of these provisions there was very little real decentralization of authority. No line was drawn between the jurisdictions of the central and the provincial legislatures. The Governor-General in Council could still legislate for the whole of India and this legislation had precedence over that of the provinces. Furthermore, in certain cases, provincial acts had to receive the previous assent of the Governor-General, and in all cases they had to receive his subsequent assent. There was also, as we shall see later, a similar overcentralization of authority in the fields of finance and administration.

4. See, for example, *East India (Councils). A Copy of the Dispatches from the Governor-General of India to the Secretary of State for India, dated the 9" of December, 1859, the 15" of January, 1861, and the 26" of January, 1861, respecting the Constitution of Councils in India* (London, 1861).

5. Immediate action was taken in Bengal (1862) but Legislative Councils were not established in the North-West Provinces and the Punjab until 1886 and 1897 respectively.

The Governor-General's Executive Council was increased by the Act of 1861 from four to five ordinary members and authority was given to retain the Commander in Chief of the Indian Army as an extraordinary member. From six to twelve additional members were to be nominated by the Governor-General for a term of two years to sit with the Council when it met in its legislative capacity. One half of the additional members must be nonofficials. The Provincial Legislative Councils were constituted in a similar manner. In Bombay and Madras, for example, the Governors were authorized to nominate from four to eight additional members, of whom one half must be nonofficials. Under these provisions a few Indians were gradually introduced into the legislative branch of the government, both central and local.

In one respect the act took what was apparently a backward step. The Central Legislative Council, as expanded by the Charter Act of 1853, had not worked at all smoothly. It had modeled its procedure on the British Parliament, criticized the administrative system, and acted in general as if its chief duty was to secure a redress of grievances. Some good work might have been done along these lines if the additional members had really represented the people of India. As a matter of fact, the six additional members all held under an appointive tenure and were all representatives of the British official class. Two were lawyers who were largely interested in legal quibbles and the other four were concerned mainly in advancing the sectional interests of their respective provinces. It is, therefore, not at all surprising that the functions of the new Councils were now strictly limited. "They were expressly forbidden to transact any business except the consideration and enactment of legislative measures, or to entertain any motion except a motion for leave to introduce a Bill or having reference to a Bill actually introduced."[6]

Finally, the Indian Councils Act of 1861 extended the legislative jurisdiction of the Governor-General in Council to include all persons in British India, whether British, Indian, or foreign, all courts of justice, and all places and things in Brit-

6. *The Montagu-Chelmsford Report,* par. 63.

ish India, and also all servants of the government of India within the Indian States.

At the end of its account of this act, *The Montagu-Chelmsford Report* concludes with the following retrospective summary:

The Act of 1861 thus closes a chapter. Its main interest has lain in the gradual construction and consolidation of the mechanical framework of government. The three separate presidencies have come into a common system; much of the intervening spaces has been brought under British rule; the legislative and administrative authority of the Governor-General in Council has been asserted over all the provinces and extended to all their inhabitants; and the principle of recognizing local needs and welcoming local knowledge has been admitted, so that local councils have been created or re-created and a few non-official and even Indian members have been introduced for the purposes of advice. But, partly at least out of anxiety to prevent the authority of the executive from being impaired (as in Warren Hastings' days) by any other rival institution without administrative responsibility, it has been expressly declared that the councils are a mere legislative committee of the Government and are not the germ of responsible institutions. We think it worth noting how the innate tendency of even a few official Englishmen, assembled in a simulacrum of a legislature, to convert it into a parliamentary body positively contributed to retard the introduction of parliamentary ideas for the benefit of the people of India as a whole.[7]

The Indian High Courts Act of 1861, the third fundamental measure in the reorganization of India after the Mutiny, abolished the old Supreme Court and the Sudder Courts of the Company and established a High Court with both civil and criminal jurisdiction in each of the three presidency towns. Each court was to consist of a chief justice and not more than fifteen associate justices, recruited partly from the ranks of British barristers, partly from the Indian Civil Service, and partly from Indian lawyers who had judicial experience or who had practiced at the bar. This act, amended from time to

7. *Idem,* par. 65.

time, has served as the model for the creation of subsequent High Courts, Chief Courts, and Judicial Commissions in the other provinces.

After the work of reorganization described above was completed in 1861, Parliament virtually ignored Indian affairs for more than thirty years. The Royal Titles Act of 1876 which conferred upon Queen Victoria the title of Empress of India was merely a sentimental gesture. A few other laws relating to India were passed, but they dealt almost entirely with technical administrative details. The life tenure for members of the Council of India, for example, was abolished in 1869, and provision was made for a reduction in the size of the Council to ten members in 1889.[8]

In India itself there was a conflict of administrative tendencies. The growing concentration of authority at Calcutta was partially offset by a determined effort to strengthen and extend the organs of local government. The chief forces making for centralization were the natural tendency of a bureaucracy to absorb functions that properly belong to subordinates; the improvement in railway, telegraph, and postal communications; and finally the spread of education, the growth of a vernacular press and the development of national feeling among the educated classes. The arguments in favor of decentralization were the increasing complexity of modern government; the difficulty of administering the affairs of a great subcontinent from a single center; the fact that the provinces differ in race, language, traditions, and stages of social development and cannot all be treated alike; the importance of creating a larger sense of responsibility among the local authorities; and the desirability of beginning the political education of the people of the country.[9]

The centralization of this period took the form of an increase in the authority of the Governor-General and a wide extension of the jurisdiction of the government of India. The power of the Governor-General to overrule his Council was

8. The subsequent history of the Council will be discussed in later chapters.

9. In this connection see *East India Decentralization* (*Royal Commission*), I (Cd. 4360), 24–25.

confirmed and strengthened by the Government of India Act of 1870. Although this power has been very rarely used, the mere fact that it exists and may be used in an emergency has been sufficient to maintain executive harmony. Lord Lytton took advantage of it in 1879 to exempt cotton goods from the payment of import duties. The legislative jurisdiction of the government of India was extended in 1865–69 to include all British subjects and all native Indian subjects of Her Majesty in the Indian States, and its influence was further enhanced in 1870–74 by the institution of the system of Scheduled Districts. Scheduled Districts were certain strategic or backward tracts, designated by the Secretary of State, in which the Governor-General in Council was authorized to issue regulations having the force of law. In dealing with these tracts and others specially "Scheduled" the Governor-General could declare, in case of doubt, what laws were in operation, and he could also extend to them, with or without amendment, any enactment in force in other parts of British India. In accordance with these powers, regulations were issued for Assam, Ajmer-Merwara, the Andaman and Nicobar Islands, the North-West Frontier Province, British Baluchistan, Coorg, Upper Burma, and other territories declared to be within the Scheduled Districts. This was practically a restoration in a restricted area of the old powers of the Governor-General in Council to legislate in a summary manner for the so-called nonregulation provinces.

The revolt against centralization was characterized by the efforts of Lord Mayo (1869–72), Lord Lytton (1876–80), and Lord Ripon (1880–84) to decentralize the financial administration and the efforts of Lord Ripon to establish a system of local self-government. Until 1870 the central government had complete control of all revenues and expenditures. The provinces were entirely dependent upon annual doles and there was keen rivalry in the struggle for appropriations. To quote the words of Sir Richard Strachey:

> The distribution of the public income degenerated into something like a scramble, in which the most violent had the advantage, with very little attention to reason. As local economy brought no local

advantage, the stimulus to avoid waste was reduced to a minimum, and as no local growth of the income led to local means of improvement, the interest in developing the public revenues was also brought down to the lowest level.[10]

In 1870–71 Lord Mayo adopted the practice of making fixed annual grants to the provinces for the support of the police, jails, medical services, registration, education, printing, roads, and public buildings. Within certain limits, the provincial governments were empowered to allot this money as they saw fit and also to raise additional funds by special taxation. The next step was taken during the administration of Lord Lytton. The sources of revenue were all classified under three headings—Indian revenues, which went to the central government; provincial revenues, which went to the provincial governments; and divided revenues, which were evenly shared between them. Under the provincial and divided headings were included law and justice, excise, license taxes, forests, public works, and other sources which might be increased by provincial management. As most of these were poor revenue producers the provinces did not really become financially independent. Their incomes had to be supplemented partly by cash contributions from the government of India and partly by the allotment of a percentage of the land revenue, which was ordinarily regarded as an Indian receipt. The amounts of these supplemental grants were fixed approximately every five years from 1882 until 1904, when a quasi-permanent settlement was adopted which remained in force until 1921.

This plan worked fairly well, especially after 1904, but it was never entirely satisfactory. The provincial governments were starved. They had to face a steady increase in the cost of administration with a revenue that was practically stationary. The result was that the government of India was frequently called upon to make special appropriations, not to meet emergencies but to cover normal expenditures. In making these grants there was too much of a tendency to interfere in petty

10. Quoted in *The Montagu-Chelmsford Report,* par. 105. Sir Richard Strachey was the chief author of the reforms that followed.

administrative details that ought to have been left to the local authorities. On one occasion the government of India overruled the provincial officials on the situation of a staircase in a government bungalow and also on the amount of rent that was to be charged after the bungalow was finished. "Administrations and officers subjected to a long course of this treatment must be reduced to the condition of oxen in an oil mill which tread their little circle unconsciously with blinded eyes."[11]

But these defects were, after all, relatively unimportant. If the system had functioned perfectly, it would have meant only a devolution of authority from bureaucrats at Calcutta to other bureaucrats in the provincial capitals. The reforms initiated by Lord Ripon, on the other hand, were more fundamental. They were based upon the idea of transferring powers from the bureaucrats to the people of the country, the idea of reviving the native genius for local self-government.

Before the British came to India the people had never been accustomed to a strongly centralized administration. The Mogul Empire and its predecessors collected tribute from subject races, deposed unruly vassals and suppressed rebellions of one kind or another, but they paid very little attention to the trial of petty cases, the maintenance of village police forces, the repair of local roads and irrigation works, and the many other minor details that so closely affect the lives of the ordinary people. These matters were looked after by hereditary or elected officials who lived in the neighborhood and were amenable to the influence of neighborhood opinion. The ordinary village, for example, was governed by a sort of board, made up of heads of leading families, which was called a panchayat.

The British gradually swept this system aside as a *political* factor, and concentrated authority in the hands of men who held under an appointive tenure and who had no permanent associations with the territories which they were called upon to rule. The provinces were divided into districts which be-

11. Quoted from the memorandum submitted by the government of Bombay to the Royal Commission on Decentralization. *East India Decentralization* (*Royal Commission*), VIII (Cd. 4367), 232.

came the chief units of local government.[12] Excluding Burma, there are now 213 districts in British India with an average area of 4,100 square miles and an average population of about 1,210,000. At the head of each district is an official, usually a British member of the Indian Civil Service, who is styled collector and magistrate or deputy-commissioner. There are also a superintendent of police and a civil surgeon. The districts are usually split up into smaller areas under the charge of a junior officer of the Indian Civil Service or officers of the Provincial Service who are styled assistant magistrate or deputy-collectors. In most of the provinces there is a further division into tahsils or talukas, administered by tahsildars, or manlatdars, who are as a rule Indian members of the Subordinate Service.

Until the days of Lord Ripon these officials were unhampered by any kind of popular control. Each was an absolute monarch in his own field except in so far as he might be overruled by his official superiors.[13] It was a bureaucratic system pure and simple, but in many ways it was remarkably successful. The personnel of the Services was excellent and the highest standards of honesty, justice, and efficiency were maintained. The object of Lord Ripon's reforms, therefore, was not to improve the Service, but to train the people to take part in public affairs. He was even prepared, if necessary, to sacrifice a measure of departmental efficiency in the cause of political education.

The famous Local Self-Government Resolution was issued May 18, 1882, and steps were immediately taken to put its

12. In all the provinces except Madras there is a larger administrative area called the division, which is formed by grouping together several districts (usually from four to six), but it is relatively unimportant. The chief officer of a division is the commissioner.

13. This statement should perhaps be qualified to some extent. Municipal institutions were established in the three presidency towns in the seventeenth and eighteenth centuries and a general municipal statute was passed in 1850. The members of the various corporate boards were, however, all appointed by the government until 1870, and the elective element introduced at that time was comparatively insignificant.

principles into operation. There were established three sets of administrative bodies—district and subdistrict boards in the rural areas and municipal boards in the urban areas—to deal with education, public health, roads, and streets, and other local problems. According to an official estimate made in 1918, there were at that time about 200 district boards, 500 subdistrict boards, and over 700 municipal boards. The composition of these bodies has varied widely in different parts of the country. As a rule, the elected members have constituted a majority, but the suffrage has been very much restricted and there has been a large minority of government officials and other appointive members. The chairmen have usually been government officials. The collector and magistrate, for example, has ordinarily been the chairman not only of the district board but also of one or more of the municipal boards in his district. Two thirds of the municipalities had official chairmen as late as 1918 and the proportion in the rural boards was much larger.

This system is now being thoroughly overhauled. The boards are being brought more directly under popular control and their powers and responsibilities are being greatly increased. The real test will come in the future. It is sufficient here to say that Lord Ripon's reforms had not come up to his original expectations when the Government of India Act was passed in 1919. Except in a few municipalities and in a still smaller number of rural areas, the work had been done entirely by the official element on the boards or by the regular governmental departments. In some parts of the country boards either had not been established at all or had fallen into disuse. There were, for example, no district boards in Assam, no subdistrict boards in the United Provinces, and no rural boards of any kind in Burma and Baluchistan.

Two theories have been advanced to account for this failure, one by the members of the Indian Civil Service and the other by the Indian Nationalists. According to the former, the people were given an opportunity to exercise a wide influence in a most important field of government and they failed to take advantage of it. The voters were apathetic, a large percentage of the seats were uncontested, and the members who were elected were inclined to neglect their duties. The inference usually drawn is that it would be very unwise to extend the powers and responsibilities of a people who do not have enough public spirit to take part in the solution of problems that affect their immediate welfare. The Nationalists are willing to admit that there is a lack of interest in the boards, but not that there is a lack of interest in local government itself. According to their contention, it is the system and not the people that is to blame. The boards are kept in leading strings. They are controlled from the inside by the official members and from the outside by departmental superiors who overrule their decisions. There is an excellent summary of these criticisms in *The Report of the Royal Commission on Decentralization* which was presented to Parliament in 1909:

> Critics of the present system have dwelt on the failure to develop the principle of election, and on the appointment of official presidents. The boards, it has been urged, have practically become a department of the Government administration; their work is done by the official element within the boards themselves, or by Government Departments at the boards' expense; their proceedings are subject to excessive outside control; and in present circumstances they can never become, as Lord Ripon intended them to be, effective instruments of local self-government.[14]

There is an element of truth in both of these theories. The Indian Civil Service never approved the reforms and never really gave them a fair chance to succeed. At the same time, if the electors had shown a moderate amount of enthusiasm in using the powers conferred upon them, they could have exerted a substantial influence on local administration and their powers would undoubtedly have been increased. This local inertia is perhaps due, in some measure at least, to the tradition of the Indian educational system which is based upon the fantastic idea that if there is a good superstructure the foundations will take care of themselves. If education filters downward, political capacity may follow the same natural law. We must also remember that the leaders of Indian thought

14. *Op. cit.,* I, 269.

have been educated along Western lines at a time when Western political philosophy has been strongly nationalistic and the trend of government has been toward greater centralization.

A scheme for the reconstitution of the Central and Provincial Legislative Councils was adopted at the annual meeting of the (unofficial) Indian National Congress in 1889. Half of the seats were to be elective and the other half divided evenly between officials and nominated nonofficials. A bill embodying these Congress principles was introduced into the House of Commons by Mr. Bradlaugh. Lord Dufferin, who was at that time Governor-General, made some recommendations of a less radical character, but he also suggested that some of the members should be chosen by election. These proposals being too liberal for the Secretary of State, the so-called "Kimberley clause" was finally adopted as a compromise. Under its warrant a system of election was established, although there was no official recognition of the elective principle. A certain number of Councilors were to be nominated on the recommendation of various bodies which were mainly nonofficial in character. The final result was the passage of the Indian Councils Act of 1892, which is sometimes called Lord Cross's Act. The number of additional members in the Governor-General's Council, that is to say, the number of members added to the Executive Council when it went into legislative session, was increased from a maximum of twelve to a maximum of sixteen. In order that an official majority might be maintained it was provided that six of these should be officials and ten nonofficials. Four of the nonofficials were to be nominated by the Governor-General on the recommendation of the nonofficial members of the four Provincial Councils which existed at that time and one on the recommendation of the Calcutta Chamber of Commerce. A few seats of a similar character were also instituted in the Provincial Legislative Councils, the nominations being made by the Governor or Lieutenant-Governor on the recommendation of district boards, municipalities, universities, and various organizations representing landed or commercial interests. In other words, there was introduced for the first time into the legislative bodies of India a small quasi-elective element made up chiefly of Indians.[15] The remaining nonofficial members, most of whom were also Indians, were nominated by the Governor-General, or, in the case of a province, by the Governor or Lieutenant-Governor, acting on his own responsibility.

The Act of 1892 also marked progress by enlarging the powers of the Legislative Councils. The rigid restrictions imposed by the Act of 1861 were so modified as to give members the right of interpellation and the right of discussing the annual financial statement, provided no resolutions were moved and no divisions were taken. In the absence of any real control over either the administration or the budget, the questions and the debates were very rarely of any constructive value.

Since the passage of the Act of 1892 the growth of unrest and the development of Nationalism have been the salient features of Indian history. In 1905, at the close of Lord Curzon's vigorous, but not very tactful, administration, India seemed to be on the brink of a revolt. Lord Minto, the new Governor-General, realized the gravity of the situation and a committee of his Council was appointed under the chairmanship of Sir Arundel Arundel to consider the question of increasing the Indian element in the Legislative Councils. Lord Morley, the Secretary of State, also became interested in the matter, and, after a period of very careful investigation and deliberation, the so-called Morley-Minto Reforms were devised and put into operation in 1907–9.[16]

The object of these Reforms was to create what has been termed a constitutional autocracy. Lord Morley and Lord Minto both disclaimed any intention of setting up a system of responsible government. To quote the words of Lord Morley: "If it could be said that this chapter of reforms led directly or indirectly to the establishment of a parliamentary system in India, I, for one, would have nothing at all to do with it." The

15. The Calcutta Chamber of Commerce being a European organization, only four of the "elective" additional members of the Governor-General's Council were Indians.

16. See Lord Morley, *Recollections* (London, 1917), Vol. II; John Buchan, *Lord Minto: a Memoir* (London, 1928); and Mary, Countess of Minto, *India, Minto and Morley, 1905–1910* (London, 1934).

British were to retain complete control over all branches of the government, but it was intended that in the exercise of that control they should be made more amenable to Indian opinion. This was done by increasing the proportion of Indian members and extending the functions of the Legislative Councils and by providing for Indian representation on the Executive Councils and the Council of the Secretary of State.

In one important respect the Morley-Minto plan and its successor, the Montagu-Chelmsford plan, both were based upon the same principle; namely, that the more radical changes should be made first in the provinces, the implication being that if the experiment proved successful it could ultimately be extended to the central government. The Morley-Minto plan, for example, provided for nonofficial majorities in the Provincial Legislative Councils, but not in the Legislative Council of the Governor-General; the Montagu-Chelmsford plan established the system of dyarchy in the provinces, but did not apply it to the government of India. The Indian Councils Act of 1909 increased the number of additional members in the provincial legislatures to a maximum of 50 in the larger provinces and 30 in the smaller. Although there were nonofficial majorities in all the provinces, as stated above, the change was not as revolutionary as might at first appear. A sufficient number of nonofficials were appointed by the chief executive in every province except Bengal to give them, combined with the official members, a majority over the elected members. Even in Bengal, where there was a clear elective majority, the balance of power was held by two or three European elective members who generally voted with the government on important issues. The Indian Legislative Council also received a large addition of Indian members, but there was no attack even in theory upon the autocratic character of the government. Out of a total membership of 68, there were 36 officials and 32 nonofficials; 41 seats were filled by appointment and 27 by election.

Several new features were introduced into the scheme of representation by the Act of 1909. The old method of nomination by the chief executive on the basis of recommendations made by special constituencies, as established under the Act of

1892, was superseded by a regular system of election. With the exception of a very few seats the elections were indirect and the number of electors was exceedingly small. The principle was adopted that certain minority or backward religious or racial communities should elect their own members in separate constituencies. This system, which is known as communal representation, was devised at the instance of the Moslems. As will be seen later, it was accepted as one of the fundamental features of the Montagu-Chelmsford scheme in its final form and was extended to include Sikhs, Indian Christians, Europeans, Anglo-Indians, and others. Finally, the Moslems and the landed gentry were given a representation that was out of proportion to their population, wealth, or degree of educational advancement, apparently in the hope that they would serve as a conservative balance against the radicalism of the Hindu barristers and pleaders who tended to monopolize most of the seats for which they were eligible.

A few figures will illustrate the facts mentioned in the preceding paragraph. There were 5,818 electors for the Indian Legislative Council, an average of 215 for each of the 27 elective members. Some of the constituencies were much smaller than this average. Eight electors, for example, chose the Moslem representative from Bombay and 9 chose the general representative from Burma. Thirteen of the 27 were elected by the nonofficial members of the Provincial Legislative Councils, 6 by landholders, 6 by Moslems, and 2 by the Chambers of Commerce of Calcutta and Bombay.[17]

The Act of 1909 also further enlarged the functions of the Legislative Councils. Under the Act of 1892, the budget could be discussed but not until after the estimates had already been settled by the executive. No resolution could be proposed in regard to it and no division could be demanded. The members were now allowed a much fuller opportunity for discussion and they could also move resolutions and call for a vote. The right to offer resolutions and to ask for divisions was in fact conceded in the case of practically all matters of public inter-

17. *East India (Constitutional) Reforms: Lord Southborough's Committees,* I (Cd. 141), 81–82.

est whether financial issues were involved or not. The right of interpellation was likewise extended so as to allow a member who had asked a question to supplement it by asking another.

The other features of the Morley-Minto Reforms may be summarized very briefly. Two seats on the Council of the Secretary of State, one on the Governor-General's Executive Council and one on each of the Provincial Executive Councils were reserved for Indians. Preliminary steps were also taken to bring about a devolution of administrative, legislative, and financial control. Some of the provincial governments had long complained of the burdensome restrictions imposed upon them by the Secretary of State and the government of India. There was also a feeling that every step in the direction of self-government should logically be accompanied by a corresponding relaxation in the rigidity of the supervision exercised by the higher authorities. A Royal Commission upon Decentralization was accordingly appointed in 1907 under the chairmanship of Mr. C. E. H. Hobhouse. The report, which was presented in 1909, was exceedingly cautious in its recommendations, with the result that although a few minor changes were made the provinces were not given any real constitutional freedom of action.

Taking it as a whole, the Morley-Minto plan of reform is a landmark in the history of Indian administration. It was generally welcomed by the leaders of public opinion as a forward step in the association of the people with the government. Mr. G. K. Gokhale, for example, commended it very highly in a memorable speech made before the Indian National Congress in 1908. It is now the fashion to decry it, to say that it was a failure and to imply that its lack of success was the result of its own defects. But before we accept this judgment let us look at the brighter side of the picture. The nonofficial members of the Indian Legislative Council played a more or less important part in framing the Indian Court-Fees (Amendment) Bill, the Indian Factories Bill, the Indian Patents and Designs Bill, the Indian Companies Bill, the Patna University Bill, and various other measures enacted during the years from 1910 to 1918. They also introduced a number of private bills, some of which were accepted by the government and placed on the statute books. Although the government rejected Mr. Gokhale's Elementary Education Bill because of the financial burden that it involved, the discussion to which it gave rise will probably bear fruit ultimately in the adoption of some measure of educational compulsion. It is more difficult to get exact information in the case of the Provincial Councils, but there is evidence to show that the unofficial members were able to exert a certain amount of influence upon both legislation and administration.[18] Finally it may be said that the loyalty of the great masses of the people of India during the war was itself a tribute to the wisdom of Lord Morley and Lord Minto. If the old bureaucratic system of Lord Curzon's day had still been in force, it is not likely that the people would have remained even moderately contented. It is perhaps significant that the most serious troubles during the war and afterwards occurred in the Punjab, where, under the rule of Sir Michael O'Dwyer as Lieutenant-Governor, the old conditions were most nearly approximated.

But when all has been said in favor of the plan, the fact must be admitted that as a permanent solution it was not a success. This was due in part to its own imperfections, but it was probably due far more to the rapid development of national consciousness in India which could not have been foreseen in 1909. To quote the words of *The Montagu-Chelmsford Report* (par. 100), it failed because it "ceased in the brief space of ten years' time to satisfy the political hunger of India." The fundamental defect of the plan was that it left the entire responsibility of government in the hands of one set of men while it transferred a large measure of power to another set of men. The nonofficial members of the councils could criticize and embarrass the government without being restrained by the prospect that they might be called upon to change places. The presidential system of government works fairly well in the United States because the executive is elected for a short and definite term and is ultimately responsible to the same electorate that chooses the legislature. In India, however, the

18. For more detailed information see *The Montagu-Chelmsford Report,* chap. iv.

opposition party in the legislature was responsible to the people of India whereas the executive was responsible, through the Secretary of State, to the British Parliament and ultimately to the people of Great Britain. Furthermore, the conflict was embittered by race antagonism, the executive being British and the legislative opposition being Indian.

The other defects were of somewhat lesser importance. The system was still overcentralized, the provincial governments being kept in complete subordination to the government of India and the latter to the Secretary of State and Parliament. This failure to trust the man on the spot may have protected the people from the tyranny of the Indian Civil Service, but it did not make for efficiency. The electoral system was also faulty. The number of voters was small and, in those constituencies in which the indirect method of election prevailed, there was too wide a gap between the member and the primary electors. The large percentage of lawyers elected to the Councils might likewise be regarded as a misfortune. In the elections of 1916, 70 per cent of the general constituencies returned lawyers. In many cases these members were mere political agitators who made no effort whatever to give the government any constructive assistance. Finally, the official bloc was the cause of a great deal of friction. As a rule the official members of the Councils, both ex-officio and additional, were not allowed to speak, ask questions, or move resolutions without the approval of the government, and they were expected to vote according to government orders.

Notwithstanding these defects and the rapid growth of national sentiment, the reorganization of the government would probably not have come so soon or been so complete, if it had not been for the great events of the period from 1914 to 1918. Owing to India's loyal coöperation in the war, the emphasis placed by the Allied and Associated Powers upon the principle of self-determination, the feeling aroused among Moslems by the conflict between Great Britain and Turkey, the restrictions imposed by the Indian authorities to prevent seditious agitation, the breakdown of the administrative machinery during the first Mesopotamian campaign, and other causes too numerous to mention, the British government found it advisable, while the war was still in progress, to announce a fundamental change of policy in its relations with India. On August 20, 1917, Mr. Edwin Samuel Montagu, the Secretary of State for India, declared in the House of Commons that the policy of the government was "that of the increasing association of Indians in every branch of the administration and the gradual development of self-governing institutions with a view to the progressive realization of responsible government in India as an integral part of the British Empire."

The Montagu-Chelmsford Act of 1919, which attempted to implement this promise, was concerned exclusively with British India, but since that time the Indian States have been drawn into the general stream of constitutional evolution and steps are now being taken to incorporate them in a federal plan of government. It will be advisable, therefore, to survey their early relations with the British authorities before an attempt is made to discuss the problem as a whole.

During the century from Plassey to the Mutiny (1757–1857) more than half of the best territory in the State area was absorbed into British India. The movement was especially vigorous after 1841 when the Company was advised by its Board of Directors to "persevere in the one clear and direct course of abandoning no just and honourable accession of territory or revenue." Various methods were employed. Sind and the Punjab, for example, were acquired by conquest; Satara, Nagpur, and Jhansi by utilizing the feudal doctrine of lapse; and Coorg and Oudh by asserting the right to annex a state which was suffering from maladministration.

In dealing with the states that remained the policy of the Company was at first based on the principle of nonintervention beyond its own ring fence. Treaties of alliance and mutual amity were concluded with a few of the principal rulers, but there was no attempt to assert rights of sovereignty or overlordship. Although Lord Wellesley, who was Governor-General from 1798 to 1805, was inclined to be somewhat aggressive, there was no permanent change until about 1815 when Lord Hastings initiated the policy of subordinate isolation. By 1857 all of the states had been brought completely under

British control, so far as their foreign and interstate relations were concerned, although the Company still generally refrained from interfering in their internal affairs. The origin and the nature of these powers have been admirably described by Professor Dodwell:

> Beside the rights created by treaty in the Company, there had arisen under no sanction but that of superior power on the one side and reluctant acquiescence on the other a body of precedents relating to successions and to interference in the internal administration of the states. Together these constituted the Company's paramountry, undefined, undefinable, but always tending to expand under the strong pressure of political circumstances.[19]

The Crown was the heir of the Company and also of the Mogul Empire and in both cases it asserted the widest possible claims. According to the legal experts, it took over all of the powers that the Company had acquired by 1858 and all of the rights of sovereignty that had been exercised by the Empire in the days of Akbar and Shah Jehan. On these broad foundations the Political Department of the government of India[20] has built up a body of political rules which grows with every new encroachment on the rights claimed by the princes. The general tendency of the rules is to weaken the force of treaty obligations that might interfere with the exercise of the paramount authority of the Crown. Treaties may be given a constructive rather than a literal interpretation and "all treaties must be read together," which means that an agreement made with a small state may establish a principle that is binding on all of the other states. It is perhaps an exaggeration to say that the treaties have become *scraps of paper*, but they have frequently been violated when so-called moral con-

19. *The Cambridge History of India,* VI, 492.

20. The powers of the Crown in relation to the states have hitherto been exercised by the Governor-General in Council, but when the new federal system of government is put into operation they will be taken over individually by "His Majesty's Representative for the exercise of the functions of the Crown in its relations with the Indian States." This post will normally be held by the Governor-General although a separate appointment is possible.

siderations have seemed to make it desirable.[21] The net result was aptly summarized by Lord Curzon in a speech at Bhawalpur in 1903: "The sovereignty of the Crown is everywhere unchallenged; it has itself laid down the limitation of its own prerogative."[22]

This still holds good. The liberal reaction which followed Lord Curzon's administration has influenced British policy without affecting its theoretical foundations. The princes have received more considerate treatment, but the effort to have their relations with the Crown defined and put on a treaty basis has so far been unsuccessful. Their position will be clarified to some extent when the new federal system of government is established, but they will continue to be subject to the paramount authority of the Crown in the broad fields of activity which lie outside of the Constitution.

In taking over the powers of the Company the Crown did not take over its policies. There were two essential changes. In the first place, the policy of annexation was abandoned and the state boundaries were frozen as they existed in 1858.[23] This was done partly because it was believed that annexation was the chief cause of the Mutiny and would give further trouble if it were continued and partly because the princes had remained loyal during the crisis itself and therefore deserved to be rewarded. The other change was not so favorable. The Company made a distinction between the treaty states and the small feudatory principalities and practically never interfered in the domestic affairs of the former group. The Crown, on the other hand, has tended to ignore these distinctions and to subject all of the states to the same amount of control. *The Montagu-Chelmsford Report* implies that the princes are

21. A. P. Nicholson, *Scraps of Paper: India's Broken Treaties* (London, 1930). See also Professor Dodwell in *The Cambridge History of India,* VI, 503–504.

22. Lovat Fraser, *India under Curzon and After* (London, 1912), p. 209.

23. The only change in India proper was the creation of the small state of Benares in 1911. Mysore was restored to native rule in 1881, after fifty years of British administration, but technically it was never a part of British India.

justified in their fear "that usage and precedent may be exercising a levelling and corroding influence upon the treaty rights of individual States."[24]

As a matter of fact, absolute uniformity is impossible. The states may be divided into three groups: (a) those that have a population of more than two millions, 8; (b) those that have a population of less than two millions, but are entitled to representation in the Chamber of Princes, 227; and (c) those that are very small and are not represented in the Chamber of Princes, 393.[25] The rulers of the first group have to yield when important issues are at stake, but by using their political influence and appealing to treaty rights they are usually able to protect themselves against encroachments of the ordinary bureaucratic variety.[26] The states in the middle and lower categories are not so fortunate. About thirty of them have treaties with the Paramount Power and a somewhat larger number have agreements or sanads, but they are not much better off than the still larger group that have no direct written guarantees of any kind.

In 1918, five states dealt directly with the government of India through their Residents, 172 were under agents to the Governor-General, and about 500 were in political relations with the local governments. *The Montagu-Chelmsford Report* recommended that they should all be brought under central control and placed as far as possible in the first category. This has been done in the case of nearly all of the important states and of many of the smaller ones. The control is exercised by the Political Department of the government of India which is

24. Par. 304.

25. The figures for the first two groups are based on the census of 1931 and the list of states that are represented, directly or indirectly, in the Chamber of Princes. The figures for the third group are those given in *The Montagu-Chelmsford Report* (par. 310) minus the states in Burma.

26. Kashmir and Jammu, the largest state in area and the fourth largest in population, is apparently an exception to this rule. Its administration has been subjected to a wide measure of British control since 1931 because of a conflict between the Hindu Raja and his Moslem subjects.

under the charge of the Governor-General himself and is manned almost exclusively by British officers selected from the Indian Civil Service and the Indian Army. "Political officers are accredited as individual Residents to the greater States. In each of the Agencies, namely, Rajputana, Central India, the Punjab States, the Western India States, the Madras States and Baluchistan there is an Agent to the Governor-General with a staff of officers, many of whom are accredited to particular States or groups of States."[27] These Residents and political agents are the normal channels of communication between the states and the outside world. Their powers of intervention are wide and many of them are the real masters of the states to which they are accredited. Sometimes the government also exerts control by nominating the Prime Ministers of the states or by "lending" British officials to serve in key positions of one kind or another.

The control exercised by the Crown over the external affairs of the states is practically the same as it was in 1858. The foreign relations of Kashmir and a few other border states have been brought under more effective supervision, but the general conditions have not been changed. The princes cannot correspond or carry on any negotiations with a foreign power and they are prohibited from employing foreigners without the consent of the government of India. They are bound by extradition treaties, neutrality agreements, and other international obligations incurred by the British government. They have no jurisdiction over European British subjects and foreigners in their states[28] and their own people, when they are outside of India, are treated as British subjects. There has been some coöperation between the rulers since the

27. *Report of the Indian Statutory Commission,* commonly called *The Simon Commission* (London, 1930), I, 90–91. The Bombay states were also brought into direct relations with the government of India in 1933 and a group of them was reorganized as the Gujarat States Agency.

28. These people are subject to the extraterritorial jurisdiction of the government of India which is normally exercised by the Resident or the political agent. The state authorities, however, usually have jurisdiction over Indian British subjects.

Chamber of Princes was formed in 1921, but interstate agreements are prohibited and interstate disputes must be settled by the adjudication of the paramount authority.

There are various powers claimed by the Crown on the basis of sovereignty. In the first place, it has the right to grant honors and decorations, regulate salutes, and settle questions of precedence. These matters are taken very seriously in local court circles and would cause a great deal of friction if the power of the Crown to deal with them was not absolute and exclusive.[29] There are, however, a number of other sovereign rights that are fundamentally more important. The princes have been permitted since 1858 to adopt heirs and the doctrine of lapse has ceased to be used as an excuse for annexation, but every succession "must be recognized by the British Government, and no succession is valid until recognition has been given."[30] The government has the power, in other words, to settle a disputed succession and even to veto the succession of the nearest heir if it seems desirable. The leading case is that of the Juvraj of Manipur who was not only deprived of his right of succession in 1891, but was put to death because he was implicated in the murder of some British officials. Another sovereign right is the power to set up a regency or to take control of the administration of a state when the ruler is a minor or is unable for some other reason to perform his duties. This is of course a temporary arrangement, but it affords an opportunity to establish new rights and precedents which tend to increase the permanent authority of the government of India. The power of the government to depose a ruler or compel him to abdicate has frequently been enforced. The Gaekwar of Baroda was deposed in 1875 because his state was badly governed and he was apparently unable to carry out the reforms which the government recommended. The resignation of the Maharaja of Kashmir "was accepted" in 1889 on the

29. For a full discussion of this question see Sir William Lee-Warner, *The Native States of India* (London, 1910), pp. 318–322 and K. M. Panikkar, *An Introduction to the Study of the Relations of Indian States with the Government of India* (London, 1927).

30. *Parliamentary Papers,* 1890–91, No. 392, p. 13, quoted in *The Cambridge History of India,* VI, 497.

ground of maladministration, although the real cause was probably the belief that he was too friendly in his attitude toward Russia. These are the outstanding examples, but there have also been more recent cases in Bharatpur, Alwar, Indore (2), Nabha, Udaipur, and other states of lower rank.

The responsibility for the defense of India is the source of other powers claimed by the Crown. His Majesty's military forces have the right to pass through the states, to establish forts and cantonments within their limits, to demand assistance in the procuring of supplies and to claim the extradition of deserters. There are no exceptions to this rule. One of the largest cantonments in India is at Secunderabad in the Nizam's dominions and there is another at Bangalore in the state of Mysore. The normal function of the troops is to insure the maintenance of law and order, but they are also available to coerce an obstinate ruler or to suppress a rebellion against the paramount authority. The cantonments are entirely under British jurisdiction and they are sometimes used by Indian politicians as centers of intrigue against the state governments. A large amount of extraterritorial jurisdiction is also exercised over railway, telegraph and telephone lines, and the postal service on the ground that they are parts of the system of defense. In all of these cases the sovereignty of the ruler is merely suspended, which means that each bit of territory will revert to his jurisdiction if and when it ceases to be used for defense purposes. Another phase of the military problem is the power of the Crown to deal with the armies which the rulers themselves maintain. The figures vary from time to time, but there are now some thirty states which have their own military forces and the total strength is approximately 45,000 men. These armies were regarded by the British authorities as a source of potential danger until Lord Dufferin (1884–88) and his advisers made a virtue of necessity and established the system of Imperial Service Troops which worked so well during the Great War. The troops are trained by British army officers lent for that purpose, but they are subject to the orders of the Commander in Chief only when they are on active service. Lee-Warner's theory that the Crown has the power to make unlimited demands on the states in time of war[31] has never been tested. No attempt was made during the war either to tax the states or to draft their men for the army.

In all of these fields of activity the Crown followed the general course marked out by the Company, but it had a method of its own in dealing with the internal affairs of the states. When the policy of annexation was abandoned and the immunity of the rulers against domestic insurrection and foreign invasion was strengthened, something had to be done to protect the people of the states from misgovernment. One solution has already been discussed: an incompetent or tyrannical prince may be deposed or compelled to abdicate. This is a serious remedy, however, and it has rarely been used in recent years as a punishment for maladministration alone. The Maharaja of Indore (1926) was involved in a murder committed in British India and the Maharaja of Nabha (1925) had repeatedly trespassed on the rights of his neighbor, the Maharaja of Patiala. The more normal method of procedure is to interfere directly in the internal administration of the states on the broad ground that the Paramount Power is responsible for their general welfare. This responsibility, according to Lee-Warner, covers the right of intervention to prevent the dismemberment of a state, to suppress rebellion against its lawful sovereign, to prevent gross misrule, to check inhuman practices or offenses against natural law or public morality and to secure religious toleration.[32] Some of these obligations are very elastic and can be utilized to justify a wide measure of intervention. In dealing with a case of "gross misrule" the government of India may authorize the British Resident to exercise a rigid supervision over the state administration or it may devise a reform program and nominate Ministers to put this into execution. British officials may also be "loaned"

31. See Lee-Warner, *op. cit.,* pp. 234–238. Mr. Panikkar criticizes this theory in so far as it affects the states which had early treaties with the Company. See Panikkar, *op. cit.,* pp. 86–87.

32. Lee-Warner, *op. cit.,* pp. 282–308. He contends that these rights apply to all of the states even though some of them have treaty guarantees that the government of India will never interfere in their internal affairs.

to reorganize the police force, the financial system, and other branches of the administration that have been mismanaged.

The difficulty about a system of this kind is to determine the minimum level of efficiency that should be required. If it is too low, the people of the states will suffer; if it is too high, the intervention will be aggressive and both the people and their rulers are likely to feel humiliated and embittered. The state of Mysore, which was restored to native rule in 1881 after fifty years of British control, has sometimes been taken as a model. The conditions under which the restoration was made warrant a considerable amount of British supervision and the rulers of other states are often compelled to submit to similar restrictions if they are unable to bring their administrations up to the Mysore standard. The solution has not been altogether satisfactory. There has been enough interference nearly everywhere to arouse the hostility of the princes without winning the gratitude of their subjects, but except in Mysore, Travancore, Baroda, and possibly one or two other states the level of efficiency is still much lower than it is in British India.

The states have become involved in the problem of constitutional reform because the Nationalist movement, the industrial revolution, and the improvement of transportation facilities have all combined to draw them closer to British India. For several years there has been a steady increase in the range of matters that should receive uniform treatment. The tariff is a good example. Although the majority of the states are landlocked they were not much affected by the tariff legislation of British India as long as it was on a revenue basis. The adoption of the policy of protection (1922), however, forced their people to make heavy indirect contributions to the government and industries of British India. When they try to retaliate by raising their own tariff walls they merely increase the cost of living, encourage smuggling, and interfere with legitimate business in an area where fiscal unity is highly desirable. There are many other subjects—defense, currency, banking and exchange, salt revenue, opium, railways, posts and telegraphs, prevention of the spread of epidemics, *et cetera*—which should likewise be regulated by a central government representing the whole country.[33] The attitude of the states toward federation is also influenced by political considerations. As hereditary rule depends on British support most of the rulers would like to secure a guarantee of their constitutional position before that support is withdrawn. They believe that they can get better terms now while they hold the balance between the Nationalists and the Imperialists than they can later if they have to deal with the Nationalists alone. There are others who believe that a guarantee of this kind is worthless and that they should either come to terms with the Nationalists[34] or prepare to fight them when the British evacuation occurs.

The growth of Nationalism is the chief factor in the struggle for constitutional progress in India, both as it affects the states and as it affects British India. It will be advisable, therefore, to sketch the early history of this movement and to analyze some of the grievances upon which it feeds before we discuss the efforts that have been made to implement the reforms promised by Mr. Montagu in 1917.

33. For a more detailed discussion of this subject, see *The Montagu-Chelmsford Report,* pars. 298–300, and *The Simon Report,* II, pars. 13–20.

34. This view is held by some of the best informed students of Indian affairs. See, for example, Edward Thompson and G. T. Garratt, *Rise and Fulfilment of British Rule in India* (London, 1934), p. 652: "We believe that, no matter what the Paramount Power may 'guarantee' to Indian Princes of their former status and unimpaired authority, they must come to terms with the majority, as nobles did in mediaeval Europe and the Samurai in Japan; and it is obvious that they know this themselves."

CHAPTER II

THE NATIONALIST MOVEMENT (1885–1917)

THE history of Indian Nationalism is sometimes traced back to the Mutiny of 1857, but it did not assume practical importance until the founding by Indians of the National Congress in 1885. Since that date there have been three main periods or stages of development, the first extending to the close of Lord Curzon's administration and the close of the Russo-Japanese War in 1905, the second from 1905 to Mr. Montagu's announcement of the new Indian policy in 1917, and the third from 1917 to the present time. The first two periods will be discussed in this chapter and the third in later chapters in connection with the Montagu-Chelmsford Reforms and the Constitution of 1935.

The events which led to the organization of the Indian National Congress may be summarized very briefly. During Lord Lytton's administration (1876–80) several measures were adopted which aroused opposition among the educated classes in India. Lord Salisbury, who was at that time Secretary of State for India, reduced the maximum age limit for the Indian Civil Service examinations from twenty-one to nineteen years. His intention was obvious. As the examinations were held only in Great Britain and were based on the curricula of the British universities, it was difficult for Indian students to complete their preparation before they were twenty-one and almost impossible to do it two years earlier. The premier Civil Service in India was to remain a special preserve for European British subjects. The second Afghan War (1878–79) was also unpopular because it imposed a financial burden on India which was apparently not justified by its results. Finally, there were the Arms Act and the Vernacular Press Act, under which Indians were disarmed and their newspapers gagged, although neither act applied to Europeans.

Better things were expected when the Gladstone government came into office in 1880. Lord Ripon, the new Governor-General, did all in his power to meet these expectations, but he was not very successful. His local government reforms have already been discussed. He brought about the repeal of the Vernacular Press Act and was also an advocate of the Ilbert Bill, a measure designed to place Europeans and Indians on an equality in the administration of the criminal laws. The principle involved in this bill does not now seem especially important. With a few modifications, it has recently been adopted by the reformed government of India without attracting much attention or producing any dire results. It created immense excitement, however, at the time and aroused stronger racial prejudices than any other measure which had been proposed since the Mutiny. The emasculation of the bill through the opposition of the European community in India was a valuable lesson to the Nationalist leaders and their British advisers. It showed what could be accomplished by organized agitation and thereby prepared the way for the creation of the National Congress.

It is difficult to say who first suggested the idea of the Congress, but the credit for its actual establishment is usually given to Mr. Allen O. Hume, an ex-official of the Indian Civil Service. The first session was held in Bombay in 1885 and the second in Calcutta in 1886. Since then there has usually been a regular annual meeting, although there was a gap from February, 1931, until October, 1934, when the organization was banned by the government. Special sessions have also been held occasionally in times of emergency; for example, the meeting in Bombay in August, 1918, to consider *The Montagu-Chelmsford Report* and the meeting in Calcutta in September, 1920, to consider the Turkish peace treaty, the Report of the Hunter Commission, and the advisability of adopting Mr. Gandhi's policy of noncoöperation.

There were 72 delegates at the first Congress and 412 at the second. The numbers slowly increased although for many years a large proportion of those who attended lived in or near the city in which the meeting was held. Since the war, the attendance has averaged more than 6,000 and every province in India has been represented. This is too large a number for effective work and the membership has recently been somewhat reduced. The delegates are chosen by the various provincial and district bodies affiliated with the Congress and every adult British subject without regard to sex, class, race, or creed is eligible.

The procedure of the Congress is simple. At the opening session an address of welcome is made by the chairman of the local committee, and the president of the year delivers what might be called the keynote speech. The presidency is usually held by a popular national leader, such as Mr. Dadabhai Naoroji, Sir P. M. Mehta, Mr. Gokhale, Sir Surendranath Banerjea, or the Pandit Jawaharlal Nehru, although the honor has, at one time or another, been conferred upon Sir William Wedderburn, Sir Henry Cotton, Mrs. Annie Besant, and other British radicals. The proceedings have been ordinarily conducted in Hindustani, although English or another vernacular may be used if there is good reason. The sessions usually last about three days and conclude with the adoption of a series of resolutions criticizing the government and recommending schemes for reform.

There are several organizations affiliated with the Congress, including the All-India Congress Committee, which has approximately 350 members, the Subjects Committee, which is composed of the same personnel, and an executive board of 15, which is called the Working Committee. Each province also has its Provincial Congress and its Provincial, District, and Subdistrict or Taluka Committees. A British Committee of the Indian National Congress was founded in 1889 by Sir William Wedderburn, Mr. Dadabhai Naoroji, Mr. W. S. Caine, and others to carry on propaganda in Great Britain. Sir William Wedderburn was chairman of this committee from the time it was founded until his death in 1918. He likewise helped to organize the Indian Parliamentary Committee in 1893, a body made up of members of Parliament who were pledged to attend Indian debates and to take a general interest in Indian affairs. A journal called *India* was established in February, 1890, as the official organ of the British Committee. Issued at first at irregular intervals, it became a monthly in 1892 and a weekly in 1898. The circulation was not extensive but it exerted a wide influence through the material it furnished to other papers, especially to those of radical tendencies. As a consequence of the theory, now generally accepted in India, that the people can work out their own salvation, there is a feeling that propaganda in Great Britain is illogical and unnecessary. The Nagpur Congress of 1920 decided, therefore, to discontinue the publication of *India* and the farewell issue appeared on January 14, 1921.

The Nationalist movement during the first period of its history, 1885–1905, was confined largely to Hindus of the student and professional classes, very little interest being shown by the other communities or by the merchants, landlords, and peasants of the Hindu community. It is true that there were always a few Parsees and Moslems associated with the movement, but, so far as the Moslems were concerned, the great majority followed the lead of Sir Sayyid Ahmad and would have nothing to do with it. Even as late as 1906, when the All-India Moslem League was formed, they were still inclined to be lukewarm, the objects of the League being communal rather than nationalistic. The League and the Congress were gradually drawn together, however, and after 1916 they were practically amalgamated until the recrudescence of communal animosity in the last few years began to drive them apart again.

Bombay was the chief center of disaffection in the early years. The leading parts were taken by two small communities in that presidency whose influence was out of all proportion to their numbers, the Chitpavan Brahmans and the Parsees. The Chitpavans are found mainly in the Poona section of the Deccan and the Parsees in the city of Bombay. Both communities have a high level of ability and a strong educational tradition. The Chitpavans are noted for their political and administrative capacity and the Parsees for their ability to make money. A few Parsees are, however, interested in politics and some of the most distinguished representatives of the Nationalist movement have come from their ranks.

The Nationalists were at that time divided into two fairly

well-defined groups: the Moderates, who tried by purely constitutional methods to bring about a few mild social, financial, and administrative reforms; and the Extremists, who were not very scrupulous about the methods employed and who occasionally resorted to the policy of terrorism that was being popularized by the Nihilists of Russia. As the people of India are especially addicted to hero worship, it may be useful to give brief sketches of the lives of some of the leaders. Mr. Dadabhai Naoroji, Mr. Justice Ranade, and Mr. Gopal Krishna Gokhale were the most influential members of the Moderate faction, and Mr. Bal Gangadhar Tilak was the undisputed leader of the Extremists. All were residents of the Bombay presidency and all except Mr. Naoroji were Chitpavan Brahmans.

Dadabhai Naoroji, affectionately called the Grand Old Man of India, was the son of a Parsee priest. He was born in the city of Bombay on September 4, 1825, and was educated there at Elphinstone College. He went to England in 1855 and spent a large part of the adult years of his life in that country. He founded the London Indian Society and the East India Association and served three years (1892–95) in Parliament, being the first Indian member of the House of Commons. While he was in Parliament he worked hard to secure the admission of Indians to the Civil Services in India and he also procured the appointment of a Royal Commission to investigate Indian expenditures (the Welby Commission, 1895). He assisted in the organization of the Indian National Congress in 1885 and was president of it in 1886, 1893, and 1906. He died in 1917 in his ninety-second year.

In addition to his other activities, Mr. Naoroji also helped the Nationalist cause by his numerous speeches and writings on financial and economic subjects. He read a series of papers before the Bombay branch of the East India Association in 1876, which were revised and published two years later under the title *Poverty of India*. This work and some other material were brought together in 1901 to form a larger book called *Poverty and Un-British Rule in India*. His main thesis was that the wealth of India had long been drained for the benefit of Great Britain and that this is the fundamental cause of India's poverty. In other words he originated the theory of the economic drain which bulks so large in modern Nationalist literature.[1]

Madhava Govinda Ranade, the oldest of the three Chitpavan leaders mentioned above, was born at Niphad in the Nasik district of Bombay presidency on January 18, 1842. Although for many years a judge of the High Court of Bombay and a very distinguished jurist, he was always chiefly interested in social and economic problems. He was one of the founders of the Prarthana Samaj, a Hindu reform sect in Bombay similar to the Brahma Samaj in Bengal, and he was also the principal founder of the Indian Social Conference which held its first meeting in 1887. He advocated the abolition of child marriage and the right of widows to remarry and was actively interested in the education of girls. In the field of economics he was one of the pioneer advocates of the protectionist policy which is now so popular in Indian political circles. He died on January 16, 1901.

The careers of Mr. Gokhale and Mr. Tilak were in some respects very much alike. In addition to the fact that they were both Chitpavan Brahmans, they were both born in the Ratnagiri district of Bombay and were interested in educational reform before they entered the arena of politics. For several years they were associated in the work of the Deccan Educational Society and the Fergusson College at Poona. Temperamentally, however, they were very different and it was not long before they drifted apart, Gokhale to become the most distinguished leader of the Moderates, and Tilak, of the Extremists.

Gopal Krishna Gokhale was born on May 9, 1866. From 1884 until 1902, he was engaged in educational work, most of the time as a professor in the Fergusson College. He began to take an active part in politics in 1899, first as a member of the Provincial Legislative Council of Bombay and later, from 1902 to 1915, as a member of the Imperial Legislative Coun-

1. For an account of the economic drain theory, see chap. v, "Economic and Financial Grievances."

cil. He was also President of the National Congress in 1905 and a member of the Royal Commission on the Public Services of 1912–15, although he died in 1915 before the report of the commission was completed. In knowledge of public affairs and skill in debate he had no rival among the Indian members of the Imperial Council. He was an unsparing critic of the government when he felt it deserved to be criticized, but he abhorred the revolutionary methods of Tilak and the Extremists. He favored Dominion Home Rule as an ultimate goal for India, but he realized that it ought to be preceded by a large measure of educational and social reform. His name will go down in history as an advocate of universal compulsory education and as the founder of the Servants of India Society.[2] Sir Valentine Chirol says that "Gokhale was perhaps the finest character that India has produced, blending accurate knowledge of Western history and Western thought with a profound understanding of the Indian mentality and of the ancient civilization that has moulded it."[3]

Bal Gangadhar Tilak, the stormy petrel of modern Indian political history, was born July 23, 1856, and died on the first of August, 1920. He graduated at the Deccan College in 1876 and shortly afterwards he and a few of his friends founded the New English School at Poona which later developed into the Fergusson College. They also organized the Deccan Educational Society (1884) and started two newspapers to further their educational activities, the *Mahratta*, printed in English, and the *Kesari* (Lion), printed in Marathi. Tilak was, however, more than a mere organizer. He was

2. The Servants of India Society was organized by Mr. Gokhale in 1905. The idea was apparently derived from the Jesuits. The young men who join the Society agree to devote their lives to the cause of their country and to promote, by constitutional means, the national interests of the Indian people. They assist educational movements, especially those for the education of women, and help to improve the conditions of the depressed classes. Mr. Gokhale was the first president of the Society.

3. *The Modern World, India* (London, 1926, V, 108. See John S. Hoyland, *Gopal Krishna Gokhale. His Life and Speeches* (Calcutta, 1933).

an eminent Sanskrit scholar and the author of several articles and books dealing with the antiquity of the Vedas.

The second stage of his career dates from 1889, when he became associated with the Indian National Congress. Almost immediately he won recognition as the leader of the Extremists. To quote again the words of Sir Valentine Chirol, he "was the most striking personality in the India of our times, except, perhaps, Gandhi, whose essential gentleness and humility he lacked, while he possessed on the other hand far greater gifts of intellect and far more political acumen." His great influence was due partly to his powers of oratory and partly to his newspapers, especially the *Kesari,* which for many years had the largest circulation of any paper published in India. It may also be attributed in some measure to the fact that he had a single-track mind. He wanted a political revolution and nothing else. Outside the field of politics his views were ultraconservative. He vigorously opposed the Act of 1890 raising the age of consent for child wives from ten to twelve years of age, and he led the fight in the Poona Congress in 1895 to prevent the Congress hall from being used as a meeting place for the Indian Social Conference. It is said that he became more liberal in his later years, but there is no evidence that he ever really appreciated the importance of social reform. On this issue he differed widely from Ranade and Gokhale, but his views were more in harmony with orthodox Hindu public opinion.

In the early days of Tilak's political activity it is doubtful whether he should be regarded as a Nationalist at all. He made a special appeal to religious and communal bigotry, arousing prejudice against Moslems and Indian Christians as well as against Europeans. Festivals were organized through his efforts in honor of Ganesh, the elephant-headed god of the Hindus, son of the god Shiva. There was also established a cult of Shivaji, the famous Maratha leader, whose chief title to fame was the tradition that he had assassinated a Moslem general during an uncertain truce. Tilak applauded this treacherous deed and apparently regarded it as a worthy precedent in justification of political murder.

One of the Shivaji festivals was held at Poona on June 12,

1897. In the account of the proceedings published in Tilak's paper, he is reported to have used the following language:

> Did Shivaji commit a sin in killing Afzal Khan [the Moslem general] or not? The answer to this question can be found in the Mahabharat itself. Srimat Krishna's advice in the *Gita* is to kill even our own teachers and our own kinsmen. No blame attaches to any person if he is doing deeds without being actuated by a desire to reap the fruits of his deeds. Sri Shivaji did nothing with the view to fill the void of his own stomach. With benevolent intentions he murdered Afzal Khan for the good of others.

It might be well to note the circumstances in which this speech was made and the events which immediately followed it. India had just been visited by the first great outbreak of the bubonic plague in modern times. The epidemic was especially violent in Poona, and the government in trying to suppress it had been searching private houses, establishing isolation camps, and adopting other measures of a similarly drastic character. Tilak had denounced these measures in the *Kesari* and had been especially severe in his criticism of Mr. Rand, the president of the Poona Plague Committee. On June 27, only fifteen days after the Shivaji festival speech, Mr. Rand and Lieutenant Ayerst of the Commissariat Department were assassinated by the brothers Chapekar, who were Tilak's followers. The Chapekars were convicted and executed. There was no evidence that Tilak had any direct connection with this horrible crime, but he was imprisoned for a year on the charge of publishing a seditious article in the *Kesari*. After his release he modified the tone of his criticism and the use of terroristic methods was abandoned until after the partition of Bengal.

The Nationalist movement did not become truly nationalistic until the second period of its history, from 1905 to 1917, when it spread over the whole of India and affected all communities and all social and industrial classes. The way was prepared for it by the terrible famines of 1896 and 1899–1900 and the ravages of the plague, which the political agitators used to discredit British rule. Its growth was unwittingly assisted by government activities, both in India and in other parts of the British Empire. The Bengalis, for example, were antagonized by the Universities Act, the Calcutta Municipal Act, and the partition policy of Lord Curzon; and the loyalty of the Punjabis was shaken by fiscal and agrarian measures of one kind or another. The British government added to the discontent of the Moslems by permitting Moslem countries to be despoiled by European powers and by taking a share of the spoils for themselves. A great deal of feeling was also aroused in all parts of India and among all classes by the exclusion of Indian immigrants from the self-governing Dominions and the ill-treatment of Indians already domiciled in the Union of South Africa. The Sikhs were especially aroused by the refusal of the Canadian authorities to allow the *Komagata Maru*, with several hundred Sikh passengers aboard, to land at Vancouver in 1914.

As Nationalism increased in strength its program became more radical. There were still Moderates and Extremists, but they both moved rapidly toward the Left. If *The Montagu-Chelmsford Report* had been made in 1905 or even in 1914 it would have been regarded as distinctly revolutionary. As a matter of fact, when it did appear in 1918, it was accepted very reluctantly by the Moderates and was rejected altogether by the Extremists, who insisted that a specific date should be set for the establishment of Dominion Home Rule. In spite of the general trend toward radicalism, the Moderates secured control of the National Congress at the famous meeting at Surat in 1907 and retained it until 1916. Their success was due partly to the Morley-Minto Reforms, partly to the masterly leadership of Mr. Gokhale, and partly to the fact that Mr. Tilak was compelled to spend most of these years in exile. These advantages were soon lost. By 1914, the Morley-Minto Reforms had come to be regarded as hopelessly inadequate even by the Moderates; Mr. Gokhale died in 1915; and Mr. Tilak returned from exile in 1914. A so-called compromise was adopted at the Lucknow Congress in 1916, but it was a compromise in which the Moderates had to accept the terms dictated by their opponents.

Mr. Gokhale continued to be the outstanding leader of the Moderates as long as he lived. Among his associates should be mentioned Sir Surendranath Banerjea, Sir Pherozeshah Mehta, and the Moslem Aga Khan. Sir Sankaran Nair, the Rt. Hon. V. S. Srinivasa Sastri, and Sir Satyendra (later Lord) Sinha might also be included, although they were not especially prominent until after 1917. Mr. Tilak retained his supremacy among the Extremists during this period, but in the latter part of it he had to share the honor with Mrs. Besant. Of somewhat less importance in the movement as a whole, though very influential in their own provinces, were Lala Lajpat Rai in the Punjab and Mr. Bepin Chandra Pal and the Ghose brothers in Bengal.

Sir Surendranath Banerjea was born in Calcutta in 1848. His father was a liberal Brahman and he was himself one of the first Brahmans to break caste rules and go to England. He was also one of the first Indians to pass the open competitive examinations for the Indian Civil Service. The regulations at that time provided that candidates should be not more than twenty-one years of age. Banerjea was just under twenty-one, but an application blank which he had previously filled out as a candidate for the matriculation examination at the University of Calcutta seemed to indicate that he was several months older. The discrepancy was due to the fact that in India a person's age is calculated from the date of conception and not from the date of birth. The Civil Service Commissioners refused to accept this explanation and Banerjea was compelled to appeal to the courts for justice. He received an appointment, but after a short time some trivial charges were brought against him and he was dismissed from the Service. He and his friends always believed that he was badly treated, that he was punished not because of his official delinquencies, but because he had the temerity to break into the most exclusive of all the Indian Services.

Banerjea now determined to practice law. He had already spent eight terms at the Middle Temple and he returned for the remaining four terms, but when he had complied with all of the usual conditions he was refused admission to the bar because of his dismissal from the Civil Service. Excluded both from the government and the bar, he decided to enter the teaching profession. He returned to India in 1875 and taught

English Literature in various schools in Calcutta, one of which ultimately developed into Ripon College. He continued to teach until 1912. In the meantime he had also made a great reputation as an orator and a journalist. He bought the *Bengalee*, a small weekly newspaper in Calcutta, in 1879. The circulation increased rapidly, but Banerjea's other interests took up so much of his time that he did not convert the paper into a daily until 1900. It was for many years one of the most influential papers in India.

The political career of Banerjea began about 1876 when he and a few of his friends founded the Indian Association which developed into the most powerful political organization in Bengal. He was a member of the Provincial Legislative Council from 1893 to 1901 and of the Imperial Legislative Council from 1913 to 1916. In the latter body his influence was distinctly inferior to that of Mr. Gokhale because his emotional Bengali style of oratory, though effective in dealing with large public audiences, was not well adapted to the Council chamber. He was a faithful member of the Indian National Congress, of which he was elected president in 1895 and again in 1902. The outstanding feature of this earlier and more radical stage of his public life, however, was the bitter fight which he waged against the partition of Bengal. He was defeated, but he aroused the spirit of the Bengalis as it had never been aroused before, and he did more than anyone else to bring them into the main current of the Nationalist movement. His influence indeed was so great that he was popularly acclaimed "the uncrowned king of Bengal."

It is difficult to say when Mr. Banerjea became a Moderate. His point of view really never changed. He was merely unable or unwilling to move as rapidly toward the Left as the majority of his former colleagues. In the split at Surat in 1907 he sided with the conservatives and signed the so-called creed which stated that the goal of the Congress was the attainment of self-government for India within the Empire by purely constitutional means. He also strongly supported the Empire in the crisis of 1914, and made recruiting speeches in various parts of Bengal. He could hardly be classed as a pronounced Moderate, however, until the beginning of the conflict over the

Montagu-Chelmsford Reforms in 1918. He served for a time as Minister of Local Government in Bengal, was knighted in 1921, and died in 1925.

Next to Dadabhai Naoroji, Sir Pherozeshah Mehta was probably the ablest leader that the Parsee community has produced during the last hundred years. Born in Bombay, August 4, 1845, he was educated at Elphinstone College, and received the degrees of B.A. and M.A. from Bombay University in 1864. He then went to England to read law and was called to the bar in 1868. Shortly after his return to India, he became a member of the Provincial Legislative Council and a Fellow and member of the Senate of Bombay University, all of which positions he continued to hold during the greater part of the rest of his life. He was also for a few years (1894–96, 1898–1901) a member of the Imperial Legislative Council. He was one of the founders of the Indian National Congress and was president of it in 1890. He was keenly interested in municipal and educational reform, in the movement to secure the admission of Indians to the Public Services, in the efforts to ameliorate the conditions of Indians in South Africa, and in other questions too numerous to mention. In the conflict between the Moderates and the Extremists he played the role of peacemaker, but when the final split came at Surat in 1907 he definitely allied himself with the Moderates. He opposed Mr. Gokhale's efforts to heal the schism in 1914 because he believed that it would lead to the control of the Congress by the Extremists who would use it for revolutionary purposes. He was not, however, a sycophant and was never entirely trusted by the more conservative government officials. Lord Sydenham, who was Governor of Bombay from 1907 to 1913, seems to have regarded him as a very dangerous radical. Furthermore, he founded the Bombay *Chronicle* (1913), which, in the days when Mr. B. G. Horniman was editor, could scarcely be called an organ of conservatism. He was knighted in 1904 and died on November 5, 1915.

His Highness the Aga Khan was born at Karachi, November 2, 1875. He is rich and well educated and a famous sportsman, his horses having won many prizes on the race courses of England and France, including three victories in the Derby.

Since the death of his father in 1885 he has been the spiritual head of the Ismailia Shi'as, a small Moslem sect found mainly in India and British East Africa. Although regarded as religiously unorthodox by the great majority of Indian Moslems, Sunnis, he has for many years been their most influential political leader. He was apparently the first member of their community to realize the significance of the Morley-Minto Reforms. If political authority was gradually to be delegated to the people of India, the Moslems must abandon their old attitude of aloofness or be prepared to see all the benefits go to the Hindus. He was the head of the Moslem delegation which waited on Lord Minto in 1906 and convinced him of the necessity of liberal Moslem representation in the enlarged Legislative Councils. He also played a leading part in the founding of the All-India Moslem League (1906), of which he became a kind of perennial president. Among his many other interests and activities there might be mentioned his efforts to abolish the purdah system among Indian Moslems, his efforts to help the Indians in East Africa, his work in raising the Moslem Anglo-Oriental College at Aligarh to the rank of a university, his loyal services during the war, and the interesting analysis of Indian and Middle Eastern affairs which he made in his book on *India in Transition* in 1918. He was an admirer of Mr. Gokhale and Sir Pherozeshah Mehta and used his influence among the Moslems to further their ideal of progress by evolution rather than revolution.

The other Moderate leaders mentioned above may be dismissed very briefly so far as their activities before 1917 are concerned. Sir Sankaran Nair was a Hindu who was born in the Malabar district of Madras, July 11, 1857. He was at various times judge of the High Court of Madras, member of the Madras Legislative Council, President of the Indian National Congress (1897), and President of the Social Conference. At the close of this period he was the Educational Member of the Governor-General's Executive Council, a position which he held from 1915 to 1919. He was one of the pioneer advocates of social reform, especially in the Madras presidency, where there are so many millions of "untouchables." The Rt. Hon. V. S. Srinivasa Sastri, also a native of the province of Madras, was born September 22, 1869. He joined the Servants of India Society in 1907 and succeeded Mr. Gokhale as its president in 1915. He was a member of the Madras Legislative Council, 1913–16, and of the Imperial Legislative Council, 1916–20. During the period before 1917 he was primarily interested in the social and humanitarian work of the Servants of India Society and was a devoted disciple of Mr. Gokhale. Lord Sinha, the first Indian member of the Viceroy's Executive Council and the only Indian member of the House of Lords, was born in Bengal in 1864. He was educated at the Presidency College in Calcutta and at Lincoln's Inn and was called to the bar in 1886. After a distinguished career as a barrister, he served as Advocate General of Bengal, 1907–9, as Law Member of the Governor-General's Executive Council, 1909–10, again as Advocate General of Bengal, 1916–17, and member of the Bengal Executive Council, 1917–18. He died in 1928.

We come now to one of the most remarkable figures in the history of the Nationalist movement. It is said to be the privilege of a well-born Englishman to be eccentric. Mrs. Annie Besant was not especially well born and was not a man, but she was English, at least on the paternal side, and her life is convincing proof that the men of her country have no monopoly of eccentricity. She was born on October 1, 1847. Her father was Dr. William Page Wood, a London physician, and her mother was Irish. She married the Reverend Mr. Frank Besant in 1867, but separated from him in 1873 when she found she could no longer accept the orthodox teachings of Christianity. For a few years she was under the influence of Mr. Charles Bradlaugh and in consequence was very much interested in atheism and birth-control. She also wrote and published a number of pamphlets attacking British Imperialism in Ireland, Egypt, and India. In 1884 she was converted to socialism by Mr. Hyndman and Mr. Bernard Shaw. This resulted in a break with Mr. Bradlaugh, who was an individualist. About 1889 she became a theosophist and a follower of Madame H. P. Blavatsky and shortly afterwards went to India, where she spent the remainder of her life. In 1898, with the assistance of Colonel Olcott and a few Hindus, she founded the Central Hindu College, which subsequently became the nucleus of the Hindu University at Benares. She started a weekly newspaper at Madras in 1914, called the *Commonwealth*, and she also purchased the Madras *Standard*, which was renamed *New India* and published as a daily.

During the Great War she came to the conclusion that Britain's need was India's opportunity, and in 1916 founded the All-India Home Rule League at Madras, which soon had branches all over India. This and the Indian Home Rule League founded by Mr. Tilak greatly strengthened the organization of the Extremists. According to Mrs. Besant, two leagues were formed instead of one because many of her friends disliked Mr. Tilak and many of his friends disliked her. It was simply a question of getting as large a membership as possible. The two organizations worked in harmony with each other and also with the Congress and the Moslem League, their first task being to advertise and popularize the so-called Congress-League plan of government. It was chiefly Mrs. Besant who brought about the reconciliation between Tilak and his former associates, which made it possible for the Extremists to capture the Lucknow Congress in 1916. She and Tilak attended that meeting and when they appeared on the platform together they received a tremendous ovation. Shortly afterwards, she got into trouble with the Madras government and was interned in her summer cottage at the mountain station of Ootacamund. She was released a few months later, through the intercession of Mr. Montagu, and as a reward for her "martyrdom" was elected president of the Congress in 1917. Her attitude toward the Montagu-Chelmsford Reforms and Mr. Gandhi's policy of noncoöperation will be considered later. She died in 1933.

Lala Lajpat Rai was born in 1865 in the town of Jagraon in the Ludhiana district of the Punjab. His father was a devout follower of the Swami Dayanand Saraswati, the founder of the Arya Samaj. The chief object of the Arya Samaj is to bring about social and religious reform through the renaissance of early Hindu doctrines, its favorite mottoes being "Back to the Vedas" and "Aryavarta for the Aryans." Efforts are also made to check the conversion of Hindus to Islam and to Christianity and to bring back into the fold those who have already been converted. The work is largely humanitarian and educational. Lajpat Rai became associated with this movement early in life and he always devoted to it a liberal share of his time and the large income that he received from his law practice. He was also its best-known historian. He was one of the founders of the Dayanand Anglo-Vedic College at Lahore in 1886 and was very active in humanitarian work during the great famines of 1896–97 and 1899–1900. He was especially concerned about the welfare of Hindu children whose parents had died of famine and was anxious to prevent their falling into the hands of Christian missionaries. It was in fact largely due to his efforts that the Punjab government laid down the principle that no orphans were to be made over to persons or institutions of different religions until all attempts to find persons or institutions of their own religion willing to take care of them had failed.

The reputation of the Arya Samaj as an anti-British political organization is partly due to the influence of Sir Valentine Chirol's book on *Indian Unrest*, but it is doubtful whether his views of the movement would have been so generally accepted in England if they had not apparently been confirmed by the activities of Lajpat Rai. In 1905, he joined Mr. Gokhale on a mission to England to protest against the partition of Bengal and other unpopular measures of Lord Curzon's administration. After his return to India, he supported the swadeshi[4] movement and is said to have played a very active part in arousing disaffection among the peasants of the Punjab. He and Ajit Singh, the leader of the Sikh agitators, were deported in 1907 under the authority of Bengal Regulation III of 1818. They were soon allowed to return, but, after a short interval, Lajpat Rai again left India and remained away until 1920, spending a considerable part of his exile in the United States, where he became the best-known representative of Indian Nationalism. The secret of his great influence was to be found in

4. Swadeshi, *lit.*, "of one's own country," means the encouragement of Indian trade and industry. It is usually associated with the boycott of British and other foreign goods.

the austere simplicity of his life, the fervor of his oratory, and the cleverness of his pen. He was the author of many books and articles, both in English and in Urdu, including lives of Mazzini and Garibaldi, which have had wide circulation in the Punjab. He died November 17, 1928.

In Bengal, as Mr. Surendranath Banerjea grew more conservative, Mr. Bepin Chandra Pal, Mr. Aravinda Ghose, and Mr. Barendra Kumar Ghose became the chief representatives of the radical point of view. These men were educated in the English tradition and they were also very much influenced by the Brahma Samaj. They were more liberal than Mr. Tilak in their attitude toward social reform, although they were loyal to ancient Hindu ideals and ardent exponents of Tilak's political program. During the most active stage of their careers they were journalists, and their newspapers exerted a powerful influence in organizing the agitation against the partition of Bengal and in upholding those principles of swaraj (Home Rule), swadeshi (economic independence), boycott, and national education, which played such an important part in the history of India after 1905.

Mr. Pal was born November 7, 1858, and was educated partly at the Presidency College at Calcutta and partly in England. He started his journalistic career in 1883 as subeditor of *Bengal Public Opinion*, but for a number of years his interests were divided among journalism, foreign travel, library work, and missionary work for the Brahma Samaj. He started *New India*[5] in 1901 and afterwards *Bande Mataram* (Hail Motherland) and the *Hindu Review*. Mr. Pal was also a forceful public speaker. He delivered some lectures at Madras in 1907 which were long regarded as the classic exposition of the Extremist creed. They had an enormous influence in bringing the Madras presidency into the militant Nationalist movement and also in preparing the way for the split between the Moderates and the Extremists at the Surat Congress in 1907. In discussing "The Gospel of Swaraj" in these

5. This paper, published in Calcutta from 1901 to 1907, should not be confused with Mrs. Besant's *New India,* which was started in 1914 and was published in Madras.

lectures he apparently advocated national independence, although he later denied any such intention and said that he really favored Imperial Federation. His influence with the Extremists began to decline about 1911 as his criticism of the government became more temperate and more constructive and he became more committed to the idea of Imperial Federation.

Aravinda Ghose was born in Calcutta on August 15, 1872. At the age of seven he was taken to England to be educated, first at St. Paul's School and later at King's College, Cambridge. He passed the examinations for the Indian Civil Service in 1890, but failed in the riding test. He graduated two years later, taking a first class in the classical tripos, and then returned to India, where he entered the service of the Gaekwar of Baroda. His promotion was rapid and he finally became the vice-principal of the Baroda State College. At the beginning of the contest over the partition of Bengal, he sacrificed his position and a promising future for a life of poverty and hardship in the service of his motherland. He soon became associated with the *Bande Mataram* and, through its columns, carried on a vigorous fight not only against the partition of Bengal, but also against British rule in all of its aspects and against Western civilization in general. A poet and a religious ascetic, he inspired the younger generation of Bengali Nationalists with a kind of mystical fervor that was unknown in other parts of India. Although it was believed in government circles that he was primarily responsible for the violent character of the Nationalist movement in Bengal, it was difficult to secure evidence against him that could be used in a court of law. He was arrested in 1908 on a charge of conspiring to provide rifles and ammunition for revolutionary purposes, but after a long and expensive trial he was finally acquitted. When charges were again brought against him early in 1910, he retired to the French colony of Pondicherry to practice yoga or to escape arrest, and is still living there at the present time. His political influence has waned and he is now known chiefly as a poet and a popularizer of the sacred literature of the early Hindus.

Barendra Kumar Ghose, a younger brother of Aravinda,

was born in England in 1880. He was taken to India as a child and lived for a time with his brother in Baroda. He went to Bengal in 1902 and tried to organize a revolutionary movement, but was not very successful and soon returned to Baroda. He would probably have abandoned his efforts altogether if Lord Curzon had not provided him with a popular issue. Shortly after the partition policy was announced, both the brothers returned to Bengal and Barendra became the leader of what might be called the extreme Left wing of the opposition movement. His method of procedure was to get hold of groups of school boys, give them religious instruction, and use their religious zeal for political ends; to organize secret societies for purposes of propaganda, for collecting arms and ammunition, and for learning how to manufacture bombs; and to further the cause by establishing vernacular newspapers. With the assistance of two of his friends he started the *Jugantar* (New Era) in 1906. This paper was from the outset more radical and more outspoken than Banerjea's *Bengalee*, Pal's *New India*, or the *Bande Mataram*. It was also written in fluent and eloquent Bengali. "The Government translator confessed in the High Court that he had never before read, in Bengali, language so lofty, so pathetic and so stirring, that it was impossible to convey it in an English translation."[6] The editors and printers were fined and imprisoned time and time again, but the paper continued to appear under new auspices and with a rapidly increasing circulation. It was finally suppressed in 1908 under the Newspapers (Incitement to Offenses) Act, which was enacted primarily for that purpose. Ghose ceased to play an active part in politics about that time, but the revolutionary movement in Bengal still bears the stamp of his influence and that of the *Jugantar*.

Some of the characteristics of the period from 1905 to 1917 have already been indicated. One of the most striking features was the organized propaganda carried on outside of India, especially in England, France, and Germany, and on the Pacific coast of the United States. There are people in

6. Sir Valentine Chirol, *Indian Unrest*, p. 95.

Great Britain who look upon this propaganda and that conducted more recently by the Soviet government of Russia as the chief source of discontent in India, just as there are equally credulous people in the United States who attribute the major part of American industrial and political unrest in the last few years to the malign influence of Lenin, Trotsky, and Stalin. In the case of India there are a few facts which seem to lend an air of plausibility to this theory. The report of the Rowlatt Sedition Committee in 1918 describes in great detail the activities of Indian exiles in England, France, and the United States and the efforts of Germany to stir up trouble in India during the Great War. But, however extensive this propaganda may have been, it would be an incomplete diagnosis to regard it as the chief cause of dissension. It would not have gained any headway if India had not already been seething with discontent.

In India itself there were three main centers of activity—Bombay, Bengal, and the Punjab. There were no indigenous movements of a revolutionary character in the other provinces, although there were occasional indications of outside propaganda and a few sporadic crimes of violence. In the next few pages an effort will be made to summarize the progress of the movement during this period and to pay some attention to the encouragement that it received from the outside. The chief source of authority is the report of the Sedition Committee.

Shortly after the Rand-Ayerst murders in 1897, there went to England from Kathiawar in the Bombay presidency a young man by the name of Shyamaji Krishnavarma. Very little is known of his movements in the next few years, but early in 1905 he started in London the Indian Home Rule Society, appointed himself president and issued the first number of the *Indian Sociologist*, a monthly periodical which openly glorified political murder. He also founded India House at Highgate as a meeting place for Indian students and other Indians living in London who were in sympathy with the Extremist party. A celebration of the Mutiny of 1857 was held at India House in May, 1908, in which the Mutiny was referred to as the Indian War of Independence.

Another meeting was held in June, at which an Indian student lectured on the making of bombs and attempted to justify their use as political weapons. He is reported to have said, "When one of you is prepared to use a bomb at the risk of his life, let him come to me and I will give him full particulars." In 1909, Krishnavarma got into trouble with the police and fled to Paris, where he continued to publish the *Indian Sociologist*.

Krishnavarma's chief associate was Vinayak Damodas Savarkar, a young Chitpavan Brahman from the Nasik district of Bombay who had been educated at the Fergusson College in Poona. Savarkar went to England in 1906 and became the leader of the India House group in 1909. At the Sunday meetings he often made incendiary speeches and read passages from a book he had written entitled *The Indian War of Independence, 1857, by an Indian Nationalist.* In June, 1909, he received word from India that his elder brother, Ganesh Savarkar, had been convicted on a charge of abetting war against the King and sentenced to transportation. As a consequence of this news, his language was especially violent at the Sunday meeting of June 20, and he vowed his intention to wreak vengeance on the British. Eleven days later (July 1), Colonel Sir W. Curzon Wyllie, an official of the India Office, was assassinated at the Imperial Institute in London. It would be difficult to prove any direct connection between Savarkar's speech and this crime, but it is significant to note that the assassin, Madan Lal Dhingra, was a member of India House and was entirely under Savarkar's influence.

The primary object of the India House group, however, was not to murder British officials in England, but to organize revolutionary Nationalism in India. Incendiary literature was smuggled into the country in large quantities, including Savarkar's *War of Indian Independence, 1857*, the *Indian Sociologist*, and various newspapers and pamphlets published on the continent of Europe. On one of the prisoners arrested in connection with the Nasik conspiracy there were found several copies of a pamphlet entitled *Bande Mataram*, which glorified the murder of Curzon Wyllie. "Terrorise the officials, English and Indian," says this pamphlet, "and the collapse of the whole machinery of oppression is not very far. . . . This campaign of separate assassination is the best conceivable method of paralysing the bureaucracy and of arousing the people." There were also secret shipments of arms and ammunition, including at least one fairly large consignment of Browning pistols.

Although the members of India House represented all parts of India, the connections with Bombay were naturally the most intimate because both Krishnavarma and Savarkar came from that presidency. The opportunities for propaganda were also unusually good in Bombay owing to the pioneer work that had already been done by Mr. Tilak. Tilak was comparatively inactive for a few years after his release from prison in 1899, partly perhaps because he had become cautious and partly because he was involved in a long and expensive lawsuit. The partition of Bengal brought him again into prominence. The Bengalis adopted the swadeshi program that he had long advocated, and the newspapers founded by Bepin Chandra Pal and the Ghose brothers were to a large extent modeled upon his own *Kesari*. He played an important part in the National Congresses of 1905 and 1906 and, with the aid of the younger Bengali element, tried to capture the Congress at Surat in 1907. As a result of the defeat at Surat, he and his followers practically withdrew from the Congress movement altogether for nearly ten years. This was unfortunate. The Congress is a public body and its control involves a certain amount of responsibility, whereas the secret organizations which flourished among the Extremists during these years were almost entirely free from the restraining influence of Indian public opinion.

The murder of Mrs. and Miss Kennedy in 1908 will be discussed later in connection with Bengal. Here it will be sufficient to say that Tilak excused this crime and praised the use of bombs. For two articles published in the *Kesari* in May and June, 1908, he was convicted and sentenced to six years' transportation, which was subsequently commuted to simple imprisonment at Mandalay. When his sentence expired in 1914, he reëntered the political arena, coöperated with Mrs. Besant in organizing a Home Rule campaign and secured control of the Congress at Lucknow in 1916. Shortly after this, he and

Mrs. Besant drifted apart and were both eclipsed by the rising fame of Mr. Gandhi. Tilak died August 1, 1920, while Gandhi's star was still in the ascendant.

During this period and especially after the imprisonment of Tilak, Nasik became a rival of Poona as a seat of disaffection. Nasik is a city of about 25,000 inhabitants situated near the headwaters of the Godavari River, 107 miles northeast of the city of Bombay. It is one of the holiest of Hindu cities and a famous pilgrimage center, a kind of Benares on a smaller scale. More than a third of the population are Brahmans, including a small group of Chitpavans. An association called the Mitra Mêla was formed here in 1899 in connection with the Ganpati celebrations. Under the leadership of the Savarkar brothers, it developed into a political organization known as the Adhinav Bharat (Young India). Reference has already been made to the transportation of Ganesh Savarkar in June, 1909, and to the probable connection between this affair and the assassination of Colonel Sir W. Curzon Wyllie. There was also another victim. The district magistrate of Nasik who committed Savarkar for trial was Mr. Jackson. "Pundit" Jackson, as he was called by his friends, was a scholar widely known for his sympathy with the Hindu people and his knowledge of their institutions and sentiments. He was shot and killed on December 21, 1909, with a Browning pistol which was afterwards identified as one of those that had been sent to India by the India House conspirators in London. The crime was committed by Ananta Luxman Kanhere, a young Chitpavan Brahman, who was convicted and executed. In the general investigation of the Nasik conspiracy that followed 38 men were put on trial, of whom 27 were found guilty and sentenced to various terms of imprisonment. With one exception, all of these conspirators were Brahmans and nearly all were Chitpavans.

In addition to the troubles in Poona and Nasik there were also some disturbances in the state of Gwalior and in the city of Ahmedabad, where an attempt was made to assassinate the Viceroy and Lady Minto in November, 1909. The conditions in the Bombay presidency as a whole were relatively normal, however, from the close of 1909 until the outbreak of the riots in 1919. The center of revolutionary agitation had, in fact, already shifted from Bombay to Bengal as early as 1905.

The local causes of discontent in Bengal may be summed up briefly. In the first place, Bengal has a larger English-educated class than any other province. The Bengalis, together with the Parsees, were the first Indians to send their sons to England to qualify for the bar and for the higher grades of the Civil and Medical Services and they are still sending them in large numbers to British and American universities. There are also many colleges in Bengal itself where the instruction is given in English and a network of English preparatory schools which extends to the remotest villages. The members of the English-educated class are called bhadralok, which means respectable people. In the early days, as British authority was extended over northern India, the bhadralok established a kind of monopoly on all the most important official and educational positions except the few which the British reserved for themselves. Those conditions obviously could not last. With the spread of English education in the other provinces more local candidates for office were able to qualify and they were naturally given preferential treatment. Although the field of enterprise was thus restricted, the Bengalis continued to increase their educational output and to retain the old system of education without any change. The emphasis was still on literary, historical, and legal subjects and the student was still taught to look forward to a government appointment, to a teaching position, or to a successful career as a lawyer. If he was disappointed, there was practically nothing else that he could do without loss of prestige. He had to be supported by his family, who had already probably made great sacrifices to give him an education. There were thousands of young Bengalis in Lord Curzon's time who found themselves in this position. It would be difficult to imagine a better system of recruiting the forces of political agitation. Other conditions were also propitious. There has probably never been any other period of Bengali history when it was so easy to appeal to religious enthusiasm and national idealism.

The majority of the population of Bengal are Moslems, but, as the Moslems have not made very much educational progress, nearly all of the bhadralok are Hindus. The proportion was even larger in the days of Lord Curzon. Western-educated Hindus were long inclined to abandon the manners and customs of India and to imitate those of Europe; were prone to abjure their religion, either to become atheists or to associate themselves with the Brahma Samaj or some similar organization designed to bring Hinduism into harmony with Western ethical ideals. About 1890 these conditions began to change. There arose a group of men and a woman (Mrs. Besant) who were convinced that the Hindu religion is the best in the world. If it has any defects, the remedy can be found in its own sacred writings. For a time, the educated classes held themselves aloof from this movement, but they were soon swept into it and are now among its most ardent adherents.

For Bengal, the forerunner of this Hindu revival was Sri Ramakrishna, a religious ascetic who made an enormous impression on the popular imagination by the purity and simplicity of his life. But while Ramakrishna prepared the way for the movement he was not really a part of it. It developed along lines that were alien to the spirit of his teachings. According to his gospel, all religions are true. If we follow any path in the right spirit, God will guide us, and we will ultimately reach our destination. "The only thing necessary for realization is whole-hearted and whole-souled devotion to God."

Ramakrishna died in 1886. His work was continued by his disciples, of whom the chief was Narendra Nath Dutt, better known as the Swami Vivekananda. At the Parliament of Religions held at the World's Fair in Chicago in 1893, Vivekananda was by far the most impressive figure. He organized Vedanta societies in various parts of America and Europe and, on his return to India in 1897, he was hailed as a great prophet of the Hindu faith. Religious and philosophic centers were established under the auspices of the Ramakrishna Mission and Vedantism was proclaimed as the future world religion. This was a departure from the broad liberalism of Ramakrishna. A still greater departure was made after Vivekananda's death in 1902, when his writings and teachings were popularized and made the basis of a Hindu renaissance in

Bengal. In this movement there was a subtle and indefinable blending of religion and politics. If there was a Golden Age in religion, why was there not also a Golden Age in politics? If Hindus were capable of creating the greatest of all religions, why were they not capable of governing their own country? If "Back to the Vedas" was a good motto, why was not "Aryavarta for the Aryans" equally good? The Bengalis are a temperamental people and these arguments appealed to their emotions as well as to their intellects. Bepin Chandra Pal and the Ghose brothers were great emotional artists and they knew exactly when and how to make their appeal in the most convincing manner. Vivekananda's brother was one of Barendra Ghose's associates in the establishment of the *Jugantar*.

It was while this revival was in the first vigor of its youth that Lord Curzon decided to partition the province of Bengal. From a purely administrative point of view, an argument could be made in favor of the partition policy; a very good argument, in fact, was made by the late Mr. Lovat Fraser in his book on *India under Lord Curzon and After* (1911). It would even be possible to defend the particular scheme advocated by Lord Curzon in comparison with that subsequently carried out in 1911. Administrative efficiency is not, however, the only factor that should be considered. The partition was a bad political measure and it was carried out at the worst possible time. The psychological results were similar to those produced in later years by General Dyer's conduct at Amritsar in 1919. The Extremists were given an issue which made it possible for them to rally merchants, landlords, and other normally conservative groups to the support of a radical program.

The old Bengal, as it existed before 1905, was the most difficult province in India to govern. Its area was 189,837 square miles and it had a population of over 78,000,000, as compared with 48,000,000 in the United Provinces, the next largest provincial area. The transportation facilities were bad and the huge mofussil or rural area was overshadowed by the city of Calcutta, which at that time was the capital, not only of Bengal, but of all British India. Furthermore, owing to the permanent settlement of the land revenues, there was less contact between district officials and the people than there was in the other provinces.

The most neglected part of the province was the great rice- and jute-growing region lying east of the Ganges. This is a land of rivers and swamps and terrifically enervating heat. It is also a land of wealth and a land in which most of the people are their own bankers. The police force in those days was small and badly equipped and the nature of their morale may be judged by the fact that service in the river patrol boats was regarded as a punishment. The consequence was a tremendous amount of robbery (dacoity), murder, and other crimes of violence. This section was also neglected in various other ways. Although it contributed heavily to the support of the government, it received very little public money for education or railways or the development of its shipping facilities.

Mr. Lovat Fraser gives in the book mentioned above a detailed account of the origin of the partition scheme. Early in 1903, a suggestion was made by Sir Andrew Fraser, the Lieutenant-Governor of Bengal, that a part of the eastern section of the province where the administrative difficulties were most acute should be detached from Bengal and annexed to Assam. Lord Curzon endorsed this suggestion in principle, but, after a further investigation, he changed its character by greatly increasing the area that was to be affected. He also provided for a rectification of the frontier between Bengal and the Central Provinces. His plan was approved by the India Office with a few slight modifications and was put into operation in 1905.

The three divisions of Chittagong, Dacca, and Rajshahi and some smaller pieces of territory were joined with Assam to form a new province called Eastern Bengal and Assam. At the same time, the district of Sambalpur and a few tiny Indian states were transferred from the Central Provinces to the old province of Bengal. In the new province the area of the two sections was approximately the same—50,000 square miles in Eastern Bengal and 56,000 in Assam—but there was a great disparity in the population, which was about 25,000,000 in Eastern Bengal and 6,000,000 in Assam. Instead of annexing a part of Eastern Bengal, Assam was itself absorbed by Eastern Bengal. The area of old Bengal was reduced from 189,837 to 141,580 square miles and the population from 78,000,000 to 54,000,000.

In defense of his policy, Lord Curzon argued that it would lighten the burden of the Bengal government, improve the administration of Eastern Bengal, and give Assam a seaport at Chittagong. These were sound arguments, but they were based on administrative and economic considerations while other aspects of the problem were ignored. The lower Ganges runs through the heart of the Bengali country. The people on both sides of the river in eastern and central Bengal belong to the same racial stock and speak the same language. The partition was, therefore, a dismemberment of the "Bengali nation" and there was no reason to doubt the sincerity of Mr. Surendranath Banerjea and other leaders who opposed it on that ground. Their opposition was justified in 1911 when the British government approved the reunion of the "two Bengals" and endeavored to solve the administrative problem by carving the new province of Bihar and Orissa out of the western or non-Bengali section of the old province.

The religious issue was also involved. The lower Ganges may not be a racial or linguistic frontier, but it is to a large extent a religious frontier, the Hindus predominating west of the river and the Moslems east of it. The Hindus are also strong a little further toward the northeast frontier and, before 1905, they were in the majority both in Bengal and in Assam. Their predominance in Bengal was of course increased by the partition, but in the new province the Moslem majority in Eastern Bengal exceeded the Hindu majority in Assam, the total figures for the entire area being about 18,000,000 Moslems and 12,000,000 Hindus. There was a common belief among Hindus at that time that the British authorities in general were partial to the Moslems and that Lord Curzon was especially predisposed in their favor. The partition was, therefore, naturally regarded as a glaring act of favoritism. A great Moslem political area was deliberately created in the east of India where none had existed before. When representative institutions were established the Hindus would be subjected to the domination of an ignorant and fanatical Moslem majority. This argument was used extensively in purely Hindu circles, but as there was a danger of antagonizing the Moslems if it was pushed too far, the chief emphasis was placed on the appeal to Bengali national sentiment.

There were still other motives underlying the antipartition agitation. The city of Calcutta would suffer if a provincial capital were created at Dacca and a good seaport developed at Chittagong; the bar of Calcutta, if a separate High Court were established in the new province; and the vernacular press of Calcutta, if it had to meet the competition of new papers published at Dacca and Chittagong. The absentee zamindars (landlords) of Eastern Bengal, who spend most of their time and money in Calcutta, might also be caused some inconvenience. According to Mr. Fraser, Lord Curzon's Universities Act was another important factor. The educated Bengalis opposed that measure on the ground that it would increase the cost of higher education and bring educational institutions too completely under bureaucratic control. They were defeated and, in their rage, they seized upon the partition as a pretext for an attack upon Lord Curzon.

The agitation was almost entirely restricted to Hindus, partly because they predominated in the bhadralok and partly because of the peculiar nature of the religious issue. With a few exceptions, the Moslems either favored the partition or were too ignorant and apathetic to take any interest in the matter at all. Calcutta furnished most of the leaders and organizers of the opposition, although a large proportion of the active participants came from Eastern Bengal. An effort has already been made to sketch the careers of Mr. Banerjea, Mr. Pal, and the Ghose brothers and to give some idea of the great influence exerted by their newspapers. The organization and the methods of the revolutionary wing may now be described.

Through the efforts of Barendra Ghose and his associates, there was formed a body called the Anusilan Samiti (society for the promotion of culture and training). There were two headquarters, one at Calcutta for Bengal proper and the other at Dacca for Eastern Bengal and Assam. The Dacca society at one time had about five hundred separate branches. The object of these societies was to arouse public opinion against the government by circulating seditious literature, popularizing revolutionary songs, and organizing secret associations. The wide circulation of *Jugantar* was largely due to their influence. A series of textbooks was also prepared, including lives of Mazzini and Garibaldi, the writings of Vivekananda, the *Bartaman Rananiti* (The Modern Art of War) and the *Mukti Kon Pathe* (What Is the Path of Salvation?).

The methods of procedure varied from time to time. The boycott of British goods (swadeshi) was a favorite weapon in the early days of the agitation, but it proved ineffective and the Extremists then resorted to more violent measures. An effort was made to institute a reign of terror through the assassination of magistrates, police officers, witnesses, and informers. The funds necessary to carry on the work were raised by dacoities (gang robberies) committed on their own people. *Mukti Kon Pathe*, which was made up largely of articles reprinted from *Jugantar*, explained and attempted to justify this system. If the revolution is for the benefit of society, then society should pay for it. Ordinary dacoity (dakaiti) is a crime, but political dacoity is a virtue. "If revolutionaries extort money from the miserly or luxurious members of society by the application of force, their conduct is perfectly just." These arguments made a deep impression on the younger generation. The Report of the Sedition Committee gives a long list of dacoities, assaults, and murders committed between 1907 and 1918, and in nearly every case where convictions were secured the criminals were school boys or young men of the bhadralok class under twenty-five years of age.

A few cases will be sufficient to show how these methods were applied. At Muzaffarpur in the north of Bengal (now Bihar), on April 30, 1908, a bomb was thrown into a carriage in which two ladies, a Mrs. Kennedy and her daughter, were driving and they were both killed. The crime took place just outside the house of Mr. Kingsford, the judge of Muzaffarpur, for whom the bomb was obviously intended. Two students were arrested. One confessed and was hanged and the other committed suicide. Nanda Lal Banerjea, the Indian subinspector who arrested one of these boys, was assassinated in Calcutta a few months later. Terroristic methods were also used in connection with the trial of the Alipur Conspiracy case in 1908. Narendra Gosain, one of the young men arrested, became an approver and was murdered in jail by two of his fellow prisoners. The public prosecutor in these cases and a deputy superintendent of police involved in them were likewise assassinated. A typical example of a dacoity was one which occurred at Barrah in the Dacca district of Eastern Bengal on June 2, 1908. A body of fifty young men, armed with rifles, revolvers, and daggers and wearing masks, came in boats and attacked the house of one of the wealthiest residents. They secured Rs. 25,000 in cash and a considerable amount of jewelry. The village watchman attempted to stop them and was killed. The villagers and a small police force soon started in pursuit of the robbers and in the fighting which followed three more men lost their lives and several were wounded.

The conflict continued year after year without any appreciable improvement. The hopes aroused by Lord Morley's constitutional reforms in 1908–9, by the reunion of the Bengals in 1912, and by Mr. Montagu's announcement of the new Indian policy in 1917 were all doomed to disappointment. The European war did not improve the situation. Although the educated classes in general were loyal and Mr. Banerjea in particular was active in the recruitment campaign, the revolutionaries were obsessed by the prospect of help from Germany and were more zealous than ever in their attempts to plunge the country into anarchy. A good example of their activity may be found in the first month of the war. On August 26, 1914, fifty Mauser pistols and 46,000 rounds of ammunition were stolen from a gun-making firm in Calcutta. As the pistols were numbered and could easily be identified, it is known that they were used in 54 cases of dacoity and murder by the beginning of 1918. These were only a few of the many political offenses committed in Bengal during that period, although the crime wave was checked to some extent in 1916 and 1917 by the vigorous application of the Defense of India Act.

The influence of German propaganda and the ghadr (mutiny) movement will be considered more fully in connection with the Punjab. Here it will be sufficient to say that a number of Bengalis were connected with these schemes, that Batavia in Java was the headquarters for operations in Bengal and that a serious effort was made to smuggle into the province a cargo of firearms, which was said to consist of 30,000 rifles and 12,000,000 rounds of ammunition. The *Maverick*, an old Standard Oil tank steamer, was purchased by a German firm in San Francisco. It sailed from San Pedro, April 22, 1915, with about 30 men and officers, all of them Indians. Through the German Consulate in San Francisco, it was arranged that the ship was to proceed to a small island about 600 miles west of Mexico and wait there for the schooner *Annie Larsen*, which was to bring a cargo of rifles and ammunition. The cargo was then to be transferred and taken to Bengal. The junction was never effected. After waiting for several weeks, the *Maverick* sailed for Batavia, where it was received by German agents and subsequently sent back to America. This was as near as Germany ever came toward giving any really useful assistance. The revolutionists were of course disappointed and they were also weakened by the attacks of the Bengal government, but they continued their campaign and at the close of the war were preparing to expand their activities.

To understand the troubles in the Punjab a knowledge of a few essential facts is necessary. In the first place, the Punjabis are a martial people. They furnished over 50 per cent of the fighting men raised in India during the Great War although they constitute only about 8 per cent of the Indian population. With 24,000,000 people, the Punjab supplied 350,000 recruits, whereas Bengal, Bihar and Orissa, and the Central Provinces, with a combined population of over 100,000,000, supplied less than 20,000. This predominance may have been due in some measure to the special efforts made by Sir Michael O'Dwyer to encourage recruiting in the Punjab, but that was not the main reason. The number of Punjabis in the Indian Army, in time of peace as well as in time of war, is always disproportionately large.

A second factor is the conflict of interests between city and country which exists in all parts of India, but is especially strong in this province. About ten million acres of arid or semi-arid land have been brought under profitable cultivation in the last forty years. This has meant a great increase of wealth and population in the rural districts. The government has aided the movement not only by constructing irrigation works and organizing a system of mass colonization, but also by protecting the peasant's land tenure and improving his credit facilities. The Punjab Land Alienation Act of 1900 was designed to prevent moneylenders, shopkeepers, and other city people from acquiring the land of hereditary cultivators through purchase or through the foreclosure of mortgages. Lord Curzon's Coöperative Credit Societies Act of 1904 led to the establishment of a network of rural credit organizations in the Punjab as well as in other provinces. Both measures have been highly beneficial to the agriculturalists, but they have reduced the profits of the moneylenders and the lawyers and are not profitable in the cities. There was also another controversial problem in which the government was involved. Until 1902, nearly all public service positions in the Punjab were filled by the urban literati, but during the administrations of Sir Charles Rivaz, Sir Denzil Ibbetson, Sir Louis Dane, and Sir Michael O'Dwyer, a systematic effort was made to break this monopoly through the appointment of rural candidates whenever they were able to qualify. These facts will help to explain why the revolutionary agitation was so bitter in the cities and why the government was in general loyally supported by the landed gentry and the peasants.

Religious rivalry is another important factor. About 55 per cent of the people are Moslems, 33 per cent Hindus, and 11 per cent Sikhs. The balance among the three communities is, however, more even than these figures would indicate. The Hindus are wealthier and better educated than the Moslems. They are also shrewder politicians and are more concentrated in the cities and towns where political influence can be most effectively exercised. They would probably control the Punjab Legislative Council if its members were elected in general or noncommunal constituencies. In an appeal to physical force, it is equally probable that they would be defeated, although they include in their ranks several million Jats and Rajputs and other representatives of the so-called fighting races. The strength of the Sikhs lies in their martial prowess, their supreme confidence in themselves and their tradition of former political supremacy. From the dissolution of the Mogul Empire in the eighteenth century until their defeat by the British in 1849 they were the dominant power, not only in the Punjab but in nearly all of northern India. Although they are not very clever at the political game, they have been able to exercise considerable influence in the Reformed Council by holding the balance of power between Hindus and Moslems.

The revolutionary agitation in the Punjab began in 1907. There was considerable trouble from 1907 to 1909, followed by a peaceful interlude which lasted until the attempt to assassinate the Viceroy, Lord Hardinge, in December, 1912. In its first stage, the movement was mainly urban and political, although the leaders tried to arouse the agricultural classes by emphasizing their economic grievances. It is difficult to say whether the agitation was primarily indigenous or the product of influences emanating from Bengal and Bombay, and, in so far as it was indigenous, it is also difficult to estimate the parts played by Mr. Lajpat Rai and the Arya Samaj. It is well known, however, that most of the participants were Hindus and a large proportion of them were associated with the Arya Samaj. Ajit Singh, one of the other leaders, was a Sikh, but his efforts to stir up that community were not especially successful. The Moslems took very little part in the movement until after 1912, when they began to be influenced by Pan-Islamic propaganda.

When the agitation started in 1907 the chief pretext was the Canal Colony Bill which had just been passed by the Punjab Legislative Council. The object of this bill was to modify the system of land tenure in one of the large canal colonies. It was a bureaucratic measure and some of its provisions were unnecessarily rigid and restrictive. Another source of trouble was the Punjab Land Alienation Act which has already been mentioned. The government was criticized when it protected the peasant from the moneylender as well as when it failed to protect him. There was also some trouble caused by the increase of land revenue rates in the Rawalpindi district and by a proposal to increase the water rate in the Bari-Doab canal. These grievances were thoroughly ventilated by Lajpat

Rai and Ajit Singh and there were serious riots at Lahore, Lyallpur, and Rawalpindi. The authorities acted promptly with a combination of firmness and conciliation. Lajpat Rai and Ajit Singh were deported under Bengal Regulation III of 1818 and the Governor-General, Lord Minto, refused to approve the Canal Colony Bill.

The excitement was checked for a time, but was renewed in 1908 when the leaders were permitted to return. Ajit Singh soon got into trouble with the authorities again and fled to Persia in 1909. After that, the Punjab was comparatively quiet until December 23, 1912, when an attempt was made to assassinate the Viceroy, Lord Hardinge of Penshurst, as he was making a state entry into the new capital city of Delhi.

In the meantime the movement had passed into the hands of younger and more radical leaders. Har Dayal, a native of Delhi, after a successful career as a student in Delhi and Lahore, went to St. John's College, Oxford, in 1905 on a state scholarship. He soon gave up his scholarship and returned to India about 1908. He lived for a time with Lajpat Rai in Lahore and organized a class of young men, to whom he preached the value of passive resistance and the boycott as weapons for driving the British out of India. He went back to Europe late in 1908 and spent two years, mainly in Geneva and Paris, where he fell under the influence of Krishnavarma and other advocates of more violent measures. In 1910–11, he was again in India teaching young men the technique of revolution. Among those associated with him were Rash Behari, a Bengali clerk in the Forest Department, and Amir Chand, a schoolmaster at Delhi. They took charge of the work when he went to America in 1911. Shortly after the attack on Lord Hardinge, an Indian orderly was killed at Lahore by a bomb which was evidently intended to be used for the murder of British officials. The crime was traced to this group. Amir Chand and several others were convicted and hanged, but Rash Behari escaped. There is every reason to believe that the same conspirators were responsible for the assault on Lord Hardinge.

Har Dayal arrived in San Francisco in the latter part of 1911. He addressed meetings in various parts of the United States, especially on the Pacific coast, and organized associations sworn to destroy British rule in India.[7] He also started a newspaper in San Francisco called the *Ghadr* (Mutiny), of which the first issue appeared on November 1, 1913. The character of the paper is indicated by its name. A mock advertisement which appeared in it is illuminating: "Wanted:—Brave soldiers to stir up *Ghadr* in India; Pay—death; prize—martyrdom; pension—liberty; field of battle—India." This paper was widely circulated among the Indians of California, Oregon, Washington, and British Columbia. It was also translated into various dialects and smuggled into India. In one lot seized in Burma in 1915 there were 220 copies printed in Gujarati, 10 in Hindi, and 3 in Urdu.

At a meeting at Sacramento, December 31, 1913, Har Dayal told his audience that Germany was preparing for war with Great Britain and that it was time for patriotic Indians to go home and get ready for the revolution. His speeches finally attracted the attention of the United States authorities and steps were taken to deport him as an undesirable alien. Arrested and released on bail, he absconded to Switzerland in March, 1914, with one of his associates, a Moslem by the name of Barkatulla. The management of the ghadr movement was then taken over by Ram Chandra, a Hindu, who had previously been editor of two seditious newspapers in India.

A crisis in the history of the movement was precipitated by two events which happened in 1914, the *Komagata Maru* episode and the outbreak of the European war. The *Komagatu Maru* affair was connected with the immigration policy of Canada. There were several thousand Indians, mostly Sikhs, living on the Pacific coast of the United States and Canada at that time. They were grieved by the immigration laws which made it practically impossible for their relatives and friends to join them, and Har Dayal and his associates saw to it that their grief was fanned into a white heat of rage. It was useless to protest against the laws of the United States, but, as Canada was a part of the British Empire, it was felt that a little agitation might be effective. In the summer of 1913 three Sikh delegates were sent from Canada to the Punjab to stir up

7. Har Dayal subsequently recanted and became an ardent defender of British policy in India.

public opinion. A series of protest meetings was held and a great deal of interest was aroused. At some of the meetings the speakers diverged from the main issue and indulged in a general criticism of British rule in India. This was soon checked by the intervention of Sir Michael O'Dwyer, Lieutenant-Governor of the Punjab, but it was discovered later that the delegates carried on a very extensive secret propaganda of a seditious character.

Early in 1914, a plan was devised to test the Canadian laws and incidentally to embarrass the British government by compelling it either to interfere with Canada's immigration policy or to suffer a further loss of popularity in India. A Japanese vessel, the *Komagata Maru*, was chartered and it sailed from Hong Kong to Vancouver with 351 Sikhs and 21 Punjabi Moslems, recruited at Hong Kong, Shanghai, Moji, and Yokohama. The ship arrived at Vancouver on May 23. A few of the passengers were able to comply with the Canadian laws, but the great majority could not do so and were refused permission to land. The ship remained in the harbor for two months and was finally driven out by force of arms. The feelings of the would-be immigrants were then further embittered by the fact that they were not returned to the ports from which they had sailed, but for some reason connected with the war, which had begun while they were in mid-ocean, they were all sent to India instead. When they arrived at Budge-Budge, near the mouth of the Hugli, on September 29, there was a special train waiting to take them to the Punjab. The Moslems and a few of the Sikhs boarded the train, but about 300 Sikhs refused to do so and started to march to Calcutta. They were turned back by force and eighteen were killed. Of the others, some disappeared, some were arrested and imprisoned, and the rest were sent on to their original destination.

These men constituted the nucleus of the agitation in the Punjab. They were soon joined by thousands of other Sikhs, mainly from the United States and Canada, who were persuaded by the ghadr agitators to go home and avenge the grievances of their community. Active assistance was also received from the German consuls in San Francisco and New York. Rash Behari, who had been active in the troubles at

Delhi and Lahore in 1912–13, returned to the Punjab to take charge of the operations. He was assisted by a young Maratha Brahman named Vishnu Ganesh Pingley. The worst outrages occurred between October, 1914, and September, 1915. Police were murdered, rural officials were terrorized, wealthy Indians were robbed to secure funds for the cause, attempts were made to wreck trains and blow up bridges, factories for the manufacture of bombs were established, war material was collected in secret depots, and strenuous efforts were made to tamper with the loyalty of the Indian soldiers. The propaganda among the troops was carried on actively at Meerut, Lucknow, Cawnpore and various other stations in the United Provinces, and in the Punjab. It met with a considerable degree of success and a general mutiny was avoided only by the prompt and vigorous action of the Punjab government. On February 19, 1915, several houses in Lahore were raided by the police and thirteen of the leaders were captured along with a supply of arms, bombs, incendiary literature, flags, and other revolutionary material.

During the early part of the war, the government of India used summary methods to combat external propaganda, but the internal agitation was handled through the ordinary criminal courts. This policy was not very successful. Under the Ingress Ordinance of September 5, 1914, about 400 returning Indians were interned in jail during the first two years of the war, about 2,500 were restricted to their native villages, and about 5,000 were released without any serious restrictions. Most of the trouble was caused by members of the last group and by a few agitators who slipped into the country without being examined by the police. Sir Michael O'Dwyer urged the government to adopt more strenuous methods and the Defense of India Act was finally passed in March, 1915. The authorities were given emergency powers to intern suspicious characters and Special Tribunals were created to deal with revolutionary crimes. These powers were used ruthlessly in the Punjab. Sir Michael O'Dwyer says that 175 persons were tried before the Special Tribunals on general conspiracy charges, of whom 20 were hanged, 58 were transported for life, and 58 were transported or imprisoned for shorter periods.[8] The rebellion was suppressed by the end of August and there were no further serious disturbances in the Punjab until the riots of 1919.

We have now considered the troubles in the three main centers of revolutionary activity during this period (1905–17). The other provinces were relatively quiet. A small group of young men in Madras were aroused by the lectures of Mr. Bepin Chandra Pal in 1907 and their zeal was further stimulated from time to time by influences emanating from the French colony of Pondicherry, but, with the exception of the murder of Mr. Ashe, the district magistrate at Tinnevelly, in 1911, there was very little resort to revolutionary methods. It is true that Mrs. Besant lived in Madras and that she was in those days an uncompromising foe of the Moderate party, but she was never an advocate of violence and always believed that radical results could be accomplished by peaceful agitation. The movement also failed to take root in Bihar and Orissa, the United Provinces, the Central Provinces, Assam, and Burma, although there were occasional crimes and disorders of a political character. With the assistance of the German consul at Shanghai, the ghadr agitators conducted an especially active campaign in Burma, but they failed to make any impression on the Burmese people, although they did succeed in stirring up a mutiny among troops of the 130th Baluchi Regiment stationed at Rangoon (1915). This uprising and a similar one in the 5th Light Infantry at Singapore both were suppressed and the ringleaders severely punished.

In emphasizing the revolutionary aspect of the Nationalist movement it should not be forgotten that there is another side to the picture. The Moderates and a section of the Extremists have always been opposed to the use of violent methods. If they and the vast majority of the people of India had not been loyal during the war they would have risen in rebellion when the British regular troops were withdrawn and the reserves of artillery and ammunition were denuded. They would also have protested against the contribution of £100,000,000 voted by the government of India in 1917 for the support of the war.

8. Sir Michael O'Dwyer, *India As I Knew It* (London, 1925), p. 107.

On the other hand, they felt that India was entitled to a greater measure of self-government and, as a general rule, were unwilling to wait for it until the war was over. Mr. Montagu's famous declaration of policy on August 20, 1917, was mainly intended to meet this demand. It was the product of motives that were more or less contradictory. India was to be rewarded for her loyalty and at the same time bribed to keep quiet while the Empire was fighting for its life.

CHAPTER III

THE MONTAGU-CHELMSFORD REFORMS (1917–1921)

THE advocates of Indian constitutional reform at the time of the war were divided into two main groups: the British and the majority of educated Indians, who believed that a certain degree of preparation was necessary for self-government; and a small group of radical Indians, who believed that self-government should be established immediately in the provinces and in all of the departments of the central government except those dealing with defense and foreign relations. In the first group there was a difference of opinion as to the amount and the quality of the training that was required. The British naturally wanted to make haste slowly and the Indians were anxious to reach the goal as soon as possible. So far as the quality of the training was concerned, one of the chief points at issue was the relative merits of the presidential and parliamentary forms of government. Presidential government is believed by many students to be more suitable for an oriental community where a strong executive is necessary to maintain order and to prevent political disintegration. Curiously enough, this view has long been popular among the Indians themselves, but the British have not appreciated its merits. The majority of the British seem to believe that because parliamentary government has worked well in the United Kingdom it must necessarily be the best system for other countries. But it is one thing to argue that the presidential form would be more suitable for the permanent government of India and quite another thing to argue that it would be better adapted for a period of transition. In the former case, the executive and the legislature both would be elected; in the latter, the executive would be largely under British control while the legislature would be responsible to the people. At the same time, it should be remembered that India has always been accustomed to a kind of presidential government and it might be unwise to drag in another system unless it is to be adopted permanently. Among the reform schemes that attracted most attention in 1916–18 the Congress-League plan was based on the presidential theory and the Montagu-Chelmsford plan on the parliamentary theory.

In October, 1916, nineteen members of the Indian Legislative Council submitted to the government of India a memorandum proposing reforms in the system of government. With a few additions and alterations, this scheme was approved by the National Congress and the Moslem League at their annual meetings at Lucknow in December, 1916, and it soon came to be known as the Congress-League Plan of Government. It began with three resolutions, the substance of which was that the Crown was requested to recognize Dominion Home Rule as the ultimate goal for India and to accept the scheme outlined in the plan itself as an initial step in that direction. Four fifths of the members of the various Legislative Councils and one half of the members of the Executive Councils were to be elected. This meant that the Indians would have fairly complete control over legislation and would probably be able to exert some influence over the administration. They could not, however, compel officials to resign and they could not interfere in military affairs or in the foreign and political relations of India.

Another interesting feature of the plan was the "Lucknow Pact," which provided for the distribution of the elective seats in the legislative bodies between the Hindus and the Moslems and accepted the principle of communal electorates, i.e., that each community should elect its own members in separate constituencies.[1] This system was bitterly criticized by the Hindus when it was first put into operation as a part of the Morley-Minto Reforms in 1909, but they now reversed their attitude and joined with the Moslems in arranging for the allocation of seats. The agreement applied to the Central Legislature and to the Legislative Councils of all the provinces except Assam and Burma. The seats were allotted on an All-India

1. For a more detailed discussion of this subject, see chap. xi, "Hindu-Moslem Relations."

basis, which meant that when a community was in a minority its representation was weighted; that is, it was given more seats than its population justified in order that it might have a more effective position. This is illustrated in the following table:[2]

Legislative Body	*Percentage of Moslems to the total population of the electoral area (1921)*	*Lucknow Pact percentage*
Punjab	55.2	50
Bengal	54.6	40
United Provinces	14.3	30
Bihar and Orissa	10.9	25
Central Provinces	4.4	15
Madras	6.7	15
Bombay	19.8	33.3
Central Legislative Assembly	24.0	33.3

This plan was discussed in some detail in *The Montagu-Chelmsford Report* and two main objections were urged against it. In the first place, it gave the legislature the power to paralyze the executive, but not the power to remove it from office, which is, of course, only another way of saying that it was based on the presidential rather than the parliamentary theory of government. The second objection was more fundamental. The legislature was responsible to the people of India while the executive was responsible to the Secretary of State and Parliament and ultimately to the people of Great Britain. "It is unsound," says the Report, "that the legislature and executive should derive their powers from, and be responsible to, different authorities." The Report also criticized communal representation, but admitted that it was a necessary evil and even proposed that it should be extended to include the Sikhs in the Punjab.

The origin of the Montagu-Chelmsford plan may be explained in a few words. Shortly after the Boer War, some

2. See *The Simon Report,* I, 189. In Assam, 32.3 per cent of the population in the electoral area was Moslem, and under the Montagu-Chelmsford Reforms they were allotted 37.5 per cent of the seats in the Indian general (communal) constituencies. There is no Hindu-Moslem problem in Burma, where 85 per cent of the population is Buddhist.

young men who were associated with Lord Milner in his reconstruction work in South Africa organized a campaign of political education which led to the formation of the Union of South Africa in 1910. As soon as victory in this field was assured, they conceived the more ambitious project of reviving the Imperial Federation movement which had been very active at one time but had now fallen completely into oblivion. Mr. Lionel Curtis, the leader of the group, visited Canada, Australia, and New Zealand in 1909–10. A number of clubs were formed, mainly in the university centers, to study the problem of federation. These clubs corresponded with one another and a quarterly magazine, called the *Round Table*, was started in London to serve as a sort of clearinghouse of information. In 1916, Mr. Curtis published two books which were based partly upon the information received from the various clubs and partly upon his own investigations—*The Problem of the Commonwealth* and *The Commonwealth of Nations.*

The scheme of federation originally included only the United Kingdom and the self-governing Dominions. The first suggestion that India should also be admitted was apparently made in 1912 by Sir William Marris and Lord Meston, two Indian Civil Service officials who belonged to the Round Table group. Mr. Curtis approved the suggestion and decided that as a preliminary step in this direction India ought to be granted a large measure of local autonomy. At his request, a tentative plan of constitutional reform was prepared in 1915 by Sir William Duke, who had been Lieutenant-Governor of Bengal and was at that time a member of the Council of India. This document was discussed and thoroughly revised by Mr. Curtis and his friends and was finally published under the title of *The Duke Memorandum.* It contains the first statement of the theory of dyarchy or dual government in the provinces which constitutes the essential feature of the Montagu-Chelmsford plan. So many changes were made in the original draft of the Memorandum that it is difficult to say whether the theory originated with Mr. Curtis or with Sir William Duke. It was popularized, however, by Mr. Curtis and it came to be definitely associated with his name.

Mr. Curtis went to India and studied the problem at first

hand during the cold season of 1916–17. In 1917, he published the results of his investigation in two small volumes, one entitled *A Letter to the People of India* and the other, *Letters to the People of India on Responsible Government.* In these books the principle of dyarchy is further elaborated and there is an excellent discussion of the problem of responsible government as applied to India. Another interesting feature is the effort made to prove that most of the provinces of India are too large and heterogeneous for the development of an efficient system of government. In the Legislative Council of Madras some of the members speak Tamil, some Telugu, and others Canarese, and it is impossible for them to understand one another. There are also several other smaller linguistic groups to whom all three of these languages are unknown. An even more striking example was to be found in Bombay, where the people of Sind differed from the population in the remainder of the presidency, not only in language, but also in religion and to a large extent in race.[3] In the Central Provinces there is considerable rivalry between the northern Hindi-speaking districts and the southern Marathi-speaking districts. Mr. Curtis thinks that British India might very well be divided into about twenty-four provinces with an average population of approximately 10,000,000. The facts he gives cannot be denied, but Mr. Montagu and Lord Chelmsford ignored his remedy because they remembered all too well the bitter controversies aroused by Lord Curzon's partition of Bengal in 1905. When the people of India obtain complete self-government they will probably see the advantages of a more logical arrangement. The British are wise not to force the issue.

From 1914 until 1917, the British government used all of its[4] energy in the prosecution of the war. Other problems were neglected at a time when the abnormal conditions created by the war tended to increase its difficulties. This policy was especially dangerous, so far as India was concerned, and the officials who were responsible for the conduct of Indian affairs

3. In 1936 Sind was detached from Bombay and made a separate province.

4. The singular is used in reference to "government," as in Western practice.

soon began to realize it. Lord Chelmsford, who succeeded Lord Hardinge as Viceroy and Governor-General in April, 1916, was apparently convinced before he went to India that Dominion Home Rule should be the goal of Indian constitutional progress and that an official declaration to that effect ought to be made immediately. His opinion was probably strengthened when he read a copy of *The Duke Memorandum* which was sent to him in May, 1916.[5] Mr. Austen Chamberlain, the Secretary of State for India, also appreciated the gravity of the situation and was about to issue a liberal statement of policy when he was forced out of office by the report of the Mesopotamian Commission in the summer of 1917. He supported Mr. Montagu's program in Parliament and it was largely through his efforts that enough Conservative votes were obtained to secure its adoption.

Mr. Edwin Samuel Montagu, the new Secretary of State, made the following declaration of policy in the House of Commons on August 20, 1917:

The policy of His Majesty's Government with which the Government of India are in complete accord, is that of the increasing association of Indians in every branch of the administration and the gradual development of self-governing institutions with a view to the progressive realization of responsible government in India as an integral part of the British Empire. They have decided that substantial steps in this direction should be taken as soon as possible, and that it is of the highest importance as a preliminary to considering what these steps should be that there should be a free and informal exchange of opinion between those in authority at home and in India. His Majesty's Government have accordingly decided, with His Majesty's approval, that I should accept the Viceroy's invitation to proceed to India to discuss these matters with the Viceroy and the Government of India, to consider with the Viceroy the views of local Governments, and to receive with him the suggestions of representative bodies and others.

I would add that progress in this policy can only be achieved

5. Lionel Curtis, *Dyarchy* (1921), p. xxvi; E. A. Horne, *The Political System of British India* (1922), p. 70.

by successive stages. The British Government and the Government of India, on whom the responsibility lies for the welfare and advancement of the Indian peoples, must be the judges of the time and measure of each advance, and they must be guided by the co-operation received from those upon whom new opportunities of service will thus be conferred and by the extent to which it is found that confidence can be reposed in their sense of responsibility.

Ample opportunity will be afforded for public discussion of the proposals which will be submitted in due course to Parliament.

Mr. Montagu went to India during the next cold season (1917–18) to study conditions at close range with the idea of discovering the best method of putting his announcement into practical operation. He was accompanied by Lord Donoughmore, a member of the House of Lords; Mr. Charles Roberts, a member of the House of Commons; and Sir William Duke and Mr. B. N. Basu, members of the Council of India. Mr. Basu was a native of India. They were joined in India by Lord Chelmsford and they traveled all over the country, gathering information and receiving complaints and suggestions from men of all classes, creeds, and colors. The result of their efforts was the famous *Montagu-Chelmsford Report*, known officially as *The Joint Report on Indian Constitutional Reforms*, 1918. The main principles of the document were unanimously approved by the Executive Council of the Governor-General in India and by the Council of the Secretary of State in England. It was more difficult to secure the approval of the cabinet, where Lord Curzon was a somewhat uncertain factor, but Mr. Montagu was loyally supported by Mr. Chamberlain and their efforts were finally successful.[6]

6. Lord Curzon was the author of the famous clause in the Declaration of 1917 relating to the "progressive realization of *responsible government* in India," but he criticized the Report on the ground that it sowed the seeds of parliamentary government and even considered the possibility of resigning his seat in the cabinet to secure freedom of action. For a detailed account of his tortuous policy at this time, see The Earl of Ronaldshay (now the Marquess of Zetland), *The Life of Lord Curzon* (London, 1928), Vol. III, chap. x.

The central idea of the Report is the application of the principle of dyarchy in the government of the provinces. The traditional method of dealing with popular aspirations for self-government in the non-European parts of the Empire had always been to allow the people to elect a minority of the members of the legislature or the majority of the members of a so-called legislature that did not have any real legislative power. No one was ever satisfied and the only result was usually an increase in the amount of rabid and irresponsible criticism. It was hoped that under a system of dyarchy these difficulties might be avoided.

There were two forms of dyarchy considered by the committee. Under the form proposed in *The Duke Memorandum*, the departments of the provincial governments were to be divided into two groups, one of which was to continue under the old bureaucratic system of administration while the other was to be administered in accordance with the principle of responsible government. The other form was suggested in a document known as the *Joint Address*, which was written by Mr. Curtis in November, 1917, after a series of informal conferences with some of the leaders of the Moderate party in Bengal and a few of the more influential members of the European community. Each of the larger provinces was to be divided into areas of approximately equal size and in each area there was to be established a so-called state government. The state government was to consist of an elective assembly and a responsible ministry chosen from the majority party. It was to have charge, in whole or in part, of one group of executive departments while the other group was to continue to be administered by the existing provincial government.

Both systems were based on the same fundamental idea. The provincial departments were to be divided between the representatives of British authority and the representatives of the people of India and there was to be a gradual transfer of functions from the former to the latter. There were, however, some important differences. The Memorandum provided for a division of function only, the Address provided for a division of both functions and areas. The Memorandum divided the provincial governments into two parts, the Address created an entirely new set of governments. Mr. Montagu's committee recommended the adoption of the former plan, partly because it involved less change in the existing machinery and partly because it avoided the difficult problem of partition.

The system was intended to apply to eight of the larger provinces, namely, Bengal, Bombay, Madras, Assam, Bihar and Orissa, the Central Provinces, the United Provinces, and the Punjab. Burma was added to this list in 1922, the North-West Frontier Province in 1932,[7] and Sind in 1936. In each of these provinces the chief executive was to have the title of Governor. He was to be assisted by an Executive Council in charge of what were called Reserved Subjects and a Ministry in charge of Transferred Subjects. The Governor and the Executive Council were to be responsible to the Governor-General and the Secretary of State. The Ministers were to be responsible to a Provincial Legislative Council which had a large elective majority. The Executive Council was to consist of an equal number of British and Indian members; the personnel of the Ministry would presumably always be Indian. Reserved Subjects were those of vital importance which it was felt could not as yet be safely entrusted to Indian control, such as the Police and the Administration of Justice. Transferred Subjects were those which it was believed could safely be turned over to Indian Ministers for a long enough period of time to give the system a trial. Among these were Agriculture, Local Self-Government, and a large part of the field of Education. In most of the provinces there were twenty-one Transferred Subjects in 1936.

At the end of five years, the government of India was to conduct an investigation to determine whether further subjects should be Transferred or whether some of those already Transferred should be brought back into the Reserved class. Every twelve years a Royal Commission was to be appointed to review the whole system and to suggest methods of improving it. These recommendations were adopted in a modified

7. There are backward tracts in Madras, Bengal, Assam, Burma, the Punjab, and Bihar and Orissa, covering 207,900 square miles, which were wholly or partially excluded from the Reforms. Burma was detached from India in 1937.

form. Parliament authorized a rule under the Government of India Act, 1919, to arrange for the transfer of subjects from one category to another and it also provided for the appointment of a Statutory Commission in 1929.[8]

Although the section dealing with the provinces was the most original part of the Report, it also contained other interesting features. The suggestions made for separating the powers of the central and provincial governments on some kind of federal lines were especially important. Indian administration had been overcentralized since the passage of the Charter Act of 1833. The efforts of Lord Mayo, Lord Lytton, and Lord Ripon to remedy this defect have already been discussed and some reference has also been made to the *Report of the Royal Commission on Decentralization* in 1909. A few minor reforms had been introduced, but the system as a whole had remained unchanged. As long as the whole administration was bureaucratic the Nationalists did not complain. They had more confidence in the Secretary of State and Parliament than they had in any of the authorities in India and more confidence in the government of India than they had in the bureaucrats who presided over provincial affairs. Under the new regime these conditions would be entirely changed. With the progressive realization of responsible government there must be a progressive devolution of authority. This would be true especially in the field of finance because the control of the purse is the real test of official responsibility. The Report, therefore, recommended a scheme of decentralization and discussed the financial arrangements in considerable detail.

Aside from this recommendation, which would tend to strengthen the government of India in its relations with the India Office and His Majesty's government, and weaken its control over the provinces, there was very little in the Report dealing with the power and authority of the government at Delhi. It was assumed that dyarchy might ultimately be extended to the central government, if it worked well in the provinces, but for the time being the executive was to remain unified and to be free from legislative control. The Legislative

8. The act was subsequently amended and the Simon Commission was appointed in 1927.

Council was to be superseded by a bicameral legislature, in which the upper house was to be called the Council of State and the lower house the Legislative Assembly. The government was to appoint a majority of the members of the Council of State, but there was to be a large elective majority in the Legislative Assembly. This recommendation was strongly criticized in Nationalist circles and it was finally decided that there should be elective majorities in both houses.

The other recommendations may be summarized in a few words. The India Office in London was to be reorganized and its expenses, except those connected with its agency functions, were to be transferred from the Indian budget to the budget of the United Kingdom. There was to be no change in the administration of the Indian States, but provision was made for a Council of Princes which should be summoned from time to time by the Viceroy to consider questions affecting their interests.

The Report was attacked in India by the majority of Europeans both in the Government Service and in the commercial community because they felt that it granted entirely too much to the Indians. It was opposed by the radical wing of the Nationalists for exactly the opposite reason. The liberal elements in both races supported it. Through the efforts of Mr. (later Sir) Surendranath Banerjea and Mr. Srinivasa Sastri, a Moderate conference was held at which the plan was approved although certain changes were suggested to make it more liberal. In England it was commended by all the liberal newspapers and was generally hailed as the most important document in Imperial history since the publication of Lord Durham's report on Canada in 1839. The more conservative papers, however, criticized it with great bitterness. This was especially true of the *Morning Post*, which in these modern days best represents the point of view of George III and Lord Eldon. The reactionaries tried to sidetrack the Report by arguing (1) that nothing should be done until the close of the war and (2) that the whole question should be reëxamined by a Joint Parliamentary Committee. In reply to the first argument, *India*, which was at that time the official organ of the Indian National Congress in England, quoted the famous words of Lord Macaulay in connection with the Reform Bill of 1832. Responding to the question whether he would legislate in times of great excitement concerning matters of deep public concern, Macaulay said: "Yes, Sir, I would. . . . Reformers are compelled to legislate in times of excitement because bigots will not legislate in times of tranquility."

There were three problems outlined in the Report which had to be considered in further detail by special investigating committees. A Franchise Committee was appointed to deal with the number of members of the various legislative bodies in India, the apportionment of elective and nominated members, the communal allotment of elective members, the methods of election, and the qualifications of the electors. A Committee on Function was to inquire into the division of functions between the central and provincial governments and to draw the line in the provinces between Reserved and Transferred Subjects. A Committee on the Home Administration of Indian Affairs was to consider the reorganization of the India Office in London, the word "Home" being used in its customary insular connotation. The president of the first two committees was Lord Southborough and they are, therefore, usually called the Southborough Committees. They were appointed in October, 1918, their work was done in India, and their reports were presented to the Governor-General in Council on February 26, 1919. The chairman of the third committee was Lord Crewe. It sat in England and its report was completed on June 21, 1919.

A Government of India Bill was introduced in the House of Commons by Mr. Montagu on June 2, 1919, and was referred to a Joint Select Committee of Parliament. There were fourteen members of this body, seven from each house, and they were selected to represent all shades of opinion. Lord Selborne was chairman and there were also included Mr. Montagu, who was of course strongly in favor of the plan, Lord Sydenham of Combe, who was equally strongly opposed to it, Mr. Ben Spoor, who criticized it because it was not sufficiently democratic, and Lord Sinha, the first and only Indian member of the House of Lords. The work of the Committee was based largely on the reports of the four bodies mentioned above, namely, the Montagu-Chelmsford Committee, the two Southborough Committees, and Lord Crewe's Committee. It also held public sessions during July and August and examined a large number of witnesses, many of whom were summoned from India for that purpose. Mr. Montagu's bill was thoroughly revised and a special report was presented to Parliament in November. The bill in its amended form passed both houses and received the assent of the Crown on December 23, 1919.

This measure is cited as the Government of India Act, 1919. It was consolidated with other Statutes relating to India to form the Government of India Act, in accordance with the system of condensing the organic law of India which has already been mentioned. The Statutes, however, are merely outlines, the details of which are filled in by so-called Statutory Rules made by the Governor-General in Council with the sanction of the Secretary of State in Council. These Rules have to be laid before Parliament, but unless the Secretary of State requests it they do not require parliamentary approval. That is to say, they are usually put into operation at once and they remain in force if neither house of Parliament expresses its disapproval within thirty days. The original Rules framed under the Act of 1919 were revised by the Joint Select Committee of Parliament. The Government of India Act and its schedules, as amended up to December 23, 1919, cover 92 printed pages; the Rules and their appendices and index cover 292 pages.

The Montagu-Chelmsford Reforms are chiefly embodied in these two documents. There are, however, a few important principles, enunciated in the Report of the Joint Select Committee, which are supposed to be binding although they do not have any statutory sanction. A good example is the recommendation in favor of Indian fiscal independence. Another example is the arrangement that three members of the Viceroy's Executive Council must be Indians. The Government of India Act itself makes no racial distinctions of this character.

The plan as a whole may be summarized in a few words because its most important features have already been anticipated. Beginning with the so-called Home Administration, the chief reform was the relaxing of Imperial control. This was to be accomplished mainly through the adoption of self-denying resolutions, and time and experience alone would determine how far it was to be carried. Except in very rare cases, which were carefully defined in the Statutory Rules, the Secretary of State was forbidden to interfere in the management of Transferred Subjects in the provinces. The government of India and the officials of the provincial governments in charge of Reserved Subjects were still under the control of the Secretary of State and Parliament, but it was hoped that there would be no interference when the officials and the popular element of the government were in agreement. The application of this principle to the tariff has been discussed in one of the chapters on "Economic and Financial Grievances."

In addition to its general work of supervision, Parliament was assigned two specific functions under the Reform scheme. It was to pass upon amendments to the Rules framed under the Government of India Act and also upon laws enacted by the Governor-General or the Governor of a province over the heads of the legislature. Owing to the excellent work done by the Joint Select Committee on the Government of India Bill, it was decided that there should be elected at the beginning of each session a Standing Committee of Parliament on Indian Affairs. There were twenty-two members of this committee, evenly divided between the two houses, and all political views were supposed to be represented. They were to prepare the material upon which Parliament acts in exercising the functions mentioned above, but their chief duty was to keep alive the interest in Indian affairs and to improve the quality of the Indian debates.

There was no material change in the establishment of the Secretary of State for India. Lord Crewe's Committee recommended that the corporate idea of the Secretary of State in Council should be abandoned and the Council of India transformed into a purely advisory board. The recommendation was rejected. The Council retained its control over expenditures and the rules relating to the Civil Services. The Council had formerly consisted of not less than 10 and not more than

14 members, of whom 9 must have recently resided or served in India. It was usually controlled by retired members of the Indian Civil Service. Under the new regulations, the membership was reduced to a minimum of 8 and a maximum of 12, of whom only one half were required to have Indian experience. There were 9 members in 1936, of whom 5 were retired members of the Indian Civil Service. Three of the members, including one of the representatives of the Indian Civil Service, were Indians and it is generally assumed that their number will be increased until they constitute one half of the total membership. The reduction in the normal term of office from seven to five years was made for the benefit of the Indian members.

There was an interesting provision about the salaries of the members of the Council. The regular remuneration was £1200 a year, but there was an annual subsistence allowance of £600 extra for any member who at the time of his appointment was domiciled in India. This was intended to strengthen the British argument that European civil servants in India are entitled to extra pay because of the additional expense of being so far away from home. The reciprocity is a little one-sided, however, because it is not likely that there will ever be more than six Indian members of the Council of India.

The decision to retain the Council in its old form was probably a mistake from the point of view of administrative efficiency. It was also a disappointment to the Indian Nationalists who had been clamoring for more than twenty years that it should be abolished. There were, however, two important concessions made to Indian opinion. The political charges of the India Office were transferred to the British budget and provision was made for the appointment of a High Commissioner for India in the United Kingdom. The transfer of the India Office charges not only settled a long-standing grievance, but it also brought the administration of that Office more directly and continuously under the control of Parliament. The policy of the Secretary of State for India can now be challenged on the vote of his salary. The famous debate of July 8, 1920, on the conduct of General Dyer at Amritsar was brought about in this way. The second concession was hardly less important. The High Commissioner is the business agent of the government of India in London; the agency functions formerly exercised by the India Office are gradually being turned over to him, and he has apparently been given a free hand to purchase government supplies wherever it can be done to the best advantage. He acts under orders from the government of India and his position is similar to that of the High Commissioners of the self-governing Dominions. The present High Commissioner is an Indian.

Although these reforms were important they were not revolutionary. The system of Imperial control was modified, but in all of its essential features it was still the old system. The radical part of the Reforms was that which dealt with the Constitution and powers of the various governmental authorities in India itself. In this field, the most significant changes were the attempt to devise a quasi-federal system of government,[9] the reorganization of the central legislature, the establishment of dyarchy in the provinces, the creation of central and provincial electorates, and the general effort to bring the government more directly under Indian control.

The first point to emphasize was the trend toward federalism. A line was drawn between central and provincial subjects and an effort was made to restrict the authority of the government of India to interfere in the provincial field. The division of functions was about the same as it is in the United States although it was based upon a different principle. In the United States the powers of the central government are enumerated and the reserve powers are left to the states. In India the powers of both were enumerated, 47 subjects being listed as central and 51 as provincial. The reserve powers were really vested in the central government, however, because the final clause in the All-India list gave it jurisdiction over all other matters not included in the list of provincial subjects.

In the United States the division of function is determined by the Constitution. If Congress or a state legislature exceeds its jurisdiction, the validity of its acts may be challenged in

9. The federal or devolution principles apply to Coorg as well as to the Governor's provinces. A Legislative Council, consisting of 15 elected members and 5 nominated members, was created in Coorg in 1923.

the courts. This was not the case in India. The division of functions was made, not in the Government of India Act or in any other statute, but in the Statutory Rules. The central and provincial legislatures were nominally confined to their respective spheres, but there was a curious statutory provision which gave the Indian legislature as regards British India, and each of the provincial legislatures as regards its own province, a theoretical concurrent jurisdiction over the whole legislative field. A system of this kind would be inconsistent with federalism if India were an independent nation. It worked very well, however, because the Secretary of State and Parliament were in a position to act as umpires and prevent either the Indian legislature or the provincial legislatures from encroaching upon each other's domain.

The subjects enumerated as All-Indian were, for the most part, those of an obviously general character. The most important were Foreign and Indian State Relations; Military and Naval Affairs; Railways, Tramways, and Inland Waterways, except those of a purely local character; Coinage, Currency, and Banking; Commerce, Shipping, and Navigation; the Public Debt; Emigration and Immigration; Posts, Telegraphs, and Telephones; Census and Statistics; Patents and Copyrights; Customs, Excise Duties on Cotton, Salt Tax, and Income Tax. Among the provincial subjects were the Police; the Administration of Justice; Local Self-Government; Education; Public Health and Sanitation; Excise and Land Revenues; Agriculture; Famine Relief; Public Works; Fisheries and Forests. There were a few subjects in the provincial list, such as Prison and Factory Legislation, which were fully provincialized only in respect to the administration. They were classed as "subject to Indian legislation," which meant that the laws would be enacted either in whole or in part, by the central legislature, but would be enforced by the authorities of the province.

The control of the government of India over the provinces was still very extensive. The provincial governments were under the supervision, direction, and control of the Governor-General in Council and they were required to obey his orders and keep him constantly and diligently informed of their proceedings and of all matters which ought, in their opinion, to be reported to him or as to which he required information. Every act passed by a provincial legislature had to be submitted to the Governor-General and no act was valid until it received his approval.

These powers were absolute in that part of the local government which was still under bureaucratic control, although they were considerably relaxed in the departments which were brought under the supervision of the legislature. The Statutory Rules provided that the general powers of superintendence, direction, and control vested in the Governor-General in Council should, in relation to Transferred Subjects, be exercised for only three purposes: (1) to safeguard the administration of central subjects, (2) to decide questions arising between two provinces in cases where the provinces themselves were unable to arrive at an agreement, and (3) to enforce certain provisions of the Government of India Act relating to contracts and liabilities and to the Civil Services in India. The authority of the Secretary of State (and, by inference, the authority of Parliament) to intervene in this field was limited in a similar manner; but he might, in addition, exercise his powers (4) to safeguard Imperial interests, and (5) to determine the position of the government of India in regard to questions arising between India and other parts of the British Empire. The Speaker of the House of Commons ruled out of order questions addressed to the Secretary of State in regard to Transferred Subjects.

This may be regarded both as a concession to the demand for Home Rule and as a step in the development of a federal system of government. It would not have been very effective, however, in either respect, if it had not been accompanied by a reform of financial arrangements. The early history of the financial relations between the government of India and the provinces has already been considered.[10] Subject to the supervision of the Secretary of State in Council, the central government had complete control over all revenues and expenditures until 1870. The provinces were dependent upon doles and there was keen rivalry in the struggle for appropriations.

10. See chap. i, "Historical Survey."

During the period from 1870 to 1921 a few sources of revenue were earmarked for the provinces, but they were inadequate and had to be supplemented partly by cash contributions from the government of India and partly by the allotment of a percentage of the land revenue, which was ordinarily regarded as a central receipt.

As long as this system prevailed there could be no real provincial autonomy. The problem was considered in *The Montagu-Chelmsford Report*, but it involved some very complicated details, and in 1920 a special committee under Lord Meston was appointed to make it the subject of further study. The new plan was to a large extent based on the report of this committee. The heads of revenue were still classed as central and provincial, but as land revenue and a few other important sources of taxation were transferred to the provinces, the old conditions were nominally reversed. It was the provinces which were now self-supporting and the central government which received contributions. The provinces also were empowered under certain restrictions to prepare their own budgets; borrow money on the security of local revenues; purchase supplies through the High Commissioner in London and impose or authorize additional taxation for provincial purposes or for the purpose of local agencies, such as municipalities and district boards.

The Meston Committee estimated the deficit in the central budget which would have to be liquidated by provincial contributions. As a matter of fact, the change in the relations between the government of India and the provinces was relatively insignificant. The former still had the more flexible sources of revenue and the power to prevent any reduction in the provincial contributions. Fortunately, the financial situation gradually improved and the government was able to reduce the quotas and finally in 1927 to suspend the contributions altogether.

The second important constitutional change was the reorganization of the central legislature. Before the Reforms, there was a single Legislative Council with an official majority. The new system was bicameral with elective majorities in both houses. The upper house or Council of State consisted of 60 members, of whom 34 were elected and 26 were nominated. Not more than 20 of the nominated members could be officials. In 1936, there were 13 officials and 13 nonofficials. The Legislative Assembly consisted of 145 members, of whom 105 were elected, 26 were officials, and 14 were nominated nonofficials.[11] These figures could be changed within certain limits by an alteration of the Statutory Rules, but the law forbade any reduction in the proportion of elective members. The president of the Council of State was appointed by the Governor-General. The president of the Legislative Assembly also held under an appointive tenure until 1925, when the post was made elective. Sir Alexander F. White was the first president of the Assembly (1921–25) and Mr. V. J. Patel was the first elective president (1925–30).

The Council of State was to continue for five years and the Legislative Assembly for three years from its first meeting although either could be dissolved or, in special circumstances, have its period of duration extended by the Governor-General.[12] In order to avoid prolonged disputes between the two houses there was a provision that, if a bill was passed by one house and was not passed by the other within six months, the Governor-General might refer the matter for a decision to a joint sitting of both houses. Every member of the Executive Council was an official member of either the Council of State or the Legislative Assembly. He could not be a member of both houses, but there was a curious provision, taken apparently from the Constitution of the Union of South Africa, which permitted him to attend both houses and to take part in the debates.

11. There was one member in each house from the Berar section of the Central Provinces who was nominated by the government after a preliminary local election. This was purely a technical arrangement based on the theory that Berar still belonged to Hyderabad, and these members are here classed as elective. Delhi and Ajmer-Merwara had one elective representative each in the Legislative Assembly.

12. The election for the Legislative Assembly that should nominally have been held in the autumn of 1929 was postponed until September, 1930.

There were no other changes of any importance in the constitution of the central government. The Executive Council was no longer limited to six ordinary members and the old distinction between ordinary and extraordinary members was abandoned. A more significant reform, which was made independently of the Government of India Act, was the decision to appoint three Indian members of the Council. For several years, the Law Member had been an Indian, but his office was one that required technical knowledge rather than administrative skill. The positions occupied by the new members were supposed to need more constructive ability. In 1936, one of them was head of the Department of Education, Health, and Lands and the other was head of the Departments of Railways and Commerce.

The most radical reform in the Constitution of the provinces, the establishment of the system of dyarchy, has already been discussed. Each of the major or Governor's provinces had a Governor, an Executive Council, a Ministry, and a Legislative Council. The minor provinces—British Baluchistan, Delhi, Coorg, Ajmer-Merwara, and the Andaman and Nicobar Islands—were still administered by chief commissioners.

In the Governor's provinces, Reserved Subjects were administered by the Governor in Council and Transferred Subjects by the Governor and the Ministers. The chief Reserved Subjects were the Police, the Administration of Justice, and the Administration of the Land Revenues. The Transferred Subjects included Local Self-Government, Medical Administration, Public Health and Sanitation, Education, Public Works, Excise, and Agriculture. There were at first a few restrictions and exceptions. Public Works, Excise, and Fisheries, for example, were not Transferred in Assam and the Forest Administration was Transferred only in Bombay and Burma. On the recommendation of the Reforms Inquiry (Muddiman) Committee (1925) some of these inequalities were rectified, but except in the two provinces mentioned, the Forest Administration was still Reserved.

There was another type of inequality among the provinces which was based upon custom and historical tradition and not upon the Government of India Act. In the three presidency provinces of Bombay, Bengal, and Madras, the Governors were chosen from men prominent in public life in Great Britain, usually members or ex-members of the House of Commons, but in the other provinces the appointments were practically restricted to the European members of the Indian Civil Service. There were usually four Executive Councilors and three Ministers in the presidencies and two Councilors and two Ministers in the other provinces. While Lord Sinha was Governor of Bihar and Orissa in 1920–21 there were three members of the Executive Council. As two of these were British, the arrangement was obviously designed to prevent the Indians from having a majority. There were three Ministers in the Punjab and there were short periods when political conditions made it impossible to have any Ministers at all in Bengal and the Central Provinces. The North-West Frontier Province had one Councilor and one Minister.

Although the law did not prescribe any racial qualification for membership in the Executive Councils, it was an accepted convention that as far as possible half of the members should be Europeans and the other half Indians. All the Ministers were Indians. The minimum membership in the various Legislative Councils was fixed by law,[13] but the number could be increased by Statutory Rule, provided at least 70 per cent of the members of each Council (60 per cent in Burma) were elected and not more than 20 per cent were officials. As a matter of fact, the actual membership exceeded the statutory minimum in every province. There were, for example, 113 elective members in Bengal in 1936, though the legal minimum is 98. The total membership figures varied from 40 in the Frontier Province and 53 in Assam to 139 in Bengal.

One of the most difficult tasks that confronted Mr. Montagu and his associates was to create an electorate and establish a system of representation that would be just and fair to all creeds, races, and economic interests. Lord Southborough's

13. The Council of State was an exception. The Government of India Act prescribed a maximum membership of 60 members, but did not fix a minimum.

Committee on Franchises collected some valuable information on this subject, although many of their recommendations were subsequently rejected. The plan finally put into operation was based on general principles approved by the Joint Select Committee of Parliament, the details being worked out in the Statutory Rules.

There were three separate electoral systems, each having its own constituencies and its own suffrage qualifications—one for the Council of State, another for the Legislative Assembly, and a third for the Provincial Legislative Councils. These systems were not uniform throughout the country or even in the same province. A person qualified to vote for a member of the Council of State in Bengal, for example, would not necessarily be able to qualify in Bombay or Madras. He might qualify in the Dacca division in Bengal and yet fall below the requirements set for the Burdwan division or the presidency division. In each of the three systems there were both general and special constituencies. It is difficult to define these terms without anticipating the subject of communal representation, but it may be said that a general constituency usually had a religious or racial as well as a territorial connotation. A Moslem who had the necessary general qualifications was entitled to vote for one or more Moslem representatives for the district in which he lived. The special constituencies were based on the Soviet principle of representation of special interests, usually economic or educational.

The attempt to define the suffrage qualifications in the general constituencies presented some very serious difficulties. About 93 per cent of the population of India are illiterate and there is an equally large percentage who are desperately poor. As the vast majority of these people are obviously unfit to exercise electoral privileges, the only question that arose was, what should be the basis of exclusion? Most of the Nationalists believed that the basic test should be educational, but the British authorities were unwilling to accept that solution because they were afraid that a small urban minority, composed mainly of Brahmans and other high-caste Hindus, would dominate the government and work for the advancement of their own interests at the expense of other classes and communities. The general test adopted, therefore, in all three of the electoral systems was the holding of property or the payment of a certain amount of taxes. The electorate for the Council of State was practically restricted to wealthy landlords and the large income taxpayers in the cities. The requirements were much lower for the Legislative Assembly and lower still for the Provincial Councils, but they were high enough even in the latter case to exclude the vast majority of the adult population.

There were a few exceptions to the general property test. The only one that affected a considerable number of people was the provision that any retired, pensioned, or discharged officer or soldier of the Indian Army might vote in the Provincial Council elections. Village headmen also had the provincial franchise in the Central Provinces and the Punjab. In the Council of State electorate there was a small and exclusive group which included past and present unofficial members of Indian legislative bodies, past and present members of University Senates, and past and present chairmen and vice-chairmen of municipalities, district boards, and coöperative central banks.

Woman's suffrage was another difficult problem. Lord Southborough's Committee reported against it and emphasized the fact that most of the women who would have enough property to qualify as voters would belong to a social class which keeps its women in seclusion. This argument did not appeal to the women of Great Britain. It seemed to them to be merely a variation of the ancient platitude that "woman's place is in the home." A vigorous protest was also made by a group of women in India, including Mrs. Annie Besant, Mrs. Sarojini Naidu, and Mrs. Herabai Tata. The electoral rules as finally adopted provided that women might be admitted to an electorate by a resolution of the legislature concerned, on the condition that no woman might vote in an All-India electorate unless she had also been admitted to the provincial electorate. Beginning with the Provincial Council of Madras in April, 1921, all of these bodies had passed the necessary resolutions by 1936. The law excluded women from the right to sit in the legislatures until April, 1926,[14] when each body was empowered to decide the question for itself. By 1936, they had become eligible for membership in the Legislative Assembly and in all the Provincial Councils. The first woman member of an Indian legislature was Dr. Mathulakshmi Ammal, who was appointed by the Governor of Madras to the Legislative Council of that province in 1927. Dr. Ammal is a well-known medical practitioner and social worker.

In all three electoral systems the general constituencies were divided along communal lines. While the Hindus and the Moslems are the two main communities there are several smaller religious or social groups which are strong enough, in some of the provinces at least, to demand separate representation. The general method of procedure was to create Moslem and non-Moslem constituencies, the latter including all voters who were not Moslems or members of other communities having separate representation. The Sikhs had their own constituencies in the Punjab, but in other parts of India they were classed as non-Moslems. The number of Sikhs, Parsees, Indian Christians, and Anglo-Indians voting in non-Moslem constituencies was so small that for all practical purposes the term non-Moslem and Hindu were synonymous.

The division of seats between the two major communities was based upon the Lucknow Pact, the agreement reached by their own leaders when they prepared the Congress-League Plan of Government in 1916. The Moslems were allowed a representation in both houses of the Indian legislature and in six of the Provincial Councils that was out of proportion to their population and wealth, but they were underrepresented in Bengal and the Punjab. The distribution of seats among the minor communities was made by the Joint Select Committee of Parliament and the details of the whole system were worked out by the officials who framed the Statutory Rules.

14. The position of Burma was somewhat different from that of the other provinces. There was a provision in the Electoral Rules adopted in 1922 that women should be eligible to membership in the Provincial Council whenever the Council and the Governor expressed a desire for their admission.

There were 34 elective members of the Council of State, of whom 31 were chosen in general, and 3 in special constituencies. Ten of the representatives of the general constituencies were elected by Moslems, 17 by non-Moslems, 1 by Sikhs (Punjab), and 3 by voters in real general constituencies (Burma, the Central Provinces and Berar) without any religious or racial qualifications. The three special constituencies were the Chambers of Commerce of Bombay, Bengal, and Burma. Of the 105 elective seats in the Legislative Assembly, 30 were filled by Moslems, 48 by non-Moslems, 2 by Sikhs (Punjab), 9 by Europeans, 3 by non-Europeans of Burma, 2 by real general constituencies in Delhi and Ajmer-Merwara, and 11 by special constituencies representing Indian Commerce and Indian Landholding.

Except in Burma, there was a similar distribution of seats in the Provincial Legislative Councils. In addition to Moslem and non-Moslem constituencies, there were European constituencies in Madras, Bombay, Bengal, the United Provinces, and Bihar and Orissa; Anglo-Indian constituencies in Madras and Bengal; Indian-Christian constituencies in Madras; and Sikh constituencies in the Punjab. Twenty-eight of the 65 non-Moslem seats in Madras were reserved for non-Brahman Hindus and 7 of the 46 non-Moslem seats in Bombay were reserved for Marathas. There was also a provision for separate urban and rural representation in these general constituencies. In the Bombay Legislative Council, for example, there were 5 Moslem urban and 22 Moslem rural seats, 11 non-Moslem urban and 35 non-Moslem rural seats.[15] The interests most commonly represented in the special constituencies were European Industry and Commerce, European Planters, Indian Commerce, Indian Landholders, and the Universities. There was a European Mining representative in the Central Provinces and both a European and an Indian Mining representative in Bihar and Orissa. In Burma, where a vast majority of the population is Buddhist, communal representa-

15. This system was not in general adopted in the two All-India electorates, although it was used in Bombay, Madras, Bengal, and the United Provinces for the election of members of the Legislative Assembly.

tion was the exception rather than the rule. Of the 79 elected members, 14 were classed as general urban and 44 as general rural. There were, however, 15 communal seats—8 Indian urban, 5 Karen rural, 1 European, and 1 Anglo-Indian. There were also 6 special seats, 5 representing Commerce and 1 representing Rangoon University.

The number of electors in all constituencies registered for the elections of 1925–26 was 32,126 for the Council of State, 1,125,602 for the Legislative Assembly, and 8,258,823 for the Provincial Legislative Councils. As the total population of the provinces affected by the Reforms was about 240,000,000, it is obvious that the suffrage was very much restricted, especially in the All-India electorates. If Burma, which is not really a part of India, were eliminated, the system would appear still more aristocratic. Nearly one half (15,555) of the Council of State electorate and more than one fifth (1,821,155) of the provincial electorates were enrolled in that province. Five of the six provinces which had woman's suffrage in 1926 kept a separate record of women voters. The total enrollment of women in the provincial electorates was 346,614, the largest number (114,199) being in Madras and the smallest (16,655) in the Punjab. If the figures for Assam were available, the total would probably be brought up to about 350,000.[16]

The Reforms were clearly not democratic. As a matter of fact, however widely the suffrage may be extended, no government in India can be democratic until the caste system is very much modified and a great deal of progress has been made in popular education. But that is not the question. What we really want to know is whether the plan conformed to the principle of Home Rule. Did it transfer to any class of Indians an appreciable control over the government and administration of their country? Assuming that it was given a fair trial, could it have been utilized to bridge the gap between bureaucracy

16. See *Return Showing the Results of Elections in India in 1925 and 1926* (Cd. 2923), (London, 1927). These figures differ slightly from those given in *The Simon Report* (I, 291) mainly because the figures for Burma are for the election of 1928. The Report says that there were 3,000 women electors in Assam.

and self-government? These are difficult questions to answer. The concessions in the government of India were nearly all hedged about with elaborate safeguards because the experiment was new and the Indian Nationalists had already given notice that it did not meet with their approval. It should be remembered, however, that most of the powers retained by the British were intended to be used only in case of emergency and that the whole system was to be revised at the end of ten years.

The British still had absolute control of the central executive and of that part of the provincial executive that dealt with Reserved Subjects. It was also possible, in a crisis, for the Governor of a province to assume the temporary administration of a Transferred Subject and for the Governor-General in Council, with the previous sanction of the Secretary of State in Council, to revoke or suspend the transfer of any subject in any province.

The control over legislation and finance was likewise still very extensive. The Indian legislature, for example, could not deal with certain classes of subjects without the previous sanction of the Governor-General. Among these were the public debt, the religion or the religious rites of any class of British subjects in India, the discipline or maintenance of His Majesty's military, naval, and air forces, and the relations of the government with foreign princes or states. There was a similar, but somewhat larger, list of forbidden subjects in the field of provincial legislation. It is interesting to note that the previous sanction here must also be obtained from the Governor-General and not from the Governor. The Governor-General had the further power to certify that any bill or amendment introduced or proposed to be introduced in the Indian legislature affected the safety or tranquillity of British India or any part thereof and the measure must be immediately dropped. Governors had the same power in dealing with the provincial legislatures. If, in spite of all these restrictions, an undesirable bill was passed, it might still be vetoed by the Governor, the Governor-General, or the government of Great Britain.

These powers were all negative. There also had to be devised a method of insuring the enactment of legislation essential to the needs of the government of India and the Reserved Departments of the provincial governments. *The Montagu-Chelmsford Report* recommended a plan that was based on the perpetuation of the old official bloc, against which the Nationalists had been protesting for so many years. This was rejected by the Joint Select Committee and a new method was evolved which imposed personal responsibility on the Governor-General or the Governor of the province. If the Indian legislature refused to pass a bill in the form recommended by the Governor-General, he could certify that its passage was essential for the safety, tranquillity, or interests of British India or any part thereof and it would become a law. A similar power was vested in the Governors of the provinces in the case of bills relating to Reserved Subjects. These laws went into effect immediately, if, in the opinion of the Governor-General, a state of emergency existed; otherwise their operation was suspended until they had been laid before Parliament and approved by His Majesty's government. When the emergency was urgent it was necessary to put a rough-and-ready plan into temporary operation while a better one was being devised. The Governor-General was, therefore, authorized to issue ordinances having the force of law for not more than six months.

The procedure by certification was first used by Lord Reading in 1922, when the Press Act of 1910 was repealed, to secure the enactment of a law protecting the princes of the Indian States against the dissemination of literature calculated to excite disaffection among their subjects. It was used again in 1923 to double the salt tax. A good example of the procedure in all its stages is to be found in the measures taken to deal with revolutionary anarchy in Bengal in 1924–25. An ordinance issued by the Governor-General in October, 1924, was followed by the Bengal Criminal Law Amendment Act, certified by the Governor of Bengal in January, 1925. Inasmuch as some of the provisions of the ordinance were beyond the competence of the provincial government, but were regarded as essential, the Governor-General enacted by certification the Bengal Criminal Law (Supplementary) Act, 1925. All of these measures were approved by His Majesty's government.

There were similar restrictions in the domain of finance. The

Government of India Act, for example, provided that certain items in the central and provincial budgets should not be subject to legislative vote, although they might be discussed with the approval of the chief executive. More than half of the net expenditures were nonvotable, which meant that the legislatures could exercise no control over them except indirectly by appealing to public opinion through the budget debates. The nonvotable items included military, political, and ecclesiastical expenditures; interest and sinking fund charges on loans; expenditures of which the amount is prescribed by law; and the salaries and pensions of various officials. The provincial contribution to the government of India was also nonvotable in the provincial budgets. In the case of votable items, the Governor-General or the Governor, in dealing with Reserved Subjects, had the power to restore any grant that had been rejected or reduced by the legislature, if he was satisfied that it was essential to the discharge of his responsibilities. The Joint Select Committee of Parliament asserted that this "restorative power" was real and that it was meant to be exercised. It was, in fact, used on several occasions—by Lord Reading, for example, to restore the grant for the Lee Commission on the Public Services which the Assembly had rejected, not for reasons of economy, but as an expression of their disapproval of the general policy of the government toward the Services.

"The progressive realization of responsible government" was not seriously hampered by these restrictions. The extension of popular control over Indian affairs could be shown by a catalogue of central and provincial legislation since 1921, or by quotations from the *Morning Post* and the writings of "Al. Carthill," Sir Michael O'Dwyer, and Sir Reginald Craddock. If the educated classes in India had been willing to cooperate, the progress would have been greater still. The chief obstacle was political rather than constitutional. There was only one large and well-organized party or political bloc in India and it was irreconcilable. It boycotted the elections of 1920 and participated in the later elections primarily for obstructive purposes. The more moderate groups were small and badly disciplined and they were not very successful in forming the coalitions which are necessary when the majority party is unwilling to assume its constitutional obligations. This weakened the whole system. One especially unfortunate result was that the Ministers were usually unable to command an elective majority in the Provincial Councils and were kept in office partly by the votes of the official members.

CHAPTER IV

THE REFORMS IN OPERATION (1921–1930)

THE Reforms were carefully devised and worked out with a meticulous regard for details. Unfortunately, this required a great deal of labor at a time when the British government was occupied with the war and the Peace Conference, so that, while the new policy was announced by Mr. Montagu in August, 1917, it was not put into operation until February, 1921. During this interval India passed through a severe economic depression and the worst influenza epidemic (1918) that was ever known. She also suffered from the Amritsar "massacre" of 1919 and from the Caliphate agitation that grew out of the abortive peace negotiations with Turkey in 1920. The people were tremendously stirred by these events, especially by the "massacre" which stimulated their sense of racial solidarity and by the Caliphate agitation which swept the Moslems into the full tide of the Nationalist movement. They were further aroused by the declaration of the Allied and Associated Powers in favor of the principle of self-determination and by the repudiation of that principle in India when the civil authorities passed the Rowlatt Act and the military authorities treated the Punjab like a conquered province. Their attitude toward the Reforms was determined by these factors in combination with the great personal influence of Mr. Gandhi.

Mohandas Karamchand Gandhi is the best known of all the Indian Nationalist leaders. The details of his early life are familiar history—his birth at Porbandar in one of the small Kathiawar states of the Bombay presidency on October 2, 1869, his education in England, his career in South Africa, and his loyalty to the Empire in the Great War. His campaign against the Rowlatt Act, which culminated in the Amritsar "massacre," is discussed in a later chapter. The method used in that conflict was called satyagraha, which means holding on to truth, or letting truth itself prevail. A redress of grievances was to be secured by self-sacrifice, by refusing to obey the law and suffering the consequences without resorting to any form of violence. There is a little of George Fox in this, but rather more of Tolstoy. Gandhi is really a philosophical anarchist. He believes that our modern machine-made civilization imposes a burden on the individual, subverting his higher nature and his spiritual aspirations. The object of all human activity should be the freedom of the individual soul, a freedom which can be attained only by the mastery of spiritual forces over material might.

This philosophy explains the strategy of the campaign waged against the Reforms during the first few years, but it does not altogether account for Gandhi's immense personal popularity. An idealistic philosopher and a mahatma, or holy man, may be greatly admired and reverenced, but he is not usually accepted, even in India, as a practical political leader. The chief secret of his hold on the popular imagination is the fact that, while he would be the last person in the world to encourage any kind of racial bigotry, he really personifies, more than anyone else, the racial and cultural antagonism of Indians toward Europeans. In spite of his broad human sympathies, he represents the spirit of exaggerated nationalism which afflicts India as well as the rest of the world. He is also, and again without very much conscious effort on his part, an exceedingly clever politician. During the years of his greatest influence (1920–23), he held the upper classes by advocating swaraj (Home Rule), the lower classes by his campaign for the removal of untouchability, the factory workmen by his efforts to improve their industrial and social position, the peasants by trying to revive the cottage textile industry as a subsidiary employment in slack seasons, and the millowners by urging the people to boycott British cloth. He won the Moslems by his support of the Caliphate movement, and all classes and creeds by his denunciation of the "atrocities" in the Punjab.

He began to advocate the Turkish cause as early as November, 1919, when he attended the Caliphate Conference at Delhi. Shortly after the publication of the draft of the peace terms with Turkey in May, 1920, he and the Ali brothers organized a nonviolent noncoöperation campaign to compel a revision of the treaty.[1] He also started a similar movement to secure a redress of grievances in the Punjab. In this effort, his hands were strengthened by the report of the commission appointed by the Punjab Subcommittee of the Indian National Congress, by the Report of the Hunter Committee, by the refusal of the House of Lords to approve the rebuke administered by the government to General Dyer, and finally by the action of the *Morning Post* in raising a subscription fund to reward General Dyer for his "brutality."

It was inevitable that the noncoöperation movement should become involved in the working of the Reforms. At the beginning of 1920 the Extremists were uncertain whether it would be wiser to boycott the Council elections that were to be held later in the year or to take part in them and try to secure control. Those who favored the latter policy were subdivided into two groups: some wished to work the scheme and agitate for further concessions while others preferred obstructive tactics, to wreck the Councils from within and compel the British to grant full responsible government at once as an alternative to anarchy. With the growth of Gandhi's influence, it became more and more obvious that the final decision would rest with him and that it would be in favor of the boycott, the only plan that harmonized with his panacea. The boycott was unpopular with the intellectual aristocracy who drew their inspiration from Tilak and, if Tilak himself had been a younger man, he might have entered the conflict. His mind was too keen and his political judgment too sound for him to be taken in by such a fantastic program. His health was broken, however, and he died on August 1, 1920.[2]

A special session of the National Congress was held at Calcutta early in September (1920) to consider the Turkish

1. For a more detailed account of the Caliphate movement and the early careers of Shaukat and Mohammed Ali, see chap. x, "Religious Grievances."

2. There is a story current in India that Tilak, shortly before his death, approved Gandhi's campaign, but this probably means that he approved Gandhi's objects rather than his methods.

peace treaty, the Report of the Hunter Committee, and the feasibility of adopting Gandhi's program. The principle of noncoöperation was approved and a committee was appointed to work out the details. The committee recommended (1) the surrender of all titles and honorary offices and the resignation of nominated seats in local bodies, (2) the boycott of government levees, durbars, and other official and semi-official functions held by government officials or in their honor, (3) the gradual withdrawal of children from schools and colleges, owned, aided, or controlled by the government and the establishment of so-called national schools, (4) the gradual boycott of British courts by lawyers and litigants and the creation of private arbitration courts, (5) the refusal on the part of the military, clerical, and laboring classes to volunteer for service in Mesopotamia, and (6) the refusal to participate in the coming elections either as electors or as candidates. These recommendations were adopted by the Congress and also by the Moslem League at their regular annual sessions held at Nagpur at the end of December. As a matter of fact, very few Indians surrendered their titles and honors—only 21 out of about 5,000 by February, 1921—and only a few lawyers gave up their practice. The troubles in Mesopotamia (Iraq) had already been settled and the Indian forces there were being reduced. The educational system was, however, badly dislocated for two or three years and the Left-Wing Nationalists were not represented in the first Legislative Councils.

When the Extremists secured control of the Congress, the Moderates—Sir Surendranath Banerjea, Mr. Sastri, Mr. Chintamani, and others—formed a new organization called the National Liberal Federation. Their policy was to take part in the elections and try to make the Reforms succeed while keeping up a constant agitation for further progress along constitutional lines. At their annual conference held at Calcutta in December, 1919, they outlined their policy and also demanded a radical revision of the Press Act and the repeal of the Rowlatt Act.

The first elections under the new system were held in November and December, 1920. The boycott was moderately successful. It was more effective in the constituencies of the Legislative Assembly and the Provincial Legislative Councils than it was in those of the Council of State, in the general constituencies than in the special constituencies, in the cities and towns than in the country, and among Moslems than among Hindus. The proportion of qualified electors who voted in the contested constituencies was 55 per cent for the Council of State, 25 per cent for the Legislative Assembly, and from 22.5 (Central Provinces and Berar) to 39.7 (Bihar and Orissa) per cent for the Provincial Councils. The Moslem percentages varied in the urban constituencies from 4.4 in Bombay to 16.1 in Bengal and in the rural constituencies from 14 in Madras to 59.9 in Bombay. The figures for the Hindus were higher in almost every case. In Bombay, for example, 32.3 per cent of the urban non-Moslem electors voted and only 4.4 of the Moslems. The corresponding figures for Madras were 52.7 and 8.4, for Bengal 40 and 16.1, and for the United Provinces 14 and 9. It can be shown by a comparison with the elections of 1923 and 1925–26 that these low percentages were mainly the result of the noncoöperation campaign, although the proportion of the electors who never vote is probably about as large in India as it is in the United States. The percentage of votes polled to the number of registered electors in contested constituencies of the Legislative Assembly was 25.0 in 1920, 41.9 in 1923, and 48.07 in 1926. In some of the Provincial Council constituencies the comparison is even more striking, the figures for the Central Provinces and Berar being 22.5 in 1920, 57.7 in 1923, and 61.9 in 1926. At first glance, the statistics for the Council of State seem to tell a different story. The percentage fell from 55 in 1920 to 34 in 1925, but this was due entirely to a lack of interest in Burma, where only 5 per cent of the vote was polled in 1925 in a constituency which contained nearly one half of all the Council of State electors in India. With the exception of a slight decline in Bombay, there were increases in all of the other provinces.

The chief result of the boycott was that the elective seats in the various legislative bodies were filled by Moderates and Independents. This had its disadvantages as well as its advantages. It made it possible for the Reforms to work fairly smoothly during the first three years, but it created an atmosphere of unreality. The elected members were tempted to play politics, to engage in irresponsible criticism for the purpose of impressing people who preferred to work outside of the regular machinery of government. Except in Madras, where there was a strong non-Brahman organization, it was almost impossible for the Governors to select Ministers who could command a majority of the elected members of the Legislative Councils.

The new system was inaugurated at Delhi by the Duke of Connaught on February 9, 1921. It was put into operation in the provinces of India proper about the same time and in Burma in 1922.[3] The first important measure passed by the Legislative Assembly was a resolution dealing with the troubles in the Punjab which committed the government of India to the principle of race equality, expressed regret that the martial law administration had departed from that principle, and promised that adequate compensation should be made to the families of those who had suffered. There was also a clause in the original draft demanding the punishment of the officers who were guilty of the abuses in the Punjab, but it was eliminated before the resolution was accepted by the government. Most of the other Reforms carried out during the period of the first Legislative Assembly (1921–24) are discussed in later chapters. Among them should be mentioned (1) the repeal of the Press Acts, (2) the repeal of the Rowlatt Act and many other repressive laws of the old regime, (3) the removal of practically all racial discriminations in the administration of the criminal law, (4) the rapid Indianization of the Civil Services and the beginning of the more difficult task of Indianizing the army, (5) the application of the principle of fiscal independence through the creation of a Tariff Commission and the imposition of protective duties on steel, (6) the adoption of a program of retrenchment in public expenditures, and (7) the adoption of a policy that is ultimately intended to bring about the complete nationalization of the rail-

3. The Reforms were extended to the North-West Frontier Province in 1932 and to Sind and Orissa in 1936.

ways.[4] The provincial governments also made considerable progress although they were badly handicapped by a lack of funds.

This was a good record but it did not arouse any enthusiasm for the Reforms or weaken the forces of radicalism. Every opportunity was seized by the Extremists to appeal to racial and religious prejudice and to demonstrate that the new Constitution was inadequate. They were helped by Lord Reading's use of the power of certification to protect the Indian princes from criticism and to increase the salt tax and by the controversy over the treatment of Indians in Kenya and the Union of South Africa. They also continued to take advantage of the unfriendly relations between Great Britain and Turkey although that issue was partially neutralized by the famous dispute between Mr. Montagu and Lord Curzon in 1922. Mr. Montagu's resignation made the government of India at least relatively popular by dissociating it from the foreign policy of His Majesty's government. The whole question was of course settled later by the Treaty of Lausanne and the abolition of the Caliphate.[5]

Mr. Lloyd George's "Steel Frame" speech in the House of Commons on August 2, 1922, was another contribution to the radical cause. In the course of his remarks, which were probably in large measure extemporaneous, he made several references to the Indian Reforms as an *experiment*. He also spoke of the British Civil Service as the steel frame of the Indian administration and said that he could see no time when India could dispense with its guidance and assistance. This language was regarded in India as a repudiation of the Reforms. In addition to the uneasiness aroused by the use of the word *experiment*, which seemed to imply that the Reforms might some day be withdrawn, there was a general feeling that

4. The government decided to take over the management of the East Indian and the Great Indian Peninsula railways when the contracts with the operating companies expired.

5. For a discussion of the treatment of Indians in Kenya and South Africa, see chap. ix, "Social and Racial Grievances." For the Turkish problems, see chap. x, "Religious Grievances."

the retention of the Service in its existing form would be incompatible with the further process of Indianization and with the ultimate realization of responsible government. The government of India tried to put a conciliatory interpretation upon the Premier's language, but the Legislative Assembly, by a vote of 48 to 34, passed a resolution expressing the grave apprehension of the people of India. The question was kept alive by the appointment of the Lee Commission on the Public Services. The fear that India would have to pay larger salaries and pensions to European officials and that the improved conditions would encourage European recruitment was too strong to be offset by the prospect that the commission would also recommend a more speedy rate of Indianization. It is doubtful whether the feeling would have been so bitter if the British civilians as a class had not been so obviously hostile to the Reforms.

These issues were handled with marvelous skill. The people of all classes were aroused as they had never been aroused before, and, for the first time, there was a real popular demand for swaraj. It is, however, much easier to agitate than to secure practical results. There were only two possible methods of attaining swaraj, to risk everything on the fortunes of rebellion or to participate in the Reforms.[6] What was needed was either a soldier or a popular political leader who was willing to be an opportunist. Mr. Gandhi was neither. He refused to sanction the use of force or to coöperate with a "Satanic" government. The only people in India who showed that they appreciated the logic of the situation were the two extremes, the Revolutionists who used bombs and the Moderates who preferred to use ballots.

The disillusionment of Mr. Gandhi was painful although it apparently did not have any effect on his policy. He was constantly lamenting the absence of an "atmosphere of nonviolence" and engaging in penitential fasts, but he continued to

6. The latter method was at last attempted. The Working Committee of the Congress decided on July 9, 1937, that all M.L.A.'s (Member Legislative Assembly) who had previously been duly elected should accept office.

advocate schemes that were certain to lead to bloodshed. He proclaimed a boycott against the visit of the Prince of Wales, for example, in 1921, and there was a riot in Bombay in which several hundred people were killed or injured. He also sanctioned the National Volunteers, a kind of militia force organized under the auspices of the Congress and the Caliphate Conference. As long as the members of this organization served without pay they came from a class of society that had a sense of responsibility and some regard for the principles of nonviolence, but when they began to receive compensation from the Tilak Swaraj Fund their ranks were flooded with recruits of a less scrupulous character. Although technically unarmed, they were often equipped with guns and bombs and cruder weapons that could be used in an emergency. These volunteers came into conflict with the police at Giridih in Bihar and Orissa and at Malegaon in Bombay. They also led the fanatical peasants in the terrible affair at Chauri Chaura in the United Provinces in February, 1922, when twenty-one policemen and rural watchmen were atrociously murdered.

The chief offenders were the Moslems. As a community, they are temperamentally unfitted for passive resistance and at that time they were especially excited by the Turkish question. The Ali brothers evidently tried to live up to Gandhi's principles, but they found it impossible to restrain their exuberance. The government was about to have them arrested in May, 1921, when Gandhi interceded and persuaded them to apologize "for the unnecessary heat of some of the passages" in their speeches and to promise that they would not "directly or indirectly advocate violence at present or in the future, nor create an atmosphere of preparedness for violence." This weakened their influence among their own people and they soon relapsed. In speeches made at the Caliphate Conference at Karachi in July, they urged Moslems to desert from the army and even suggested the possibility of the establishment of an Indian republic. One of the resolutions proposed by Mohammed Ali and adopted by the conference reads as follows:

> This meeting clearly proclaims that it is in every way unlawful for a Musalman at the present moment to continue in the British Army or to enter the army or to induce others to join the army,

and it is the duty of all Musalmans in general and of the Ulema in particular to see that these religious commandments are brought home to every Musalman in the army.

Lord Reading accepted the challenge. Both brothers were arrested, tried, convicted, and sentenced to two years' imprisonment. The outstanding product of this agitation was the Moplah (Mappilla) rebellion with its ten thousand victims, most of whom were innocent Hindus.[7]

Mr. Gandhi gradually enlarged his original program in 1920–21 by announcing his intention to raise a Tilak Swaraj Memorial Fund of ten million rupees, to secure ten million members of the Indian National Congress, and to install two million spinning wheels in two million homes. The Swaraj Fund was oversubscribed although it is impossible to say how much was actually collected. The success in the other fields was not so spectacular, in spite of the fact that a part of the Tilak money was used to finance the membership drive and to subsidize the installation of spinning wheels and hand looms. A temperance movement was also started about this time and was formally approved by the All-India Congress Committee at its meeting in Bombay in July, 1921.

More important than any of these schemes, so far as the immediate results were concerned, was the proposal to inaugurate a campaign of mass civil disobedience. Mass civil disobedience is a logical outgrowth of noncoöperation, but it goes a great deal further. Noncoöperation affects only a small group of educated people, those who would ordinarily practice law, hold administrative or judicial posts, sit on legislative councils or send their children to government schools. Mass civil disobedience means the opposition of all the people to the laws and institutions of a "Satanic" government. It appeals to baser motives because it offers the prospect of evading the payment of taxes and of looting and committing other crimes without the risk of punishment. It would lead straight to violence and bloodshed and, if successful, it could result only in anarchy. Although Gandhi insisted at first that it should not be put into operation until a "nonviolent atmosphere" was

7. See chap. x, "Religious Grievances," pp. 314 ff.

created, he finally yielded to the pressure of the Left Wing of his followers and agreed to give it a trial at Bardoli in the Bombay presidency. His faith was shaken, however, by the violence which attended the arrival of the Prince of Wales and the date selected for the beginning of the experiment was postponed. The National Congress approved this action, but in deference to the radicals it was also resolved that mass civil disobedience should be tried as soon as possible at Bardoli and in other areas where there had been sufficient preparation. The situation was again altered by the Chauri Chaura tragedy in February, 1922, and the scheme was still further deferred.

From this time onward, Gandhi's political influence gradually declined. He had not driven the British out of India or redressed the grievances of the Turks and he was apparently afraid to carry out his own program. The All-India Congress Committee continued to give him its nominal support, but it really undermined his position by authorizing the Provincial Congress Committees to sanction what was called individual civil disobedience. The futility of this method of procedure was soon recognized, however, by the Extremists, and it was never actually put into operation until 1930, when it was found to be impossible to enforce it by peaceful methods.

Mr. Chitta Ranjan Das, the leader of the opposition to Gandhi, was a curious combination of a practical business man and an emotional idealist. He was for years the most successful lawyer in Calcutta, but his large income, estimated at about £60,000 per annum, was nearly all spent on the causes in which he was interested. His enthusiasm for the Nationalist movement was largely due to the influence of Aravinda Ghose. He defended the Ghose brothers and their adherents in the courts and it is believed that he also contributed liberally to their newspaper ventures. He was elected president of the Bengal Provincial Congress in 1917, but was never very widely known outside of his own province until 1919 when he spoke against the Montagu-Chelmsford plan in the special session of the National Congress at Delhi. When Gandhi proclaimed the policy of nonviolent noncoöperation, Das gave up his practice and joined the movement. In 1924, he deeded his fortune to a board of trustees to be used to advance the cause of Nationalism and he and his wife retired to a small cottage and lived on an allowance of £5 per week.

On most issues, Mr. Das and Mr. Gandhi were in complete agreement. They both believed that India should be emancipated from Western culture, that cottage industries should be revived, and that a Hindu-Moslem entente should be maintained even if the Hindus had to sacrifice some of their legitimate rights. They both were convinced that swaraj means democracy, that India must be governed by the masses of the people and not by the upper classes. There was one question, however, about which they held different views, although, even here, it was more a matter of procedure than a matter of principle. Mr. Das was more of a realist. He believed that the Nationalists, instead of ignoring the Reforms, should participate in the next elections and then wreck the Councils from the inside. In other words, he was an obstructive rather than a passive noncoöperationist.

Mr. Das was assisted in his campaign by the Pandit Motilal Nehru, a distinguished lawyer and the leading Nationalist of the United Provinces. Mr. Nehru was born May 6, 1861. He was president of the Provincial Conference of the United Provinces in 1907 and of the National Congress in 1919, and was for several years a member of the Provincial Legislative Council. When the National Congress approved the policy of noncoöperation he gave up his large law practice and supported the cause with so much enthusiasm that he was sentenced to prison for six months. But he too was a realist and he soon began to appreciate the futility of an absolute political boycott. In fact, it was probably he, rather than Mr. Das, who originated the idea of entering the Councils in order to destroy them.[8]

An active propaganda was carried on by these two men during the latter half of 1922. Defeated at the Gaya Congress in December, they organized the Swaraj party, secured the adhesion of the Ali brothers, and kept up the fight until the victory was won. A resolution was adopted at a special session of the Congress, held at Delhi, September 25, 1923, authorizing each Congressman to decide for himself whether he would take

8. He died February 6, 1931.

part in the elections. The policy of noncoöperation was repudiated, partly because it failed to produce results and partly because Mr. Gandhi, who was in prison at this time, was unable to assume personal leadership. In addition to being badly led, his followers were also stunned and demoralized by the calm assurance of Mr. Mohammed Ali that he had received a telepathic message from the Mahatma approving the modification of the boycott.

The second elections for the Legislative Assembly and the Provincial Legislative Councils were held in November and December, 1923. There were two main parties in the field, the Swarajists and the Liberals, and also a number of Independent candidates who had enough local influence to make the race without the support of a party organization. The Swaraj leaders were of course Mr. Das and the Pandit Motilal Nehru while the best-known representatives of Liberal or Moderate opinion were still Sir Surendranath Banerjea and Mr. Sastri. In making their appeal to the electorate, the Swarajists pledged themselves to present an ultimatum to the government demanding Home Rule. If it were not accepted, they would follow a policy of "uniform, continuous and consistent obstruction with a view to make government through the Assembly and the Councils impossible." The Liberals promised to continue their old policy which was to coöperate in working the Reforms and at the same time to insist that they should be further liberalized.

The results of the election were not decisive. The radical element was weakened by the refusal of the No-Changers, a small group of Mr. Gandhi's adherents, to take any part in the campaign. In spite of this defection, the Swarajists won nearly half of the elective seats in the Legislative Assembly and the largest group of seats in several of the Provincial Councils, but they had an absolute majority only in the Central Provinces and Berar.

Shortly after the campaign was over (December, 1923), the National Congress met at Cocanada in Madras and formulated the ultimatum that was to be presented to the government. It demanded the release of all political prisoners, the repeal of all repressive laws and the summoning of a National

Constitutional Convention. The Liberal Federation, which met at Poona, also worked out a more definite program. It resolved that it would strive by legal means to secure an immediate revision of the Constitution, a more rapid Indianization of the army and the Public Services, a retrenchment of military expenditures and a redress of the grievances of Indians overseas.

The first session of the second Legislative Assembly was opened by Lord Reading, January 31, 1924. In a total membership of 145 there were 40 nominated members, 45 Swarajists, and 60 Independents and Liberals. Through the efforts of Mr. Nehru, a coalition was formed between the Swarajists and a considerable number of Independents which came to be called the Nationalist party. The first test of strength was the vote on the Swarajist ultimatum, presented February 18, in the form of a request for a Round Table Conference to recommend a scheme for the establishment of full responsible government in India. The resolution was adopted by a vote of 64 to 48. The refusal of the government to grant this request strengthened the coalition and it gained several other victories. Resolutions were passed, for example, calling for the release of certain political prisoners, the repeal of Bengal Regulation III of 1818, and the appointment of a committee to inquire into the grievances of the Sikhs.[9] But their greatest triumph was the refusal to permit the introduction of the Finance Bill for the year, which Lord Reading was compelled to enact by certification.

Similar tactics were adopted in the Central Provinces and Berar and in Bengal. In the Central Provinces, the Governor, Sir Frank Sly, requested the Swarajist majority to take office. They refused to do so, voted their lack of confidence in the Ministers who were appointed and then fixed the ministerial salaries at Rs. 2 per annum. They also indiscriminately rejected the budget and all other government measures that were laid before them. The Governor was compelled to take over the administration of Transferred Subjects and to use his emergency powers to solve the budget problems.

In Bengal, where the Swarajists were in a minority, they

9. See chap. x, "Religious Grievances."

were able to form a coalition with some of the Independents, especially with the Moslems, who were won over by the Bengal pact proposed by Mr. Das as a solution of the Hindu-Moslem problem. On March 24, 1924, the Council rejected the demand for salaries of the Ministers by a majority of one vote. The Ministers decided for the time to carry on without pay. A supplementary demand for a salary grant was also defeated on August 26 by a vote of 68 to 66. The Ministers then resigned and Lord Lytton, the Governor, assumed temporary charge of the Transferred Subjects. On February 17, 1925, the Council voted to provide ministerial salaries in the annual budget, but the Ministers selected by Lord Lytton were not satisfactory and the salaries were again refused by a vote of 69 to 63. As this could not go on indefinitely, the Governor-General in Council, with the previous sanction of the Secretary of State in Council, issued a formal decree on June 13 giving the Governor control over Transferred Subjects until January 21, 1927.

There was no anarchy in either Bengal or the Central Provinces. The Reforms were merely replaced by the old autocratic system of administration until the majority of the Legislative Council were prepared to coöperate. Furthermore, the Swaraj tactics were apparently not approved by the electors. The party was badly defeated in 1926 in the Central Provinces and the new Council passed the demand for the Ministers' salaries by a majority of 55 to 16. The defeat was not so decisive in Bengal, but the Independent Moslem members abandoned the coalition and the salary grant was carried by a vote of 94 to 38.

The policy of obstruction had in fact been challenged from the very beginning. Mr. Gandhi, who was released from prison in February, 1924, made a strenuous effort to recover control of the Congress machinery and restore the original principle of noncoöperation. He was also disgusted by the action of the Bengal Provincial Congress in the Saha case. In January, 1924, Gopi Nath Saha shot and killed Mr. Ernest Day, mistaking him for the commissioner of police of Calcutta. The Provincial Congress passed a resolution which stated in substance that while it still adhered to the ideal of nonviolence it paid homage to the patriotism of Saha.

Although most of the intellectuals were opposed to Gandhi, his popularity with the masses was so great that he had to be handled very tactfully. A mild resolution approving the boycott of the Councils was passed by the All-India Congress Committee, but no penalties were provided for enforcing it. Saha's crime was condemned and Gandhi's campaign to encourage the spinning of yarn by hand, to remove untouchability, and to settle the Hindu-Moslem difficulties was endorsed.

In spite of these concessions, there would probably have been a serious split among the radicals if the government had not come to their support. There had been a recrudescence of revolutionary violence in Bengal and the ordinary judicial machinery proved inadequate for its suppression. On October 25 (1924), Lord Reading issued the Bengal Criminal Law Amendment Ordinance, which revived, for a period of six months, most of the autocratic powers exercised by the Bengal government during the war for the suppression of sedition.[10] This measure was bitterly denounced by Indians of all factions and parties. In November, Mr. Gandhi joined with Mr. Das and Mr. Nehru in urging the radicals to bury their differences and present a united front to the enemy. The main questions at issue were compromised. The approaching Congress at Belgaum was advised to approve Gandhi's program for encouraging cottage industries, removing untouchability, and promoting communal amity, but noncoöperation was to be suspended except in so far as it related to the wearing of foreign cloth.

The Nationalist coalition suffered also from internal dissensions. During the first session of the new Legislative Assembly (January–March, 1924) the party machinery worked smoothly. As has already been indicated, several government bills, not at all unpopular in themselves, were rejected for purely obstructive reasons. The first real test, however, came

10. For the history of this Ordinance and the more permanent legislation that followed, see chap. viii, "Political Grievances."

in May when a special session was called to consider the report of the Tariff Board based on the steel industry. The Board recommended and the government approved a moderate measure of protection. The issue was tremendously important. It was the initial step toward fiscal independence and the adoption of a tariff policy in accordance with Indian public opinion. Would the Nationalists dare to throw out a bill of this character merely in order to embarrass the government? As a matter of fact, reason and the pressure of economic interests proved stronger than logic. The bill was passed and the policy of obstruction was doomed.

The Independents gradually drifted away from the Nationalist coalition and formed a separate bloc under the leadership of Mr. Mohammed Ali Jinnah, a Moslem member from Bombay. They held the balance of power between the Swarajists or Nationalists and the government. Their general policy was to support the Swarajists when popular issues were at stake without accepting obstruction as a regular political weapon; to vote with the Swarajists, for example, against the Report on the Public Services, but not against the Railway Budget or protectionist measures that would help the manufacturing interests of Bombay.

This movement spread and in time began to affect the Swarajists themselves, especially after the death of Mr. Das on June 16, 1925. Mr. Nehru accepted an appointment on the Indian Sandhurst Committee and Mr. V. J. Patel was elected president of the Legislative Assembly. A few other leaders were prepared to go further still. In October (1925), Mr. S. B. Tambe, the most influential Swarajist in the Central Provinces, accepted office as Executive Councilor of his province. Mr. Nehru hastened to condemn Tambe and a violent controversy arose. Mr. M. R. Jayakar, the leader of the Bombay Swarajists, came to Tambe's rescue, saying among other things that he could see no essential difference between Tambe's acceptance of office and that of Patel. Similar views were expressed by Dr. B. S. Moonje of the Central Provinces and Mr. N. C. Kelkar of Bombay.

Mr. Nehru reacted violently against this heresy and swung back toward the old policy of noncoöperation. The Cawnpore

Congress (December, 1925), which was completely under his influence, resolved that the Home Rule ultimatum of February 18, 1924, should be revived and that, if the government refused to take favorable action, the Swarajist members of the Assembly should not attend any meetings except enough to prevent their seats being declared vacant. Mr. Jayakar, Dr. Moonje, and Mr. Kelkar immediately issued a public statement disapproving the resolution and urging the adoption of what they called a policy of responsive coöperation. Their protest was ineffective. On March 8 (1926), Mr. Nehru and his orthodox followers walked out of the House.

There now remained in the Assembly three groups of elected members—Liberals, Independents, and Responsivists. The cleavage between them was not very well marked. They all felt that the Reforms were inadequate, but that it would be wise to coöperate in working them until something better could be secured. The effort to form a coalition failed, however, partly because there was an unusually bitter outbreak of communal antagonism in April which lasted for more than a year. During the third elections held in November and December, there was a tendency for the Hindus who refused to follow Mr. Nehru to draw together under the leadership of the Pandit Madan Mohan Malaviya, Lala Lajpat Rai, and Mr. Jayakar. Out of this movement there developed the Nationalist or Independent Congress party, which was closely associated with the Hindu Mahasabha. The Liberal and Responsivist parties practically disappeared and Mr. Jinnah's Independent bloc, which had played such an important part in the second Legislative Assembly, dwindled down until it contained only two Hindus and a few Moslems. There were also about fifteen or twenty other Moslem members in the new Assembly, who, in the course of time, were organized as the Moslem Center party, under the leadership of Sir Zulfiqar Ali Khan of the Punjab.

The Swarajists returned to the Assembly on August 23 (1926) during the debate on the Indian Currency Bill, but they walked out again immediately afterwards. They soon discovered, however, that this policy did not meet with public approval, and the Congress, which was completely under their control, tacitly authorized them to abandon it. The annual meeting of the Congress was held at Gauhati in Assam at the end of December. A resolution, passed by a large majority, pledged the members not to accept office, but nothing was said about boycotting the legislative bodies. The Pandit Motilal Nehru and his followers attended the first session of the new Assembly in January, 1927, and took an active part in the proceedings.

It is difficult to compare the Swarajist vote of 1926 with that of 1923. So far as the Legislative Assembly was concerned, the general result was about the same. The party still held approximately forty seats. There was, however, a wide variation in the distribution of their strength, which was especially noticeable in the Provincial Legislative Councils. As a rule, they were strongest in those provinces where communal feeling was least aroused and it was still possible for Hindus and Moslems to work together. Local issues also played an important part. In Madras, for example, the Swarajists were successful because of popular dissatisfaction with the Justice party, the non-Brahman Hindus, who had controlled the Council during the previous six years. They also improved their position in Bihar and Orissa. In Bengal, they won about the same number of seats that they had before, but communal friction weakened party discipline and made it difficult to secure the support of the Independent members. They were badly defeated in Bombay, the Punjab, the United Provinces, and the Central Provinces.

The first session of the third Legislative Assembly was held in the new capitol at Delhi in January–March, 1927. Although the Swarajists were in a minority, their leaders were able to discover several issues upon which they could secure enough Nationalist and Independent support to embarrass the government. At the beginning of the session, Mr. Nehru moved an adjournment of the House to discuss the absence of Mr. Satyendra Chandra Mitra, who had been elected to the Assembly while he was a political prisoner in Bengal. Mr. Nehru said that his motion involved the question of parliamentary privilege rather than the general question of repressive legislation, but the real issue was the autocratic administration of the criminal law in Bengal and the resolution was carried by a majority of thirteen votes.

The government's fiscal proposals were also bitterly attacked. In the case of the Railway Budget the burden of criticism was the delay in Indianizing the Service and the inadequate character of the accommodation provided for third-class passengers. Amendments were also made to the General Budget reducing the salt duty 50 per cent and rejecting the government's proposal to abolish the export duty on hides. The salt duty was restored to the original level by the Council of State, but the export duty on hides was retained in order to encourage the tanning industry. The issue of protection was further involved in the Steel Protection Bill. The government agreed to an increase of the import duties on steel, but only on the condition that there should be a preferential in favor of British steel. After a spirited debate, the Assembly finally yielded because it was obvious that the protection desired could not be secured on any other terms. This settlement was very unfortunate. It convinced the people of India that the fiscal independence promised by the Joint Parliamentary Committee in 1919 was really a farce. The government of India is not a free agent. It must obey orders from Whitehall and there is no difference in principle whether those orders are dictated by the British textile industry or the British steel industry. There could be no stronger argument in favor of independence or Dominion Home Rule.

Great Britain's policy in China was likewise used to good advantage by the Swarajists. In Lord Irwin's address at the opening of the session, he referred to the fact that Indian troops were to be sent to Shanghai. This aroused keen excitement which was especially reflected in the vernacular press. It was alleged that the British were waging an aggressive war on China to prevent the establishment of a Nationalist government. The day after the Viceroy's speech was delivered, Mr. Srinivasa Aiyangar, one of the Swaraj leaders, announced his intention of moving an adjournment of the Assembly as a protest against the sending of Indian troops to China. This involved not only the relations of Great Britain and India with China, but also with other countries having interests in China.

Lord Irwin, therefore, disallowed the motion under a Statutory Rule which authorizes such action when the relations of His Majesty's government or the government of India with any foreign state are affected. The discussion was continued, however, outside of the Assembly until it died from lack of nutrition, that is to say, until it became clear that the British government merely intended to protect the interests of its nationals in China and had no desire to interfere in the internal affairs of the Chinese people.

The chief debate of the session was over the Currency Bill, which involved the old familiar conflict between the advocates of inflation and contraction. The technical aspects of the question are discussed later in connection with "Economic and Financial Grievances." Here it need only be said that, after the closing of the mints to the free coinage of silver in 1893, India had a good exchange standard, that the value of the rupee was stabilized at 1*s.* 4*d.* in foreign exchange, that the system broke down with the rise in the price of silver during the war, that the attempt to stabilize at 2*s.* in 1920 was also a failure and finally, that the Hilton-Young Commission, in 1926, recommended the establishment of a gold bullion standard, which provided that gold bars should be exchanged for silver rupees and rupee notes at the rate of 1*s.* 6*d.* for each rupee. Although no provision was made for a gold coinage, this was to be a real gold standard and not merely a government guarantee of the stability of external credits.

A Currency Bill designed to carry out this recommendation was prepared by Sir Basil Blackett, the Finance Member of the Governor-General's Council, and introduced into the Assembly in March, 1927. It was opposed by the majority of the nonofficial members, partly because it did not provide for the establishment of a gold mint in India, but mainly because it overvalued the rupee, which would encourage imports and discourage exports. In other words, they favored the traditional ratio of 1*s.* 4*d.* in the belief that the higher ratio proposed by the commission would penalize Indian industry and commerce. This was not merely the view of politicians to whom all government measures are anathema; it was also shared by the majority of Indian bankers and manufacturers and it was based upon the same principle which has led the British government since 1931 to depress artificially the exchange value of the pound. On the decisive vote about twenty elected members supported the government and they won by the narrow margin of 68 to 65. Great Britain and India both abandoned the gold standard in September, 1931, but the rupee is still linked to sterling at the ratio of 1*s.* 6*d.* and the grievance still rankles.

The Hilton-Young Commission also proposed the establishment of a central Reserve Bank in India to control currency and exchange, which precipitated an even more acrimonious controversy. The government preferred a Shareholders' Bank, free from political influence, but the majority of the Legislative Assembly wanted a State Bank in which a large proportion of the directors would be chosen by the elected members of the various Indian legislative bodies. They also wanted a statutory provision that the governor or deputy governor should always be an Indian. Sir Basil Blackett tried hard to compromise their differences, but he was unsuccessful and the bill was finally dropped.[11]

There was a similar controversy when the government of India proposed that the Royal Indian Marine should be reconstructed as a combatant force, "to enable India to enter upon the first stage of her own naval development, and ultimately to undertake her own naval defense." The Royal Indian Marine was to be converted into the Royal Indian Navy, which would have a status equal to that of the Royal Navy and the Dominion Navies and would in the course of time be entirely subject to the control of the Indian legislature. The scheme was approved by the Secretary of State and the Admiralty, the details were worked out by a committee under the late General Lord Rawlinson, and the necessary changes in the Government of India Act were made by the British Parliament. The force was normally to be controlled by the government of India and used only for the defense of India, but, in an emergency, they could place it at the disposal of the Admiralty.

11. The bill was finally passed in 1934 in the form desired by the government.

All that remained to be done was for the Indian legislature to establish a code of discipline, based on the legislation for the discipline of the Royal Navy, with such modifications and adaptations as might be needed to meet Indian conditions. An Indian (Navy) Discipline Bill was accordingly introduced in the Legislative Assembly in February, 1928, and there was a debate on the merits of the plan as a whole. The chief arguments of the opposition were that the Indian legislature had not been consulted in regard to the constitution of the navy, that it would have no control over naval expenditures, that it would have no voice in the decision to place the force at the disposal of His Majesty's government, and that the rate of Indianization proposed by the Rawlinson Committee was inadequate. In reply, the government representative said that the Assembly had shown no desire to discuss the plan, although it had been kept fully informed of its progress during the past two years; that expenditures on the Royal Indian Marine had always been nonvotable, so there was no change in this respect; that it was possible under the existing law for the Admiralty to take over ships of the Royal Indian Marine without even waiting for the consent of the government of India; that the ratio of Indian recruitment[12] was as large as could be expected in a small and highly technical service in which there was no established Indian tradition; and finally, that the plan was purely transitional, the first step toward the ultimate goal of a navy entirely officered by Indians and controlled by the Indian legislature. His efforts were wasted. A motion to refer the bill to a Select Committee was rejected and the whole plan had to be abandoned.[13]

There were also acrimonious disputes over many other measures. In 1928 and again in 1929, the government urged the Legislative Assembly to enact a Public Safety Bill[14] giv-

12. The committee had recommended that one third of the officers recruited in the immediate future should be Indians.

13. With a few amendments, the bill was finally passed in 1934.

14. These measures are discussed in later chapters, the Public Safety Bill in chap. viii, "Political Grievances," and the Cotton Textile Bill in chap. v, "Economic and Financial Grievances."

ing them the power to deport foreign and British Communists, but they were defeated by the president of the Assembly on a point of order and were finally compelled to proceed by means of an ordinance. In 1930, a controversy was precipitated when the government forced the Assembly to grant a preferential duty on British cotton cloth by refusing to increase the general rates under any other conditions, as they had done in the case of the steel duties in 1927. The Assembly, on the other hand, wished to build up the Indian mercantile marine by restricting the coastal traffic to vessels owned and registered in India, but this was rejected by the government. There were similar conflicts in most of the provincial legislatures, especially in Assam and Bengal, where the Councils had to be dissolved in 1929 because it was impossible to find Ministers who could command support.

The government of India decided in 1929 that it would be unwise to hold a general election until after the publication of the *Simon Report* and the life of the Legislative Assembly was, therefore, prolonged for another year. The Report was published in June, 1930, and the election was held in the following autumn. The new Assembly did not attract much attention because public interest was concentrated on the struggle for constitutional reform. The members themselves were sometimes tempted to engage in constitutional debates. As a matter of fact, this was true of the Montagu-Chelmsford system from the very beginning and it has constituted a serious handicap. The views of the Simon Commission on this subject were illuminating. They believed that a constitution which attempts to measure the successive stages of progress and marks each step with a commission of inquiry is bound to fail. At the beginning of their recommendations, therefore, they criticized the makeshift character of the existing system and exposed the evils of a temporary constitution with a fixed timetable:

> Those who have to work a temporary constitution tend inevitably to fix their minds upon the future instead of on the present. Instead of making the most of the existing constitution and learning to deal with practical problems under existing conditions,

they constantly endeavour to anticipate the future and to push forward the day for the next installment of reforms. There is little incentive to try to make the system a success; on the contrary, those who are not satisfied with the advance already made are eager to prove that the temporary constitution is unworkable.

CHAPTER V

ECONOMIC AND FINANCIAL GRIEVANCES

PART I

THE economic system of India is more rigid than that of the United States or the countries of western Europe. As the majority of the people live almost constantly on the verge of starvation, anything that affects their supply of food and clothing is a matter of immediate and tremendous consequence. An industrial depression or a crop failure that would merely cause a temporary hardship in the West would be likely there to result in famine and the loss of millions of lives. The British seem to ignore these facts. Their reforms are nearly always concerned with political questions and when they do make an economic concession, it is likely to favor a privileged minority. They have, for example, allowed protective import duties to be levied on cotton cloth and steel products which increased the profits of a few wealthy manufacturers, but they have done practically nothing to improve the condition of the workmen in the mills or to lighten the burden of a land revenue system that bears with exceptional severity upon the poorest class of the people. This failure to remedy economic grievances is the most vulnerable spot in their armor and it bulks large in the literature of Indian Nationalism. There is, of course, a tendency to play up grievances that are purely imaginary. If that were the whole story, if it were only necessary to counteract the effects of a campaign of misrepresentation, the government of India would probably be able to handle the situation without very much difficulty. Unfortunately, that is not the case. There are real economic abuses of far-reaching consequences which the government has never made any serious effort to remedy. This chapter will deal with imaginary as well as legitimate grievances, partly because an attempt to draw a line between them would be arbitrary and invidious and partly because an analysis of both is necessary in appraising the causes of discontent.

Nationalists of all shades of opinion are practically united in the belief that India has been impoverished by British rule and that her resources and her labor force are exploited for the benefit of British capitalists. Among the concrete charges the following are the most important: there is a heavy annual "drain" of Indian revenue to England; the taxes are exorbitant and India has not been given complete freedom to impose the tariffs necessary for the protection of her industries; the administration is extravagant and too much money is spent on the army and not enough on education, sanitation, and other "nation building" services; the exchange value of the rupee has been stabilized in the interest of British exporters; Indian government funds—Treasury Balances, Gold Standard Reserve, and Paper Currency Reserve—have been manipulated for the benefit of British trading and banking interests; railways and shipping rates have been regulated to encourage the importation of manufactured goods and the exportation of food and raw materials; and India has not been allowed to enact navigation laws for the protection of her coastwise trade.

The "drain" theory was apparently first put forward by Mr. Dadabhai Naoroji about 1876, but it was not fully explained until the publication in 1901 of Sir William Digby's *Prosperous British India* and of Mr. Naoroji's own book on *Poverty and Un-British Rule in India*. Since that time it has been further elaborated by Mr. Lajpat Rai, Mr. R. C. Dutt, Professor C. N. Vakil, and various other writers. One of the strongest arguments against the theory is that given by Sir Theodore Morison in his book on *The Economic Transition in India*, published in 1911. Strictly speaking, there is no direct tribute levied in British India at all, but more than £30,-000,000 sterling has to be remitted annually to Great Britain irrespective of the ordinary trade balances. The chief items in this total are (a) interest on the public debt, (b) payment for services performed by the British merchant marine, (c) payment of civil and military pensions, gratuities, and furlough allowances, (d) remittances sent home by British officials, and (e) commercial earnings remitted to Great Britain.

A study of the first two items naturally suggests some

points of resemblance between the economic history of India and that of the United States during the half century preceding the Great War. Both countries were debtor nations. Large amounts of capital were borrowed in Europe by the government of India and by private American corporations for the construction of railways and other public works. The external trade of both countries was conducted mainly in foreign bottoms. The result was that both had to export a great deal more than they imported in order to pay interest, sinking fund, and transportation charges.

Was this an economic drain? Would it have been wiser if they had developed more slowly and had depended entirely on their own resources? In attempting to answer these questions, so far as India is concerned, we must remember that native capital is exceedingly conservative and that there is a dearth of administrative capacity and engineering skill. We must also bear in mind the fact that European executives and engineers will usually not work under Indian Boards of Directors. In other words, the real alternative to a rapid development with foreign capital was not a slow development with native capital, but a lack of any development on a large scale at all. It might have been better if India had been allowed to accept this alternative. The population would now be smaller, the cottage industries would be more prosperous, the country people would not be drifting into the cities, and it would not be so easy to export food which is really needed at home. A plausible argument could be made for this thesis, but it would apply equally well to other countries. If, on the other hand, we accept modern industrialism as an accomplished fact and consider the question from its point of view, it is difficult to see that India has any grievance. The money was borrowed at a low rate of interest and as a rule it was wisely invested. There were some initial difficulties and some irreparable blunders, but the ultimate results were on the whole highly satisfactory. After the payment of operating expenses and fixed charges there is in normal years a large annual surplus derived from the railway, telegraph, and irrigation works which either becomes part of the general revenue or is used for further expansion. The productive capacity of the country has been greatly augmented, the people have found wider markets for their goods, and there has been an enormous increase of national wealth. It ought not to be any greater hardship for a nation than it is for an individual to pay interest on borrowed money that has been profitably invested.

Although the parallel between India and the United States no longer exists, there is a fairly close analogy between India's financial position at the present time and that of the debtor nations of Europe. This is especially true in the case of the ordinary or unproductive debt. The European nations are richer than India. If it is an economic burden for them to pay interest on their foreign war debts, it is certainly more burdensome for her to pay interest on that part of her foreign debt that represents unproductive expenditure. The fact that the Allied debts are payable to the United States government while the Indian debt is payable to private investors in Great Britain does not affect the validity of the argument. In both cases the money is sent out of the country and nothing of tangible value is received in return. In 1934–35 the interest charge payable in England was approximately £7,000,000.

The history of the ordinary or unproductive debt of India may be summarized very briefly. The people were conquered and the Mutiny of 1857 was suppressed largely by their own troops and at their own expense. They were also called upon to support the East India Company's establishments at Bencoolen, Malacca, Canton, and St. Helena and to share the cost of British expeditions to Mauritius, China, the Cape of Good Hope, and other places remote from their own shores. In 1860, the public debt amounted to £93,000,000, nearly all of which had been borrowed for unproductive expenditure. The amount was increased later by the redemption of the East India Company's stock in 1874, by wars in Afghanistan and Burma, by the famines of 1874–77 and 1896–1900, and by various other emergencies, but, owing to the adoption of a new system of bookkeeping about 1870, it did not appear in the official statistics. Under this system, all expenditures on productive public works were treated as borrowed money and, when surplus revenues were so employed, the amount was deducted from the ordinary debt and added to the productive debt. As there were budget surpluses in fourteen out of the sixteen years immediately preceding the war (1898–1913), the ordinary debt was practically liquidated by 1914. It was, however, greatly increased in the next decade mainly by the war contributions of £112,000,000 in 1917–19 and the budget deficits of 1918–23, which amounted to about 100 crores of rupees.[1] There was some reduction later, under the financial administration of Sir Basil Blackett, and another increase after 1929. On March 31, 1935, the figures were 203.19 crores or £152,390,000. The productive debt was 1,032.55 crores or £774,420,000.

There are two methods of dealing with the problem. One is to get the latest possible figures and try to find out how much of the amount is held in England and how much represents an ethically sound obligation. If this method is employed, the case for India is not very convincing. The government has floated many of its loans in India since 1914 and a large proportion of the obligations are held by the people of India themselves. Furthermore, the war loans were approved by the Indian representatives in the Legislative Assembly and there is no good reason to question the validity of the loans contracted to meet the deficits in the budget. The other method of procedure is to ascertain the total sum of all unproductive loans from the beginning, deduct those which India would have been compelled to contract, if she had been an independent nation, calculate the compound interest on the remainder, and then present Great Britain with a bill for the whole amount. This is a favorite sport with the Nationalists and the bill usually amounts to about £1,000,000,000 sterling, which would be more than enough to pay off the whole of the public debt, productive as well as unproductive.

The merchant marine problem is also rather complicated. From an economic point of view, it is justifiable for a nation to use foreign ships in its external trade, or even in its coast-

1. The figures are given in rupees because the exchange fluctuated so widely during this period that it is impossible to state exactly the sterling equivalent, although it would be somewhere between £90,000,000 and £100,000,000.

wise trade, if they offer the cheapest and most efficient service. Domestic capital which might be coaxed by subsidies to enter the field of shipping had much better be employed in other enterprises where there are greater natural advantages. It is true, perhaps, that a wise government will encourage a mercantile marine as a means of national defense, but that is a political and not an economic issue and we are here concerned only with economic grievances. As long as India is a part of the British Empire and her goods are carried primarily in British bottoms it is not even a political issue. The Nationalists are, however, very sensitive on this subject and the government to be established under the new Constitution will undoubtedly restrict the coastwise traffic to Indian ships if they are allowed to discriminate.

The third and fourth items in the "drain" may also be treated together. An average of about £10,000,000 sterling is sent to Great Britain every year for the payment of civil and military pensions, furlough allowances, and the recruitment and training of troops; and about £1,500,000 more is sent by the official community for investment or for the support and education of their families. If India employed only native officials and native soldiers this money would be kept at home, but it is doubtful whether her financial and economic position would be any stronger. Sir Theodore Morison argued in 1911 that India, as an independent nation, would have to spend at least £4,000,000 per annum for the support of a navy as compared with £400,000 which she was then contributing to the Imperial Navy and the Royal Indian Marine, and she would also have to maintain a diplomatic and consular service. Furthermore, the political connection with Great Britain made it possible for her to borrow money at an average rate of 3½ per cent, whereas, judging from the example of Japan, she would otherwise have to pay at least 5½ per cent. The saving of 2 per cent interest on a total debt of £267,000,000 (in 1911) amounted to £5,340,000 a year. As nearly 78 per cent of the public debt was held by Europeans, over £4,000,000 would have been "drained" abroad in any case.[2]

2. *The Economic Transition in India,* pp. 182–242.

The last item, commercial earnings remitted to Great Britain, varies widely from year to year and is of course very difficult to estimate. There is a considerable amount of British capital invested in private enterprises and there is a large residential commercial community. The Nationalists, as a rule, do not complain that British business profits in India are excessive, but they seem to feel that it is a serious economic injury to India if any part of these earnings is sent abroad. They do not adequately consider the value of the services rendered or the fact that the money sent abroad is probably more than offset by (a) remittances sent to India by Indian merchants and laborers in other parts of the world, (b) remittances sent to India for the support of Christian missions and other benevolent enterprises, and (c) expenditures made by foreign travelers in India in so far as they exceed the expenditures of Indian travelers in other countries.

With a few exceptions, Nationalist writers believe that India needs industrial development. They also believe that this could be accomplished entirely by native enterprise if there were sufficient tariff protection. In making this assumption they overlook a few very obvious difficulties. It is true that India has enough potential capital to expand her industries as rapidly as economic conditions would warrant. The greater part of this capital, however, is hoarded and the remainder follows obstinately certain traditional lines of investment. An Indian will take chances on a cotton mill, but he is very wary of jute. The cotton industry of Bombay is almost entirely owned and operated by Indians (mostly Parsees) and the jute industry of Calcutta by Europeans. There is a similar racial specialization in other industries. British capital and British financial and technical experts, therefore, perform a very useful service. Without them, India's industrial development would be greatly retarded and some fields would be entirely neglected.

The amount of money remitted to India by her people in other lands can be only roughly estimated. A thorough study of this subject was made by Mr. K. M. Panikkar in a prize essay written for the *Indian Emigrant* of Madras in 1916. According to his figures, the average annual amount was somewhere between Rs. 1,15,00,000 and Rs. 1,25,00,000 or £760,000 and £830,000.[3] As money wages have increased in Ceylon and British Malaya the amount now would probably be considerably larger.

An excellent illustration of the tendency of the Nationalists to overemphasize the "drain" as a grievance may be shown by comparing their attitude toward the India Office charges and the ecclesiastical charges. From the time that the Indian National Congress was founded in 1885 until the point was finally yielded in 1919, it objected most bitterly to the inclusion in the Indian budget of a sum of about £200,000 a year for the support of the India Office in London. With the possible exception of the salary of the Secretary of State himself, this is a perfectly reasonable and logical charge. It is true that the Colonial Office is supported by the Imperial government, but that was probably due originally to the difficulty of apportioning such a small amount among so many colonies and protectorates. It is an illogical arrangement. The ecclesiastical charges, however, are in an entirely different category. The poverty-stricken people of India have for many years been taxed about £120,000 annually for the support of the Anglican bishops of Calcutta, Bombay, and Madras and other Christian clergymen. Although India is not in any sense a Christian country, for many years no serious complaint was ever made against this unjust and unreasonable burden, probably because the beneficiaries live in India and most of the money is spent in that country.[4]

The purchase of government stores in the United Kingdom is sometimes regarded as a "drain," although it should really

3. K. M. Panikkar, *An Introduction to the Study of the Problems of Greater India,* pp. 20–21.

4. Mr. Purshotamdas Thakurdas made a formal protest against the ecclesiastical charges in a note appended to the Report of the Inchcape Committee on Retrenchment in 1923, and the General Purposes Retrenchment Subcommittee in 1931 recommended that the Ecclesiastical Department should be abolished. Under the Constitution of 1935 the department will be Reserved and its budget will remain nonvotable.

be considered as an ordinary import transaction. There was, however, at one time a legitimate grievance. The rules for the purchase of these stores issued in 1870 and 1875 forbade the purchase of certain classes of goods in India and required all contracts to be made through the Stores Department of the India Office in London. The system was slightly relaxed in 1883 and, about twenty years later, railway materials and iron and steel products were added to the list of supplies that might be purchased in India. Since that time all of the old restrictions have been removed, rupee tenders for contracts have been authorized, and the purchase of stores in India has received official encouragement. The Sea Customs Act of 1924, for example, makes government stores liable to the same import duties as goods imported on private account. An Indian Stores Department has also recently been created and rules have been put into force (January 1, 1931) requiring the government of India to purchase "stores for the public service in such manner as to encourage the development of industries in India to the utmost possible extent consistently with economy and efficiency." These rules provide that, if the quality is satisfactory, preference in making purchases should be given in the following order: first, to articles produced in India in the form of raw materials or manufactured in India from Indian materials; second, to articles wholly or partially manufactured in India from imported materials; third, to articles of foreign manufacture held in stock in India; fourth, to articles manufactured abroad which must be specially imported.

The Stores Department in London was transferred from the India Office to the new office of the High Commissioner for India in 1921. On September 23, 1921, Sir Vithaldas Thackersay introduced the following motion in the Indian Legislative Assembly: "That the High Commissioner for India in London be instructed by the Government of India to buy ordinary stores required for India in the cheapest market consistently with quality and delivery." Speaking in support of this motion, he said that the High Commissioner was being pressed to sacrifice the interests of the Indian taxpayers by buying supplies from British manufacturers when he could get them cheaper in other countries. The government of India accepted this motion and the Secretary of the Industries Department stated that the government had no intention of making India a tied-house for British industry. Shortly after that, a large locomotive contract was let in Germany, because the German bid was lower than that offered by any British firm. If the British authorities can continue to resist the pressure brought to bear upon them by British industry, this question may now be regarded as settled.

The Indian system of taxation is similar to that of the United States, but it is more scientific because the line of demarcation between central and provincial revenues is more clearly drawn and there is no double taxation. The customs tariff is the chief source of revenue and its history, as in other countries, is closely involved with the issue of protection. The cotton schedule has caused the most trouble, partly because cotton goods usually constitute about one third of India's total imports and partly because cotton manufacturing is primarily an Indian industry. During the seventeenth and eighteenth centuries, when India had an advantage over England in the cost of production, her cotton cloth was excluded from English markets by an absolute embargo; but when conditions were reversed by the industrial revolution and Great Britain secured the advantage, India was not allowed to take any steps for the protection of her home market. Enormous quantities of Lancashire cloth poured into the country and the native industry was practically destroyed. As a matter of fact, cottage industries were doomed in India as they were in other countries. If there had been a high protective tariff or even an embargo the hand loom would have been largely displaced by the power loom. The process would merely have been a little slower, there would be more cotton mills in India, the Parsees would be richer, and the masses of the people would have to pay more for one of the essentials of life.

Before the Mutiny, the general import duty on cotton cloth was 5 per cent, the special rate on yarns was 3½ per cent, and there was a preferential in favor of British goods. The preferential was abolished in 1859, and the general rate was raised to 10 per cent and the rate on yarns to 5 per cent. The primary object of this increase was the production of revenue to meet the cost of suppressing the Mutiny. The financial situation having steadily improved, the old rates were restored in 1862 on both cloth and yarn.

The manufacturers of Great Britain did not object to the incidental protection afforded by these duties as long as the industry in India was still in the hand loom stage. Although the first cotton mill was started at Calcutta as early as 1818, the progress was very slow and the first mill at Bombay, which is now the center of the industry, was not established until 1851. The growth was more rapid during the next three decades while the trade in Great Britain was suffering a severe depression. The American Civil War affected the industry in the two countries in exactly opposite ways. It stimulated the production of cotton in India and thereby increased the amount of raw material available for Indian mills and at the same time it practically cut off the chief source of supply for Lancashire. Lancashire was also adversely affected by the adoption of high protective tariffs in the United States, Germany, and other foreign countries, and in the British Dominions.

During the panic of 1873, when the depression was at its lowest ebb, the trade began to attack the Indian cotton duty as one of the causes of the trouble. Pressure was brought to bear on the government and on May 31, 1876, Lord Salisbury, who was then Secretary of State for India, denounced the duty in a dispatch to the government of India, as "at once wrong in principle, infamous in its practical effect, and self-destructive in its operation." The House of Commons also passed resolutions in 1877 and 1879 declaring that the duty was contrary to sound commercial policy and that it ought to be repealed. The government of India had to obey these orders, but it did so with great reluctance. In fact, it is the only important instance in the history of India in which the Governor-General was compelled to overrule a majority of his Executive Council. The duties on the different grades and varieties of cotton goods were gradually removed between 1878 and 1882. With their abolition, the remainder of the tariff was of little financial importance and it was also repealed.

Most students of economics would admit the fundamental truth of the free-trade principle upon which the action of the government was based. The student of politics, however, might well question the wisdom of forcing the principle upon a dependent people who still believe in the fallacies of protection. The moral position of the government was further weakened by a reasonable doubt as to the purity of its motives. The two great political parties in the United Kingdom were at that time very evenly balanced and both Lord Beaconsfield and Mr. Gladstone appreciated the value of the Lancashire vote. The government also weakened its position by its subsequent inconsistency. It acquiesced in the imposition of a duty on petroleum in 1888, which clearly violated the free-trade principle, apparently for the reason that it did not affect British trade, the United States and Russia being the chief external sources of India's supply of oil.

The Lancashire influence was the dominant factor in Indian tariff policy until 1917. India was practically on a free-trade basis from 1882 until March, 1894, when the financial difficulties growing out of the fall in the price of silver made it necessary to restore the old 5 per cent tariff of 1875. The Secretary of State insisted at first that cotton goods should be retained on the free list, but this seriously crippled the measure as a revenue producer, and a compromise was finally reached under which they were to pay the regular duty and there was to be a countervailing excise of the same amount levied on cotton goods manufactured in Indian mills. In spite of strong opposition in India, this system was maintained until 1917. The rates were revised in February, 1896, the duty on yarns being removed, and the customs and excise duties on cotton cloth being reduced to 3½ per cent.

Early in 1917 the government decided to borrow £100,000,000, and present it to the Imperial government as a war contribution. To meet the recurring charges on this loan it was proposed, among other things, that the customs duty on cotton cloth should be raised to the general tariff level of 7½ per cent[5] without a corresponding increase of the excise. The Indian members of the Legislative Council voted in favor of this offer and it was submitted to the Imperial government for

5. The general tariff had been raised to 7½ per cent in 1916.

ratification. Although it was not stated in so many words, the issue involved was really very simple: the government and people of India were willing to make a gift of £100,000,000 toward the expenses of the war on condition that a net protection of 4 per cent was granted on cotton cloth. This proposition was so important that it was made the subject of a special debate in the House of Commons. It was bitterly attacked by the members from Lancashire without regard to party. They were joined in the division lobby by the Irish Nationalists, and the government would have been overthrown if it had not been for the Asquith Liberals, who were unwilling to precipitate a cabinet crisis.

Further progress has been made since the war. The general principles of the case were considered by the Joint Select Committee on the Government of India Bill in 1919 and the following recommendation, subsequently known as the Fiscal Convention, was made in its report to Parliament:

> Nothing is more likely to endanger the good relations between India and Great Britain than a belief that India's fiscal policy is dictated from Whitehall in the interests of the trade of Great Britain. That such a belief exists at the moment there can be no doubt. That there ought to be no room for it in the future is equally clear. A satisfactory solution of the question can only be guaranteed by the grant of liberty to the Government of India to devise those tariff arrangements which seem best fitted to India's needs as an integral portion of the British Empire. . . . Whatever be the right fiscal policy for India, for the needs of her consumers as well as for her manufacturers, it is quite clear that she should have the same liberty to consider her interests as Great Britain, Australia, New Zealand, Canada, and South Africa. In the opinion of the committee, therefore, the Secretary of State should as far as possible avoid interference on this subject when the Government of India and its Legislature are in agreement, and they think that his intervention when it does take place, should be limited to safeguarding the international obligations of the Empire or any fiscal arrangement within the Empire to which His Majesty's Government is a party.[6]

6. *Joint Select Committee on the Government of India Bill,* I, 11.

This convention was soon put to the test. Owing to the heavy expense of the campaign on the North-West Frontier, there was a large deficit in the budget at the close of the fiscal year 1920–21. The additional revenue that was needed for the coming year could not all be raised by direct taxation without increasing the difficulties of the political situation, so the government of India followed the line of least resistance and fell back upon the only form of taxation that was not likely to arouse opposition. With the approval of the Indian legislature and the Secretary of State, the general level of customs duties, including the duty on cotton cloth, was raised to 11 per cent. As the cotton excise remained unchanged, there was now a protection of 7½ per cent in favor of Indian power looms and 11 per cent in favor of hand looms. Lancashire made a vigorous protest, but the British government refused to interfere.

The issue was brought up again in March, 1922. There was a deficit of about £34,000,000 in the fiscal year then drawing to a close and, on the basis of existing taxation, it was estimated that there would be a further shortage of £32,000,000 in the year to come. The government proposed, among other things, that the general tariff level should be raised to 15 per cent and that there should be a corresponding increase in the excise on cotton cloth from 3½ to 7½ per cent. A bitter controversy was immediately precipitated. The Indian members of the Legislative Assembly were practically unanimous in denouncing the excise and also in demanding that cotton goods should remain in the general tariff schedule. The government of India, however, refused to sanction any further increase of the customs duty on cotton cloth unless there was a corresponding increase in the excise.

This was not a technical violation of the recommendation of the Joint Select Committee. The convention provides that India is to have fiscal freedom, but only when the government of India and the Indian legislature are in agreement. The difficulty, of course, about any arrangement of this kind is that the government of India is not a free agent. It may have acted on its own initiative on this occasion, but if a similar crisis were to arise in the future and secret orders were sent from England it would have to obey them. It would have been hard to convince the people of India that Lancashire was no longer in a position to influence Indian fiscal policy.

As a matter of fact, it is reasonably certain that the government of India was influenced primarily by fiscal considerations. The cotton manufacturers are the wealthiest class of people in British India. If the figures given by Mr. Waddington in the House of Commons on July 12, 1921, are correct, the Sholapur Company had paid dividends as high as 1,000 per cent a year, the Lakshmi and Maneckji Companies as high as 500 per cent, and many others amounts varying from 100 to 375 per cent. There are other statistics which show that the mills on the Island of Bombay paid average dividends of 53 per cent on a capital of Rs. 12½ crores from 1915 to 1922 and that large profits were also made in Ahmedabad and Sholapur. The tax on incomes and excess profits was comparatively low at that time, so it was quite natural that the government should try to make the manufacturers give up at least a part of the swollen profits which the war and the tariff together had enabled them to take from the consumers. An argument in favor of the government's policy could also be made from the protectionist point of view. Mr. Gandhi and other Nationalist leaders have long been advocating a revival of cottage industries, especially the weaving of cotton cloth. They have tried to popularize the use of khaddar or homespun by wearing it at meetings of the National Congress and on other occasions when large numbers of people are gathered together. They admit that the hand loom cannot exist without protection, but they ignore the fact that it needs protection against Bombay as well as against Lancashire. A moderate amount of protection against both was offered in the government's proposal.

The cotton excise was never judged on its merits. It was treated as a political issue and was condemned, not because it violated the principle of protection, but because it was regarded as a symbol of Indian subordination to Great Britain. Since the British finally realized that this was the case, it was suspended in December, 1925, and abolished in March, 1926. It will probably never be revived until the Indians themselves achieve financial responsibility and recognize its possibilities as a revenue producer.

There were other protective items in the general tariff at the close of the war and a few cases of special rates levied partly for protective purposes. Sugar is a good example. Although India is one of the greatest sugar producing countries in the world, she has not been able to meet the home demand, and for many years sugar ranked next to cotton in the list of imports. The duty has usually been above the general rate. In 1922, for example, when the general rate was raised from 11 to 15 per cent, the sugar duty was raised from 15 to 25 per cent. This was replaced later by a specific duty, which of course increased the *ad valorem* equivalent when the market price declined. The rate was finally made prohibitive and to compensate for the loss of revenue an excise duty was imposed on the domestic output in 1935. The duty on motor cars, motorcycles, and bicycles and their tires, parts, and accessories was raised to 20 per cent in 1921 and to 30 per cent in 1922. Although this was primarily designed as a luxury tax, there was no doubt some hoped that it would encourage home industry.

A Fiscal Commission was appointed by the government of India in 1921 to examine tariff policy and consider the desirability of adopting the principle of Imperial preference. Seven members of the commission, including the president, Sir Ibrahim Rahimtulla, were Indians and four were British. The report,[7] which was signed on July 6, 1922, recommended a "policy of protection to be applied with discrimination," and proposed that a Tariff Board should be established to investigate the claims of particular industries to protection, to observe the operations of the tariff, and to advise the government and the legislature in applying the policy in detail. A few main principles were laid down for the guidance of the board. An industry that wishes protection must satisfy three conditions: (a) it must have natural advantages, (b) it must be an industry that, without the help of protection, is not likely to develop as rapidly as is desirable, and (c) it must be an industry that will ultimately be able to face world competition without protection. These conditions might be relaxed to some extent in the case of industries that are essential for purposes of na-

7. *Report of the Indian Fiscal Commission* (Simla, 1922).

tional defense. The cotton excise was unreservedly condemned and it was recommended that the excise policy in the future should be regulated solely in the interests of India. The introduction of a general system of Imperial preference was disapproved, but the suggestion was made that preferential duties might be imposed on a limited number of commodities with the sanction of the Indian legislature.

The findings of the commission were technically unanimous, but there was a long Minute of Dissent, signed by five of the Indian members, which was practically a minority report. The chief difference between this document and the report itself is that it is more extreme in its demand for unadulterated protection. Its criticism of the conditions under which protection was to be applied is a good index of Indian public opinion, but otherwise it is important because when a government once begins to hand out tariff favors it soon loses the capacity to discriminate. There is also in the Minute of Dissent an interesting reference to a grievance which was agitating the people of India at that time, although it had very little connection with the tariff.

> The conditions precedent to any agreement with a British Dominion in trade matters on the basis of reciprocity should be the recognition of the right of the Indian people to a status of complete equality and the repeal of all Anti-Asiatic laws so far as they apply to the people of India.

The government and the legislature approved the recommendation of the commission and a Tariff Board was appointed in 1932. The first work of this board was the preparation of a report on the steel industry, which was suffering badly from continental European competition. They recommended that the industry was entitled to protection and a Steel Industry (Protection) Bill was accordingly introduced by the government at a special session of the Indian legislature, held in May and June, 1924. The existing duties of 10 and 15 per cent on a variety of iron and steel products were raised to an average of about 33⅓ per cent and, in addition, bounties were granted on the production of steel rails, fishplates, and railway wagons.[8] The Swaraj members were inclined to favor bounties rather than protective duties, partly in the interest of consumers, but mainly because they wished to prevent foreigners from erecting mills in India behind the tariff walls. In accordance with a recommendation of the Fiscal Commission, the bounties were payable only to companies that were incorporated and registered in India with rupee capital, had a reasonable number of Indian directors, and provided facilities for the training of Indian apprentices. The payments were, as a matter of fact, all made to the Tata Iron and Steel Company, which was also the chief beneficiary of the protective duties. During the three years that the act was in force (1924–27), this company received 2 crores of rupees in bounties and about 1½ crores in benefits from the duties, or a total of approximately £2,625,000 sterling.

The passage of this act marks the beginning of a new epoch in the fiscal history of India. The free-trade policy, under which she had become one of the great commercial nations of the world, had been slowly undermined and was now definitely abandoned. It is one of the ironies of history that the Labor party was then in power in Great Britain and was compelled to approve this momentous change. Mr. Sydney Webb (now Lord Passfield) submitted the legislation to the House of Commons in his capacity as President of the Board of Trade.

> Whatever may be the views of the Board of Trade on Protection [said he], at any rate the Board of Trade does not like Protection in India, and there is going to be a tariff on steel and steel goods there which His Majesty's Government has not felt it right to interfere to prevent. We have carried on the policy of what is called fiscal autonomy in regard to India, and we have said that, if the Indian Legislature and the Indian Government pressed for this tariff, the British Government ought not to stand in the way to prevent it.

He then went on to express the hope that the approval of the house would be unanimous. The Conservatives must believe

8. Bounties were also paid on finished steel after September 30, 1924.

that protection is good for India if it is good for the United Kingdom, and the Liberals and the Laborites should certainly be willing to let India settle the matter for herself. His plea was effective and the action of the government was approved.

Since that time, the Tariff Board and other bodies organized on a similar basis have investigated applications for protection made by the cement, magnesium chloride, printer's ink, paper and paper pulp, match, coal, mineral oil, plywood and tea chest, salt, gold thread, and other industries, and a number of applications for a reduction of duties on articles used as raw materials. It is impossible to deal with these investigations here, although it should be noted that the board has shown considerable courage in rejecting some of the applications especially those made by the coal and mineral oil industries.[9] It will, however, be advisable to follow the history of the iron and steel industry a little further and to say something more about cotton textiles because they affect the largest amount of trade and also involve the issues of preferential tariffs.

The modern principle of Imperial preference was first applied in India in 1919. An export duty of 15 per cent was levied on hides and skins, partly to protect revenue, but mainly to protect the Indian tanning industry. Two thirds of the duty was rebated if the hides and skins were exported to, and tanned within, other parts of the Empire. As this measure was unpopular in India and was not of any special benefit to the tanning industry of Great Britain, the rebate was withdrawn in 1923 and the export rate itself was reduced to 5 per cent. It was not until 1927, when the iron and steel duties were revised, that Imperial preference really became a live issue. The Tariff Board published a new report on the steel industry in January, 1927, and shortly afterwards the government introduced a bill in the Legislative Assembly to replace the Steel Industry (Protection) Act of 1924. This provided for the abolition of the bounty system and the imposition of basic duties on a large number of iron and steel products with additional duties, in some cases, when the products were of non-

9. For a more detailed discussion of this subject the reader should consult Mrs. Vera Anstey's excellent book on *The Economic Development of India* (2d ed., 1931).

British origin. The basic rates were generally lower and the basic and additional rates together were generally higher than the rates in force from 1924 to 1927. In other words, there was to be a considerable preference in favor of British goods.[10] The bill was severely criticized by the Pandit Motilal Nehru, Lala Lajpat Rai, and other leaders of the Congress and Nationalist parties, and a motion was made to reconsider the report of the Select Committee in order to eliminate the preferential. Absent members were summoned and the government was compelled to apply the closure to force a vote before they could arrive. The motion was defeated by a vote of 60 to 49, but it was obvious that a large majority of the elected members were opposed to any form of Imperial preference. The protective rates are to remain in force until March 31, 1941.

The prosperity of the cotton industry during the war and the period that immediately followed has already been mentioned. The rate of progress was checked in 1922, but the industry as a whole has continued to move forward and it is probably in a stronger position in India today than in any other country in the world. Although there has been keen competition from Japan and the export trade has been seriously crippled,[11] the Indian mills have acquired a steadily increasing share of the home market. They produced 29 per cent of the mill cloth consumed in India in the prewar period (1909–14), 54 per cent in the postwar period (1919–24), and 77.5 per cent in 1934–35. From 1922 to 1934 the number of mills increased from 298 to 352, the number of spindles from 7,331,219 to 9,613,174, the number of looms from 134,620 to 194,988, and the average number of hands employed daily

10. The basic rate on fabricated steel and a few other heavy products was Rs. 21 per ton or 17 per cent *ad valorem* whichever was higher, and the additional rate was Rs. 15 per ton.

11. There was a great decrease in the exports of twist and yarns and of gray and bleached piece goods. The trade in colored piece goods increased until 1927–28, but since that time it has also suffered a decline. The Far-Eastern market has been almost entirely lost, but there is still a fairly good trade with Ceylon, Iran, Iraq, Arabia, and East Africa.

from 343,723 to 384,938. Including the goods woven on hand looms, India now supplies about 83 per cent of her total needs. She also spins about 96 per cent of her yarn, importing American cotton for the higher counts.[12]

But there is one serious flaw in this picture. The prosperity has not been evenly distributed. Although there has been a steady expansion in Ahmedabad and other up-country centers, the Island of Bombay has never fully recovered from the depression of 1922. Her share in the total Indian production of yarn fell from 52 per cent in 1912–13 to 38.2 in 1924–25 and 26 in 1934–35. Her production of cloth has declined in about the same relative proportion and she was actually surpassed by Ahmedabad in 1934–35. It is true that Bombay was hampered by a strike in the early part of that year, but Ahmedabad is forging ahead and will probably attain the front rank in a few years. The fact is that the cotton industry is gradually being transferred from the Island of Bombay to the other parts of India just as in America it is being transferred from New England to the South. No amount of protection can check this movement until wages, taxes, and other costs of production are equalized and there is no logic in giving further assistance to up-country producers under favorable conditions. Higher tariffs are likely to reduce the per capita consumption, which is already below the level of 1913–14, and injure the manufacturer as well as the poverty-stricken consumers.

The position of Lancashire is somewhat similar to that of Bombay. There has not only been a decline in the importation of cotton goods into India since 1914, but, until 1933, there was a still greater decline in Lancashire's share of what was left. In 1913–14, 97.1 per cent of the piece-goods imports came from the United Kingdom and .3 per cent from Japan. In 1932–33, the figures were almost even, 49.1 for the United Kingdom and 48.5 for Japan. The history of the yarn trade was much the same. The United Kingdom furnished 80 per cent of the imports in 1913 and Japan 2 per cent. In 1932–33

12. The *Indian Year Book, 1935–36,* pp. 34–36. See also *Review of the Trade of India in 1934–35.*

about one third was British and most of the remainder came from Japan or from mills in China owned mainly by Japanese.

The people of India are not interested in Lancashire, but so long as the political connection with Great Britain is maintained Lancashire will exercise a certain amount of influence on Indian tariff policy. So far as India is concerned, the only problem is to help the industry on the Island of Bombay without increasing the cost of living, stimulating overproduction in up-country mills, or enacting tariff laws that will provoke Japanese retaliation, but the British authorities also insist that it shall be done without unduly damaging the interests of Lancashire. The Bombay Millowners' Association made a plea in 1925 for an increase of the tariff and the repeal of the cotton excise duties. An attempt was also made to reduce wages, but it caused one of the worst strikes in the history of India and completely demoralized the industry for several months. A compromise was finally reached in December, under which the wage-cut was withdrawn and the government of India agreed to suspend the excise. The final abolition of these duties in March, 1926, has already been mentioned.

The repeal of the excise automatically increased the net protection on mill cloth from 7½ to 11 per cent. There was no improvement, however, on the Island of Bombay, and in 1926 a special Tariff Board was appointed to investigate the industry and report whether it needed any additional protection. The Board reported in June, 1927, that the textile depression was world-wide, but that the Bombay mills were also suffering from competition in other parts of India and that the industry in general needed protection against Japan and China. Several recommendations were made to improve the internal organization of the industry and it was also proposed that the duty on cotton piece goods should be raised from 11 to 15 per cent for three years, that a bounty should be paid on the grades of yarn which were most subject to Japanese and Chinese competition, and that the duties on textile machinery and certain mill stores should be remitted. The government rejected the first two proposals, but the duties on textile machinery and mill stores were repealed and a duty of 1½ annas per pound (or 5 per cent *ad valorem,* whichever was higher) was imposed on yarn.[13]

In spite of these remedies, the industry still languished on the Island of Bombay and on April 16, 1928, it was plunged into another terrible strike which lasted for nearly six months and is generally regarded as the worst industrial conflict in the history of India. The Millowners' Association found it impossible to reduce wages to the Japanese or the up-country level, and in June, 1929, a deputation was sent to the Viceroy to urge the need for further protection. Mr. G. S. Hardy, Collector of the Customs at Calcutta, was authorized to conduct an investigation, and his report, published at the end of November, emphasized the growth of Japanese competition. The government then invited millowners from all over India to attend a conference at Delhi and proposed that the tariff should be increased on condition that a preferential was established in favor of the United Kingdom. The conflict that followed was similar to that in the iron and steel industry in 1927. The manufacturers were all opposed to the preference, but the Bombay group were inclined to yield in order to secure additional protection against Japan. Another group, led by Mr. G. D. Birla, the head of the Birla Cotton Mills of Delhi, preferred to suffer rather than to pay the price demanded.

The fight was transferred to the Legislative Assembly on February 28, 1930, when the budget estimates were presented by Sir George Schuster, the Finance Member of the government. The Assembly was informed that there had recently been some correspondence between His Majesty's government and the government of India on the subject of the cotton duties. His Majesty's government fully recognized the fiscal

13. The 5 per cent *ad valorem* duty had been in force since 1922. The addition of the specific alternative duty meant a considerable increase in the rate on the lower counts where the competition was most acute. The rates were modified later and extended to March 31, 1939. On counts above 50 the rates are now 5 per cent *ad valorem* on British yarn and 6¼ per cent on foreign yarn. On counts below 50 the *ad valorem* rates are the same, but there are alternative rates of 1¼ annas per pound on British yarn and 1⅞ annas on foreign yarn.

freedom of India, but urged the Indian authorities to handle these rates in a manner that would not injure either British or Indian industry. Sir George proposed, therefore, that the ordinary duty on cotton piece goods should be raised from 11 to 15 per cent and that an additional duty of 5 per cent (or a total minimum of 3½ annas a pound on plain gray cloth) should be imposed on goods of non-British origin. The extremists bitterly attacked the latter proposal, but a moderate group, led by Mr. R. K. Chetty, supported it and induced the government to accept an amendment which provided that the alternative duty of 3½ annas a pound on plain gray cloth should apply to British as well as foreign cloth.[14]

This settlement was unsatisfactory both to Lancashire and to the Extremists in India. If the preferential rate had been fully effective, it would not have been sufficient compensation for the extra duty that Lancashire had to pay on her own goods. As a matter of fact, owing to the Chetty Amendment, it was at first very largely ineffective. Plain gray goods imported from the United Kingdom paid 15 per cent *ad valorem* or 3½ annas per pound, whichever was the higher; the same goods coming from other countries paid 20 per cent or 3½ annas per pound, whichever was the higher. As prices were low at that time, the specific rate was usually more than the equivalent of 15 per cent and consequently the preference was reduced or even wiped out altogether. The 5 per cent differential was effective on white, colored, printed, or dyed goods, but plain gray cloth is the principal item in the British cotton trade with India. The discontent of the Indian Extremists was also detrimental to Lancashire. The Pandit Malaviya and eight other members of the Nationalist party resigned their seats in the Assembly as a protest against the adoption of the preferential policy and announced that a boycott would be inaugurated against all foreign cotton goods. The use of the

14. The general increase from 11 to 15 per cent was a part of the Finance Act, but the additional protection was provided by a separate Cotton Textile Industry (Protection) Act. The latter was enacted for a period of three years and the government promised that during that period the whole question should be thoroughly investigated by the Tariff Board.

boycott as an economic weapon was sanctioned by the Irwin-Gandhi Agreement in 1931, and for a time it was rigidly enforced, with Lancashire as the chief victim.

The cotton industry received additional protection in 1931, when the regular duties were increased (March) and a surcharge of 25 per cent was made in order to balance the budget (October). This brought the British rate up to 25 per cent and the foreign rate to 31¼ per cent. There was no improvement, however, and the Millowners' Association of Bombay and Ahmedabad clamored loudly for still higher duties. The government of India refused to impose any further penalties on Lancashire, but they agreed that the fall in the rupee value of the yen gave Japan an artificial advantage in the Indian market. The Tariff Board was asked to consider (a) "to what extent, if any, should the duty on cotton piece goods not of British manufacture be increased and . . . (b) whether the duty should be increased generally or only against a specified country or countries." On their recommendation, the duties were raised on foreign piece goods to 50 per cent and on foreign rayons to 100 per cent (August 31, 1932). The increase was not made against Japan alone because that would have constituted a violation of the Indo-Japanese Trade Convention of 1905, but Japan was the only country that was seriously affected.

Owing to the further depreciation of the yen, the dumping was continued and, on April 10, 1933, Japan was notified that the most-favored-nation clause of the convention of 1905 would lapse in six months. A few days later the Indian legislature passed the Safe-Guarding of Industries Act, under which the Governor-General in Council was empowered for a period of two years to impose additional duties on goods which in its opinion were being imported at abnormally low prices. Without waiting for the convention to expire in October, the government of India announced on June 6 that the minimum emergency tariff on plain gray cotton cloth of non-British origin would be raised to 75 per cent "due to the depression of the Japanese yen and also to the pressure of Japanese competition." The Japanese spinners retaliated by proclaiming a boycott on Indian cotton, which was called "a suspension of buying" because the Japanese government, in its relations with China, regarded a "boycott" as an act of war. But whatever it was, it was enforced with remarkable efficiency. In August, 1933, 391,000 piculs of cotton were imported from India and 315,000 from America. In November, the figures were 3,871 from India and 816,839 from America.[15]

An economic war between India and Japan would be disastrous for both countries. Under normal conditions, Japan is the best customer for Indian cotton and India absorbs large quantities of Japanese textiles and other industrial products. India would probably suffer more than Japan because the balance of trade between the two countries has usually been heavily in her favor. The Indian peasant in the cotton-growing area would be especially penalized as he would receive less for his crop and pay more for his clothing. It was obvious that the dispute would have to be settled as soon as possible and equally obvious that Bombay and Lancashire would have to join their forces against a common danger. Two settlements were accordingly negotiated in the latter part of 1933, an informal agreement between representatives of the textile interests of India and the United Kingdom and a protocol dealing with the cotton trade which was part of a new Indo-Japanese Trade Agreement. The essential provisions of these documents were embodied in the Indian Tariff (Textile Protection) Amendment Act of 1934.

The settlement between the Millowners' Association of Bombay and the United Kingdom Textile Mission, commonly known as the Mody–Clare Lees Agreement, was signed October 28, 1933.[16] The principal terms were (1) that the Indian cotton textile industry was entitled to a reasonable amount of protection against the United Kingdom, but it needed additional protection against certain foreign countries with lower production costs, (2) that when the financial situation made it possible to remove the general surcharge duties on cotton

15. The London *Times,* January 5, 1934. A picul is about 133⅓ pounds.

16. The chairmen of the two delegations were Mr. H. P. Mody and Sir William Clare Lees.

piece goods imposed in 1931 the Indian side of the industry would not press for further protection against the United Kingdom, (3) that a liberal preferential rate on cotton yarn and silk piece goods should be guaranteed to the United Kingdom, and (4) that the British would endeavor to secure an increase in the use of Indian cotton in the United Kingdom. It was of course implicit in the agreement that both groups would use their political influence to obtain the best possible terms from Japan.

The Indo-Japanese Protocol was completed early in January, 1934, after several months of negotiation at Simla and Delhi between a Japanese delegation, headed by Mr. Setsuzo Sawada, and an Indian delegation, headed by Sir Joseph Bhore, the Commerce Member of the government of India. It was to be in effect until April 1, 1937, when either party could terminate it by giving six months' notice. The settlement involved a reduction of the import duty on foreign cotton cloth and the establishment for Japan of a sliding-scale quota based on the Japanese importation of Indian raw cotton.

The duty on plain grays was to be 50 per cent *ad valorem* or 5¼ annas per pound, whichever was higher, and the duty on other piece goods was to be 50 per cent *ad valorem*. The *ad valorem* rate was to be adjusted to fluctuations in exchange so that the barrier would not be lowered by the depreciation of the yen. The maximum amount of Japanese piece goods which could be imported into India was fixed at 400,000,000 square yards per annum. In order to secure this allotment Japan must import at least 1,500,000 four-hundred-pound bales of Indian cotton.[17] If she imports less than that amount, her quota is proportionally reduced; if she imports more, the excess is credited to her account in the following year. The quota is divided into four categories on a percentage basis—plain gray, 45 per

17. The "cotton year" was to begin on January 1 and the "cotton piece-goods year" on April 1. In other words, if Japan should import 1,500,000 or more bales of Indian cotton in 1934, she would be entitled to export to India 400,000,000 yards of cloth between April 1, 1934 and April 1, 1935. Japanese cloth reëxported from India could be deducted from the quota.

cent; bordered gray, 13 per cent; bleached, 8 per cent; and colored, 34 per cent—but a limited variation is permitted provided the total does not exceed the prescribed quota.[18]

The Protocol averted a serious economic conflict, but it has proved unsatisfactory to both parties and they have announced that they will not renew it in its present form. The Japanese feel that they should not be required to pay such high duties, because the quota system itself is a guarantee against excessive competition, and they bitterly resent the large preference enjoyed by the United Kingdom. They cannot understand why Japanese cloth made from Indian cotton should be so heavily penalized for the benefit of British cloth made from American cotton.[19] They also feel that the division of the quota into four categories is unfair because it prevents them from concentrating on the kind of goods which they are best qualified to produce.[20] The Indians, on the other hand, are dissatisfied because fents (cotton remnants) are not included under the quota and also because the Protocol does not deal at all with woolens, artificial silks, glassware, and numerous other articles which are being imported from Japan in increasing quantities. The importation of Japanese fents rose from 8 million yards in 1933–34 to 23 million in 1934–35; of worsted yarns, from 50,000 pounds in 1932–33 to 1,300,000 pounds in 1934–35; and of artificial silk piece goods from 39.6 million yards in 1933–34 to 66.6 million in 1934–35. There is

18. See Japan No. 2 (1934), Cd. 4660 and Treaty Series No. 31 (1934), Cd. 4735 (London, 1934).

19. The United Kingdom is gradually increasing her imports of Indian cotton, but in 1934–35 they were less than one fifth the amount imported by Japan.

20. In 1934, Japan imported 2,053,534 bales of Indian cotton. She was, therefore, entitled to export 400,000,000 yards of cloth to India during the corresponding "cotton piece-goods year." Counting in the preliminary allotment for the period from January 8 to April 1, 1934, her total quota for the whole period, January 8, 1934—April 1, 1935, was 477,997,260 yards. Owing to the high duties and the dangers of exceeding the quota in some of the separate categories, she actually sent only 401,169,574 yards. Her percentage of the total imports of cotton piece goods fell from 44.8 in 1933–34 to 39.6 in 1934–35, while the British percentage increased from 54.5 to 58.5.

also keen competition in woolen piece goods, shawls, and hosiery.

The British secured their preferential position in the cotton piece-goods market without giving anything in return. The Indian legislature was permitted to raise a high tariff wall against foreign countries only on condition that the British side of the wall should be kept on a much lower level. But when we come to other commodities there is a different story to tell. The Ottawa Agreements of 1932 were based on mutual concessions and if there was any balance of advantage it was probably on the side of India. The negotiations for India were conducted mainly by Indian delegates, the approval of the Indian legislature was required, and provision was made that, after three years, the agreements could be denounced by either party on six months' notice.

Two main ideas were emphasized by the Indian delegation at Ottawa: "the extension and development of the export trade of India and the preservation unimpaired of the protection enjoyed by certain Indian industries." They wished to improve India's position in the British market without injuring her export trade with other countries or sacrificing the principle of protection at home. The essential features of the General Agreement of August 20 may be summarized in a few words. Early in 1932, the United Kingdom imposed a duty of 10 per cent *ad valorem* on all imports with the exception of a few commodities that paid a special rate and a few essential foodstuffs and raw materials that were kept on the free list. This duty was suspended on Indian and Dominion products pending the result of the Ottawa conference. The agreement continued the exemption and thus gave India a more or less permanent preference of 10 per cent on goods to which the duty applied. It was also stated that the duties on certain foreign goods had been or would be raised to higher levels and the preference enjoyed by India would be correspondingly enhanced. His Majesty's government also promised that it would endeavor to secure a greater use of Indian cotton in Lancashire.

India, on her part, agreed to give a 7½ per cent preference on certain classes of motor vehicles and a 10 per cent preference on a few articles of food and drink, a few oils and minerals, and a long list of manufactured goods. The concessions are hedged about, however, with a number of complicated provisions and exceptions. "In the class of iron and steel goods," for example, "the 10 per cent preference extends only to those commodities which are not subject to protective duties, and in the class of machines only to those articles which pay the ordinary revenue rates of 25 per cent *ad valorem.*" It is also stated that no decision is possible as regards goods made of silk, cotton, or artificial silk until the Indian Tariff Board makes its report on the textile industry. "But it has been agreed that when the decisions have been reached, the 10 per cent preference will be extended to these goods, with the exception of artificial silk yarns and articles on which protective duties may be imposed." This apparently means that the existing preferences on iron and steel and cotton piece goods will be abolished. If this is a correct interpretation, it is difficult to see any advantage in the agreement from the point of view of the United Kingdom.[21]

21. The text of the agreement is published in the London *Times,* August 22, 1932, p. 15. There are a number of duties in the Indian tariff which afford a certain amount of protection, but they are not regarded as "protective" unless they are so classified by the Tariff Board.

CHAPTER VI

ECONOMIC AND FINANCIAL GRIEVANCES
PART II

THE income tax is the second most important source of revenue for the central government. Before the war the rate was rather low, and considering the conditions in India, there was a high limit of exemption. Since 1914 the rate has been gradually enhanced, the progressive principle adopted and a supertax imposed on large incomes. An additional tax or surcharge of from 12½ to 25 per cent has also been imposed since 1931. As the rates are still below the British level and agricultural incomes are exempted, the yield is comparatively small, usually about one third of the amount produced by the tariff. The exemption of agricultural incomes is the worst defect in the system. Wealthy landlords who have already received special favors in the settlement of land revenues are practically exempted from other forms of direct taxation. The income tax has not in general been a subject of controversy, although there is always a conflict between the government and the Legislative Assembly whenever the rate is increased. There is also a chronic dispute between the central government and the provinces over the allocation of revenue from income and corporation taxes, but that is discussed elsewhere as a constitutional problem.[1]

Owing to the comparative failure of the income tax, India still relies far too much on revenue that bears heavily on the poor. Next to the tariff, the worst examples of this are the salt duty in the case of the government of India and the land revenues in the case of the provinces. Mr. Gandhi demonstrated his shrewdness as a political leader when he marched to the sea and began his illegal manufacture of salt and also when he championed the cause of the people of Bardoli in their

1. See chap. xii.

fight for remission of land revenues. His failure to protest against the tariff is probably due either to ignorance of its economic effects or to a feeling that the people should make every sacrifice to secure economic independence. It is possible that he has also been influenced to some extent by contributions which the millowners make to the Nationalist cause.

The salt consumed in Bengal, Assam, and Bihar and Orissa is mostly imported, but the other provinces depend mainly on local production. Although the revenue is collected as an import duty or excise, it is listed in the budget as a separate item. The amount of the duty formerly varied widely in the different provinces, but it was everywhere high enough to encourage smuggling from the Indian States, and the government was compelled to establish an expensive and burdensome system of inland customs lines. The rates were gradually equalized, however, and arrangements were concluded with the salt-producing states which made it possible to abolish the customs lines in 1879.[2] From 1878 until 1903 the duty was usually Rs. 2/8 per maund (82 pounds). There was a constant agitation for reduction and, with the improvement of the financial conditions, the rate was gradually cut until it was fixed at R. 1 in 1907. In 1916, it was raised to Rs. 1/4, in spite of very strong opposition from the unofficial members of the Legislative Council. A proposal to double the rate was rejected by the Legislative Assembly in 1922, but it was revived in 1923 and finally incorporated in the Finance Act by the use of the Viceroy's extraordinary powers of certification. This aroused very bitter feelings and, when the conflict was renewed in 1924, the government yielded and the old rate was restored. Owing to the financial difficulties that followed the depression of 1929, a temporary surcharge of 5 annas was imposed in 1931, so that the excise rate is now Rs. 1/9 per maund. The excise and the import duty were formerly the same, but a small additional import duty has been levied since 1931 for protective purposes. It has been estimated that the cost of producing salt in India varies from 2½ to 6 annas per maund, which

2. There is still an inland customs line between British India and Cutch and the small states of the Kathiawar peninsula, but it will probably be abolished in the near future.

means that the duty on an *ad valorem* basis runs from about 400 to 1,000 per cent. This burden is exorbitant, not because the per capita payments are large, but because the consumption of salt is reduced to a minimum which is detrimental to the health of the people and also to their cattle.

The land revenue, formerly a perquisite of the central government, has been the chief source of provincial income since 1921. There are three main systems of assessing and collecting this revenue. When the East India Company assumed the diwani (revenue administration) of Bengal in 1765 the land revenue was collected by hereditary zamindars or tax-farmers. The efforts of the Company to control these zamindars and enforce the principle of periodical assessments were not very successful and finally in 1793, on the recommendation of Lord Cornwallis, the so-called Permanent Settlement was concluded. The zamindars received a guarantee that the land revenue assessments then in force would never be altered. This meant that they would pay the government a fixed annual sum or quitrent and that they and not the government or the cultivators would benefit by the natural increase in the economic rent. It also meant the final evolution of the zamindars from tax collectors to landlords. The system was gradually extended and the Permanent Settlement area now includes almost five sixths of Bengal, and Bihar and Orissa, one fourth of Madras, one eighth of Assam, and one tenth of the United Provinces (the portion near Benares). There is a similar system of indirect collection in the Central Provinces, the Punjab, and the greater part of the United Provinces; but the assessments, instead of being permanent, are subject to periodic revisions. The Talukdars of Oudh and the landlords of Agra and the Central Provinces intervene between the government and the cultivators and are primarily responsible for the payment of the revenues. The Punjab is the home of peasant proprietors, but the responsibility for the payment of the land revenue rests on the village community and not on the individual cultivator. In other parts of the country, especially in Madras, Bombay, and Assam, there is a third system, under which the state is regarded as the landlord and the revenue is collected directly from the cultivator by government officials. This form of tenure is called ryotwari from ryot (raiyat), the Hindi word for peasant.

According to the British official theory, the title to all agricultural land is ultimately vested in the state and the revenue derived from it is a rent and not a tax. The state is entitled to the net assets or economic rent, which may be defined as the gross assets or total value of the crop minus an allowance for labor, seeds, and other necessary costs of production. Government apologists contend that the state has never taken the whole of this amount and that there has in fact been a decline in the proportion of land revenue to rental value from 90 per cent in 1812 to about 50 per cent at the present time. The state has undoubtedly been liberal if its policy is judged according to the ethics of a private landlord, but there are a few facts that should be emphasized before it is given a clean bill of health.

Under an equitable system of taxation the taxpayer is always left a minimum amount for the support of himself and his family. This principle is applied in the case of the income tax. An artisan whose income is Rs. 200 a year is permitted to keep it all, but a peasant who earns the same amount receives a very moderate allowance for his labor and certain essential expenditures, and then pays about 50 per cent on what is left. It makes no difference to him whether the payment is called rent, land revenue, or a tax, the burden is just as heavy. So far as the government is concerned this argument really applies only to the ryotwari area and to the village community or mahalwari area in the Punjab, but it can also be used against the landlords in the zamindari area.

The landlord system is seen at its worst in the region of the Permanent Settlement. The government's share of the economic rent in this zone has dwindled from 90 per cent in 1812 to less than 25 per cent at the present time. Only a part of the difference goes to the peasant. In Bengal alone about £4,000,000 a year are being taken from the poverty-stricken cultivators and used to support idle and unprogressive landlords while the provincial government is seriously hampered for lack of funds. The Permanent Settlement is, however, generally regarded in India not as a grievance but as a benefit whose advantages should be spread over the whole country. This would seem to indicate that the Tory conception of Nationalism as an oligarchic movement is correct, that the average politician is more interested in preserving the privileges of the landlords than he is in advancing the welfare of the masses of the people. The Nationalists, of course, do not accept this explanation. According to their version, they approve the Permanent Settlement because they distrust the British and are convinced that if the government could get hold of the revenue that now goes to the landlords it would simply mean an increase of expenditure and not a remission of taxation. But there are a few radical leaders who are bitterly opposed to the Permanent Settlement and the whole landlord system. The no-rent campaign organized a few years ago by the Pandit Jawaharlal Nehru was intended primarily to embarrass the government, but it might easily have developed into an agrarian revolution.[3]

In the Temporary Settlement area, which includes about four fifths of British India, the assessments are revised every thirty or forty years. The payments are based on an estimate of the average annual net assets for the whole period. In other words, the principle of elasticity is disregarded, although farming is a highly speculative business, especially in India where so much depends on a favorable monsoon. The peasant gambles on the vagaries of nature. The size of his crop is determined by weather conditions at home and the price that he gets for it is largely determined by weather conditions in other parts of the world.[4] But he is expected to pay the same cash revenue for thirty or forty years without regard to the fluctuations in the value of what he produces. There is probably no other system of taxation in the world so unfair in its incidence except the general property tax in the United States. British officials frequently cite figures to prove that the burden is lighter than it was in the old days of native rule. The govern-

3. The center of Mr. Nehru's activities was the United Provinces, most of which is outside of the Permanent Settlement area, but it has the same agrarian conditions.

4. The chief crops in the Temporary Settlement area are cotton, wheat, and millet.

ment now takes the equivalent of from 7 to 10 per cent of the average total crop, whereas the Indian rulers of the eighteenth century took at least 25 per cent. But there is a difference. The Indian rulers were usually paid in kind on the basis of each year's harvest. They shared the peasant's prosperity, but they also suffered with him in his periods of adversity. The burden was heavier, but it was more equitably distributed.[5]

The old system had another advantage. A general improvement in agricultural conditions was shared by the government automatically without attracting the attention of the cultivator, whereas, under the present system, the government can secure these benefits only once in thirty or forty years and then only at the cost of a great deal of friction and resentment. There was of course one serious disadvantage. The land being the chief source of income, there was a wide fluctuation of revenue which would be enough to bankrupt a modern government, with its heavy fixed charges. This handicap could be overcome by setting aside reserves in good years and by making the income tax a provincial source of revenue, a proposal which is now being considered.

Under the present system, the peasant may be comparatively prosperous in a good season, but he is apt to suffer severe hardship when his crop falls below the average. If, as often happens, he borrows money to meet his obligations to the government, he has to pay exorbitant rates of interest and run the risk of losing his holding under foreclosure proceedings. This evil was at one time especially serious in the Punjab. Mr. S. S. Thorburn, financial commissioner to the government of that province, stated in 1893[6] that many of the peasants had been ruined beyond redemption because they had been "borrowing from money lenders to pay the land revenue." The bania or moneylender formed an alliance with the pleader

5. The Mogul Emperors had already taken steps to commute the payments into money and the system had accordingly lost some of its elasticity before 1765.

6. Quoted in C. J. O'Donnell, M.P., *The Causes of Present Discontent in India,* p. 94. It is well known of course that the peasants also borrow money for other purposes, especially for elaborate marriage ceremonies.

which threatened to establish an absentee landlord regime in the place of the old village community (mahalwari) system of land tenure. The government was finally compelled to interfere. The transfer of land from agriculturists to nonagriculturists was forbidden by the Punjab Alienation of Land Act of 1900, a measure which unfortunately antagonized the politically minded classes among the people whom it was designed to benefit.[7] It has been to some extent nullified by legal subterfuges of one kind and another. Legislation was also enacted in 1904 to encourage the establishment of coöperative credit societies and a more liberal policy was adopted in the matter of remitting and suspending land revenues. The cultivator might perhaps have been more grateful if the government had not with singular lack of wisdom proceeded at the same time to increase the land revenue assessments and to impose high water rates in the canal colonies.

If the land revenue is not paid within a certain time, the government may seize the movable property of the defaulter, arrest and confine him for a limited period or sell his holding and evict him from the premises. Sales and evictions were very common a generation ago. According to a dispatch sent by Mr. A. Rogers of the Indian Civil Service to the Under-Secretary of State for India in 1893, there were sold at auction in the presidency of Madras alone in the eleven years from 1880–90 the occupancy rights of 840,713 ryots and also Rs. 2,965,-081 worth of personal property. Mr. C. J. O'Donnell quotes this dispatch and comments upon it as follows:

> Roundly, one-eighth part of the entire agricultural population of the Madras Province was sold out of house and land in little more than a decade. Not only were their farms brought to auction, but their poor personal belongings, their furniture and their cooking utensils, their beds and everything but their scanty clothes were sold to provide money for "Imperial" expenditure.[8]

Conditions have greatly improved in recent years, partly

7. This act applies only to the so-called agricultural tribes, but they hold about five sixths of all the cultivated land in the province.

8. *Idem,* pp. 109–110.

because the growth in the value of landholdings[9] has made it easier for the cultivator to borrow money to carry him over a bad year and partly because agricultural incomes have been supplemented in an increasing degree by other sources of revenue. More peasants are working part of each year in the industrial centers and more money is being sent home by Indian laborers employed outside of India.[10] There are also other factors at work, but most important of all is the change in the policy of the government. The British authorities in India are finally beginning to realize, probably as a result of the troubles in the Punjab, that their rule is doomed if the rural masses are ever swept into the Nationalist movement. But while their motives may be political rather than humanitarian, there can be no doubt that their agrarian program has steadily been growing more enlightened. They have put an end to wholesale evictions, encouraged the formation of coöperative agricultural credit associations, endeavored to protect the peasant from moneylenders, and have been more liberal in suspending or remitting the land revenue in times of distress.

These are all steps in the right direction, but they do not go far enough. It may be impossible to disprove the theories of Ricardo and Henry George. It may be true that the value of agricultural land is increasing and that the state has the right to take the whole or any part of this increase, but when 100,000,000 people rarely get more than one scanty meal a day it is no time to spin theories about economic rent and unearned increment. The government should buy out the interests of the landlords and establish a paternalistic system of peasant proprietorship. Under such a system it could forbid anyone to own agricultural land who did not live on it and cultivate it, and could guarantee that no cultivator should ever be required to pay rent, land revenue, or any form of direct tax until a definite and fairly liberal minimum had been set aside for the subsistence of himself and his family. Some income would of course

9. The value of a holding is determined theoretically by capitalizing at the prevailing rate of interest the difference between the land revenue and the net assets or economic rent.

10. The remittances sent home by Tamil coolies employed abroad have especially improved conditions in Madras.

still be secured in the more fertile sections of the country, but this would probably all be needed to take care of the financial obligations incurred in purchasing the interests of the landlords. The whole of the £28,000,000 a year now derived from the land revenue would, therefore, have to be raised from other sources. There is reason to believe that the greater part of this sum could be obtained by applying the theories of Henry George where they ought to be applied, that is, by taxing to the full limit the unearned increment on urban land. If it should seem desirable, out of regard to vested interests, to proceed rather slowly along these lines, the income tax and the supertax might be considerably increased and a graduated inheritance tax imposed. A financial system based on these principles would help redress the balance between the city and the country. The people of the city who now prosper at the expense of the peasant would be compelled to pay their share of the public expenditure.

This solution of the problem is open to at least two objections, but whether they are sufficient to warrant its rejection is a question about which there will be a difference of opinion. There is first the objection that it will antagonize the people who are already most discontented. The Nationalists talk a great deal about exorbitant land revenues, but they usually have bourgeois connections and would certainly not like to have the burden shifted to their own shoulders. Their ranks could be broken, however, if the British were to advocate reforms of a more sweeping character than these Nationalists were generally prepared to accept. The chief difficulty about this solution is that the field has already been in large measure preëmpted by Mr. Jawaharlal Nehru.

The second objection is more fundamental. Would the peasants use their additional resources to raise the standard of living, or would they merely increase the size of their families? If as a class they did the latter, their condition would still be hopeless, but at least they would not be able to blame the government. Their chief grievance being removed, they would not be so easily swayed by political agitation. What the people of India need most is a campaign of education on the subject of birth control. A few clinics conducted by women doctors in every city, town, and rural district would gradually break down the walls of prejudice and superstition and do more to improve social and economic conditions than any amount of legislation.

The only other source of revenue about which there has been very much criticism is the excise tax. The use of alcohol is contrary to the religious precepts of both Moslems and Hindus and the leaders of both communities are in favor of complete prohibition. The British authorities have opposed this movement partly on financial grounds and partly on the theory that prohibition could not be enforced. Their policy has been to tax liquor as heavily as possible without stimulating illicit production to a degree which would increase instead of diminish the total consumption and without encouraging the substitution of deleterious drugs. As a matter of fact, the consumption has increased more rapidly than the population since the beginning of the century, even when allowance is made for the higher rates. The excise revenue rose from Rs. 5.5 crores[11] in 1899 to Rs. 19.24 crores in 1920. According to the official point of view, this is an evidence of prosperity, but that theory is quite properly rejected by the Indians. "An increase in the excise revenue in India," says Mr. C. N. Vakil, "does not show an increased capacity on the part of the people; it shows an increasing tendency toward moral and physical degeneration."[12] Since 1921 nearly every provincial legislature in India has passed resolutions advocating a reduction in the consumption of liquor with prohibition as the ultimate goal. The boycott of the liquor shops is probably the most popular feature of Mr. Gandhi's campaign against British rule in India. It was a clever move on the part of the British to make the excise a powerful source of revenue because its abolition would reduce the amount of money available for schools, hospitals, and other "nation-building" purposes, but would not affect the expenditures on the army or the public debt services.

Turning to the other side of the ledger, the chief bone of contention is the military expenditures. The army of India

11. 55 million rupees.

12. *Financial Developments in Modern India, 1860–1924*, p. 480.

consists of about 150,000 Indian troops, for which India bears the whole charges, and about 60,000 British troops, for which India bears in full the direct charges for maintenance, the charges for sea transportation, and a part of the "home effective charges" incurred by the War Office in recruiting and training British officers and soldiers for the Indian Establishment. India also pays a part of the pension charges in respect of these troops. The government and the people of India have long contended that His Majesty's government should share the burden as a whole and that the "home effective" and "capitation" charges should be more equitably apportioned.

So far as the main issue is concerned, their chief argument is "that the Army in India serves an Imperial as well as an Indian purpose, and is always available and sometimes used for other purposes than the Defense of India." The government of India in a dispatch to the Secretary of State, as far back as March 25, 1890, stated the case as follows:

> Millions of money have been spent in increasing the Army of India, on armaments and fortifications to provide for the security of India, not against domestic enemies or to prevent the incursions of warlike people of adjoining countries, but to maintain the supremacy of British power in the East. The scope of all these great and costly measures reaches far beyond Indian limits, and is an Imperial policy. We claim, therefore, that in the maintenance of the British forces in this country a just and even liberal view should be taken of the charges which should legitimately be made against Indian revenues.[13]

The point is also made that other parts of the Empire do not contribute to the same extent to the cost of Imperial defense. The Dominions pay very little and the Crown Colonies and Protectorates are never assessed more than 20 per cent of their total revenues. Taking the central and the provincial governments together, the defense charges in India are 29 per cent of the total expenditures, and if the central government alone is considered, it amounts to 54 per cent.

13. *Report of the Indian Defense Expenditure Tribunal* (The Garran Tribunal), 1933.

Two main issues are involved in this controversy, one dealing with the expenditures incurred in time of peace or when the army is fighting at home and the other dealing with the support of the troops when they are employed on foreign service. So far as the first issue is concerned there was no serious trouble until after the so-called forward policy on the frontier was adopted at the beginning of Lord Dufferin's administration in 1885. The military expenditures, which had varied very slightly during the previous twenty years, increased about 65 per cent between 1885 and 1905. The army was considerably enlarged and huge sums were spent on frontier defense, on military railways that did not pay operating expenses, on Lord Kitchener's army reconstruction plans and on such costly military enterprises as the Waziristan expedition of 1884–86 and the Chitral expedition of 1895–96.

These expenditures were bitterly resented by the people of India and they constituted, probably, the most important single factor in the early development of Indian Nationalism. There was a long struggle in the government of India between the military experts and the men who were responsible for the financial policy and the general political condition of the country.[14] The military experts were generally supported by the Secretary of State and the British government and in consequence were able to maintain their supremacy until the close of 1905. Lord Kitchener's triumph over Lord Curzon in the dispute over the military representation in the Governor-General's Executive Council was their last decisive victory. Since 1905, the India Office has in the main been dominated by the broad and liberal ideas of Lord Morley, Lord Crewe, and Mr. Montagu. The government also found it easier to adopt a new military-financial policy because of the general change in the international situation. The Russian menace on the North-West Frontier was to a large extent removed by Russia's defeat in the war with Japan and by the Agreement of 1907 between Russia and Great Britain defining their respective interests in Persia and Afghanistan. Military expenditures in India were kept practically stationary at about £20,000,000 a year from 1905 until after the outbreak of the war and the

14. In army circles this struggle was facetiously called the "dog fight."

principle was definitely accepted that the army was to be maintained on a strictly defensive basis.

The results of the new policy were not altogether satisfactory from either the political or the military point of view. The Nationalists felt that even £20,000,000 a year was excessive and they were continually comparing this sum with the pittance that was spent on education. At the same time, according to the militarists, the army was being starved. The equipment and transport facilities were allowed to become obsolete and they broke down completely in the first Mesopotamian campaign. Nationalists admit these facts, but they contend that the trouble was due to bad management rather than to lack of funds. They also argue that India has nothing to do with Mesopotamia and that if the British wish the army to be always prepared to wage an offensive war they ought to pay the expenses and not to impose the burden on the people of India.

The military budget ordinarily chargeable[15] to the government of India did not increase much during the war, but the growth was very rapid just after the Armistice. The total expenditure in crores of rupees was 66.72 in 1918–19, 86.97 in 1919–20, and 87.38 in 1920–21.[16] There was almost constant fighting on the Afghan Frontier for nearly three years. Whether this was necessary to protect India from invasion or merely a recrudescence of imperialism is a question about which there is wide difference of opinion. The Nationalists generally accept the latter view, although there were a few Extremists at the time who believed in the possibility of an invasion and were inclined to welcome it as a means of getting rid of the British.

There was a decrease in the expenditures to Rs. 69.81 crores in 1921–22 and Rs. 65.26 crores in 1922–23. In 1923, the Inchcape Retrenchment Committee recommended a gradual reduction to a sum not exceeding Rs. 50 crores a year. A con-

15. The special contribution of £112,000,000 made by the government with the approval of the Indian members of the Legislative Council will be considered later.

16. The figures are given in rupees instead of pounds sterling because of the wide fluctuations in exchange. At the prewar rate of exchange Rs. 87.38 crores would be £58,250,000.

siderable amount was saved in 1923–24 by demobilizing 4,500 British and 8,500 Indian troops. The budget for that year was Rs. 56.23 crores. It declined slowly until March, 1928, when a financial control system, planned by Sir William Birdwood, the Commander in Chief of the Indian Army, was put into operation. Under this system, expenditures were to be stabilized for four years at Rs. 55.10 crores a year and the army authorities were encouraged to economize by an assurance that the savings could be spent on their modernizing program. Owing to the financial depression, the contract was modified in 1930, the appropriation being cut to Rs. 54.30 crores, while the scheme itself was extended for another year, that is, until March, 1933. As a matter of fact, the financial situation did not improve and the expenditures were reduced to Rs. 51.90 crores in 1931–32, to Rs. 46.74 crores in 1932–33, and to Rs. 44.38 crores in 1933–34.

We come now to the other main issue connected with the military expenditures which has to do with the support of Indian troops when they are employed on foreign service. There were fourteen different wars or military expeditions, before the South African War, in which Indian troops were sent abroad. In six of these—the first Afghan War (1838–42), the first Chinese War (1839–40), the Perak expedition of 1875, the Abyssinian expedition of 1885–86, and the Sudanese expeditions of 1885–86 and 1896—India paid the ordinary, but not the extraordinary charges.[17] In three cases—the Persian expedition of 1856, the second Afghan War (1878–80) and the Egyptian expedition of 1882—India paid the ordinary and part of the extraordinary charges.[18] The government of

17. Ordinary charges are those that India would have to pay if the troops had remained at home. Extraordinary charges are the additional expenses incidental to active foreign service. In all the expenditures mentioned above, with one exception, the extraordinary charges were paid by the United Kingdom. The extraordinary charges of the Perak expedition were paid by the Straits Settlements.

18. In the four remaining cases—the second Chinese War (1856–57), the third Chinese War (1859), the Malta expedition of 1878, and the Mombasa expedition of 1896—all the charges were paid by the United Kingdom.

India took the stand in all these cases, with one exception, that the issues involved were imperialistic and that India should not be called upon to bear any part of the financial burden, either ordinary or extraordinary. The exception was the Burmese War of 1885. Lord Dufferin's government assumed without protest the entire burden of that enterprise, but they did so in defiance of Indian public opinion. The war was not popular in India and the people resented having to pay for it.

In settling these cases no general principle was followed and there was apparently very little attention paid to precedent. There was no logical reason, for example, why India should have paid the ordinary charges for the first expedition to China and not those of the second and third expeditions, or the ordinary charges of the Abyssinian and Sudanese expeditions and not those of the expedition to Mombasa. There was also no logical reason why Lord Salisbury should have compelled India to meet the ordinary expenses of the Perak expedition (1875) after he had severely criticized the Liberal government for taking similar action in the case of Abyssinia (1867–68). Mr. Gladstone's inconsistency was even more glaring. He attacked Lord Beaconsfield's government for imposing the greater part of the cost of the second Afghan War (1878–80) upon the people of India and then did the same thing himself in the case of the Egyptian expedition of 1882, although India's interest in Egypt is obviously more remote than her interest in Afghanistan.[19]

When the ordinary charges alone were imposed the British government justified its action on the ground that India would have to pay the troops in any case and that she ought not to expect to make a profit when they were employed abroad. There were two answers generally advanced in reply to this argument. The first was that if Indian troops could be sent out of the country without being replaced by other troops, that in itself was proof that the ordinary military establishment was too large for India's own needs. It should, therefore, have been reduced or Great Britain should have contributed

19. *Indian Contingent (Egypt) Expenses,* London, 1883 (C.–3507); *Parliamentary Debates* (3d ser.), CXC, 406; CCLXXIII, 255–307.

to its support in so far as it exceeded the minimum necessary for defensive purposes. The second answer was an appeal to precedent. Indian troops have often been borrowed by the British government. The conditions have been reversed only once. British troops were borrowed by the government of India for the suppression of the Mutiny in 1857. Did the British say, "We will pay the ordinary expenses because we do not wish to make any profit out of this affair"? Not at all. The people of India bore the whole burden, including the cost of drilling and training the recruits before they left England, and the British government even refused to guarantee the bonds that were issued to raise the necessary funds.[20]

The extraordinary charges, however, were the chief source of controversy. Although the amount involved was not very large, India paid one half of the extra cost of the Persian expedition of 1856. The extraordinary charges of the second Afghan War (1878–80), including £3,614,000 spent on military railways, were approximately £20,000,000, of which India had to contribute all but £5,000,000. In criticizing the action of His Majesty's government in this matter, Mr. Gladstone declared "that they [the people of India] were wholly guiltless, and had washed their hands in innocence as far as that war was concerned." This remark was quoted by a political opponent two years later, when Mr. Gladstone himself proposed that India should be forced to pay all of the extraordinary charges of her contingent in the Egyptian expedition. Under the compromise that was finally reached India was compelled to assume the responsibility for all but £500,000 of the total extra charges of £1,241,634.[21]

The dispute over expenditure in general and military expenditure in particular finally became so acute that the government decided in 1895 to appoint a Royal Commission to make an exhaustive study of the whole question. This body, which was popularly known as Lord Welby's Commission, made its report in 1900. The general principle was laid down

20. *Indian Contingent (Egypt) Expenses; Parliamentary Debates* (4th ser.), XII, 874.

21. *Parliamentary Debates* (3d ser.), CCLXXIII, 255–307; *Indian Expenditure Commission,* III, 467; LV, 151–190.

that if either Great Britain or India borrowed troops from the other, the country that borrowed the troops should pay all the expenses unless the lending country had a "direct and substantial interest in the result." That is, of course, not a final solution. Who is to decide in each case whether the interest of the lending party is direct and substantial and how is the degree of directness and substantiality to be measured as a basis for apportioning the charges? The commission took it for granted that these questions would ordinarily be settled by a conference between the governments of the two countries, but it was proposed that in case of dispute no contribution should ever be made by India until the sanction of Parliament had been obtained. It also laid down a geographical criterion for deciding the main question. India, it was assumed, had no direct and substantial interest in Europe, in Africa west of the Cape of Good Hope, or in Eastern Asia. In accordance with these recommendations, the entire cost of the Indian troops used in the South African War and in the Chinese expedition at the time of the Boxer Rebellion was borne by the United Kingdom.

In 1914 there were 80,000 British officers and men in India and 230,000 Indian ranks, combatant and noncombatant. Practically all of these were used on foreign service—in Europe, Mesopotamia, Syria, East Africa, and elsewhere—being replaced in India by English territorials and India recruits. Resolutions were passed by Parliament in September and November, 1914, which provided that India should meet the ordinary charges of the foreign service troops, while the extraordinary charges and the expenses of replacing these forces in India were to be borne by the United Kingdom. In other words, it was intended that no part of the financial burden of the war should be imposed on India. This policy was followed both in theory and in practice until 1917, when the government of India, with the approval of the nonofficial members of the Legislative Council, made a voluntary contribution of £100,000,000 toward the support of the war. In September, 1918, the government, again with the approval of the nonofficial members, voted to take over as from April 1, 1918, the normal cost of 200,000 more troops than it was then paying for and a further 100,000 after April 1, 1919.[22] It was estimated that this would entail an expenditure of £45,000,000, but as the Armistice was signed shortly afterward the amount really involved was only about £112,000,000. A few extreme Nationalists try to represent this as a grievance, but in view of the fact that their own representatives voted in favor of the appropriations it is difficult to see the justice of their contention. They would, however, as already stated be able to make a good case in favor of the cancellation of that part of the debt held in the United Kingdom, if the British foreign debt should ever be canceled by the United States.

The cost of recruiting and training British soldiers for service in India is the chief item in the "capitation charges," which are paid by the government of India to the War Office on the basis of the number of officers and men in the British military establishments in India. For example, if the rate is £25 and there are 60,000 British troops in India the annual payment would be £1,500,000. The rate varied from £7 10*s*. to £11 8*s*. until 1920, when it was increased to £28 10*s*. for a provisional period of two years. It was reduced to £25 13*s*. in 1922–23 and to £25 in 1923–24. Since 1920–21, £100,000 a year has been paid to the Air Ministry for the cost of recruiting and training men for the Royal Air Force in India. The government of India contends that the charges should be based on a period of training of six months instead of twelve months as claimed by the War Office and that India should receive a rebate proportional to the average term served in the Reserve after the conclusion of their Color Service.

The problem has been the subject of several official investigations,[23] culminating in *The Report of the Indian Defense Expenditure Tribunal*, which was published in November, 1933. The chairman of the Tribunal was Sir Robert Garran,

22. There were recruited in India during the war 800,000 combatants and 400,000 noncombatants, most of whom were employed abroad.

23. See the Reports of the Tulloch Committee in 1861, the Seccombe Committee in 1872, the Welby Commission in 1900, the Romer Committee in 1908, and the recommendations presented by Lord Cave as arbitrator in 1927.

a former Solicitor General of Australia, and there were four other members, two selected by the War Office and two by the government of India. They rejected the claim that the Imperial government should make a substantial contribution to Indian military expenditures, but were inclined to lean toward India in the settlement of the capitation charges. The net result was equivalent to an Imperial contribution of approximately £1,500,000 a year. It was this settlement which made it possible to reduce the military budget from Rs. 46.74 crores in 1832–33 to Rs. 44.38 crores in 1933–34.

It is difficult to say which the Nationalists regard as a greater abuse, the large sums spent on the army and the higher Civil Service or the small sums spent on education. The agitation for compulsory primary education, begun as far back as 1869 by Judge Ranade and continued by Mr. Gokhale and others, has borne very little fruit. The theory is popular and it has generally been accepted by the authorities, but there have not been funds available to put it into operation.[24] The Nationalist contention that the money can be found only by radically reducing the military expenditures is probably true, but it is probably also true that it would be unsafe to make such a reduction at the present time. The figures, however, are very discouraging. The total amount of public money spent on education is only about one fourth of the army expenditures.

There is no need to consider the system of revenue and expenditure in further detail. The general history of the central budget since the war may be divided into three periods. During the first five years, from 1918 to 1923, there was an unbroken series of deficits, amounting in all to about Rs. 100 crores or £75,000,000. A Retrenchment Committee was appointed in 1922 under the chairmanship of Lord Inchcape, the chairman of the Peninsula and Oriental Steamship Company and a member of the Geddes Committee in England. Its report, published in March, 1923, suggested retrenchments, mainly in military and railway expenditures, amounting ulti-

24. The provincial laws regarding compulsion are usually based on the principle of local option. The system has worked fairly well in a few of the municipalities and in some of the rural areas, especially in the Punjab and the Central Provinces.

mately to 19.25 crores. As only about 11 crores could be saved in 1923–24, Sir Basil Blackett, the Finance Member of the Governor-General's Council, proposed that the salt tax should be doubled in order to balance the budget. The result has been mentioned in an earlier chapter. The proposal met with strong opposition in the Legislative Assembly and Lord Reading had to use his power of certification to put it on the statute books.

The second period lasted from 1923 to 1929. Owing to the retrenchment policy and the increase of revenue that came with the improvement in business conditions, it was possible to balance the budget, reduce the salt tax, repeal the cotton excise, and remit the provincial contributions. The militarists were strong enough for a few years to prevent the reduction of the army budget to the figure (Rs. 50 crores) proposed by the Inchcape Committee and, as we have already seen, it was stabilized in 1928 at Rs. 55.10 crores for a nominal period of four years.

Since the beginning of the great depression in 1929, the trend has again been unfavorable, but Sir George Schuster, the new Finance Member, made heroic efforts to balance the budget. The lowest ebb was reached in September, 1931, when India followed the United Kingdom in suspending the gold standard. On September 29, Sir George laid before the Legislative Assembly an outline of the government's plan to restore financial stability. There were three main proposals: a drastic retrenchment in the Government Services; an emergency cut in salaries on the basis of a maximum cut of 10 per cent, including enhanced income taxes; and the introduction of fresh taxation. He also stated that the Governor-General had agreed to take a voluntary cut of 20 per cent and members of the Executive Council 15 per cent. The most important of the new taxes was an emergency surcharge of 25 per cent on all of the existing taxes except the duty on exports which was left untouched in the interest of foreign trade. Only one half of the surcharge (12½ per cent) on the income tax was to go into effect during the current year. There were also to be import duties of 10 per cent on machinery and dyes and half an anna per pound on raw cotton. It was hoped that the deficits for

1931–32 and 1932–33 would be greatly reduced and that a surplus could be anticipated for 1933–34. In that case, relief would be given first to government employees and then to income tax payers.

These proposals were bitterly attacked in the Legislative Assembly. The government was blamed because it had not carried out the recommendations of a General Retrenchment Advisory Committee,[25] which had been elected by the Assembly, and especially because it had not made a larger cut in the military expenditures. The nonofficial European group especially criticized the surcharge on the income tax, the Nationalists denounced the surcharge on the salt duty, and the Bombay industrialists were alarmed by the new import duties on cotton and machinery. Sir George Schuster demonstrated that the government had carried out most of the suggestions of the Retrenchment Committee and had cut the military budget to Rs. 47.40 crores, which was not only far below the stabilization agreement for the year (54.30 crores) but was Rs. 2.60 crores under the minimum recommended by the Inchcape Committee. He said that the government could not accept recommendations that would abolish or cripple the Forest, Indian Medical, and other essential Services and implied very strongly that it regarded the proposal to abolish the Ecclesiastical Department as a bit of impertinence that would not be tolerated. The cotton manufacturers were assured that the surcharge on the tariff, which applied to British as well as foreign goods, was more than enough to compensate them for the new duties on raw cotton and machinery. The cotton duty was popular with the agricultural interests and was carried by a majority of 60 to 48. Most of the other items were rejected and the bill as a whole was defeated on its third reading by a vote of 63 to 48. It was passed, however, by the Council of State and was enacted in its original form by the Governor-General under his power of certification.

The problems of currency, exchange, and banking in Brit-

25. This committee was split up into a number of subcommittees, of which the most important was Sir Abdur Rahim's General Purposes Retrenchment Subcommittee.

ish India are complicated and highly controversial. The mints were closed to the free coinage of silver in 1893 and a so-called gold exchange standard was gradually put into operation. Gold coins were not minted in India and the local currency was not redeemable in gold, but the government provided foreign remittances in sterling at approximately a fixed rate of exchange. This meant that the rupee was tied to gold as long as the United Kingdom was on a gold standard. The system worked very well except for a short period in 1907–8 and it was able to survive the exchange difficulties of 1914–15. It then gradually broke down because it was called upon to protect the paper sovereign with weapons that were designed to protect the silver rupee. Owing to the appreciation of silver and the depreciation of sterling, the exchange problem was reversed. Instead of raising the rupee to 1*s*. 4*d*., which was the official rate, it was a question of keeping its value down to that level. As a matter of fact, the exchange fluctuated and the government was not able to do very much about it from 1917 until a gold bullion standard was established in 1927. The return to normal conditions was delayed by an error of judgment. On the recommendation of the Babington-Smith Committee on Indian Exchange and Currency, the government tried in 1920 to stabilize rupee exchange at 2*s*. in gold, but the price of silver soon began to fall and the task proved impossible.

The chief features of the system as it existed before 1927 may be described in a few words.[26] The local currency was composed mainly of silver rupees and government notes in denominations of from R. 1 to Rs. 10,000. The notes were ordinarily convertible into silver, but when payments were to be made abroad, both the notes and coins were convertible into sterling at a fixed rate of exchange. To accomplish this there were three reserves, which were nominally kept separate, although in the last analysis they really constituted a single fund. These were the Treasury Balances, the Gold Standard Reserve, and the Paper Currency Reserve. The names indicate the primary function of each portion of the fund, "but neither in theory

26. The greater part of this description still holds good because the radical changes adopted in 1927 have not been put into full operation.

nor in practice have the separate portions . . . been entirely reserved for the objects indicated by their respective names."[27]

The Treasury Balances were kept partly in India and partly in London. The London portion was designed primarily to meet the home charges, but it was also used to stabilize the exchange value of the rupee. If at any time it was insufficient to meet these demands, the Secretary of State could draw upon the Gold Standard Reserve or the Paper Currency Reserve. The Gold Standard Reserve, created in 1900 out of the profits derived from the coinage of silver,[28] was allowed to accumulate until it amounted to £40,000,000 in 1931 and it was subsequently maintained at that figure. The greater part of this fund and a large fraction of the Paper Currency Reserve were usually deposited in London.

This system was severely criticized by Indian Nationalists and by some of the leaders of the European business community in India. They felt that India should have her own gold coinage and her own monetary system, a gold standard and not merely a government guarantee of the stability of external credits. They also felt that the Reserves were badly managed. The Gold Standard Reserve should have been composed of gold and the greater part of it should have been kept in India, but, as a matter of fact, it was made up almost entirely of sterling securities deposited in London. In a lesser degree, the same was also true of the Paper Currency Reserve. The accumulation of these large sums in London checked the normal flow of gold to India and increased the stringency of the Indian money market. There was likewise a loss to the Treasury because the yield on liquid funds was lower in England than it was in India. But the real difficulty was that a financial crisis was likely to affect both countries at once and India would be unable to make full use of her resources when they were most needed.

The Nationalists especially disapproved the management

27. *The Report of the Chamberlain Commission on Indian Finance and Currency* (1914), par. 9.

28. The profit on the coinage of a rupee is the difference between the face value and the bullion value. A part of the growth of the Reserve was also due to the accumulation of interest on its securities.

of these funds during the war. In 1914, 84 per cent of the Gold Standard Reserve was held in England and 16 per cent in India; of this total, 16 per cent was in gold, 16 per cent in silver, and 68 per cent was invested in sterling securities. In 1919, it was all held in England in the form of sterling securities (83.2 per cent) and "cash at short notice" (16.8 per cent). The statistics of the Paper Currency Reserve tell a similar story. In 1914, 20 per cent was held in England; 48 per cent was in gold, 31 per cent in silver, and 21 per cent was in rupee (15) and sterling (6) securities. In 1919, 54 per cent was held in England; 11.4 per cent was in gold, 24.3 was in silver and 64.4 was in rupee (10.4) and sterling (54) securities. The two Reserves together increased nearly 100 per cent, the Indian portion 20 per cent and the English portion 200 per cent. The balance of trade was in India's favor and her funds were piling up in London because the British government was unwilling to let her have gold and was unable to get an adequate supply of silver. A serious crisis was averted by the passage of the Pittman Act (April 23, 1918), under which 200 million ounces of silver were purchased from the United States government and shipped to India between July 1, 1918 and July 17, 1919.

A Royal Commission on Indian Currency and Finance, commonly known as the Hilton-Young Commission, was appointed in 1925. In its report, published in August, 1926, it recommended the establishment of a gold bullion standard with the value of the rupee fixed at 1*s.* 6*d.* and the creation of a Reserve Bank in India to control credit facilities. A Currency Bill, designed to carry out the first recommendation, was prepared by Sir Basil Blackett, the Finance Member, and laid before the Legislative Assembly in March, 1927. The general principle of the bill was approved, but the majority of the nonofficial members urged the adoption of the traditional ratio of 1*s.* 4*d.* In the manner of Mr. Maynard Keynes, they argued that a higher rate would penalize Indian industry and commerce because it would encourage imports and discourage exports. It would also be equivalent to the paying of a bonus to British holders of rupee stocks and bonds and to British officials and businessmen who made remittances to England.

In answer to these arguments, Sir Basil Blackett called attention to the fact that since the reëstablishment of the gold standard in Great Britain in June, 1925, rupee exchange had been pegged at 1*s.* 6*d.* and prices in India had become adapted to that rate; it could not, therefore, be reduced without adopting a policy of inflation which would increase the cost of living and cause great hardship to the masses of the people. Furthermore, the acceptance of a ratio of 1*s.* 4*d.* would increase by 12½ per cent the burden of the large annual payments which the government of India must make in Great Britain. This would wipe out the budget surplus in the current year and make it impossible to remit the provincial contributions. It might even be necessary to resort to extra taxation. When the decisive vote was finally taken, about twenty elected members voted in the affirmative and the government won by the narrow margin of 68 to 65.

From the point of view of the orthodox school of finance this was perhaps a wise solution. It was generally agreed that the gold value of the rupee should be fixed by law and that the government should make every effort to maintain this valuation. If there should again be a considerable rise in the price of silver, it would be easier to maintain a ratio of 1*s.* 6*d.* than a ratio of 1*s.* 4*d.* because the melting point would be 12½ per cent higher. Then, too, inasmuch as the *de facto* ratio at that time was 1*s.* 6*d.*, its legal adoption was not the occasion for any dislocation of business. On the other hand, Mr. Keynes's theory of public finance is extremely plausible. When business is bad, a check in the progress of deflation or even a judicious inflation of the currency is sometimes an excellent tonic. If the British were afraid to use this remedy in their own country, were they justified in forbidding its use to the people of India, especially when all they asked for was a return to the conditions that existed before the war? There is still a tendency in India to criticize the Currency Act and to hold it at least partly responsible for the industrial depression and the great strikes of 1928 and 1929. This is not merely the view of the politicians to whom all government measures are anathema; it is also shared by Sir Victor Sassoon, Sir Purshotamas Thakurdas, and other well-known bankers and manufacturers of

Bombay. The efforts made by the British government since 1931 to keep down the exchange value of the pound justifies their contention.

The controversy over the Reserve Bank Bill was even more acrimonious. The Hilton-Young Commission proposed that the control of Indian currency should be transferred from the India Office in London to a central bank in India. For various reasons, the Imperial Bank of India, which was established in 1920 by the amalgamation of the three presidency banks, could not be used for this purpose. The commission, therefore, recommended the creation of a new Reserve Bank and suggested certain principles upon which it should be organized. These recommendations were considered by a Joint Select Committee of the two houses of the Indian legislature and several important amendments and additions were proposed. Still further changes were made when the bill came before the Legislative Assembly at the Simla session in August (1927). The commission, for example, had accepted the principle of a Shareholders' Bank which would be free from political pressure. The majority of the Assembly favored a State Bank. They struck out the clause which made members of the central and provincial legislatures ineligible as directors of the bank and inserted a clause providing for the selection of a large proportion of the directors by the elected members of these bodies. They also injected the race issue by providing that either the governor or the deputy governor of the bank must always be an Indian.

Sir Basil Blackett tried to save the bill by a compromise. He accepted the principle of a State Bank and agreed to a plan providing for the choice of some of the directors by a system of electoral colleges which would almost certainly have been subject to political control. Some of the staunchest supporters of the government were alarmed by these concessions, especially the nonofficial Europeans and the more conservative Moslems. The religious issue was involved because the members of the electoral colleges were to be chosen in general instead of in communal constituencies, which might serve as a dangerous precedent when the time came to revise the Constitution of India. In spite of this opposition, the Finance Member continued to negotiate with the leaders of the Congress and Nationalist parties until suddenly and without any apparent warning he was overruled by the Secretary of State and compelled to announce that the government did not intend "at present" to proceed with the measure.

An episode of this kind is humiliating to the government of India as well as to the people of India. It shows that the members of the Governor-General's Council are still mere puppets who must respond when the wires are pulled in London. There can be no give and take between them and the legislative majority on any really important issue. The unfortunate part of it is that the fiasco could probably have been avoided without a sacrifice of principle. The Congress-Nationalist coalition would almost certainly have rejected any terms acceptable to the Finance Member and his colleagues on the Front Bench. In that case, they and they alone would have been held responsible for the defeat of a bill, which, in one form or another, is approved by nearly all of the intelligent people of India. It should also be noted that the politicians would not have had a majority on the Board of Directors even if the compromise had been passed.

Sir Basil Blackett offered his resignation, but it was not accepted. He went to London in November to talk over the problem with the officials of the India Office, and a new bill, presumably approved by the Secretary of State, was drafted in time to be submitted to the Assembly when it met again at Delhi on February 1, 1928. The Simon Commission, however, had been appointed during the recess and feeling was running too high for any measure to be considered on its merits. The bill was not even discussed, permission to introduce it being refused by the Assembly on purely technical grounds. The point was made that a new bill could not be introduced when an old bill covering the same subject was still alive. The first bill had not been withdrawn, the government having merely announced that it would not proceed with it "at present." Sir Basil then said that he was prepared to go on with the original bill, but the government was soon defeated on a test vote and the measure was again dropped. The issue was mainly political. The Left-Wing parties were determined not to agree to the establishment of a Reserve Bank that was not subject to their control. Part of the opposition, however, came from vested interests—shareholders in the Imperial Bank of India, for example—who themselves feared that a Reserve Bank would interfere with their business. There was also an agrarian element in the Assembly which honestly believed that a Shareholders' Bank would be dominated by the great financial interests of Bombay.

The British government was convinced that a Reserve Bank, free from political influence, must be established before the control of currency and exchange could be shifted from England to India and it made a recommendation to Parliament that this should be a condition precedent to the inauguration of the new Constitution. In Article 32 of the White Paper of March 18, 1933, there occurs the following statement:

> The proposals relating to responsibility for the Finance of the Federation are based on the assumption that before the first Federal Ministry comes into being a Reserve Bank, free from political influence will have been set up by Indian legislation, and be already successfully operating. . . . If a situation should arise in which all other requirements for the inauguration of the Federation having been satisfied it had so far proved impossible successfully to start the Reserve Bank . . . it would, inevitably be necessary to reconsider the position and determine in the light of the then circumstances what course should be pursued.

Under the gold bullion standard no provision was made for a gold coinage, but there was a pledge that gold bars would be exchanged for silver and paper rupees at the rate of 1*s.* 6*d.* per rupee. The sale of government silver to build up the gold reserves unsettled the silver markets of the world, reduced the purchasing power of the Far East, and probably helped to bring on the great depression.[29] The system was not tried long

29. A large part of this hoard still hangs over the market, but in the International Silver Agreement, signed in London, July 22, 1933, provision was made to restrict the sales to a yearly average of 35,000,000 ounces for four years, beginning January 1, 1934. This agreement and the silver purchasing policy adopted by the United States government in 1933 have stabilized the market to a considerable extent.

enough to test its possibilities. On September 21, 1931, the day on which Great Britain abandoned the gold standard, Sir George Schuster informed the Legislative Assembly that India had followed her example and that an ordinance suspending the operation of the appropriate sections of the Currency Act of 1927 had been signed by the Governor-General. Sir Samuel Hoare, the Secretary of State for India, made a similar statement to the Round Table Conference, which was at that time holding its second session in London. As Great Britain had abandoned the gold standard, India could not adhere to gold without increasing the sterling value of the rupee. This was obviously unwise and it had therefore "been decided to maintain the present currency standard on a sterling basis."

The decision met with general approval in India, although there were a few critics who argued that His Majesty's government was robbing the Indian Reserves to bolster up British credit. There was, however, almost universal criticism of the procedure that was followed. In a speech delivered before the Round Table Conference, Mr. Gandhi declared that action had been "taken over the heads" of the Legislative Assembly. "On matters of the most vital importance to the nation they were not yet considered fit to be consulted, much less to decide, what was good for them." In the Legislative Assembly itself, Sir Samuel Hoare's tactics were denounced as an insult to India. He had imposed a policy from Whitehall not only on the Indian people and the Indian legislature, but also on the government of India itself. Sir George Schuster tried to explain why it was necessary to take such hasty action. A run on the banks had already been started and note holders were raiding the Treasury's gold supply. If the government had waited to secure the approval of the Assembly the result might have been disastrous. The Assembly, however, refused to be mollified and a vote of censure was passed by a majority of 64 to 40.

The suspension of the gold standard was inevitable and it probably averted some of the worst effects of the depression, but unfortunately it was followed by a tremendous depletion of the gold supply. The balance of trade is normally in favor of India and there are large imports of treasure, most of which is made into jewelry or absorbed into private hoards. According to the estimates of financial experts, a net total of about

£600,000,000 in gold and about 400,000,000 ounces of silver was brought into the country between 1931 and 1935. The tide then turned, at least temporarily, in the other direction. From September, 1931, to July, 1936, £211,000,000 in gold were exported. In less than five years India lost over one third of the gold which it had taken her nearly a century to accumulate.[30] The movement is still in progress and if an embargo is not imposed, it is likely to continue for some time to come.

There are apparently two main causes of this movement. In the first place, owing to the decline of Indian commodity prices, the trade balances which are generally used to pay the fixed charges in England have tended to disappear. In the second place, there has been a flight from the rupee, based on the fear that the legal rate (1*s.* 6*d.*) may have to be abandoned. Very little gold actually comes out of the Treasury or the bank reserves of India. The low price of agricultural products makes it impossible for a large proportion of the people of India to meet the fixed obligations which they owe to landlords, moneylenders and the government without sacrificing their hoards. There is also a tendency to sell gold from the hoards in order to make a profit in rupees or in depreciated sterling. This movement should ultimately be beneficial, but it is doubtful whether India will get very much benefit if the treasure is all sent abroad. There is a strong feeling in India that the government should impose an embargo and keep the gold in its own hands to strengthen the currency and to use in establishing the Reserve Bank. As long as the budget is balanced, it should be possible to borrow abroad enough money to meet the "home" charges and to stabilize the exchange.

30. It should be noted of course that India had a fairly large gold supply in 1835 and that she produces an average of about £2,300,000 a year in her own mines.

CHAPTER VII

POLITICAL GRIEVANCES: THE SERVICES

THE chief political grievances have been the lack of responsible government, the discrimination against Indians in the Civil and Military Services, and the restrictions upon personal liberty, freedom of speech, and freedom of the press. The first is obviously the most important, but it may be dismissed here with a brief summary because it is discussed more fully in the chapters on the Montagu-Chelmsford Reforms and the Simon Commission. Responsible government involves two fundamental ideas, substantial elective majorities in various legislative bodies and the control of the executive by the legislature. The former was acquired under the Montagu-Chelmsford Reforms, but the legislature was not given control over the executive in the central government or over all of the executive departments in the provinces. Even in the case of Transferred Subjects the control was not as complete as the principle of responsible government usually implies. It will be impossible to say how far the principle has been carried in the Constitution of 1935 until experience shows how the safeguards are to be applied.

The work of administration in India was performed in the seventeenth and eighteenth centuries by a miscellaneous group of writers, merchants, factors, and other employees of the East India Company. A definite organization was formed under Lord Cornwallis which was recognized by Parliament in 1793 and given a monopoly of all the principal offices in India below that of membership in the Councils. This body was styled the "Covenanted Service" because its members were required to observe certain conditions laid down in a covenant or agreement made between them and the Company. Appointments were made by the Court of Directors usually on the basis of social or political influence, until 1854, when the patronage was transferred to the Board of Control and a system of competition was established. According to Lord Macaulay, who was chairman of the committee that drafted the rules for the competitive examinations, the object of the new system was to recruit for service in India a body of young men who had received the best, the most liberal, and the most finished education that the United Kingdom could afford. The examinations were held in England in the ordinary honor subjects of the universities of Great Britain and Ireland. With the change in the method of recruitment, there was also a change of name; the Covenanted Service became the Indian Civil Service.

The monopoly exercised by this Service was soon broken. As the functions of government were widened, new positions were created which called for special technical training. The result was the establishment of a number of "Special Services" —Educational, Medical, Agricultural, and others—which narrowed the field of the older Service and checked its normal growth. These Services were recruited in England and for many years their personnel was entirely European, but their intrusion was resented by the Indian Civil Service and there was considerable friction until the European members of all the Services found it necessary to present a united front against the Indians. There were also Provincial and Subordinate Services and Provincial branches of the Special Services, recruited in India, but they held only the intermediate and subordinate posts and consequently did not compete with the Superior Services.

The system which gradually developed is now organized on the following plan. "The first broad division is between the Services engaged in matters which are under the direct control of the Central Government, such as state railways or posts or telegraphs, and those which work under the Provincial Governments." The former are quite appropriately called the Central Services, but the latter are divided into the All-India Services, the Provincial Services, the Subordinate Services, and the Provincial branches of the Special Services. The reader should remember, therefore, that the All-India Services are primarily associated with the local governments, although a few of their members, especially in the Indian Civil Service, are employed by the government of India. It should also be remembered that each of the All-India Services, "not withstanding its division among the provinces, forms a single Service with a common status and a common standard of rights and remunerations." The most important of the All-India Services are the Indian Civil Service and the Indian Police, commonly called the "Security Services," because they are chiefly responsible for the maintenance of law and order. The term "Superior Service" is applied to the All-India Service and Central Services of corresponding status. In each of the major provinces there are a Provincial Service which fills the intermediate posts and a few of the higher posts in the Transferred Departments, and a Subordinate Service which fills the lower posts. There are also Provincial branches of the Special Services. The Central Services are recruited partly by the government of India. The All-India Services are recruited by the Secretary of State, but some of them have "listed posts" which are filled by promotion from the Provincial Services. The Provincial and Subordinate Services and the Provincial branches of the Special Services are recruited by the provincial governments.[1]

The Indian Civil Service is still the most important part of the general administrative staff. Its members are usually employed in the provinces, where they are responsible (1933) for the maintenance of law and order and the general administration of public affairs. They supervise the police force and the work of the criminal courts. They administer the system of land tenure, collect the land revenues, and control the local administration of various other sources of public income. Their hold on the District and Municipal Boards has recently been weakened, but they still exercise a strong influence in the field of local government. There are separate executive and judicial branches of this Service although both sets of functions are sometimes concentrated in the hands of the same official. On the executive side, the chief officials are the district

1. See the *Report of the Indian Statutory (Simon) Commission*, Vol. I, par. 290. The term "listed post" is explained later. The officials who hold these posts are nominally members of the All-India Services, but they are on a slightly different footing from the members, both European and Indian, who are directly recruited.

magistrates and collectors, the divisional commissioners, the financial commissioners, and the members of the Boards of Revenue. The Service also furnishes the Governors of all the major provinces except Bengal, Bombay, and Madras, the chief commissioners of the minor provinces, part of the Council of the Secretary of State, one half of the Viceroy's Council and the Provincial Executive Councils, and most of the chief secretaries in the central and provincial executive departments. The judicial branch includes district and session judges, judicial commissioners, and at least one third of the members of the various High Courts.

The personnel of the old Covenanted Service was entirely British. The declaration of the Charter Act of 1833 that no native of India should "by reason only of his religion, place of birth, descent, colour or any of them be disabled from holding any place, office or employment under the said Company" was ignored by the Court of Directors, and Indians continued to be excluded until the control of patronage was taken over by the Crown in 1854. Theoretically, there was no race discrimination in the new system of open competition, but in reality Indians were heavily handicapped because the examinations were held only in London and were based on the kind of education given in the British and Irish universities. Very few Indians entered the Service by this route and those who did found it difficult to secure promotion.

The liberal principles of 1833 were reaffirmed in the Royal Proclamation of 1858, when India came under the government of the Crown, but no further steps were taken to make them effective until the passage of the Government of India Act of 1870. Under Section 6 of that act, there was a provision that natives of India of "proved merit and ability" might be appointed to civil posts without taking the ordinary examinations in London, and the Governor-General in Council was authorized to prepare the rules necessary to put the plan into operation. At this stage the members of the Service began to exert their influence. Although the Secretary of State urged immediate action, the drafting of the rules was delayed, on one pretext or another, and was not finally completed until 1879. These rules provided that one sixth of the recruits for the Indian Civil Service positions each year should be statutory natives of India, appointed by the Governor-General in Council on the nomination of the Provincial governments. The term *statutory native* was defined by an act of Parliament to include Asiatic natives and Anglo-Indians or Eurasians, but not members of the domiciled European community.

This experiment was a failure. Of the sixty-nine officials who were appointed while the rules were in force, none showed any high degree of merit and the majority fell far below the ordinary Service standards. The members of the Indian Civil Service regarded this as conclusive evidence that Indians were incapable of doing first-rate administrative work and used it as an argument against any further racial dilution of the Service. The Nationalists, on the other hand, placed the blame entirely on the method of selection. There was no competitive test for judging "merit and ability" and appointments were usually given to young men who had very little educational training merely because they belonged to influential families or to families who were friendly to the British connection. It was alleged that Anglo-Indians in particular were favored even when there were far more capable Asiatic natives available.

Owing to the general dissatisfaction with these rules, a Commission on the Public Services, with Sir Charles Aitchison as chairman, was appointed by the government of India in 1886. Their report was presented in 1887 and, on the basis of its recommendations, a new set of rules was issued in 1892. One sixth of the existing Indian Civil Service positions were earmarked for statutory natives, to be selected by promotion from the Provincial Services. The test of "merit and ability," in other words, was to be practical experience. Indian and Anglo-Indian officials who had demonstrated their capacity in the lower positions were to be given an opportunity to do the same kind of work in a wider field and with a greater sense of individual responsibility.

There was an improvement from the point of view of administrative efficiency, but in other respects the change was a step backwards. As the one-sixth rule was interpreted, it applied only to the posts reserved for the Indian Civil Service in

1892 and not to the annual recruitment. The number of native appointments, therefore, tended to remain fixed instead of increasing with the normal growth of the administrative staff. In actual practice the results were even more reactionary. Although the rule required that 108 posts should be reserved for statutory natives, the Secretary of State really listed only 93 and the number was later reduced to 61, the places eliminated being those that were most important and most remunerative. There was a slight increase later, through the addition of new posts in Burma and Assam, but as late as 1924 there were only 88 out of a total of 700 posts, which was far below the number that there would have been under the old rules.

These disabilities were all connected with the system of recruitment, but there were others which Indians had to suffer after they had secured their initial appointments. It was apparently the intention of Parliament that the officials recruited under the Act of 1870 should belong to the Indian Civil Service and should have the ordinary opportunities for promotion. As a matter of fact, their names appeared on a separate list, they were known as Statutory Civilians and their salaries were lower than those paid to European officials who did the same type of work. The posts reserved for them under the rules of 1892 were nominally included in the Indian Civil Service, but they were called "listed posts" and were treated as if they belonged to an entirely different Service. The occupant of a listed post had practically no chance for promotion, not only because the rules made it possible to discriminate against him, but also because he was usually not appointed until he was nearly old enough to retire.

The organization of the general administrative corps into Imperial, Provincial, and Subordinate Services was followed by a division of the more important Special Services into Imperial and Provincial branches, the former recruited in England and the latter in India. The Services so divided in 1913 were the Police, Medical, Education, Agricultural, Civil Veterinary, Forest, Public Works, Railway (Engineering), Telegraph (Engineering), and the Survey of India. Although some effort was made, especially in the Department of Education, to give the two branches an equal standing, they really constituted in every case an upper and a lower Service, with a line between them which was almost as difficult to cross as the line between the Indian Civil Service and the Provincial Service. When members of the Provincial branch of a Service were promoted to posts ordinarily reserved for the Imperial branch they were usually treated like Statutory Civilians who held the listed posts in the Indian Civil Service, that is to say, they were not really admitted to the full privileges of the upper branch and they had little chance for further advancement.

The other Special Services were homogeneous units, which means that each Service had one official list and the officials recruited in Great Britain were supposed to be on exactly the same footing with those recruited in India. As a matter of fact, until quite recently, there was a bar between them somewhat like that between the Imperial and Provincial branches in other Services and nearly all of the better-paid positions were occupied by Europeans. In 1913, the most important Services in this group were the Post Office, Telegraph (Traffic), Land Records (Burma), Railway (Stores), Registration, Northern India Salt Revenue, Salt and Excise, and General Survey (Madras)—which were recruited mainly in India—the Military Finance, Geological Survey, Mines, Mints and Assay, and Railway (Locomotive, Carriage, and Wagon)—which were recruited mainly in England—and the Customs, Indian Finance, Pilots (Bengal), Railway (Traffic), and Factory and Boiler Inspection—which were recruited in both countries in varying proportions.[2]

This account will help to explain the bitter attacks which the Nationalists have made upon the Services, especially the Indian Civil Service, during the last thirty years. There are three main factors that should be considered at greater length: (a) the lack of sympathy between European officials and educated Indians, (b) the desire of educated Indians to secure

2. *Report of the Royal Commission on the Public Services (Islington Commission)*, London, 1917 (Cd. 8382), p. 21. The Report was finished in 1915, but on account of the war it was not published until 1917.

lucrative government jobs, and (c) the belief, only too well founded, that they have been the victims of racial discrimination. The campaign itself has passed or is passing through three fairly distinct stages. The Indians struggled first to get into the Services, then they strove to increase their membership and to secure access to the better-paid and more responsible positions and now they are trying, through the extension of the principle of responsible government, to control the policy of the Services from above.

The attitude of educated Indians toward the Indian Civil Service has already been discussed. They feel that it has blocked every effort at reform in the past and that, if any power is left in its hands, it will continue to do so in the future. The following extract from a leading article published in *India*[3] on September 20, 1918, is a good example of the more extreme type of Indian criticism:

> The Service is regarded by the great bulk of thinking people in India with the deepest suspicion and distrust. Its members, whether of the Simla breed or in the districts, are universally looked upon as a race apart, unapproachable, unsympathetic, unimaginative, having eyes to see but seeing not, ears to hear but hearing not. But what is yet more to the point, the Anglo-Indian bureaucracy are charged with having, in their own interests of class and race, and either deliberately or otherwise, broken to the Indian heart the words of promise spoken to the Indian ear by a long line of British sovereigns and statesmen. To this day the solemn pledges contained in the Charter Act of 1833 remain unfulfilled.

A slightly more moderate view is expressed by Mr. K. Vyasa Rao in his interesting book on *The Future Government of India:*

> The Civil Service is an official guild, with prospects and privileges in the nature of a cherished monopoly. It has, as a body, proved its efficiency beyond question, and in coping with strenuous and

3. *India* was at that time the official organ of the Indian National Congress in Great Britain.

> responsible work, it has gained the unstinted admiration even of its unsparing critics; but its outlook has never been that of the statesman at the helm of affairs. . . . However admirable, therefore, for the purpose of executive duty, the Civil Service is not likely to furnish men who may be expected to bring to the direction of the Government of a province the fervor of moral purpose, the self-surrender of a man with a mission, or the sustained faith in the regenerating influence of effort in behalf of others. . . . A bad or indifferent selection of men can easily be rectified, whereas a whole service cannot be metamorphosed in regard to its faith or faithlessness, its inherent incapacity to liberalise its political creed, or to free itself from the benumbing influence of frigid officialdom.[4]

With the exception of the Police, there is very little criticism of the other Services because their contact with the people is less frequent and less provocative, but none of them is really popular.

In the struggle for office the Brahmans have taken the lead. Although as a rule they are poor, they are willing to make every sacrifice to give their sons an education. There is a larger percentage of university graduates among adult male Brahmans of Bengal than there is among the so-called Brahmans of Massachusetts. The Chitpavan Brahmans of Poona rank high among the graduates of the University of Bombay. Caste and tradition make it difficult for them to go into business or to enter certain professions where they might be brought into close contact with people of lower castes. The great majority of those who have a university education wish to be teachers, lawyers, or government employees. The teaching profession is overcrowded and underpaid. The cities and villages are filled with lawyers, many of whom have to encourage litigation and resort to all kinds of devious practices in order to escape starvation. The salaries and pension allowances in the higher services are unusually attractive. Even in the Provincial Civil Service and in the Provincial branches of the Special Services they are high in comparison with the opportunities in other

4. pp. 112–114.

fields of work. The result is that there is keen competition for these positions not only among the Brahmans, but also among the educated classes of other castes and communities.

Unsuccessful candidates for office are naturally disappointed, but, if they believe that their failure is the result of race prejudice, they are apt to feel more than ordinarily resentful and they are also apt to have the sympathy of other members of their racial group. This has been the case in India. Europeans and Anglo-Indians have received preferential treatment both in the recruitment for the Public Services and in the subsequent struggle for promotion. Although ample proof of this statement has been given in the preceding paragraphs, it may perhaps be desirable to offer a few additional facts and statistics.

Some attention has already been called to the fact that the examinations for the Indian Civil Service were held exclusively in London and that they were based on the educational system of the United Kingdom. This was also true of the Imperial branch or its equivalent in the Special Services that used the competitive method of recruitment. Indians were allowed to compete in practically all of these examinations, but there was a rule in the Indian Police Service, in force as late as 1917, which provided that "every candidate must be a British subject of European descent." Their position was almost equally bad at that time in the Departments of Education, Finance, Military Finance, Customs, Forest, Public Works and Railways (Engineering), and Railways (Traffic), which were recruited, without a competitive examination, by the Secretary of State in Council on the recommendation of a Selection Committee.

There was also a certain amount of discrimination even in the Services that were chiefly recruited in India. Europeans and Anglo-Indians were sometimes favored in the kind of educational test that was required and they were frequently appointed or promoted over Asiatics who had higher grades or longer terms of service. In 1913 there were no Asiatics at all in the Departments of Mines, Mints and Assay, Pilots (Bengal), and Factory and Boiler Inspection, and very few in the better-paid positions in the Post Office, the Survey of India, the Salt and Excise, and the Northern India Salt Revenue Departments. They filled only 5 out of 46 positions in the Post Office paying over Rs. 500 a month, 5 out of 50 in the Salt and Excise Department, and 9 out of 45 in the Northern India Salt Revenue. There was a definite rule in the Survey of India Department that three fourths of all recruits in the provincial branch must be Europeans or Anglo-Indians. This meant that three out of every four vacancies would be filled by the three highest Europeans or Anglo-Indians on the examination list, regardless of the fact that there might be Indians with higher grades.

In the Report of the Royal Commission of 1913–15 there is a racial classification of 11,064 officials who held posts in 1913 paying salaries of Rs. 200 a month and upwards. Of this number, 4,898 or 44 per cent were Europeans, 1,593 or 14 per cent were Anglo-Indians and 4,573 or 42 per cent were Asiatics. As the salary scale increased, the proportion of Indians rapidly declined. There were 1,778 posts that paid over Rs. 1,000 a month, of which 86 per cent were filled by Europeans, 4 per cent by Anglo-Indians, and 8 per cent by Asiatics. Out of 97 posts that paid more than Rs. 3,000 a month, 96 were held by Europeans and 1 by an Anglo-Indian. When the purely administrative posts alone were considered, the disproportion was greater still, because more than one third of all Asiatic officials who received salaries in excess of Rs. 1,000 a month were in the judicial branch of the Indian and Provincial Civil Services.

The figures given by the commission do not distinguish between European officials recruited in Great Britain and European officials recruited in India. It is well known that the members of the domiciled community hold very few of the really superior posts, but it would probably be safe to assume that they held at least two thirds of the 3,330 posts in the European list that paid from Rs. 200 to Rs. 1,000 a month. If this assumption is correct, they filled almost 20 per cent of all the civil positions paying Rs. 200 a month and upwards, as compared with 14 per cent for Anglo-Indians and 42 per cent for Asiatics. There were at that time (1913) about 100,000 domiciled Europeans in British India, 102,000 Anglo-Indians, and

242,000,000 Asiatics, which means that 1 out of every 45 members of the domiciled community and 1 out of every 64 Anglo-Indians held a fairly lucrative government job, whereas the proportion among Asiatics was about 1 to 53,000.[5]

The changes brought about by the Montagu-Chelmsford Reforms were immediate and far-reaching. There was an increase in the recruitment of Indians, accompanied by a pronounced decrease in the recruitment of Europeans and an increase in the number of European officials who resigned before the expiration of their terms of service. A scale of Indian recruitment was adopted in 1919–20 which varied from 33 per cent in the Indian Police Service up to 50 per cent in the Agricultural, Educational, and Veterinary Services, and the Indian Service of Engineers. The initial rate in the Indian Civil Service was 37½ per cent and this was to be increased annually by 1½ per cent until it reached 48 per cent. These percentages were for a time exceeded in actual practice because the supply of European recruits was inadequate while the Indian quotas were always filled.

The decrease in European recruitment and the increase in European resignations from the Services were due to the same general causes. It was difficult for officials to work under the new conditions and also hard for them to live and support their families on salaries which had not been properly readjusted to meet the rise in the cost of living. On the theory that the Reforms changed the conditions of service, a scheme was adopted by the India Office which permitted All-India officials in the provinces, selected for appointment before January 1, 1920, to retire on pensions proportionate to their length of service. Nearly 200 officers retired under these terms in the first year and by 1924 the number had increased to 345. When they returned to England they aired their grievances widely and a number of young men who would normally have entered the Indian Services were deflected to other careers. The average annual recruitment in London for the Indian Civil Service for a series of years before the war was 53, of whom 93.4 per

5. These figures apply of course only to the better-paid positions. There were more than a million government employees, nearly all of them Asiatic natives, who received less than Rs. 200 a month.

cent were British and 6.6 per cent were Indian. During the three years from 1921 to 1923 inclusive there was an annual average of 20 British and 21 Indians, but the real disproportion was still greater because some of the British who qualified for appointment did not actually enter the Service. There was almost a complete cessation of European recruitment for the Indian Medical, Educational, and Agricultural Services.

The political leaders of India were not satisfied even with this record. In February, 1922, when Indian recruitment was flourishing and British recruitment had almost ceased, the Legislative Assembly adopted a resolution recommending to the Governor-General in Council "that enquiries should, without delay, be inaugurated as to the measures possible to give further effect to the Declaration of 20th August, 1917, in the direction of increased recruitment of Indians for the All-India Services." As a result of this resolution, the government of India sent a circular letter to the provincial governments discussing the subject and asking for an expression of their opinion. The letter was intended to be confidential, but a copy was secured by the press and it attained wide notoriety under the name of the O'Donnell Circular.[6] The general tone of this document was pessimistic. The arguments for and against a reduction or stoppage of European recruitment were summarized and it was strongly implied that it ought to be given up altogether, not so much because the people of India desired it, but because it was unfair to ask a self-respecting European to endure the conditions that then existed.

It was obvious by this time that the Services would soon be completely Indianized unless they were made more attractive to Europeans. Mr. Lloyd George's famous "Steel Frame" speech in the House of Commons on August 2, 1922, indicated that the British authorities were beginning to appreciate the seriousness of the problem, although it did not suggest any concrete solution.[7] What was really needed was a reorganization of the Services to bring them into harmony with the con-

6. So-called because it bore the signature of Mr. S. P. O'Donnell, Secretary to the Government of India.

7. For a discussion of the political results of this speech, see chap. iv.

stitutional and economic changes that had taken place since the passage of the Government of India Act of 1919. A Royal Commission on the Superior Civil Services in India was, therefore, appointed in 1923 under the chairmanship of Lord Lee of Fareham. Their task was to devise a scheme that would go as far as possible to satisfy the Indian demand that the Services should be Indianized and brought under legislative control without making too great a sacrifice of efficiency or of the vested rights of existing European officials. It was also necessary to increase the compensation of European members of the Services without arousing too much racial animosity and imposing too heavy a burden upon the Indian taxpayers.

The report of the commission presented to Parliament on March 27, 1924, was necessarily a compromise between conflicting interests. On the paramount issue of recruitment it leaned toward the Indians. The question was no longer "How many Indians should be admitted in the Public Services?" but "What is the minimum number of Englishmen which must still be recruited?" It was proposed that in the Central Services the recruitment for the Political Department, the Imperial Customs Department, and the Ecclesiastical Department should continue to be made by the Secretary of State. Officers of the Indian Civil Service employed by the central government would also be recruited by the Secretary of State. Recruitment for the Indian Railway Service of Engineers, the Superior Revenue Establishment (State Railways), and the Superior Telegraph and Wireless Board should be made partly by the Secretary of State and partly by the government of India. All of the other Central Services were to be recruited by the government of India.

In the case of the All-India Services, the general rule was adopted that officers working in the Reserved departments should continue to be recruited by the Secretary of State and officers working in the Transferred Departments should be recruited by the provincial governments. The former group included the Security Services (Indian Civil Services and the Indian Police Service), the Irrigation Branch of the Indian Service of Engineers, and the Indian Forest Service outside of Bombay and Burma. The latter included the Education, Agricultural, Veterinary, and Indian Engineers (Road and Building Branch) Services in all of the provinces and the Forest Service in Bombay and Burma. There was one important exception to the rule. Public Health was a Transferred Subject, which means that normally the Indian Medical Service would have been brought under the control of the Minister of Health and the Provincial Council and recruitment in England would have ceased. But this was a crucial problem. The Indian Medical Service was created partly as a military Reserve and partly to provide medical attendance for the European official community. If it were provincialized and recruitment in Great Britain were stopped, the Reserve would be inadequate in the emergency of war and all the Civil Services would be affected because British officials would not care to serve in India without a guarantee of European medical service for themselves and their families. The commission therefore proposed that each province should employ a fixed number of European medical officers loaned by the Royal Army Medical Corps (India), who would, of course, hold commissions from the Crown and be to a large extent independent of political control.[8]

These recommendations were significant because the officials recruited by the government of India and the provincial governments would nearly all be Indians. In a few years, the European element would entirely disappear from the Educational Service, the Agricultural Service, and several other important branches of the administration. But this was only part of the story. The commissioners also recommended a rapid increase in the Indianization of the Services which were still to be recruited by the Secretary of State. In the Indian Civil Service, for example, 20 per cent of the superior posts were to be filled by promotion from the Provincial Service, 40 per cent by the recruitment of Europeans and 40 per cent by the direct recruitment of Indians. It was calculated that the Service would be half Indian and half British by 1939. This

8. The Royal Army Medical Corps is primarily concerned with the medical care of British troops. The Indian Medical Service takes care of the Indian troops. The members of the latter Service may also be transferred to civil employment.

was revolutionary from the bureaucratic point of view, but it was probably expected that the effects of the change would be minimized by restricting Indians, as far as possible, to posts which were not directly concerned with the maintenance of law and order.[9] The Indianization of the Police was a still more serious problem because its members are all concerned with the preservation of order and the detection of crime. They must have not only the qualities of courage, integrity, and sound judgment—which many Indian officials undoubtedly possess—but they must also have a reputation for absolute impartiality in dealing with communal disputes. In spite of this difficulty, the commission proposed that 20 per cent of the recruitment in the Indian Police Service should be filled by promotion from the Provincial Police Service, 30 per cent by Indian recruitment and 50 per cent by European recruitment, so that the racial personnel would be approximately equal by 1949. For the Indian Forest Service, in the seven provinces in which Forests was a Reserved Subject, it was proposed that the recruitment should be 75 per cent Indian and 25 per cent European. Vacancies in the Irrigation branch of the Indian Service of Engineers were to be filled in the same manner as vacancies in the Indian Civil Service, 20 per cent by promotion from the Provincial Service, and the remainder by recruitment of Indians and Europeans in equal numbers.

Taking these recommendations as a whole, they went far toward meeting the demand for an increasing association of Indians in every branch of administration and also the demand for the progressive realization of responsible government, but they were not very palatable to the British members of the Services. In order, therefore, to prevent a wholesale resignation of officials and a cessation of European recruitment for the future it was necessary to balance the report by making a few concessions to the other side. Detailed proposals were made to improve the financial conditions of the Services and to safeguard the tenure of office and the opportunities for pro-

9. Officers promoted from the Provincial Service were still eligible only for "listed posts," which meant that they would usually become district and session judges. There was also a tendency for Indian recruits to go into the judicial branch of the Service.

motion. The scale of salaries had been increased in 1919, but not nearly enough to cover the rise in the cost of living. The fall in the exchange value of the rupee from *2s.* in 1919 to about *1s. 4d.* in 1924 also meant a decline of about one third of that portion of the European official's salary which he remitted to England for investment or for the maintenance and education of his family.

The fundamental problem which the commission had to face was that of paying enough to attract European recruits of the right stamp without imposing a heavy burden on the taxpayers of India by increasing the emoluments of Indian officials who were already paid more than their market value. The old solution of the problem was to have the same basic pay for all officials of the same grade, but to supplement it with overseas pay for all officials recruited in England. There was technically no racial discrimination in this arrangement because Indians recruited in England received the same overseas pay. The commission recommended that the basic rates should remain unchanged with the exception of a slight increase in the Indian Police Service which applied equally to both races. There was to be an increase of overseas pay for both British and Indian officers recruited in England, but a British officer could remit his overseas pay to England at the rate of *2s.* to the rupee whereas the Indian officer was denied this privilege unless he actually had a wife or children living in Europe. There was also a proposal that every officer of non-Asiatic domicile should receive during his normal term of service four return passages for himself and his wife and one child. This privilege was to be extended to Indian officers of the Indian Civil Service recruited in England, but not to their families.

The rights and privileges of the All-India Services were to remain inviolate. Their position was guaranteed by the Government of India Act and by statutory rules which could be changed only with the consent of a majority of the Council of India. They could be dismissed from the Service only by the Secretary of State in Council and, if they had any serious grievance, they could always appeal to the Governor-General in Council or to the Secretary of State in Council. Their salaries, pensions, and other emoluments were not subject to the vote of any Indian legislature. Officers serving in the Reserved field could retire on proportionate pensions if the department in which they were employed was transferred to ministerial control, provided the option was exercised within one year after the transfer was effected.[10] The commission also recommended the establishment of a Central Public Service Commission, but it was not to have very much control over the All-India Services or the members of the Central Services recruited in Great Britain.

A resolution embodying the principles of the Lee Report was introduced into the Legislative Assembly in September, 1924. It was bitterly criticized by the Indian members and an amendment virtually rejecting it was adopted by a vote of 68 to 46. The amendment declared that the Report sanctioned racial discrimination and that it was based on the illogical assumption that a reformed constitution could be operated with an unreformed administrative system. There was a demand for the complete cessation of recruitment in England, for a transfer of the control of the Services from the Secretary of State in Council to the government of India and the provincial governments under laws enacted by the Indian legislatures, and for the control by the Indian legislature of the new Public Service Commission. The British government and the government of India were convinced, however, that the recommendations of the Report were salutary and they were gradually put into operation. The result was an improvement in British recruitment as compared with the years from 1920 to 1924, a decrease in the number of British officials who retired prematurely, and a considerable increase in the Indianization of the Services.

The future of the Services was carefully considered by the Simon Commission. Its general recommendation that dyarchy should be abolished and all of the provincial departments brought under ministerial control will be discussed in a later chapter. On the assumption that this recommendation would be adopted, the commission reconsidered both the prob-

10. Officers who entered the Service before January 1, 1920, already had this privilege. The commission recommended that it should now be extended to those who had entered after that date.

lem of British recruitment and the problem of safeguarding the interests of British officials who were already in the Services. The principle laid down by the Lee Commission that officials in the Transferred Departments should be recruited in the province itself will be harder to enforce when all the departments are Transferred. The task of the Simon Commission, therefore, was more difficult than that of the Lee Commission and it was compelled to make more exceptions to the principle of local recruitment. It approved the one exception made on the advice of the Lee Commission and proposed that no change should be made in the present Devolution Rule "which gives the Secretary of State in Council power to prescribe the number of Indian Medical Service officers to be employed in the provinces." It also proposed that the Security Services should continue to be recruited by the Secretary of State and that the existing rule of Indianization should be maintained until the 50–50 basis is reached in the Indian Civil Service about 1939 and in the Indian Police Service about 1949. In the case of the other two All-India Services which are now being recruited by the Secretary of State—the Irrigation branch of the Indian Service of Engineers and the Indian Forest Service (except in Bombay and Burma)—it made no positive recommendation, but it showed how desirable it was that a European element should be retained and it urged the authorities in India to give the question the most careful consideration in the light of the general scheme of constitutional reform which was being put forward.

In dealing with the other problem mentioned above, the commission was very much influenced by what happened after the Montagu-Chelmsford Reforms were put into operation. The next few years are going to be very critical in India and it will be disastrous if there is a wholesale resignation of European officials or a stoppage of European recruitment.

It is essential for the success of the constitutional advances which we have recommended that the existing members of the All-India Services should remain in the service, and that their rights and privileges should be safeguarded. . . . We see no reason why a career in the services should not under the new constitution provide ample interest and opportunity for men of brains and character. But we cannot ensure this; and it would be idle to shut our eyes to the lesson of the years succeeding the reforms of 1920, when uncertainty about the future of the services led to the retirement of a large number of valuable officers.

The commission, therefore, recommended that there should be no change in the position of existing members of the All-India Services and "that retirement on proportionate pension should remain open without limit of time to any officer who might under the present rules have so retired upon the coming into force of the constitutional changes which we have proposed."[11] This is a valuable suggestion. If an official who is dubious about the future is told that the option of retiring on proportionate pension will expire within a year, he is likely to retire, but if he knows that he can get out at any time without a financial sacrifice, he will probably hold on and give the new experiment a fair trial.

The Indianization of the Civil Services may result in a loss of efficiency, but, if the transition in the Security branches is not too rapid, it should not lead to anarchy or the separation of India from the Empire. The demand for the Indianization of the army, however, raises a much more serious issue. The fallacy of comparing India's military problems with those of the self-governing Dominions is exposed by the authors of *The Simon Report*. None of the Dominions is compelled to maintain a large military force in time of peace as a measure of insurance against invasion and internal disorder. None of them has hungry neighbors who are always on the lookout for plunder, or rival religious communities who are in the habit of settling their disputes by an appeal to force. They are all subject to more or less remote dangers, but in a crisis they would be protected by the British Navy until they could mobilize their own resources. India also enjoys this protection and, like the Dominions, she gets it for practically nothing, but her crises

11. *Report of the Indian Statutory Commission,* Vol. II, pars. 327–340. The commission also recommended the establishment of Provincial Public Service Commissions covering the Provincial and Subordinate Services in all the provinces. There was already a Provincial Commission in Madras, established in 1929.

are numerous and imminent and they are not easily susceptible to naval treatment. The tribes of the North-West Frontier are a constant source of danger and back of them is a large area where Russian intrigue is probably more active than it was in the days of the old regime. There are likewise communal riots almost every year on so large a scale that the police cannot suppress them without military assistance.

These arguments are conclusive. The financial problem may be difficult and the constitutional problem may be even more difficult, but India must have an efficient army or she will be destroyed. The Nationalists are compelled to admit that this is true, but they contend that the army should be smaller and less expensive and that it should be completely Indianized at the earliest possible moment. It has been "artificially enlarged with a view to making some portion of it available for service elsewhere, or for the purpose of keeping on Indian soil a reserve not needed in India at the expense of the Indian taxpayer." The Imperial government asked for Indian troops, to be used outside of India, during the South African War, the Great War, the troubles in China in 1927, and on many other occasions. "Since India has been able, in response to such appeals, to land troops for service abroad, it follows that the troops assembled in India . . . are in excess of India's own needs." The Simon Commission summarizes this argument and pronounces it fallacious. The strength of the army is determined entirely by the necessity of protecting the country against internal disorder and external aggression. "The extent of the demands actually made upon it for these purposes naturally varies from time to time, but it has to be ready for the strain whenever the strain comes."

There are three main problems connected with the demand for the Indianization of the army. The first is concerned with the higher command and the ultimate political control, whether it should be exercised by His Majesty's government or by an Indian Ministry responsible to an elected legislature. The second has to do with the rank and file of the army, the relative numbers of British and Indian troops and their distribution among the various branches of the service. The third deals with the personnel of the regimental officers of the Indian

Army. As Indianization involves the elimination of the British, these problems may all be approached from the other end. *The Simon Report* does this and comes to the conclusion that "for a very long time to come, it will be impossible for the Army entrusted with the task of defending India to dispense with a very considerable British element, including in that term British troops of all arms, a considerable proportion of the regimental officers of the Indian Army, and the British personnel in the higher command." The British element is necessary to defend the frontier, to maintain internal security and to discharge the obligations of the Crown to the rulers of the Indian States.

When the Report was written (1930) there was no Indian holding the King's commission of higher rank than captain and only 25 out of 39 captains in ordinary regimental employment. Most of these had been promoted from the ranks and several had nearly reached the age of retirement.

> A Higher Command cannot be evolved at short notice out of the existing cadres of Indian officers, all of junior rank and limited experience. Not until the slender trickle of suitable Indian recruits for the officer class . . . flows in much greater volume, not until sufficient Indians have attained the experience and training requisite to provide all the officers for, at any rate, some Indian regiments, not until such units have stood the only test which can possibly determine their efficiency, and not until Indian officers have qualified by a successful army career for high command, will it be possible to develop the policy of Indianisation to a point which will bring a completely Indianised Army within sight. Even then, years must elapse before the process could be complete.

At this point the authors of the Report frankly admit that there is a dilemma. The goal of British policy in India, as announced in the famous declaration of August 20, 1917, is the attainment of responsible government. This may not mean Dominion Home Rule—there has been much ink spilled over that issue—but it certainly implies that the Military Department, in common with other departments, will ultimately be under the control of a Minister responsible to an elected legislature. Southern Rhodesia, though not a full-fledged dominion, would protest as loudly as Canada, Australia, or the Union of South Africa if she were called upon to support a British Army which she could not control and which she felt she did not need. The Report, however, assumes that the British element will be retained and that "it is impossible to relinquish control over an Army containing this element to Ministers responsible to any elected Legislature." It does not seem to be a very logical solution of the problem to suggest "that the protection of the frontiers of India, at any rate for a long time to come, should not be regarded as a function of an Indian Government in relation with an Indian Legislature, but as a matter of supreme concern to the whole Empire which can only be effectively organised and controlled by an Imperial agency." There is sure to be a proposal that the burden of finance should be readjusted, but the Indian contribution would remain nonvotable. The Provincial Governors, who would presumably still be British, would also have the power to request the use of British troops when they were needed to suppress internal disorders.

There are about 60,000 British and 150,000 Indian troops (as well as 42,500 reservists) in the army at the present time. They are divided into three categories: (a) Covering Troops, who deal with minor frontier outbreaks; (b) Internal Security Troops, who help the police maintain law and order; and (c) the Field Army, which occasionally assists the other two, but is intended mainly to be used as a striking force in time of war. A large majority of the Covering Troops are Indian, but the British predominate in the Internal Security force in the proportion of about 8 to 7. In the separate branches of the Service, the British practically monopolize the Air Force, the Tank Corps, the Armored Car Companies, the Royal Horse Artillery, the Field Artillery, and the Medium Artillery. The Nationalists object to the retention of so large a British element, partly because it offends their national pride and partly because it is very expensive. The financial aspect of the problem is discussed in the chapter on "Economic and Financial Grievances." Here it will be sufficient to say that a British soldier costs nearly four times as much as an Indian soldier and that India spends 54 per cent of her central revenues on defense. The Nationalists also feel that it is a reflection on the patriotism of Indian troops to exclude them from those branches of the service that are most important in modern warfare.

The officers in the Indian Army are divided into two classes according to whether they hold the King's commission or the Viceroy's commission. The latter are all Indians or Gurkhas, mostly promoted from the ranks, and they have a limited status and power of command. Whatever their experience and length of service, they are subordinate in rank and command to the most recently arrived British subaltern. Indians were not eligible to hold the King's commission until 1918 and there are still two restrictions imposed upon them which are very unpopular in Nationalist circles. With rare exceptions, they are employed only in the infantry and cavalry and they are segregated in accordance with the "eight-units scheme" promulgated by Lord Rawlinson, the Commander in Chief of the army in India, in 1923. Under this scheme, all Indian officers holding the King's commission are posted to five selected infantry battalions, two cavalry regiments, and one pioneer battalion. These units are now under senior British officers, but, if the system continues in operation, they should be completely Indianized by about 1946. It might perhaps be added that eight units is only a small fraction of the regular Indian Army, which has 104 infantry battalions, 21 cavalry battalions, and 7 pioneer battalions.

The first Indians to receive the King's commission were for the most part officers who already held the Viceroy's commission and noncommissioned officers who were selected for promotion. Men of this type often have good service records and are very capable in their special fields, but they are comparatively uneducated and are not likely to succeed in posts that require a greater assumption of responsibility. They are apt to be too old for further promotion when they receive the King's commission. It was necessary, therefore, to devise an alternative method of recruitment and this was done shortly after the conclusion of the war. Until 1931, ten vacancies were reserved for Indian cadets at the Royal Military College at Sandhurst, and the Prince of Wales' Royal Military Institute was established at Dehra Dun in 1922 to train boys for the Sandhurst examinations. This was the chief source of direct recruitment until the first batch of officers passed out of the new Military Academy at Dehra Dun and received their commissions in 1935.

The recruitment problem is not confined to India, but it has some features which are peculiar to that country, owing to the contrast between the so-called "martial" and "nonmartial" races. In 1930, the Punjab and the Punjab States furnished about 54 per cent of the combatant troops in the Indian Army and nearly all of the remainder came from Nepal, which is outside of India, the United Provinces, Bombay, the Rajputana Agency, Kashmir, and the North-West Frontier Province. There were none at all furnished by Bengal and Assam, only 100 by the Central Provinces, and 300 by Bihar and Orissa. It is sometimes said that this is due to discrimination on the part of the army authorities, but during the war, when the authorities were glad to get men from any source, Bengal, with a population of 45,000,000, provided only 7,117 combatant troops, while the Punjab, with a population of 20,000,000, provided 249,688.[12] The people of the "martial" area make excellent soldiers, but they do not have an educational tradition and are not as a rule very clever students. They would not be able to compete with Bengalis and Chitpavan Brahmans in the classroom of a military academy or in an open competitive examination. If the army is ever completely Indianized, therefore, and promotion from the ranks is given up, the officers will either be drawn from the "nonmartial" classes or there will have to be some form of racial discrimination.

The process of Indianization was too slow to satisfy the Nationalists and, as already stated, they were strongly opposed to the "eight-units scheme" and to the exclusion of the King's Indian officers from the Air, Tank, Signal, Artillery, and

12. The heavy recruitment in the Punjab was partly due to pressure brought to bear by Lieutenant-Governor Sir Michael O'Dwyer, but, if this were discounted, the figures would still be very onesided.

Engineer arms of the Service. They were especially anxious that the Institute at Dehra Dun should be enlarged and converted into an Indian Sandhurst which would graduate enough cadets to Indianize the army completely in fifty years. As the result of a debate in the Legislative Assembly in 1925, the government of India appointed a committee, commonly known as the "Indian Sandhurst Committee," to investigate the means of increasing the number and improving the quality of Indian candidates for the King's commission. Major-General Sir Andrew Skeen, who was at that time Chief of Staff of the army in India, was selected as chairman and there were eleven other members, all Indians except the Secretary of the Army Department. The committee presented a unanimous Report in November, 1926. It recommended (1) that the annual vacancies reserved for Indian cadets at Sandhurst should be doubled and that there should be a further progressive increase until 1933, (2) that a Military College on the lines of Sandhurst should be established in India in 1933, (3) that an Indianization timetable should be adopted under which one half of the officers in the Indian Army would be Indians by 1952, and (4) that the Rawlinson "eight-units scheme" should be abandoned and Indian officers allowed to serve by the side of British officers in every unit of the Indian Army.

These recommendations were unpopular with the military authorities and, after a prolonged effort, they were able to impose their views on His Majesty's government and the government of India. The official decision was held up for more than fifteen months, but was finally announced in March, 1928. The plan for an Indian Sandhurst, the timetable of Indianization, and the proposal to abandon the "eight-units scheme" were all rejected. It was agreed, however, that the number of direct vacancies reserved for Indian cadets at Sandhurst should be increased from 10 to 20 a year and that from 5 to 10 vacancies should be reserved for Indian officers holding the Viceroy's commission. A few vacancies were also to be open at Woolwich and Cranwell to train Indian cadets for the Artillery, Engineers, and Air Services. To meet the objection that a military education in England involves extra expense, as compared with one in India, the government proposed that grants should be made from the army funds to cover the additional outlay.[13]

When General Sir William Birdwood, the Commander in Chief of the army in India, announced the decision of the government in the Legislative Assembly on March 8, 1928, his speech was bitterly criticized by the Indian members and a motion to adjourn was made by Mr. M. A. Jinnah to express disapproval of the government for repudiating the Report of the Sandhurst Committee. Mr. Jinnah asserted that the decision was not really based on the Report at all, but had been reached by the military experts before the committee had finished its work. The motion was carried by a vote of 70 to 41, the Punjab Moslems and other friends of the government voting with the majority. The government was also censured during the debate on the military budget in March, 1929, mainly on the ground that the Indianization of the army was proceeding too slowly.

The Simon Commission held that the chief function of the army is the defense of India against external aggression. As this is largely an Imperial problem, it recommended that the control of military affairs should be transferred from the government of India to the government of the United Kingdom. His Majesty's government would continue to be represented in India by the Viceroy and the day-by-day work of administration would remain in the hands of the Commander in Chief, but he would cease to hold a portfolio in the government of India and to be a member of the Indian legislature. There

13. According to the Report of the Simon Commission, the Indian Sandhurst proposal was not definitely rejected. The government merely pointed out that it would be premature to fix 1933 as the year of opening, since that would depend on the use made of the increased facilities provided at Sandhurst. There is a statement in the Report showing the actual numbers of Indian and Anglo-Indian cadets admitted to Sandhurst since 1918 and to Woolwich and Cranwell since they became eligible in 1928. During 1928 and 1929, out of nine vacancies offered at Woolwich only two were filled and out of twelve offered at Cranwell only six were filled. The direct quota was filled at Sandhurst in 1929, but only three Viceroy's commissioned officers were nominated in 1928 and 1929.

would be a Legislative Committee on Army Affairs, on which the Indian States might in time have representatives, for the purpose of discussing and keeping informed about military questions. The appropriations would remain nonvotable and would be authorized by the Governor-General under his power of certification. The British element would remain in the army "for a very long time to come," but Indianization would "go forward steadfastly and sympathetically, subject only to the over-riding requirement of military efficiency."

The adoption of this policy would involve some very serious difficulties. The proposal to transfer the control of the army to His Majesty's government might be accepted, if the British would bear the major part of the financial burden, but that is a very unlikely contingency. The problem of Indianization is even more difficult. In a few years Indian officers will begin to qualify for promotion to the higher branches of the service. If they are promoted, the higher command will be partially Indianized; if they are not promoted because of "the over-riding requirement of military efficiency," a flood of racial bitterness will be released. In the former case, either the unity of the army will be maintained, with British officers and possibly British troops occasionally serving under Indian officers, or there will have to be two entirely separate armies. The latter alternative would be more in harmony with British psychology and it would probably be better for India. Some day the British element will have to be withdrawn and there will be less chance of anarchy if there is a well-trained Indian Army to take its place. This was evidently the opinion of the commission because it suggested that the government of India, in cooperation with the Indian legislature, might organize a military force which would be under its control and would be composed entirely of Indians. There would then be an Imperial Army, composed of British and Indian troops, with a British high command, British officers in the British regimental units, and British and Indian officers in the Indian units; and a National Army that would be exclusively Indian. The Imperial Army would be responsible for external defense and the National Army for internal order, but each would assist the other in emergencies. One difficulty about this arrangement is that while Indian troops are effective in frontier warfare, their communal affiliations tend to disqualify them from dealing with Hindu-Moslem riots. Another difficulty is that the contribution to the support of the Imperial Army and the demands of the civil administration would seriously restrict the funds available for an additional military force. This might be met by withdrawing the British troops gradually and using the funds thus released for the support of the National Army.

Since 1930 the British authorities have followed the cautious policy laid down in *The Simon Report* and have refused to fix a definite rate of Indianization or a date within which the process must be completed. At the first session of the Round Table Conference in London a Subcommittee on Defense was appointed with Mr. J. H. Thomas as chairman. In its Report, January 16, 1931, it recommended that the rate of Indianization should be accelerated, that a military training college should be established as soon as possible in India and that the government of India should set up a committee of British and Indian experts to work out the details of such a college.

This was the genesis of the Indian Military College Committee, appointed by the government of India, May 23, 1931. General Sir Philip Chetwode, the new Commander in Chief of the Indian Army, was chairman, but most of the other members were Indians, including a small representation from the Indian States. The majority of the committee favored Dehra Dun as the site of the college and recommended (July 15, 1931) that it should be established, if possible, not later than the autumn of 1932. Eighty cadets were to be admitted annually, 20 from the states for service in the state forces and 60 from British India for service in the regular army. There was considerable friction among the Indian members over the method of filling these vacancies, especially those allotted to British India. The origin of the conflict has already been explained. The so-called martial classes would prefer to have the majority of the cadets promoted from the ranks or nominated by the Commander in Chief without too much emphasis on intellectual requirements, while the nonmartial classes are inclined to insist upon competitive examinations. The committee worked out a compromise, but as the British members were in sympathy with the martial group, the decision, on the whole, was in their favor. Of the 60 cadets allotted to British India, 30 were to be chosen from the ranks, 24 appointed on a competitive basis, and 6 nominated by the Commander in Chief from those who had qualified at the entrance examinations, but had failed to secure a place in open competition. The majority of the committee also recommended that after the opening of the college, Indian cadets should no longer be admitted to Sandhurst and Woolwich. They were, however, to continue to go to Cranwell because "the cost of establishing a Flying Training School in India under present conditions would be prohibitive." Most of these recommendations were adopted by the government of India and the college was formally opened at Dehra Dun on December 10, 1932.

The army will probably be maintained in substantially its present form for many years to come. The progress of Indianization will be slow and there will be no immediate departure from the principle of segregation. Sir Philip Chetwode made this clear when he informed the Military College Committee that the government of India had decided (a) to limit to 60 cadets the annual intake of the college from British India, (b) to eliminate gradually from the Indianized units all officers who held the Viceroy's commission, and (c) to extend the scheme of Indianization to a complete division of the army with all of its auxiliary services. It was estimated that about 53 of the 60 cadets who entered each year would complete the course. If Indianization means anything, most of these 53 men should replace British officers, but under the new plan more than half of them during the first few years would merely take the place of other Indian officers who held the Viceroy's commission.[14]

The decision to Indianize an entire division of the army is liberal from the quantitative point of view, but it has been

14. A battalion in the Indian Army normally has 12 King's commissioned and 18 or 19 Viceroy's commissioned officers. This means that while 12 graduates from the college would have been sufficient to Indianize a unit under the old plan, at least 30 will now be required.

seriously criticized in India because it perpetuates the policy of segregation. It will take many years to complete the process and in the meantime nothing will be done in other parts of the army. As each division is a complete and self-supporting unit, a few Indian officers will have to be admitted to the Engineers, the Artillery, and other special branches of the Service, but the refusal to establish a Flying School means that they will practically be excluded from the service that promises to be most important in future warfare.

This is not an ideal solution, but it is probably the only one that is practical in the condition that now exists. The political intelligentsia should welcome it because, under the new Constitution, they will govern India as long as the British military element is there to protect them. If the army is ever completely Indianized, the martial classes will take charge of affairs and either establish a military despotism or plunge the country into anarchy. The leaders of the south and east are perhaps justified in trying to broaden the field of recruitment for the men as well as the officers of the army, but it is not likely that they can do much along that line to save themselves from the fighting people of the Punjab, the North-West Frontier, the Rajputana States, and the western part of the United Provinces.

CHAPTER VIII

POLITICAL GRIEVANCES: PERSONAL LIBERTY

WE come now to another set of grievances which are closely related and may be treated as a single group, namely, the restrictions upon personal liberty, freedom of speech, and freedom of the press. Some of these restrictions date back to the early days of Company rule, but their history practically begins with the troubles in Bengal and the Punjab in 1907. The most stringent of the earlier encroachments on personal liberty and freedom of speech were those embodied in Bengal Regulation III of 1818, Madras Regulation II of 1819, and Bombay Regulation XXV of 1827, which were later supplemented by the States Prisoners Acts of 1850 and 1858. In each of the three presidencies a *lettre-de-cachet* system was established which could be used in an emergency to imprison or deport, without trial, any person who the government felt was likely to give trouble. These powers had not been used for many years and were generally supposed to be obsolete when Bengal Regulation III of 1818 was revived by Lord Morley for the deportation of Lala Lajpat Rai and Mr. Ajit Singh in 1907 and Mr. Pulim Behari Das in 1908. There are many people in England who believe that, if this example had been more freely followed, the present difficulties in India might have been avoided.

As the Nationalist movement became more revolutionary, a new series of restrictive measures was enacted, including the Prevention of Seditious Meetings Acts of 1907 and 1911, the Explosive Substances Act of 1908, and the Indian Criminal Law Amendment Acts of 1908 and 1913. The Prevention of Seditious Meetings Act of 1907 made it possible for a provincial government to issue a proclamation declaring that a certain district or group of districts constituted a "proclaimed area," in which no meeting could be held for the discussion of a political subject or of any subject likely to cause a disturbance or arouse public excitement, unless three days' notice was given to the police or permission to hold the meeting was obtained. The district collector and magistrate could forbid any meeting which he thought might tend to promote sedition or to cause a public disturbance. This act was considered a temporary measure to meet the emergency then existing in Bengal and the Punjab, but it was reënacted in a slightly milder form and made permanent by the Seditious Meetings Act of 1911. Under the Explosive Substances Act of 1908, any person who caused an explosion likely to endanger life or property or attempted to cause such an explosion or made or had in his possession any explosive substance with intent to endanger life or property was liable to punishment. The manufacture or possession of an explosive substance for other than a lawful object was declared to be a substantive offense.

The Criminal Law Amendment Act of 1908 had two parts. The first provided a special procedure for the speedy trial of criminal conspiracies against the state and of other crimes mentioned in the accompanying schedule. This procedure was to be used only in cases of the most serious character and only with the sanction of the Governor-General in Council. The magistrate could make ex parte inquiries and evidence could be taken *in camera* in the absence of the accused. The final trial would be held before a special bench of the High Court judges without a jury. The second part of the act declared unlawful all associations which encouraged or assisted persons to commit acts of violence or intimidation and empowered the Governor-General in Council to declare any association to be unlawful that he regarded as dangerous to the public peace. Penalties were provided for the punishment of the members and the managers of an unlawful association and of all persons who contributed to its support. The Criminal Law Amendment Act of 1913, which grew out of the attempt to assassinate Lord Hardinge in December, 1912, amended the law of conspiracy so as to make it penal to conspire to commit an offense even though the conspiracy was not accompanied by any overt act.

These laws were all in force when the war began and they were soon supplemented by the Foreigners Ordinance, 1914, the Ingress into India Ordinance, 1914, and most important of all, the Defense of India Act, 1915. The Defense of India Act and the rules made for its interpretation and enforcement constitute the Indian equivalent for the Defense of the Realm Act in the United Kingdom. The government was, for example, empowered to exclude individuals from certain localities and to confine or intern them in others, to create new offenses, to set up special tribunals for the trial of revolutionary crimes and to exclude newspapers from certain provinces. These powers were used extensively in the Punjab in connection with the uprising of 1915 and in Bengal after the murder of Deputy Superintendent of Police Basanta Chatarji, in 1916.

The measures adopted by Sir Michael O'Dwyer, Lieutenant-Governor of the Punjab, were exceptionally severe. As a result of a series of trials conducted at Lahore in 1915 by special tribunals under the Defense of India Act, 28 persons were hanged and several hundred were sentenced to transportation or imprisonment. Under the Ingress into India Ordinance, 331 emigrant revolutionaries connected with the Ghadr conspiracy were interned between October, 1914, and December, 1917, and 2,576 were not allowed to leave their villages. The vernacular press was gagged and public meetings were held only under the most rigid supervision. Two of the Nationalist leaders, Mr. B. G. Tilak and Mr. Bepin Chandra Pal, who wished to go on a lecturing tour to spread Home Rule propaganda, were forbidden to enter the province. The more important Nationalist newspapers, published outside the province, such as *New India*, the *Amrita Bazar Patrika*, and the *Independent*, were also excluded.[1]

The number of persons interned and otherwise restricted during the war period was summarized by Mr. Montagu in answer to a question in the House of Commons on October 22, 1919. He reported that 149 persons had been interned under Bengal Regulation III of 1818, of whom 35 had been released before the Armistice and 25 afterwards. Under Madras Regu-

1. *Sedition Committee (Rowlatt) Report,* chap. xi; *Report of the Commission Appointed by the Punjab Subcommittee of the Indian National Congress.* Vol. I, *The Report,* chap. ii.

lation II of 1819, 12 had been interned, of whom 10 had been released before the Armistice and one afterwards. Under Bombay Regulation XXV of 1827, 6 had been interned, of whom 4 had been released. Under the Defense of India Act, 1915, 1,490 had been restricted in domicile and 310 (including 3 of the former category) had been subjected to minor restrictions, of whom 601 had been released before the Armistice, and 357 afterwards. Under the Ingress into India Ordinance, 1914, 942 had been restricted in domicile and 2,154 placed under minor restrictions, of whom 2,296 had been released before the Armistice and 466 afterwards. Three of the 942 were subsequently interned under Bengal Regulation III of 1818. The total number subjected to any restrictions under these acts was at that time (October 22, 1919) 1,257, of whom 91 were actively interned.[2]

The most famous cases of infringement of personal liberty during the war and the period immediately following the Armistice were those of two English radicals who sympathized with the Home Rule movement. Mrs. Annie Besant was interned by the government of Madras at the southern hill station of Ootacamund on June 16, 1917. This greatly increased her popularity and she was in consequence chosen President of the Indian National Congress. Through the intervention of the Secretary of State, she was released in time to preside at the annual meeting at Calcutta in December. The other case was that of Mr. B. G. Horniman, editor of the *Bombay Chronicle,* who was deported to England by the government of Bombay in April, 1919, under the authority of the Defense of India Act. The reasons given for his deportation were (1) that in the midst of riots resulting in loss of life he used his paper to spread and fan the flames of rebellion, (2) that he opened the columns of his paper to an accusation that British soldiers used soft-nosed bullets in the streets of Delhi, and (3) that his paper was distributed free among British troops in Bombay in the hope of exciting them to insubordination and disaffection.[3]

The Defense of India Act was passed for the duration of the

2. *Parliamentary Debates* (*Commons*) (5th ser.), CXX, 52–53.
3. *Ibid.,* 128, 593.

war and for six months afterwards. Believing that there would be a general recrudescence of political crime when it expired, the government of India began, as early as 1917, to consider the question of the permanent reorganization of the administration of the criminal law. The first step was the appointment of the so-called Rowlatt Committee to investigate the history of revolutionary conspiracies in British India and advise the government how to deal with them in the future. The Rowlatt Act, which was the chief result of their labors, was passed on March 18, 1919. Although this act was on the statute book for only three years and was never actually enforced, it aroused tremendous opposition, and its permanent influence will probably be greater than that of any other measure ever enacted by the government of India.

Mr. Gandhi's public career in India practically began with his opposition to this law, which he fought with *satyagraha*. Two weapons were employed, a pledge binding those who signed it to refuse obedience to the Rowlatt Act and "such other laws as a committee to be hereafter appointed" might think fit, and a general *hartal* or day of mourning to be observed throughout the whole of India. Everybody was urged to "follow truth and refrain from violence to life, person or property." It was intended that the hartal should be held on March 30, but at the last minute Gandhi changed the date to April 6, with the result that both days were observed in Amritsar and a few other places. The leaders in Amritsar were Dr. Satyapal, a Hindu physician, and Dr. Kitchlew, a Moslem barrister. At their suggestion, a third celebration was held on the 9th, when the Hindu festival of *Ram Navami* (Rama's Birthday) was turned into a demonstration of Hindu-Moslem unity.

There was very little violence at any of these meetings, but it was obvious that the people of Amritsar and the Punjab in general were becoming dangerously excited and that the government would have to take some steps to maintain its prestige. On the evening of the 9th, Mr. Gandhi was arrested on his way from Bombay to Delhi and sent back to Bombay, and early on the following morning, Dr. Satyapal and Dr. Kitchlew were removed from Amritsar and interned at Dharamsala. What happened after that is a subject of controversy. A large crowd immediately gathered in Amritsar and started for the bungalow of Mr. Miles Irving, the deputy commissioner of the district. Their motives may have been peaceful, but they were certainly in an angry mood and Mr. Irving felt that it was his duty to keep them out of the civil lines or the European quarter. The most direct route from the city to the civil lines is that which passes through the Hall Gate and crosses a bridge over the railway near the station. A small picket was stationed at this bridge with orders not to let the mob pass. The soldiers behaved with great forbearance, but were finally compelled to fire and there were several casualties. This increased the wrath of the mob and they rushed back into the city, bent on death and destruction. Five Europeans were murdered with fiendish brutality and Miss Sherwood, an elderly English missionary, was dragged from her bicycle, beaten until she was insensible and left in the street to die. She was picked up later by some friendly Hindus and her life was saved. Two European banks were looted and the town hall, the telegraph office, the Indian Christian Church, and several other buildings were burned.

The situation soon got beyond the control of the civil authorities, troops were sent in from the neighboring cantonments and Brigadier-General R. E. H. Dyer, C.B., assumed responsibility for the maintenance of law and order. On the morning of the 13th, General Dyer issued a proclamation which stated, among other things, that "any gathering of four men would be looked upon and treated as an unlawful assembly and dispersed by force of arms if necessary." The proclamation was ignored[4] and at four o'clock in the afternoon a mob of several thousand people collected in the Jallianwala Bagh, a rectangular open space surrounded by houses and walls which was commonly used as a place of public meeting. General Dyer went to the Bagh with a small contingent of Indian troops and opened fire without warning. The fusillade lasted

4. The contention made later by the Congress party that the people were ignorant of the proclamation is rather specious. It was well advertised and news travels rapidly in an oriental city, especially in times of excitement.

for about ten minutes until the ammunition was exhausted. The General then ordered the troops back to their quarters and made no effort to succor the wounded. There were several hundred people killed and about a thousand injured.[5]

This episode happened under the civil administration, although General Dyer acted entirely on his own responsibility. There were similar troubles on a smaller scale in other parts of the Punjab and martial law was proclaimed in the districts of Amritsar, Lahore, Gujranwala, Gujarat, and Lyallpur between the 15th and the 24th of April. The military regime was in force for an average period of about seven weeks and it aroused a great deal of bitterness. The Indians believed that it should not have been proclaimed at all, and that, in any case, it was unduly prolonged and very badly administered. On the first two points a good argument could be made in favor of the government, but the third complaint was well founded. The only object in establishing martial law should have been the maintenance of law and order with a minimum amount of friction. It certainly should not have been used to crush ordinary political opposition and to humiliate the people.

It would take too much space to describe the various summary tribunals that were created, but it should be noted that their penalties were heavy and that they frequently dealt with offenses committed before the proclamation of martial law. The most intense irritation was caused by the extensive use of whipping and other humiliating punishments. There were numerous cases of the imposition of capricious penalties. Some schoolboys had taken part in the riots at Kasur, but it was impossible to establish their identity. The six largest boys in the school were, therefore, seized and flogged, without regard to whether they were innocent or guilty. About 1,000 college students at Lahore were required to attend roll call four times a day at a place which made it necessary for most of them to walk sixteen miles daily during one of the hottest months of the year. There were various orders specifying exactly how an

5. According to the Majority Report of the Hunter Committee, there were 379 killed. The Report of the committee appointed by the Indian National Congress says that the exact figures will never be known, but that there were about 1,000 major casualties.

Indian must salute a European civil or military officer. One of these orders provided that if the Indian was riding or driving he must alight and if he was carrying an open umbrella he must close it before the salute was delivered.

Bad as these blunders were, they were surpassed by General Dyer's notorious "crawling order" issued at Amritsar on April 19. This was to the effect that any Indian who passed through the street in which Miss Sherwood had been attacked must go on all fours. Pickets were stationed at certain points along the street to see that the order was enforced. According to the testimony given by some of the victims, going on all fours was interpreted to mean crawling on the belly like a snake. The street is long and narrow and many of the houses have no back entrances. It is doubtful whether any of the mob who attacked Miss Sherwood lived on this street and, even if they did, they must have constituted only a small proportion of its total population. People were sometimes brought there against their will. Twelve persons, for example, who were arrested by the police on April 19 for being insolent, were taken that way to the police station and compelled to crawl. The government of the Punjab expressed its disapproval of this order and it was withdrawn on April 26. During the eight days that it was in force there were altogether about fifty victims.

These events[6] occurred while the Montagu-Chelmsford Reforms were under consideration and greatly increased the difficulties of Mr. Montagu. There was a danger that the Tory element in Parliament, if they fully realized the serious character of the disturbances, would balk at conferring so much power and responsibility upon the people of India. On the other hand, if the news was garbled or suppressed and no action taken at all, the success of the Reforms would be endangered in India. Popular feeling there was running high and there was an insistent demand for the punishment of General Dyer and others who were responsible for what was regarded as the national humiliation of the Indian people. Mr. Montagu handled the situation skilfully. The news from India was cen-

6. There were also some bad riots at this time in Delhi and Bombay, but they were handled by the civil authorities and did not leave such a terrible legacy of hatred.

sored and the significance of what was happening in the Punjab was minimized until Parliament was definitely committed to the Reform policy. In the meantime, Mr. Montagu, in consultation with the government of India, had taken the preliminary steps for the holding of an official investigation.

The Disorders Inquiry Committee, commonly known as the Hunter Committee, was appointed by the Governor-General in Council on October 14, 1919. The committee divided on racial lines and on March 8, 1920, presented a Majority Report signed by Lord Hunter and the other four British members and a Minority Report signed by the three Indian members. There was also a third Report prepared by a board of five (later four) commissioners, including Mr. Gandhi, appointed November 14, 1919, by the Punjab Subcommittee of the Indian National Congress. Their Report was signed February 20, 1920. Of these three accounts, the Majority Report of the Hunter Committee was naturally the most conservative and the Report of the Congress Commission the most radical.

The Hunter Committee criticized more or less severely the officers responsible for the administration of martial law, but its chief censure was reserved for General Dyer's conduct at the Jallianwala Bagh. He had fired upon an unarmed mob without warning, he had continued to fire after most of the mob had begun to disperse, and he had failed to make any provision for aiding the wounded and removing the dead. In a case of this kind, the only excuse for firing without notice is the danger that a small force of soldiers may be rushed and overwhelmed by superior numbers. But that was not the deciding factor. General Dyer himself said that his mind was made up before he reached the Bagh: he would fire at once if he found that his orders against holding a meeting had been disobeyed. His answer to the second charge was equally candid. He fired longer than was necessary because he was determined to reduce the morale of the rebels and strike terror throughout the Punjab. This is of course the doctrine of "frightfulness," the doctrine that a soldier in dealing with unruly civilians may go further than the immediate necessity warrants in order to terrorize other people. In reply to the third charge, the General said that it was not his job to take care of the wounded.

The hospitals were open and medical officers were available. If anyone needed help, all that he or his relatives had to do was to ask for it. This explanation does not take the time factor into consideration. It was nearly six o'clock when the firing ceased and it must have taken some time for the survivors to recover sufficiently from their terror and excitement to return and look for relatives and friends. Furthermore, under the terms of the proclamation issued that morning, any person found on the streets after eight o'clock was liable to be shot at sight. There was, however, another more practical excuse which the committee was inclined to accept. The soldiers had exhausted their ammunition and there was a danger that the mob might return and overpower them. The Minority admitted the force of this argument, but they felt that the General might have sent medical aid as soon as he returned to headquarters. The evidence certainly indicates that General Dyer was in no mood to be influenced by humanitarian considerations.

The Report of the commission appointed by the Punjab Subcommittee was full of wrath and bitterness. In addition to a lurid description of the facts, it presented a formal list of conclusions and recommendations. The Rowlatt Act should be repealed; Sir Michael O'Dwyer, General Dyer, Lieutenant-Colonel Johnson, and others should be relieved of all positions of responsibility under the Crown; the Viceroy should be recalled for condoning what had happened in the Punjab; the victims of martial law who were still in jail should be released; and all fines that had been collected under the decrees of special tribunals and military courts should be refunded. The strong feeling shown in this Report against Sir Michael O'Dwyer was also reflected in the Presidential Address delivered by Lala Lajpat Rai at the special session of the National Congress held at Calcutta in September, 1920, to consider the Punjab question and the Turkish Peace Treaty:

From the very moment he took charge of the Province he set before him an ideal of government which was Prussian in conception, Prussian in aim and Prussian in execution. For six long years he occupied himself in working out his ideal and carrying out his plan. Ever since he took charge of the Province the crushing of the political awakening was his principal aim. All through the period of his office he was guided by that ideal.

I charge him with having deliberately intensified the policy of "divide and rule" by keeping apart the Mohammedans from the Hindus and both from the Sikhs. . . . I charge him with having made illegal use of the processes of law and of his authority for recruitment purposes, and for getting contributions for the War Loan and other war funds. I charge him with having deliberately deceived the Government of India as to the necessity of Martial Law. I charge him with having deliberately manipulated the continuance of Martial Law for vindictive and punitive purposes.[7]

The government of India accepted the Hunter Report and, in coöperation with the military authorities, took steps to discipline the officials who were censured. General Dyer was removed from command and informed that he would receive no further employment in India. General Campbell and a few other officers were informed that the Commander in Chief of the Indian Army strongly disapproved of the salaaming orders, the whipping of schoolboys, and other abuses criticized in the Report. Some of the civilian officials were also told that their conduct in certain cases was "regrettable" or "injudicious and improper" and that they had incurred the strong disapproval of the government of India. The sum and substance was that General Dyer was made a scapegoat while everybody else was given a clean bill of health or let off with a slight reprimand. Some of Sir Michael O'Dwyer's acts were mildly criticized, but his general conduct was approved, and he was commended by His Majesty's government for his "energy, decision and courage."

Although General Dyer's punishment was regarded as inadequate in India, there was a large section of the public in England who agreed with Sir Michael O'Dwyer that the action taken at the Jallianwala Bagh "was the decisive factor in crushing the rebellion, the seriousness of which is only now being realized." Appreciating the strength of this sentiment, Mr. Montagu persuaded his colleagues in the cabinet to sanc-

7. *India* (newspaper), October 8, 1920.

tion the policy of the government of India and assume collective responsibility for its enforcement. It is well that he did so. When the crucial debate occurred in the House of Commons, July 8, 1920, there was a formidable revolt among the Tory members of the Coalition and the government was saved only by the support of the Opposition. In view of the conservative attitude that he has adopted later, it is interesting to note that the best speech in defense of the liberal policy was made by Mr. Winston Churchill.

This action was final, but the good effect which it might have been expected to produce in India was partially neutralized by other considerations. The House of Lords voted against the government and there was a great deal said during the debate in both houses which was calculated to arouse strong racial prejudices. The debates were published extensively in India and the European and Indian newspapers were inclined to emphasize the speeches favorable to General Dyer, the former because they approved the General's conduct and the latter because they wished to expose "the Prussian mentality" of the British. Another factor in the situation was the action of the *Morning Post* in raising about £50,000 by popular subscription and presenting it to General Dyer as a token of the regard and gratitude of conservative Britain.

It would be a good thing both for the British and for the Indians if this whole affair and all that it connotes could be wiped from their memories. Unfortunately, just as it was beginning to be forgotten it was dragged back again into public notice as a result of the trial in the case of O'Dwyer *versus* Nair. Sir Sankaran Nair, an Indian Liberal, published a book in 1924 entitled *Gandhi and Anarchy,* in which he severely criticized Gandhi and attempted to show that India under his leadership was drifting into anarchy. He believed that Gandhi would never have acquired his hold upon the popular imagination if it had not been for Sir Michael O'Dwyer's "reactionary" administration in the Punjab. He especially criticized Sir Michael for his support of General Dyer. This led to an action for libel and the case was tried in the King's Bench Division before Mr. Justice McCardie in May–June, 1924. Sir Michael won the suit and the damages were assessed at £500.

In summing up the case for the jury, the Justice defined the legal issue as follows:

> The question for the jury was whether General Dyer acted rightly or wrongly, whether he was guilty of an atrocity or not. Expressing his own opinion, and speaking with full deliberation and knowing the whole of the evidence given in the case, he came to the conclusion that General Dyer, under the grave and exceptional circumstances, acted rightly, and, in his Lordship's opinion, upon the evidence, he was wrongly punished by the Secretary of State for India.

The government would have ignored this decision if it had not been for the bad effect it was likely to have in India. In view of that contingency, the Ministry instructed Lord Olivier as Secretary of State for India to inform the government of India that His Majesty's government still adhered to the principle laid down by Mr. Montagu in 1920 in regard to the use of military force in support of civil authority. After a brief discussion of this principle in the light of Mr. Justice McCardie's dictum, Lord Olivier continued:

> But His Majesty's Government feel bound to dissociate themselves from the further view apparently held by the learned Judge, that the action proper to be taken by a military or police officer for dispersing an unlawful assembly may be determined by a consideration of the moral effect it may be thought likely by the officer taking it to have on other persons whom he may believe to be contemplating disorder elsewhere.

It is of course impossible to weigh the permanent results of the troubles in the Punjab in 1919. Time and tact may efface the bitter memories of Amritsar, but it cannot be done by time alone. Although the massacre of Glencoe is no longer a live issue in Scotland, the Irish still brood over the recollections of Wexford and Drogheda. But whatever the permanent results may be, the immediate reaction was very unfortunate. The people of India, acting through the National Congress, repudiated a broad and liberal plan of constitutional reform and declared that their loyalty to the Empire was optional. They followed and they have continued to follow the leadership of visionaries who would deprive them of all the benefits of Western civilization without being able to restore the best features of their own ancient culture.

This long digression has been necessary in order to emphasize the significance of the Amritsar "massacre" and to show how it was connected with the question of personal liberty. We are now ready to deal with the early history of the closely related problems of the freedom of the press and the freedom of speech.

A rigid censorship of the press was established by the East India Company in the early part of the nineteenth century, but it was intended to deal with European newspapers and it was abolished in 1835 through the efforts of Lord Macaulay. There were some temporary restrictions imposed during the Mutiny (1857–58) and vernacular publications were brought under official supervision from 1878 to 1881 by Lord Lytton's Vernacular Press Act. There were also a few restrictions in the Press and Registration of Books Act of 1867. With these exceptions, the press was left entirely to the operation of ordinary laws until 1908 and there was a great deal of rabid and irresponsible criticism of the public authorities. An occasional conviction was secured under Section 124A of the Indian Penal Code or under some provision of the Code of Criminal Procedure, but as the sedition movement grew more radical, especially after the partition of Bengal in 1905, this method of action was found to be inadequate. The printer or publisher of *Jugantar* of Calcutta, for example, was convicted and imprisoned five times between June, 1907, and June, 1908. A new printer or publisher came forward each time, and as there was no legal means of getting rid of the press itself the paper continued to appear and to indulge in its usual criticisms. The Newspapers (Incitement to Offenses) Act of 1908 gave the authorities power to deal with cases in which readers of the papers were directly incited to commit crimes of violence, but it was still possible for a clever editor to appeal to revolutionary sentiment and to cast odium upon the government without actually transgressing the letter of the law.

The government of India finally came to the conclusion that

more heroic remedies would have to be employed and the Indian Press Act, which has been so bitterly condemned by native writers of all shades of opinion, was passed in 1910. Sixteen different groups of offenses were listed as seditious and an effort was also made to safeguard the princes and chiefs of the Indian States against attempts by the press in British India to bring them into hatred and contempt or to excite disaffection among their subjects. The penalties imposed and the methods adopted to enforce them were very ingenious. Every keeper of a printing press or publisher of a newspaper established subsequent to the passage of the law was required to deposit a security of not less than Rs. 500 and not more than Rs. 2,000, according to the discretion of the local magistrate in each particular case. If an offense was committed under any of the categories referred to above, the provincial government could order the deposit forfeited. After that, if the printer or publisher wished to continue in business, he must make a new deposit of from Rs. 1,000 to Rs. 10,000. In the case of a second offense, the security was again forfeited and the press was confiscated. Presses and newspapers that were already in existence when the act was passed were not required to make an initial deposit until they had committed an offense, but the subsequent procedure was about the same as it was in the case of new establishments. Although appeals were allowed in all of these cases to a High Court of Justice, the offenses that might be committed were so numerous and so carefully described that there was very little opportunity for really effective judicial intervention. The provincial authorities were authorized, for example, to take action if they believed that any paper, pamphlet, or book, printed or published within their jurisdiction, had a tendency, directly or indirectly, by inference, suggestion, allusion, metaphor, implication, or otherwise, to bring into hatred or contempt the government of India or any class of people in British India.

The passage of this bill was strongly opposed by a large majority of the Indian members of the Legislative Council, the moderates as well as the extremists. Mr. G. K. Gokhale, the leader of the moderate faction at that time, declared that it would enable the provincial governments not only to protect themselves against revolutionary attacks, but also to suppress perfectly legitimate and reasonable criticism. A reactionary government could muzzle the press completely. Attention was also called to the fact that the bill in its original form discouraged the establishment of new printing presses even by people who were not interested in politics and who had no intention of printing or publishing any kind of political literature. In order to meet this objection a clause was inserted which permitted the magistrate in certain cases to dispense with the deposit of security.

The act was rigidly enforced. Several presses and newspapers established after it passed forfeited their deposits and had to suspend. The most famous case was that of the Zamindar Press which published the *Daily Zamindar* of Lahore. It was required to make the maximum initial deposit of Rs. 2,000 and when that was forfeited, the maximum additional deposit of Rs. 10,000. This was also declared forfeited together with the press itself. An appeal was taken to the chief court of the Punjab, which sustained the action of the government. Mr. Philip Morrell made this case the subject of a question in the House of Commons. He declared that the articles of November 19, 20, 21, 1919, upon which the prosecution was based, contained no seditious views and no incitement to violence, but only fair comment upon government officials. He also called attention "to the opinion expressed by the Chief Justice of Bengal that owing to the all-comprehensive nature of the Press Act, the task of an applicant to the Courts against forfeiture of security is almost hopeless, so that every newspaper which expresses any views of which the Local Government disapproves becomes liable to fine and forfeiture."[8]

Of the older printing establishments (those that antedated the passage of the Act of 1910), fourteen presses and thirteen papers were suppressed by the close of 1913. Among these were the Manohar Press (Poona), the Kshatramat Printing Press (Bombay), and the newspapers *Kal* (Poona), *Sakli* (Surat), and the *Daily Hitavadi* (Calcutta), all of which were unable to meet the demand that was made for the deposit

8. *Parliamentary Debates* (*Commons*) (5th ser.), LVIII, 1567; LXIV, 866.

of the maximum security. In other instances the deposits were put up and forfeited. The maximum security was also required of Tilak's paper, the *Kesari* of Poona, and the still more famous *Amrita Bazar Patrika* of Calcutta. During the war the *Hindoo*, *New India*, the *Independent*, the *Amrita Bazar Patrika* and the *Bombay Chronicle* forfeited their deposits, but were not suppressed.

So far as individual rights were concerned, the position of India during the war was very much like that of other belligerent countries. If there was any difference, it was in her favor. She was more fortunate than most of the other countries because she escaped conscription, which is the worst of all restrictions upon personal freedom. Her leaders generally recognized this fact and the war legislation was tolerated, even if it was not approved. There was, however, a powerful demand, as soon as the war was over, that the old arbitrary methods should be abandoned. This was reflected in the opposition to the Rowlatt Act and also in the resolution, adopted at the annual meeting of the National Congress in December, 1918, demanding a Bill of Rights in India's new Constitution, in which the following article should be included:

> That no Indian subject of His Majesty shall be liable to suffer in liberty, life, property or in respect of free speech or writing or of the right of association, except under sentence by an ordinary Court of Justice and as a result of lawful and open trial.

Although Parliament ignored the demand for a Bill of Rights, a large number of political prisoners were released, the Rowlatt Act was allowed to become obsolete, and two committees of the Indian legislature were appointed to consider the press laws and the general problem of repressive legislation. On the recommendation of the Press Act Committee, the Newspapers (Incitement to Offenses) Act of 1908 and the Press Act of 1910 were repealed and the Press and Registration of Books Act of 1867 was amended. The Repressive Laws Committee was composed of seven Indians and two Europeans and their chairman was Dr. (later Sir) Tej Bahadur Sapru, the Law Member of the government of India. They recommended that nine laws or portions thereof should be repealed and that

Bengal Regulation III of 1818 should be limited to its original purpose and, except on the inflammable frontiers, should not be used against British subjects. Madras Regulation II of 1819 and Bombay Regulation XXV of 1827 were also to be modified in a similar manner.

The government of India accepted these proposals, but they were subsequently compelled by the disturbances connected with the noncoöperation movement to reconsider their decision in so far as it affected the amendments of the three presidency Regulations and the repeal of the State Prisoners Acts of 1850 and 1858. The net result of the work of the two committees was that ten statutes were wholly or partially repealed, including a large section of the older legislation and all of the more stringent measures passed after 1907 except the Prevention of Seditious Meetings Act of 1911 and a part of the Criminal Law Amendment Act of 1908. These exceptions were made with the full approval of the Repressive Laws Committee, who stated that, in view of the grave situation that existed and that might become more serious, they thought "it would be prudent to defer actual repeal of these Acts until such time as the situation improves."[9]

The repeal of the Press Act was followed by a controversy between the government and the Nationalists over the question of protecting the rulers of the Indian States from attacks made in the press of British India. The matter had been brought before the Press Act Committee and they made the following recommendation, in which the European members fully concurred:

We understand that before the Press Act became law, it was not found necessary to protect Indian Princes from such attacks, and we note that the Act, in so far as the evidence before us shows, has only been used on three occasions for this purpose; we do not, in the circumstances, think that we should be justified in recommending, on general grounds, any enactment in the Penal Code or elsewhere for the purpose of affording protection in the

9. A private bill providing for the repeal of the Criminal Law Amendment Act of 1908 was defeated in the Legislative Assembly in February, 1936.

absence of evidence to prove the practical necessity for such provision of the law.

Lord Reading, in the summary of the controversy that he sent to the Secretary of State on October 12, 1922, says that the evidence before the committee was incomplete. It had been necessary to protect the princes before 1910, laws for that purpose having been passed in 1823 and 1891. The committee had underestimated the number of cases in which action had been taken under the Press Act, and they had "failed to take into account the deterrent influence exercised by the mere fact of the existence of the Act and by the instances, few though they were, in which they believed" it had been enforced. Lord Reading also argued that the government of India was bound in honor by a long series of treaties and agreements and royal proclamations "to afford to the Princes the same measure of protection as they previously enjoyed under the Press Act," and he called attention to the fact that they had asked for a continuation of this protection in a resolution adopted by the Chamber of Princes in November, 1921.

On September 23, 1922, Sir William Vincent, the official leader of the Legislative Assembly, asked leave to introduce a *bill to prevent the dissemination by means of books, newspapers, and other documents of matter calculated to bring into hatred or contempt, or to excite disaffection against princes or chiefs in India or the government or administrations established in such States.* This measure, subsequently called the Indian States (Protection against Disaffection) Act, 1922, differed in several particulars from the clauses of the Press Act of 1910 that dealt with the Indian States. The Press Act applied only to publishers and to keepers of printing presses, while the new bill applied also to editors and authors. Under the Press Act the penalty was forfeiture of security and in extreme cases the confiscation of the press. A seditious attack upon a prince was now declared to be a penal offense and was made punishable by fine or by imprisonment for not more than five years or by both fine and imprisonment. Provision was also made for the forfeiture of offending publications and for their detention in the course of transmission through the mails. In these respects, the new measures were more severe than the old. There was, however, a very important modification of procedure. The executive could proceed at any time under the Press Act, and, as already noted, there was practically no opportunity for the courts to interfere. A judicial inquiry was now required and no court could try an offense "except on complaint made by, or under authority from, the Governor-General in Council." There was also a further safeguard in the provision that no person should be deemed to commit an offense under the act "in respect of any book, newspaper, or other document which without exciting or being intended to excite hatred, contempt, or disaffection, contains comments expressing disapprobation of the measures of any such Prince, Government or Administration as aforesaid with a view to obtain their alteration by lawful means, or disapprobation of the administrative or other action of any such Prince, Chief, Government or Administration."

The bill was opposed by a large majority of the Indian members of the Assembly, and, after a short debate, leave to introduce it was refused by a vote of 45 to 41. This was the first crisis to arise after the adoption of the new plan of government. Under Section 67B of the Government of India Act, 1919, when either chamber of the Indian legislature refuses leave to introduce or fails to pass a bill recommended by the Governor-General, he may certify that its passage is essential for the safety, tranquility, or interest of British India or some part thereof, and it is laid before the British Parliament and becomes law after it has received His Majesty's assent. Lord Reading certified the bill under this clause and it was subsequently approved by the Crown and is still in force.[10]

This quarrel was unfortunate, but the issue involved was not very important and it was soon forgotten. There is no evidence, however, that the liberal policy of the government was appreciated in India or that its results were beneficial. The disturbances that followed might almost be regarded as a confirmation of the Craddock-O'Dwyer theory that concessions

10. Most of the evidence dealing with this subject will be found in an official pamphlet entitled *East India (Indian States) (Protection against Disaffection) Act, 1922,* London, 1922.

are interpreted by the Nationalists as a confession of weakness and an invitation to make further trouble. To meet these difficulties, the authorities were compelled to revive nearly all of the old autocratic powers and to assume others that had not previously been exercised. There have been three main crises involving the maintenance of law and order since 1921: (1) the recrudescence of revolutionary crime in Bengal, (2) the spread of communism, and (3) the struggle of the Congress party to attain swaraj by lawless methods.

The history of the revolutionary conspiracy in Bengal from 1908 to 1917 has already been sketched.[11] By the close of 1917, nearly all of the leaders had been confined under Bengal Regulation III of 1818 and many of their followers had been disciplined under the Defense of India Act of 1915. Most of these men were impenitent when they were released under the Royal Proclamation of Amnesty in December, 1919, but they did not cause any serious trouble until the nonviolent noncoöperation about the end of 1922. The old terrorist organizations were then revived, arms and ammunition were again smuggled into the country, a very dangerous type of bomb was manufactured, and many crimes of violence were committed. There were several dacoities perpetrated, some of them with murder, and special efforts were made to terrorize the police and break their morale. In January, 1924, Mr. Ernest Day was murdered in Calcutta in mistake for Mr. Tegert (later Sir Charles), the Commissioner of Police. In July, the Red Bengal leaflets appeared, in which it was announced that there was to be a campaign for the assassination of police officers and the public were warned that those who interfered would suffer the same fate. The local members of the Congress party apparently approved these methods; at least, the Bengal Provincial Conference passed a resolution expressing their admiration for the spirit of self-sacrifice exhibited by Gopi Mohan Saha, the young man who killed Mr. Day.

The government found it impossible to deal with these crimes through the ordinary courts because the witnesses and jurors were either intimidated or were too much in sympathy

11. See chap. ii.

with the criminals to assist in their conviction. Some of the leaders were confined under Bengal Regulation III of 1818, but new leaders appeared and the operations were resumed. Lord Lytton, the Governor of Bengal, consulted Lord Reading, and they finally came to the conclusion that the old autocratic system would have to be restored, at least temporarily, with safeguards to prevent it from being used to penalize legitimate political activity. Their decision was approved by the Labor government in England, and the Governor-General, acting under the powers conferred upon him by the Government of India Act, 1919, to issue ordinances having the force of law for a period not exceeding six months, promulgated the Bengal Criminal Law Amendment Ordinance on October 25, 1924. It was followed by legislation enacted for a period of five years—the Bengal Criminal Law Amendment Act, certified by the Governor, and the Bengal Criminal Law (Supplementary) Act, certified by the Governor-General. This legislation was intended, as far as possible, to prevent revolutionary crimes from being committed and to provide a summary method of trying persons who were accused of these crimes and who were likely to escape conviction in the ordinary courts. When there were reasonable grounds for believing that a person was about to commit an offense listed on the schedule that was appended to the act, he could be arrested and detained without a trial. If, in spite of this vigilance, a scheduled offense was committed, the accused might be tried before a special tribunal of three commissioners, where the case could be expedited, witnesses could be examined *in camera*, and the opportunities for intimidation could be reduced to a minimum. There were various safeguards adopted, including the right of appeal to the High Court and a provision that the High Court must examine the proceedings and give its approval before the death sentence could be executed.

These powers and those conferred by Bengal Regulation III of 1818 were freely used by the provincial authorities. On March 30, 1927, Lord Birkenhead stated in the House of Lords that 171 persons had been dealt with under the Bengal Criminal Law Amendment Act up to that time. Of these, 26 had been released, 13 had been placed in home domicile, 75 had been placed in village domicile, 54 were still in jail, and 3 were unaccounted for. There were 16 persons in prison at that time under the terms of Bengal Regulation III of 1818. The most famous case was that of Mr. Subhas Chandra Bose, the chief executive officer of the Municipal Corporation of Calcutta, who was interned at Mandalay from October, 1924, until he was released on account of ill health in May, 1927.

Shortly before the Bengal Criminal Law Amendment Act expired on April 23, 1930, the first ten sections providing for the trial of scheduled offenses by a curtailed procedure were extended for a further period of five years. The remainder of the act was repealed on April 1, but Sir Stanley Jackson, the Governor of Bengal, warned the Legislative Council that in case of an emergency it would be reënacted in the form of an ordinance. As a result of the serious disorders at Chittagong on April 18, the ordinance was issued on the following day and, for a period of six months, the executive authorities were again given the power to arrest and detain potential lawbreakers without the formality of a trial. According to a statement made in the House of Commons on May 5, 1930, by Mr. Wedgewood Benn, the Secretary of State for India, 27 persons were released on April 1, but 65 persons had been arrested and detained since the ordinance went into effect on April 19. There were also 43 persons who were being detained under Bengal Regulation III of 1818. When the ordinance expired, its provisions were continued in force by a statute.

The recrudescence of revolutionary crime in Bengal is a local problem and it has been handled almost entirely by the provincial government. It is they who have dealt with the leaders under Bengal Regulation III of 1818, and with the rank and file under the less severe provisions of the Bengal Criminal Law Amendment Act and the Bengal Criminal Law Amendment Ordinance. The spread of Communism and the development of the civil disobedience campaign, on the other hand, are national problems, and it is the central authorities who plan the roundup of offenders, sanction the conspiracy trials, and enact the laws and ordinances that the occasion seems to require.

It is difficult to obtain accurate information about Communism in India, as it is in other countries for the obvious reason that most of the propaganda is carried on through secret channels. It is also difficult to draw a line between Communists and Nationalists because their immediate objective is identical. Both are working for the downfall of British Imperialism. There is a great deal of significance in the fact that Pandit Jawaharlal Nehru can, at the same time, be a friend and admirer of Bolshevist Russia and the most popular of the young leaders of Indian Nationalism. In 1929, he was the President of both the All-India Trade-Union Congress, which was completely under Communist control, and of the All-India National Congress, which is supported almost entirely by people who would suffer severely if a dictatorship of the proletariat should ever be established. In spite of these difficulties, we know that Communism does exist in India, that it has spread rapidly in recent years, and that it has very little in common with the ordinary variety of Nationalism.

The movement is not indigenous, although there is no other country in the world where there is such abject poverty or so wide a gap between the rich and the poor. The theory is German, the source of propaganda is Russian, and the men who have been most successful in organizing the movement are British. There were two main channels through which the teachings of Marx and Lenin were introduced into India: (1) newspapers, books and pamphlets and (2) funds for the support of local agitators, which were either smuggled across the North-West Frontier or sent, in one way or another, through an agency established in Berlin by an Indian who carried on his work under the name of Manabendra Nath Roy. A Communist who was arrested at Cawnpore in 1923 had in his possession two pamphlets, presumably written by Roy, one of which was entitled *What Do We Want?* and the other, *India's Problem and Its Solution.* He also had a copy of a newspaper called the *Vanguard,* which was edited by Roy and which professed to be the "Central Organ of the Communist Party of India."

The local work was at first in the hands of Indians and they did it very badly. The leaders of the militant group, affiliated with the Third International, were unable to conceal their activities from the police and they were accordingly arrested and convicted, under Section 121A of the Indian Penal Code, on a charge of conspiracy to deprive His Majesty, the King-Emperor, of the sovereignty of British India, and sentenced to four years' imprisonment.[12] The pacifist group had nothing to conceal. They contended that they had a legal right to advocate the principles of Communism as long as they did not engage in any conspiracy to overthrow the existing government. Under the leadership of Mr. Satya Bhakta, they openly formed a Communist party at Cawnpore in 1924 and organized the first All-India Communist Conference in December, 1925. Their position was awkward. They needed money for their work, but could not get it without giving up their pacifist attitude and accepting the supervision of the Third International. The pressure was too strong to be resisted. Bhakta, who wished to avoid all foreign alliances, was defeated and compelled to resign, and the party was gradually brought under Bolshevist control.

The movement as a whole made very little progress until 1926. At the fifth session of the Third International, held in Moscow in June, 1924, it was decided that Communist activity in British colonies should be intensified. As the campaign has been conducted secretly, it is impossible to tell exactly what procedure was adopted. The evidence available, however, seems to indicate that the Communist party in the United Kingdom were asked to take charge of the work in India. Russia was apparently to furnish the rupees and Britain the brains. It was a formidable combination. A group of able and enthusiastic young Englishmen were sent out to India to revive a dying cause and to give it an effective organization. The pioneer of this group was George Allison *alias* Donald Campbell, who had been associated with the Communist movement in England and had spent some time in Moscow. He arrived in Bombay in April, 1926, and worked, mainly in the Bengal and Bombay presidencies, until the end of January, 1927, when he was arrested and prosecuted for entering India on a

12. This was the famous Cawnpore Conspiracy Case of 1924–25, which brought to light a great deal of information relating to the activities of Mr. M. N. Roy and his agents in India.

forged passport and sentenced to eighteen months' imprisonment. Philip Spratt, a graduate of Cambridge University, went to India in December, 1926, ostensibly on behalf of the Labor Research Department, an organization in London which was alleged to be under the control of the Central Council of Trades Unions in Moscow. He spent most of his time in Bombay and Calcutta, but he was also active in organizing the radical labor movement in the Punjab and the United Provinces. Benjamin Francis Bradley arrived in Bombay in September, 1927, and organized trade unions among the cotton-mill and railway employees of the Bombay presidency. Lester Hutchinson also arrived in September, 1928. He was the editor of a Communist paper called the *New Spark* and vice-president of the Girni Kamgar Union in Bombay. These men were apparently financed by various radical organizations in England, but it would be impossible to say how much of the money came ultimately from Russia.

According to the charges brought against them by the Indian authorities, their plan of campaign was (1) to instruct local agitators in the doctrines of Marx and Lenin, (2) to organize a Peasants' and Workers' party, which would replace the old Communist organization, (3) to form radical trade unions and help the Left Wing to secure control of the trade-union movement, and (4) to improve the conditions of the railway and factory workers by fomenting a series of strikes. Branches of the Peasants' and Workers' party were formed in Bombay and Bengal by Allison, and in the United Provinces and the Punjab by Spratt. When Mr. Saklatvala, who was at the time a Communist member of the House of Commons, was in Bombay in January, 1927, he looked with favor upon the new organization and was rather cold in his attitude toward the leaders of the old line Communist party. It was said that the revenue from abroad went entirely to the Peasants' and Workers' party.

The effort to dominate the trade-union movement was also successful. The history of trade unionism in India is sometimes traced back to 1890, when Mr. M. N. Lokhande organized the Bombay Mill-Hands' Association, but the movement did not amount to much until the period of economic distress that followed the Great War. It is still in its infancy and can scarcely be said to exist at all outside of Bombay, Ahmedabad, Madras, Calcutta, and a few other railway and textile centers. The greatest progress has been made in Ahmedabad, where Mr. Gandhi and Mrs. Anusuya Sarabhai have been the guiding spirits, and in Bombay where Mr. Ginwalla and the British Communists have been especially active.

The leaders of the Right Wing are Diwan Chaman Lal of Lahore, a member of the Legislative Assembly from 1923 to 1930, who founded the All-India Trade-Union Congress in 1920, and Mr. N. M. Joshi of Bombay, a member of the Servants of India Society, who has served in the Legislative Assembly since 1921 as a representative of labor. These men were members of the Royal (Whitley) Commission on Indian Labor, they were in favor of maintaining friendly relations with the International Labor Organization at Geneva, and were opposed to any affiliation with Bolshevism. The leaders of the Left Wing are Pandit Jawaharlal Nehru of Allahabad and Mr. Subhas Chandra Bose of Calcutta, but the spade work which made their victory possible was largely done by the Englishmen, Spratt and Hutchinson. Through their efforts, the Great Indian Peninsula Railway Union was brought under radical control and the Girni Kamgar, commonly known as the "Red Flag" Union, was formed in opposition to the Bombay Textile Labor Union, which is usually denounced as a "bourgeois" organization. There was a preliminary skirmish at the annual meeting of the All-India Trade-Union Congress at Jharia in 1928, and a decisive conflict at the Nagpur meeting in December, 1929. On the basis of what were said to be swollen membership figures, the meeting in 1929 was swamped by the delegates from the Great Indian Peninsula Railway and the Girni Kamgar Unions, and nearly all of the Left-Wing program was approved. Resolutions were adopted to boycott the Whitley Commission, to affiliate with the League against Imperialism, to break off all connections with the International Labor Organization and to establish an independent Socialist Republic. The proposal to affiliate with the pan-Pacific Trade-Union Secretariat was defeated, mainly through the efforts of Mr. Bose who did not want the movement to become too closely associated with Moscow.

We now come to the next item on the program of Allison, Spratt, and their lieutenants. Shortly after their arrival in India there was a tremendous increase in the number and the severity of strikes, and some of the most important industries in the country were almost paralyzed. The figures for 1927–28 (April 1) were about the average—129 strikes, involving 131,655 workers—but they were small in comparison with those for 1928–29, when there were 203 strikes, involving 506,851 workers. The strikes in the latter year were also on a larger scale and they usually lasted much longer. There were 31,647,404 working days lost, which was greater than the number for the whole five preceding years. The worst strike of the year was the one in the City of Bombay which affected nearly all of the cotton mills and lasted from April 26 to October 6, 1928. There were also serious and prolonged conflicts in the workshops of the East Indian Railway at Lilooah, in the Tata Iron and Steel Works at Jamshedpur, in the Fort Gloster Jute Mills in Bengal, and in numerous other smaller industries.

The object in some of these conflicts was to improve working conditions, to secure a recognition of the union, to prevent a reduction of wages, or to obtain an increase of wages. But if these had been the only motives, there would hardly have been so much activity in a period of economic depression. It is easier to win a strike in good times, when the employer can afford to make concessions, than it is in bad times, when he is on the verge of bankruptcy. The movement was obviously political. The working classes were discontented, the general public was dissatisfied with the personnel of the Simon Commission, and the government of India was supposed to be weak and vacillating. The Communist leaders naturally felt that, as India was about to become independent, it was time to prepare the way for the establishment of the dictatorship of the proletariat. They were merely carrying out their ideals and earning the wages that they received from Europe.

There was one fatal mistake: the strength of the government was underrated. Lord Irwin and his advisers showed remarkable patience in dealing with the Nationalists because they knew, if their critics did not, that the constitutional problems of India could be solved only with Nationalist support. But that consideration did not apply to the Bolshevists and they were handled with considerable severity. The rank and file of Indian Communists are illiterate workmen who would be helpless without leaders, and the leaders themselves, for the most part, would be equally helpless if they were not encouraged by European agitators and subsidized with European funds, and if they were not able to use the strike as a political weapon. The government decided, therefore, that it would do three things: (a) imprison the leaders, both Indian and European, and (b) ask the Legislative Assembly to authorize the deportation of non-Indian Communists, and (c) to penalize sympathetic political strikes and lightning strikes in public utility industries.

The first great roundup was made on March 20, 1929. This marks the beginning of the famous Meerut Conspiracy Case which lasted for nearly four years. The government of India, with the approval of the Secretary of State, authorized the district magistrate of Meerut to issue warrants for the arrest of the Communist leaders under Section 121A of the Indian Penal Code for conspiring to deprive the King-Emperor of the sovereignty of British India. Among those arrested were Spratt, Bradley, and Hutchinson and nearly all of the members of the Executive Committee of the Girni Kamgar Union. Although the arrests were made in Bombay, Poona, Calcutta, Dacca, Allahabad, and other places, the prisoners were all taken to Meerut for trial. The preliminary inquiry was prolonged for several months partly by obstructive tactics of one kind and another and partly by the volume of evidence to be considered. Thirty-one of the accused were finally committed and the formal trial was begun on January 31, 1930, before Mr. R. L. Yorke, Special Sessions judge, and a bench of five assessors. The case again dragged on slowly and the judgment was not given until January 16, 1933. One of the prisoners died during the trial, three were acquitted, and twenty-seven were convicted, including the three Englishmen. Spratt was sentenced to twelve years' transportation, Bradley to ten years' transportation, and Hutchinson to four years' rigorous imprisonment. An appeal was then taken to the High Court at Allahabad and the final decision was handed down on August 3, 1933. Hutchinson and eight of the Indians were acquitted and the sentences on the others were reduced and nearly all of them were released by the end of 1933.

This is the official version of the case. The prisoners themselves tell a different story.[13] Their only offense was attempting to improve the conditions of Indian labor by forming an independent trade-union organization. The government, at the instigation of the capitalists, decided to stop these efforts and, as no overt crime had been committed, they attributed political motives to purely economic activities and charged the prisoners with attempting to deprive the King-Emperor of the sovereignty of India. Most of the prisoners lived and worked in Bombay or Calcutta and twenty-four of them had never been to Meerut, but they were all tried in that city because there they could not demand a jury trial. It is true that five lay assessors were nominated to assist the judge, but in giving his verdict he largely disregarded their advice. Hundreds of pamphlets, books, and newspapers were admitted to prove that the overthrow of bourgeois government is a general Communist objective, although the court admitted that it was not a crime to hold Communist views and asserted definitely that the accused were not being prosecuted because of their opinions. At the same time, the court refused to accept evidence offered by the prisoners that the strikes which they had organized were justified by low wages and atrocious working conditions.

The history of the Lahore Conspiracy Case was somewhat similar. In April and May, 1929, twenty-five persons were arrested on the charge of being members of an organization which aimed to overthrow the existing government in India by the use of force. Among the overt acts attributed to this organization were the murder of Mr. J. P. Saunders, Assistant

13. See *The Prisoners' Reply* (The Prisoners' Speeches from the Dock) (London, 1931); B. F. Bradley, *Trade Unionism in India* (London, 1932); *British in India, Meerut Conspiracy Case, Specially written by a Barrister at Law* (London, 1933).

Superintendent of Police, and Head Constable Chanan Singh in Lahore on December 17, 1928; the bomb-throwing outrage in the Legislative Assembly on April 8, 1929; and the manufacture of bombs in Lahore, Saharanpur, and other places. An interesting feature of the case was the claim made by some of the defendants that persons accused of murder or attempted murder should be treated as political prisoners if there was a political motive for the crime. Bhagat Singh and Dutt, the two young men who threw the bomb in the Legislative Assembly, put forward this claim and went on a hunger strike to enforce it. The idea was contagious. There was a series of hunger strikes among all the prisoners and one of them died of starvation. As a result of these strikes and the use of other methods of obstruction, the hearing in the Magistrates' Court was prolonged from July 11, 1929 until May 1, 1930, when the Viceroy issued an ordinance entrusting the trial of the case to a special tribunal, composed of the judges of the High Court at Lahore, and investing this tribunal with power to deal with wilful obstruction. Bhagat Singh and two other young men were condemned to death for the murder of Mr. Saunders and Chanan Singh. As will be seen later, their execution, on March 23, 1931, helped to precipitate the Hindu-Moslem riots at Cawnpore and also had considerable influence on the history of the Round Table Conference.

The second part of the government program was initiated on September 4, 1928, with the introduction in the Legislative Assembly of the Public Safety (Removal from India) Bill, giving the Governor-General in Council the power to deport British and foreign Communist agents. A few amendments were proposed by the Select Committee to which the bill was referred, but they did not affect the main principle and were accepted by the government. On motion to accept the report of the Select Committee the vote was a tie, 61 to 61, and the bill was defeated by the casting vote of Mr. Patel, the president of the Assembly. As Spratt, Bradley, and Hutchinson were very active at this time, the government was determined to go on with its plans and a new bill was accordingly introduced at the next session of the Assembly on February 4, 1929. This went further than the previous measure in that it also empowered the government to seize funds remitted from abroad to finance Communist activities. Pandit Motilal Nehru criticized the bill as a whole and this section in particular as an attack on the National Congress and a scheme to isolate the Nationalist movement by depriving it of help from overseas, an argument which seemed to imply that he regarded Nationalism and international Communism as identical movements. The Swarajist and Nationalist parties were strongly hostile, but a motion to refer the bill to a Select Committee was carried on February 7 by a vote of 61 to 50.

The question did not come up for discussion again until April 2, and during that interview the Meerut roundup had occurred (March 20) and the defendants, including the three Englishmen, were in prison awaiting the result of the magisterial inquiry. When the Select Committee presented its report, Mr. Patel ruled that it could not be considered because it affected the English defendants at Meerut and was therefore *sub judice.* He suggested that the government should either postpone the bill or abandon the trials. The bomb explosion in the Assembly on April 8 convinced Lord Irwin that the powers which the bill proposed to confer were essential, and on the twelfth he issued the Public Safety (Removal from India) Ordinance, valid for a period of six months. In a speech defending his action, he questioned the correctness of Mr. Patel's interpretation of the rules of the Assembly, but he admitted that the president was the person to interpret the rules as they stood, and said that they would be amended at the earliest possible moment to prevent in the future any such interference with the normal legislative procedure. The powers conferred by the ordinance were apparently not used and the ordinance itself was not renewed.

The only other restrictive measure on the government program at this time was the Trade Disputes Act, which was passed by both houses in the ordinary manner and went into effect on May 13, 1929, for a period of five years. It provided the usual Courts of Inquiry and Boards of Conciliation, but the important sections, from our present point of view, were those which penalize lightning strikes in public utility services, strikes and lockouts that have other objects than the mere furtherance of a trade dispute within the industry to which the strikers or employees belong, and strikes and lockouts that are designed to coerce the government or to bring indirect pressure to bear upon it by inflicting hardship upon the community. This means, of course, that sympathetic and political strikes are declared illegal and those who participate in them may be punished.

In some of the provinces the All-India legislation was supplemented by local legislation. A law was enacted, for example, by the Bombay Legislative Council in 1929 giving the police broad powers to deport agitators from the presidency and to handle cases of intimidation in time of a strike. By using these powers and keeping the Communist leaders in prison, the authorities were able to reduce the number of strikes in 1929, as compared with 1928, from 203 to 141 and the number of working days lost from 31,647,404 to 12,165,691. The chief trouble was still in the City of Bombay, where the government and the Millowners' Association both made a determined effort to break up the Girni Kamgar Union. It would be unfortunate if the right to strike were taken away altogether because industrial conditions are still very bad and, without an occasional strike, it is doubtful whether they would ever be remedied.[14]

The Communist party in India is apparently dead, but its spirit survives in the Left Wing of the National Congress. This explains in part the third crisis mentioned above, the struggle of the Congress to attain swaraj by lawless methods. It also helps to explain why the encroachments of the state upon personal liberty have been carried further during the last few years than ever before. The policy of repression which was formerly restricted almost entirely to Bengal, has been extended over the whole of British India and its severity has been greatly increased. Lord Irwin was reluctantly compelled

14. It is impossible to deal here with the factory and mining laws and other constructive measures enacted by the central legislature and the various Provincial Councils. There is a good summary of this legislation, however, in Mrs. Vera Anstey's excellent book on *The Economic Development of India* (London, 1929), pp. 294–314. The Report of the Royal (Whitley) Commission on Indian Labor also contains some valuable information on this subject.

to take some steps in this direction but a great deal more was done under Lord Willingdon. Seven ordinances were issued when Gandhi began his civil disobedience campaign in 1930. The executive authorities were given greater power to control the press, to deal with pickets and boycotts, and to punish agitators who tried to persuade the peasants not to pay their land revenues; martial law was proclaimed in Sholapur, the Bengal Criminal Law Amendment Ordinance was extended for five years, and a special tribunal was constituted to take over the trial of the Lahore Conspiracy Case. There was another crop of ordinances and laws after Gandhi returned from the second session of the Round Table Conference and renewed his civil disobedience campaign early in 1932.[15] Many others have been issued since and they have all been rigidly enforced. The restrictions on the freedom of the press are as severe as they were before 1922 and the police power of the executive has been extended and put on a more permanent basis. It is to be hoped that a more moderate policy will be possible when the new Constitution is put into operation.

15. For a detailed account of these measures, see *Conditions in India, Being the Report of the Delegation sent to India by the India League in 1932* (London, 1933).

CHAPTER IX

SOCIAL AND RACIAL GRIEVANCES

THE fundamental cause of Indian unrest may be stated in the form of a paradox. The British have failed because they have been too successful. They have introduced Western ideas of medicine, surgery, and sanitation, protected people from domestic warfare and invasion, abolished suttee and other forms of religious suicide, and practically done away with female infanticide. In other words, they have removed some of the most effective restraints upon the growth of population in a country where custom and religion require people to marry early and breed large families. The results are shown in the census figures. The population increased 19,000,000 in 1901–11, 4,000,000 in 1911–21, and 33,000,000 in 1921–31 and there was a total increase of 98,000,000 in the half century from 1881 to 1931.[1]

The evil effects of overcrowding have been partially offset by the construction of railways and irrigation works and a great deal may still be done by introducing more scientific methods of agriculture. The improvement in the productive capacity of the country has not, however, exceeded the growth of population and it does not seem likely that it will do so in the immediate future. This fact is the central theme of the Report of the Royal Commission on Indian agriculture published in 1930. "No lasting improvement in the standard of living of the great mass of the population can be attained," says the Report, "if every enhancement in the purchasing power of the cultivator is to be followed by a proportionate increase in the population."

1. This increase was partly due to the greater accuracy in enumeration and partly to the inclusion of new birth areas, but most of it was the result of an actual excess of births over deaths. The fall in the rate of increase during the decade from 1911–21 was caused by the great influenza epidemic of 1918.

Anyone who has even a superficial knowledge of India knows that these facts are true, but for some curious reason the Nationalist usually closes his eyes and refuses to see them. He will argue that the standard of living is declining and that malnutrition is increasing the terrors of plague, cholera, influenza, and malaria. He is apt to go even further and contend, with blissful disregard of statistics, that famines are becoming more frequent and more deadly. This sad condition of affairs is of course entirely the product of British political and economic exploitation. He would reach a different conclusion if he studied the subject with less prejudice and a little more knowledge of the teachings of Malthus and Ricardo. India today is probably the best example in the world of the operation of the Malthusian law of population.

The Nationalist, in reply to this argument, usually quotes statistics to prove that India has a smaller population per square mile than England, Belgium, Rhode Island, and other congested regions of the West. As a matter of fact, these states are all insignificant in size compared with India, and they are all highly industrialized communities which draw the greater part of their food from outside and pay for it with manufactured goods. They should be compared not with India, but with the province of Bengal or the metropolitan districts of Calcutta and Bombay. Statistics are also used to show that on account of the high death rate the net fecundity of India is lower than that of Great Britain, the United States, and several Western countries. This may be true, but a country that is already overcrowded can hardly stand an absolute addition of 20,000,000 to 25,000,000 in each decade, even though the rate of increase is only 7 or 8 per cent.

Emigration cannot be utilized as a remedy partly because of the exclusion policies of other countries. Mr. Gokhale in his so-called political testament recommended that Tanganyika-land should be turned over to India as a sphere of influence and colonization. The suggestion was supported by the Aga Khan in his *India in Transition* and by Sir Theodore Morison in letters to the *Times* and in an article in the *Nineteenth Century and After* for September, 1918. It was strongly opposed by European inhabitants of East and South Africa and by missionaries and others interested in the welfare of the native African population. The British government has apparently never given the plan any serious consideration, but even if it were adopted, the relief would not be permanent. From 20,000,000 to 25,000,000 settlers might perhaps be accommodated in Tanganyikaland and in those portions of Kenya that are unfit for European colonization, but it would take many years to transport them and to get them established in their new homes and in the meantime the loss would be more than offset by the normal growth of population.

Another cause of discontent is the lack of friendly social relations between the British and the Indians. Practically every city, civil station, and military cantonment has two well-defined sections: the British quarters with its wide streets, spacious parks, clubs, cricket grounds, and golf links; and the Indian quarters, with its narrow alleys, its crowded bazaars, and its densely populated hovels. Even wealthy Indians who have large and luxurious homes do not as a rule live in the European section. The men of the two races see a good deal of one another during the day, but after business hours they retire to their respective quarters and usually do not have any social relations whatever. This is partly due to the caste system and partly to the fact that nearly all Indians, whether Hindus or Moslems, differ so widely from Europeans in their attitude toward the social position of women. The majority of Indians, even of the upper classes, recognize these facts and are perfectly satisfied with them. But those who have been educated abroad are inclined to resent the fact that they are so often excluded from the Englishman's clubs and in many other ways made to feel they are his social inferiors. Indian students at Oxford, Cambridge, and the University of London are treated as social equals. They are invited to teas, receptions, and dances where they meet English men and women on an equal footing. A few years later they meet the same men and women in India and may be unmercifully snubbed.

The relations between the races are far less friendly now than they were under the East India Company. In those days the civil servant was usually unmarried. Very often he lived with an Indian woman who regarded herself as his wife and who did not lose standing with her own people because of the alliance. He acquired some knowledge of one or more Indian languages, associated with Indians on terms of equality, and came to have for them a feeling of kindly sympathy. This was all changed by the steamship and the Suez Canal. London is now less than two weeks from Bombay. The servants of His Majesty, both civil and military, usually marry early in their careers and take their wives out to India with them. Those who do not marry would be socially ostracized and would find it difficult to secure promotion if they lived openly with Indian women. Furthermore, it is a well-known fact that European women, especially British women, draw the color line more rigidly than men. In other words, the conditions in India have improved so far as sexual morality is concerned, but the relations between the races have grown less cordial.

If it were only a question of ordinary social amenities the situation would not be so difficult, but, unfortunately, in the foreigner's treatment of the Indian there are many cases of downright brutality. The offenders are usually members of the domiciled Anglo-Indian community who keep small shops or hold subordinate positions in the railway, the police, the public works, and other public services. Many stories are told of the mistreatment of native servants and of the brutality of railway guards and petty police officers. Nationalist writers complain that these offenses are rarely punished in the courts and that they are often condoned by local European opinion.

The failure of the courts to act in these cases was formerly attributed to racial discrimination which existed in the code of criminal procedure in favor of Europeans. Before the Mutiny, the law enforced in the ordinary criminal courts of northern India was the old Moslem law of the Mogul Emperors. Europeans were exempted from the jurisdiction of these courts for the same reason that they were exempted from the jurisdiction of similar courts in Turkey and Egypt. They could not have been subjected to the criminal law of a Mohammedan despotism without inflicting a great injustice. They were, however, liable to the jurisdiction of special tribunals, presided over by British judges who administered the criminal law of England.

After the Mutiny, the conditions were changed. A new Penal Code was adopted which superseded both the Moslem law as applied to Indians and the English law as applied to Europeans. The special tribunals were abolished, but Europeans were not brought completely under the jurisdiction of the ordinary criminal courts. Except in the presidency towns (Calcutta, Bombay, and Madras), where Indian magistrates had jurisdiction over Europeans in certain cases, a European had a right to demand a trial before a European judge and a jury of which not less than half the members were Europeans.[2] This is said to have caused a great deal of hardship, not because the courts were favorable to Europeans, but because in remote parts of the country there were no courts at all to which an Indian could appeal for protection. A coolie employed in a tea garden in Assam would not have the means to promote a suit before a court in Calcutta or at some other distant place. The system was also unpopular with the Nationalists because it was apparently based on the theory of Indian racial inferiority.

The effort to remedy this grievance during the administration of Lord Ripon has already been discussed. The Ilbert Bill, which received its name from the Law Member of the Council who introduced it, was strongly supported by Lord Ripon. It was, however, opposed by the resident European community and their friends in Great Britain and, so far as its main object was concerned, it was finally defeated. The bitter feeling aroused by this controversy was one of the factors that led to the establishment of the Indian National Congress in 1885. After many years of agitation, the question was again brought before the government shortly after the adoption of the Montagu-Chelmsford Reforms. On the recommendation of a committee, appointed by the Governor of India at the request of the Legislative Assembly, all of the more important racial dis-

2. According to the wording of the law, these privileges were restricted to European British subjects. In practice, however, they were also enjoyed by other Europeans and Americans.

criminations in the Code of Criminal Procedure were abolished in 1922.

The revolt of the Asiatic against the European should perhaps be mentioned as still another factor in the history of Indian unrest. This revolt may be said to date from the Russo-Japanese War of 1904–5. As the news of Japan's victories spread through the bazaars of India it was received with an enthusiastic approbation, the full significance of which the British failed to appreciate. The British welcomed Japanese success because they approved Japan's Far Eastern policy and because they were united to her by a treaty of alliance. To the people of India it was far more than this; it was a triumph of Asiatics over Europeans, a symbol that the tide that had been flowing against Asia since the beginning of the nineteenth century had turned in the other direction. Strictly speaking, this is not in itself a cause of Indian discontent. It did, however, make those who were already discontented a little bolder in expressing their opinions and a little more radical in their methods of agitation. It happened to come just at the time when Lord Curzon was carrying out two of his most unpopular reforms, the partition of Bengal and the reorganization of the Indian universities.

But in speaking of a revolt of Asiatics against Europeans, we do not mean to imply that there is a conscious spirit of solidarity either in Asia or in Europe. Nevertheless the revolt is very general throughout Asia and it is more than a mere protest against political and economic exploitation. It is both a racial and a religious conflict. In India it takes the form of idealizing the past, of reconstructing an imaginary Golden Age before the coming of the British when everybody was happy, prosperous, and contented. In spite of the utter lack of racial and linguistic homogeneity there is developing a sort of pseudo-racial solidarity which is largely based upon hatred of Europeans and of European culture. Mr. Gandhi is the chief representative of this feeling of racial and cultural antagonism, although he probably does not realize it himself, and it is the secret of his great popularity. The late Lala Lajpat Rai also hated the European, but he knew that India could not afford to give up the advantages of Western civilization.

There is an interesting commentary on this subject in the London *Times* of March 16, 1922, written by their special correspondent in India:

The most distressing feature of the whole situation is that behind all immediate grievances and discontents, whether Caliphate, Sikh, or Non-Cooperationist, there is a continual growth of racial antagonism. The ignorant masses are inoculated with it, and it is not absent from the best and most loyal Indians in the highest official positions, though these themselves disclaim and condemn it. Several distinguished Indians have told me that the women are now affected. This is a new phenomenon, but I am assured that bitterness and sedition are now more rampant behind the *Purdahs* [curtains, i.e., women's secluded quarters] than among men. This is most deplorable, because it carries a menace beyond the present disturbances.

The dominance of race over religion is a new factor in India as it is in Egypt, Syria, and other parts of the Orient. But it cannot last permanently unless the whole character of the people is fundamentally changed. Should the Europeans be eliminated or self-government under European suzerainty be established, the old religious animosities would again come to the front. As a matter of fact, the striking feature of the recent glorification of India's past has been the revival of religion, a revival largely influenced by the eulogistic accounts given by Western writers of Hindu and Moslem teaching. "These eulogies [says William Archer] may be roughly divided into two classes: those of scholars whose painfully acquired knowledge of Sanscrit literature naturally inclines them to make the most of a treasure which has cost them so much; and those of a recent school of enthusiasts who find in the arcana of Hinduism the basis of certain esoteric doctrines which they believe to be the ultimate truths of religion."[3] As examples, we need only mention Professor Max Muller, Madame Blavatsky, Colonel H. S. Olcott, and Mrs. Annie Besant with respect to Hinduism; and Pierre Loti, Claude Ferrère, and Wilfred Blunt, with respect to Islam. Most of the Western writers on Eastern religions have devoted their attention

3. *India and the Future,* p. 56.

to the teachings of the Vedas and the Koran. But the revival in India has in general been on another plane. It has tended to emphasize the later and often less elevated features. Hindus are holding more anti-cow-killing conferences and, with a few honorable exceptions, are asserting more vigorously than ever the validity of caste, child marriage, and the ban on the remarriage of widows. The Sarda Act of 1930, designed to remedy the worst abuses of child marriage, was supported by a small group of liberals, but was criticized by orthodox Hindus and even by orthodox Moslems, and it is doubtful whether it can be very widely enforced. The reactionary character of the religious revival is also shown by the fact that nearly all of the Hindu reform organizations founded during the nineteenth century have declined except those that have abandoned the fight against caste. The Arya Samaj retains its popularity largely because it is anti-British and because it staunchly supports the movement for the reconversion of Hindus who have become Moslems or Christians.

The Asiatic revolt has been greatly strengthened by the immigration restrictions of the United States and the British Dominions and by the ill-treatment of Asiatics who have already been allowed to settle in those countries. It is useless to argue in these cases that the motives are economic; the Asiatic prefers to regard all discriminatory legislation as evidence of racial hostility. The resentment which the people of India feel against the United States stimulates their national self-consciousness, but it does not directly affect their relations with Great Britain. We are concerned here, therefore, only with the treatment of Indians in other parts of the British Empire.

Attention has already been called to the fact that the population of India has grown more rapidly during the last three or four decades than the supply of arable land or the capacity to pay for the importation of food. This is the chief cause of emigration, but there is a secondary motive suggested by the large number of outcaste Hindus, especially in the Madras presidency, who have expatriated themselves in recent years to improve their social status. The relaxation of caste rules abroad also results in greater industrial mobility and thereby increases the opportunity for economic advancement. A son is practically compelled to follow his father's trade if he remains in India, whereas if he goes to another country he may enter a more congenial and possibly a more profitable field of industry.

The pressure of population upon the means of subsistence has been relieved to some extent by internal migration, to the factories of Calcutta and Bombay, and the tea gardens of Assam, for example, but we are now interested only in the problem of emigration. Indian emigration for labor purposes began in the early part of the nineteenth century, but it did not make much headway until after the abolition of slavery in the British Empire in 1834. The indenture system, under which most of these men worked, was subject to a great deal of abuse. Wages were low, the cost of living was high, and the housing facilities were inadequate, while practically nothing was done to discourage prostitution, drunkenness, and gambling. Efforts were also made to prevent the laborer, when his indenture expired, from becoming a peasant proprietor or otherwise establishing himself as a free settler, the object being to compel him to renew his contract or return to India. In 1916, the indenture system was abolished by the government of India and, in 1922, assisted emigration of any kind was forbidden except to countries specially approved by both houses of the Indian legislature. Emigration of this character is now restricted to Ceylon, British Malaya, and British Guiana, and elaborate precautions are taken to prevent abuse.

These laborers have played an important part in the development of tea and rubber in Ceylon, rubber in the Federated Malay States, sugar in Mauritius, Fiji, and Jamaica, sugar and tea in Natal, coffee and sisal in East Africa, sugar and rice in British Guiana, and cocoa in Trinidad and Tobago. According to the figures compiled for the *Indian Year Book* for 1935–36,[4] there are 2,232,676 Indians living in other parts of the Empire. Of these 650,577 are in Ceylon, 624,009 in British Malaya, 265,796 in Mauritius, 140,689 in Trinidad and Tobago, 134,059 in British Guiana, 78,975 in Fiji, 39,644 in Kenya, 23,422 in Tanganyikaland, 17,950 in Jamaica, and about 30,000 in other dependent colonies and pro-

4. p. 986.

tectorates. There are 173,449 in the Union of South Africa, but the number in the other Dominions is very small—about 1,400 in Canada, 2,000 in Australia, 1,200 in New Zealand, and none in the Irish Free State.

There are really two problems of Indian emigration, one dealing with Indians who settle in the tropical colonies and protectorates and the other dealing with those who settle or who would like to settle in the Dominions. In the former case, the emigrants are brought into competition with indolent or inefficient native labor and they are welcome so long as their economic aspirations do not conflict too violently with those of the resident European population; in the latter, they compete with European labor and are usually not wanted in any capacity whatever. There are also constitutional differences. In the one case, the British government is responsible for the solution of the problem; in the other, although the British government may give advice and endeavor to arbitrate, the ultimate responsibility rests with the local authorities. In South Africa the two problems overlap. The Union of South Africa is a self-governing Dominion and it lies in the temperate zone, but in Natal, which is one of its constituent provinces, the climate is tropical, the European population is comparatively small, and there is a keen demand for plantation labor. Somewhat similar conditions prevail in Kenya and Tanganyikaland, where Indians are welcomed as unskilled laborers, although every effort is made to prevent them from encroaching upon the highland areas which are suitable for European colonization. The same problem would arise in Australia if the suggestion that Indians should be allowed to colonize the Northern Territory were adopted.

The Nationalists contend (a) that Indians are British citizens and should have free access to any part of the British Empire, and (b) that they should have equal civil and political rights with His Majesty's European subjects in all parts of the Empire. The first of these issues is practically confined to the Dominions,[5] but the other exists wherever there are enough Indians to constitute a separate community. All of the Dominions except the Irish Free State have adopted a general policy

5. Kenya is the only important exception.

of excluding Oriental emigrants. This is usually accomplished by indirect methods. In Canada, for example, the immigration laws in force since 1908 provide that the Governor-General in Council, by proclamation or order, may prohibit the landing of any immigrant who has not come by a continuous journey from a country of which he is a native or a naturalized citizen and on a through ticket purchased in that country or prepaid in Canada, and who does not also possess a minimum amount of money which "may vary according to the race, occupation or destination of the emigrant." These regulations are applied to Indians and they have proved effective. Those who have the necessary amount of money find it impossible to comply with the other requirements since there is no direct passenger service between India and Canada and no sale of through tickets. The immigration records show that 2,623 Indians were admitted in 1908 and only 118 in the twelve years from 1909 to 1920 inclusive.

There has also been a tendency in Canada to discriminate against Indians as compared with other Asiatics. A limited number of Japanese are admitted annually under a "gentlemen's agreement" concluded in 1908, and they are allowed to bring in their wives and children, although this privilege was not extended to Indians until 1921. From 1904 until 1924, there were no special restrictions on Chinese immigration except the payment of a head tax of $500. The results of this differential treatment are shown in the immigration statistics for the years 1908–20, during which 118 Indians, 7,961 Japanese, and 35,910 Chinese were admitted. The Indians are now treated better than the Chinese, who have been rapidly excluded since 1924, but they are still at a disadvantage as compared with the Japanese. During the period from 1921 to 1934, there were 641 Indian immigrants, mostly wives and children of the permanent settlers, and 4,954 Japanese.[6]

In Australia there is a dictation test for Asiatics and other colored immigrants which may be imposed in any European

6. The Immigration Acts of 1908 and 1910 and the Orders in Council of June 3, 1908; *The Canada Year Book* for 1934–35, p. 224. For an account of the *Komagata Maru* episode in 1914 see chap. ii. See also Cheng Tien-Fang, *Oriental Immigration in Canada,* 1931.

language. New Zealand formerly had a literacy test, but it was elementary in character and Indians educated in Fiji were sometimes able to pass it. To meet this difficulty, a new system was put into operation in 1920. Any person, not of British (European) birth or parentage, who wishes to become a permanent settler must make an application in writing from his country of residence, stating in detail his qualifications for settlement. If the Dominion Minister of Customs is satisfied that the application is desirable he is authorized to grant a permit of entry. The Governor-General by proclamation may exempt any country and any people from the operation of the regulation, but it is well understood that he will not do so in the case of Asiatics. The Union of South Africa passed an immigration act in 1913 which provides for the Australian type of dictation test and also empowers the executive authorities to forbid the entry of any person or class of persons who are regarded as undesirable on economic grounds or on account of standards or habits of life. These Dominions have also extended their immigration restrictions to the mandatory territories. Mr. Srinivasa Sastri called attention to this fact at the meeting of the Assembly of the League of Nations in September, 1921. He was especially concerned about South-West Africa, where there had never been any racial ban on immigration when it was a German colony.

There are other grievances connected with the immigration problem, some of which have aroused a good deal of bitter feeling, but they are of secondary importance and are now in process of settlement. The first immigrants to the Dominions were adult male laborers, either free or indentured. As soon as they could save enough money they usually sent home for their wives and children. The exclusion laws were put into operation before this process was completed, with the result that each Dominion had to decide whether it would encourage prostitution and miscegenation or permit the creation of a permanent Indian element in its population. Canada, Australia, and New Zealand chose the former alternative and, until after the meeting of the Imperial Conference of 1918, refused to make any concessions in favor of women and children. The Union of South Africa passed a law in 1914 which allows any Indian who has established a permanent residence to bring in one lawful wife and her minor children. Another grievance arises from the fact that wherever there is a considerable Indian population there is always a demand for religious and professional leaders and other educated men of their own race. Immigrants of this type are ordinarily excluded, although a few are occasionally admitted by special permit into Canada, Australia, and New Zealand and twelve are allowed annually to enter the Union of South Africa. Finally, there is the question of tourists, students, merchants, and other visitors and temporary residents. Until 1918, there was some uncertainty about their rights and they were frequently humiliated by the enforcement of administrative measures employed to distinguish between them and the permanent residents.

The whole problem was discussed at the Imperial Conferences of 1911, 1917, and 1918 and a compromise was finally adopted. The Indian representatives accepted the principle that "it is an inherent function of the Government of the several communities of the British Commonwealth, including India, that each should enjoy complete control of the composition of its own population by means of restrictions on immigration from any of the other communities." In return for this concession, the representatives from the Dominions recognized the rights of Indian visitors and temporary residents and agreed that Indians already domiciled in other British countries should be allowed to bring in their wives and minor children, on condition that not more than one wife and her children should be admitted for each such Indian and that each individual so admitted should be certified by the government of India as being the lawful wife and child of such Indian. In accordance with this agreement, steps were taken in the various Dominions to provide a more courteous method of dealing with Indian visitors and Indians who had become permanent residents were generally allowed to bring in their wives and children.

We come now to the second main question: should Indians who have established a legal domicile in other parts of the Empire have equal rights with His Majesty's European subjects? The Imperial Conference of 1921 considered this question and adopted a resolution which "recognizes that there is incongruity between the position of India, as an equal member of the Empire, and the existence of disabilities upon British Indians lawfully domiciled in some parts of the Empire" and urged that the rights of such Indians to citizenship should be recognized. The representatives of South Africa regretted "their inability to accept this resolution in view of the exceptional circumstances of the greater part of the Union," and there were other parts of the Empire in which it was equally unpopular.

The chief centers of trouble in recent years have been the Union of South Africa and the colony and protectorate of Kenya. The racial and economic conditions in these areas are substantially the same. In both cases, Europeans and Asiatics meet on neutral ground, being greatly outnumbered by a native African population which represents a lower stage of civilization. In their relations with the natives, the Europeans of all classes have developed a strong sense of racial solidarity. They keep the natives in a state of social and political subjection, but, with a few exceptions, they do not interfere very much with their economic freedom. There is in fact comparatively little economic friction between the two races because the native does most of the unskilled labor which the European is glad to escape. With the Indian the case is different. The points of contact with the Europeans are more numerous. The Indian is thrifty and exceedingly zealous in asserting what he believes to be his rights. He competes with the European in business, he wishes to live in European residential districts, he objects to being excluded from the right to own land in the salubrious highland areas which the European reserves for himself, and he bitterly resents the "Jim Crow" legislation which puts him in the same class with the blanket Kaffir. He aspires to political privileges partly because he is ambitious and partly because he regards the ballot as essential for the protection of his social and economic interests.

The first Indian immigrants to South Africa were indentured laborers brought over in 1860 to work on the sugar and tea plantations of Natal. The experiment was successful and they continued to come in a fairly steady stream until the government of India put an end to the movement in 1911. There was also a considerable immigration of free Indian settlers in both Natal and Cape Colony until restrictions were imposed by the former in 1897 and the latter in 1903.[7] The Dutch were not so hospitable as the British. Some Indian traders began to settle in the Orange Free State and the Transvaal about 1885. The Free State expelled them almost immediately and adopted a policy of rigid exclusion, although a few hotel waiters and household servants have been admitted under special permits. The Transvaal would have followed this example, if the British government had not interfered under Article 14 of the Convention of London of 1884 which guaranteed the rights of British subjects. As a result, there were several thousand Indians living in the country at the beginning of the South African War in 1899. Curiously enough, when the British acquired complete control at the end of the war, they proceeded to carry out the very policy that they had previously forbidden. Lord Milner's Peace Preservation Ordinance, 1902, provided that Indians who were then living in the province should not be disturbed and that those who had acquired a legal residence before the war should be allowed to return, but there was to be no further immigration. This policy was sanctioned by the Immigrants Regulation Act (Union), 1913, which excludes Indians and other Asiatics from the Union and rigidly restricts the freedom of interprovincial migration. The *Indian Year Book* for 1935–36 estimates that there were 150,920 Indians in Natal, 15,747 in the Transvaal, 6,665 in Cape Colony, and 127 in the Orange Free State.

There has been very little friction in Cape Colony and the Orange Free State. In the former, adult male Indians are allowed to vote in both parliamentary and municipal elections, and, so far as provincial regulations are concerned, they also

7. The educational test imposed under the Natal Immigration Act of 1897 prevented a wholesale influx of free Indians, but it did not exclude them altogether. There was in fact a fairly steady increase in the numbers admitted until 1913. The Cape legislation was more effective. Excluding the Malays, who are practically indigenous to the country, the resident Asiatic population decreased from 10,242 in 1904 to 7,690 in 1911.

have unrestricted rights to trade and to hold real estate. The municipalities, however, occasionally discriminate in the granting of trade licenses and there is a certain amount of discrimination under the laws enacted by the Union Parliament.[8] The policy of the Free State is not so liberal. Indians are excluded from both the parliamentary and the municipal franchise and are forbidden to own land or engage in trade, but they are not numerous enough to constitute a serious problem.

In Natal, the Indian population is almost as large as the European, although they are both in a small minority as compared with the native Africans. When their original indentures expired many of the Indians remained in the province as free settlers. This did not meet with popular approval and a scheme was devised to compel them either to renew the indentures or return to India. Under the authority of a provincial statute passed in 1895, a clause was inserted in all new indentures to the effect that any immigrant that remained in the province after his indenture expired must pay a poll tax of £3 a year. This regulation was interpreted to include women, and in 1903 it was extended to the children of immigrants, boys over sixteen and girls over thirteen, even when they were born in Natal. This caused a great deal of hardship and it was one of the most serious Indian grievances when the Union was formed in 1910. Its subsequent history will be considered later.

Ex-indentured Indians usually remain on the land. They and their descendants have prospered until they now occupy a large part of the fertile lowland area of Natal. Some of the younger generation have drifted into Durban and other towns where they compete with Europeans in shopkeeping, clerical work, and even in the learned professions. The mercantile business, however, is chiefly in the hands of the free immigrants referred to above, many of them Moslem traders from the Bombay presidency. Starting as humble purveyors of food and clothing to their own people, these merchants have practically monopolized the retail trade of the low country—European, native, and Asiatic. There are now three main sources of

8. Act No. 18, 1930, which confers the suffrage franchise upon European women, is a good example of this kind of discrimination.

friction in this province: the Europeans are trying (1) to restrict the number of trading licenses issued to Indians in Pietermaritzburg, Ladysmith, Dundee, and other towns in the high veld district of the north; (2) to reserve the agricultural land in these districts for European settlers; and (3) to prevent Indians from encroaching upon the native reserves in Zululand which are under the control of the provincial government. The Indians of Natal have been excluded from the parliamentary franchise since 1896, but, as will be seen later, there were no restrictions imposed upon their right to vote in the municipalities until 1924.

There has also been considerable trouble in the Transvaal, although the Indians constitute less than 1 per cent of the population[9] and have always been disfranchised. This is partly because they are increasing more rapidly than the Europeans, partly because they are concentrated in Johannesburg, Pretoria, and other urban centers, where they come into active competition with European artisans and traders, and partly because the Dutch there have always been more obstinate in their racial prejudices than the British. The anti-Asiatic fervor of the Dutch was somewhat tempered before the South African War by the opposition of the British government, but there is one important statute of that period that is still in force. This is Law 3 of 1885 which forbids Asiatics to own any fixed property in the Transvaal except in certain streets, wards, or other locations designated by the government. Another controversial measure passed before the formation of the Union is the Gold Law of the Transvaal (Act 35, 1908), which prohibits Asiatics from residing or occupying any stand on proclaimed ground except as *bona fide* servants. Nearly all

9. There were 13,405 Indians, 544,987 Europeans, and 1,535,885 Bantus and others in the province in 1921. The increase for the decade 1911–21 was approximately 33 per cent for Indians and 29 per cent for Europeans. The estimated increase for the period 1921–30 was 30 per cent for Asiatics and 20 per cent for Europeans. The Indians were not listed separately in this estimate, but it is well known that they constitute the chief element in the Asiatic population. See *The Official Year Book of the Union of South Africa,* 1929–30, pp. 861, 880.

of the Rand and some of the larger urban areas in other parts of the province have been set aside by executive order as proclaimed land. Both of these laws were contested in the courts and were generally evaded until 1919. Two methods of nullifying the Act of 1885 were commonly employed. A European, acting as a dummy, might buy land and mortgage it to an Indian for the purchase price or a limited liability company might hold it under a decision of the courts that a company is not Asiatic, whatever may be the race of its shareholders.

The Union government inherited this problem in 1910 and also a bitter quarrel over the exclusion of Asiatics from the Transvaal. Lord Milner's Peace Preservation Ordinance of 1902 checked to some extent the flood of Asiatic migration from Natal, but it was not wholly effective because it did not provide an adequate system of registration and identification. This defect was remedied after the establishment of responsible government by the passage of the Asiatic Registration Act and the Transvaal Immigrants' Restriction Act of 1907. Asiatics entitled to live in the province were required to register and have finger and thumb impressions taken as a means of identification. The story of Mr. Gandhi's passive resistance campaign against these measures is well known. It is perhaps not so well known that in the course of the struggle he took up other Indian grievances, especially the £3 tax on ex-indentured immigrants in Natal, and the decision of the Cape Supreme Court (March 14, 1913) invalidating Hindu and Moslem marriages. While the conflict was in progress the government of India stopped indentured emigration to Natal (1911) and the government of South Africa imposed more effective checks upon the immigration and interprovincial migration of free Indians (1913).

The Smuts-Gandhi Agreement of 1914 was embodied in the Indians' Relief Act and in a series of letters that passed between General Smuts and Mr. Gandhi. The £3 tax of Natal was repealed, monogamous Hindu and Moslem marriages were validated, a few "specially exempted" educated Indians were allowed to enter the country as permanent residents, and any Indian who had established a legal domicile was permitted to bring in one lawful wife and his minor children. General Smuts also agreed that existing laws should continue to be "administered in a just manner with due regard to vested rights." There has been some controversy about the interpretation and general character of this agreement. The South African authorities are willing to agree "that the vested rights of those Indians who were then living and trading in townships, whether in contravention of the law or not, should be respected," but they refuse to accept the theory that the rights of Indians should never be less than they were in 1914. General Smuts had no power to bind his government forever and the "vested rights" clause was not susceptible to that interpretation.

The agreement proved to be merely a truce. The conflict was renewed in the Transvaal in 1919 over the issue of trading licenses and the attempt to enforce Law 3 of 1885 and the Gold Law of 1908. The Indian commercial community made great progress during the war. Seventy-one new general trading licenses were issued to Indians on the Rand between 1914 and 1919 and on May 1, 1919, there were 370 limited liability companies registered in the Transvaal with exclusively Indian shareholders. There were 27 Indian and 4 European grocers in Krugersdorp, and two large European firms had recently been driven into bankruptcy and their premises taken over by their Indian competitors. The Municipal Council of Krugersdorp tried to check this movement by refusing to issue new licenses to Indians on the ground that they were not "desirable persons," but an appeal was taken from its decision and the magistrate ruled that race or color alone was not a good and sufficient test of desirability. The Council was more successful, however, in another case which involved the interpretation of the Gold Act of 1908. An injunction was secured from the Supreme Court at Pretoria restraining T. W. Becket and Company, a European firm, from permitting certain Indians to reside at a stand in Krugersdorp which that firm had leased to an Indian tailor. The whole question was brought before the Union Parliament and, after an investigation by a Select Committee, the Asiatics (Land and Trading) Amendment Act (Transvaal) (No. 37 of 1919) was passed. Vested interests acquired by Asiatics before May 1, 1919, were guaranteed, but a ban was imposed on the issue of new trading licenses in proclaimed areas and the future acquisition of fixed property by forming limited liability companies or by using European agents as trustees.[10]

Owing to the protests of the Indians against this legislation and the protest of the Europeans that the investigations of the Select Committee had not gone far enough, the Governor-General appointed an Asiatic Inquiry Commission on February 3, 1920. The commission presented an ad interim report on May 12, 1920, and the final report on March 3, 1921. The chief recommendations were (1) that the three acts discussed above—Law 3 of 1885 (Transvaal), the Gold Law of 1908 (Transvaal), and Act No. 37 of 1919—should not be repealed; (2) that there should be no compulsory repatriation of Asiatics, but that voluntary repatriation should be encouraged; (3) that there should be no compulsory segregation, but a system of voluntary segregation should be introduced to be administered by the municipalities; (4) that in Natal the right of Asiatics to acquire and own agricultural land, outside of the townships, should be restricted to an area along the coast from twenty to thirty miles wide; (5) that Law 3 of 1885 should apply to the three high veld districts which Natal acquired from the Transvaal at the close of the Boer War; (6) that the existing laws excluding Asiatics from the native reserves in Zululand and the Transkei territories should continue in force; (7) that a uniform license law should be enacted or, if that was impossible, the provincial laws should be consolidated by an act of Parliament which should lay down certain common principles of action; and (8) that the immigration laws should be rigidly enforced and Asiatics who had entered the country illegally should be deported. Some of these recommendations require a little further explanation. Voluntary segregation apparently meant that a municipality could compel Asiatics to live or to do business in certain prescribed areas, provided they were compensated for the loss of vested rights already acquired outside of those areas. The recommendation dealing with the ownership of agricultural land in

10. For a full discussion of the investigations of the Select Committee see *The Round Table,* X, 445–462.

Natal was the most serious in that it affected the largest number of people. It was obviously intended that the bulk of the Indian population should be confined forever to the low coastal belt of the province which is unsuitable for European settlement.

The Indian community bitterly denounced these proposals and its indignation was shared by the government and the people of India. The question was brought before the Imperial Conference of 1921, with the result already mentioned. A resolution was adopted calling attention to the incongruity between the position of India as an equal member of the Empire and the existence of disabilities upon Indians lawfully domiciled in other parts of the Empire and recommending that their rights to citizenship should be recognized. The resolution was not accepted by the Union of South Africa, but it probably exerted considerable influence on its Indian policy, especially during the period while General Smuts and the South African party were in power. There was no immediate effort to carry out the recommendations of the Inquiry Commission, and the Governor-General, acting on the advice of the Ministry, vetoed two successive Natal ordinances to exclude Asiatics from the municipal franchise[11] and also a Natal ordinance to restrict the number of trade licenses issued to Indians. General Smuts was finally compelled, however, to make some concessions to the rising tide of racial prejudice. Although they were not mentioned by name, the Class Areas Bill, introduced in the Union Parliament in 1923, provided for the segregation of Asiatics in residential and trading areas to be set aside by the municipal authorities. The bill lapsed when the Assembly was dissolved preliminary to the general election of 1924.

The new Nationalist government under General Hertzog was committed to a still more drastic racial policy. The Natal Boroughs Ordinance was revived and approved (1924) and the Mines and Works Amendment Bill, commonly called the

11. The Natal Boroughs Ordinances safeguarded the rights of Asiatics who already had the borough franchise, but forbade its acquisition by Asiatics in the future.

Color Bar Bill, was introduced in the Assembly in February, 1925. Before the great strike on the Rand in 1922, a number of skilled and semiskilled positions in the mining industry were reserved for Europeans. There was a conventional color bar, which was based on agreements between the Chamber of Mines and the trade unions, and a legal color bar, which was established by administrative regulations issued under the Mines and Works Act of 1911. The conventional bar was abolished at the time of the strike and the legal bar was practically nullified by a judgment of the Transvaal Provincial Division of the Supreme Court in the case of Rex *versus* Hildick Smith in 1923. The chief object of the Color Bar Bill was to legalize the practice which had been invalidated by this judgment. In its original form the bill provided that certificates of competence to hold the reserved jobs should not be issued to African natives or Asiatics, but, as a result of representations made by the government of India, the form was changed from the negative to the positive. Certificates were to be issued only to Europeans, Cape Colored people (mulattoes), and Cape Malays.[12] The government of India was also alarmed because the bill applied to the entire Union, whereas the Mines and Works Act of 1911 was in force only in the Transvaal, and because it made it possible for the administrative authorities to bring new positions under the protection of the color bar. There was a danger that Indians everywhere would be excluded from all skilled and semiskilled occupations. The only assurance that they could obtain from the Union government was that there was no present intention of going beyond the position reached before the Hildick Smith decision and that if any further extension was contemplated in the future an opportunity would be given to the Indians of South Africa to receive a hearing. There were other objections to the bill and it became a subject of political controversy. It passed the As-

12. The inclusion of Cape Colored and Cape Malays with Europeans is in harmony with the general racial policy of the Hertzog government, but it naturally increases the irritation and humiliation of Asiatics to be the only people who are put in the same class with the African natives.

sembly twice and was defeated in the Senate, where the South African party had a majority, but was finally enacted at a joint session of the two houses in May, 1926.

The Hertzog government also renewed the Class Areas Bill and greatly widened its scope. The ban on the ownership of land by Asiatics which was already in force in the Transvaal and the Orange Free State, was to be extended to Cape Colony and the highlands of Natal. A coast belt thirty miles wide was to be set apart in Natal, but even in that area Asiatics could acquire land only from other Asiatics. A more rigid immigration scheme was also proposed and the measure finally became known as the Areas Reservation and Immigration (Further Provision) Bill. At the request of the government of India, action on this bill was delayed and a conference was held at Cape Town from December 17, 1926, to January 11, 1927, to consider the Indian problem in South Africa in all its aspects. The chairman of the Indian delegation was Sir Mohammed Habibullah and the settlement that was finally reached is known as the Hertzog-Habibullah Agreement, or simply as the Cape Town Agreement of 1927. It was to remain in force for a period of five years, from January, 1927, until January, 1932.

The government of India recognized the right of South Africa to use all just and legitimate means to maintain Western standards of life and the government of South Africa agreed that Indians domiciled in the Union, who were prepared to conform to Western standards, should be enabled to do so. Indians who wished to emigrate to India or to other countries where Western standards were not required would be assisted by the Union government.[13] They might return within three years, on refunding the money advanced by the government, but after three years of continuous absence their Union domicile would be lost. The government of India agreed to look after such emigrants on their arrival in India. The resolution of the Imperial Conference of 1918 relating to the admission into the Union of the wives and minor children of

13. This is called *assisted emigration.* The old term *repatriation* was dropped, at the request of the government of India, because most of the emigrants were born in South Africa.

Indians who have established a permanent domicile was reaffirmed. The Union government promised not to proceed further with the Areas Reservation . . . Bill and both governments agreed to watch the workings of the settlement and exchange views from time to time as to any changes that experience might suggest. The eighth and last article contains a formal request from the government of South Africa that the government of India should appoint an agent in the Union in order to secure continuous and effective coöperation between the two governments. The essence of the compromise was this: The Union government recognized the right of the Indian government to take an interest in the Indian population in South Africa and to make representation about domestic legislation that might affect their welfare, and the Indian government accepted the policy of the Union government to reduce its Indian population by assisted emigration and agreed to cooperate.

The history of this settlement was similar to that of the Smuts-Gandhi Agreement of 1914. It relieved the immediate tension and impressed some of the political leaders with a sense of imperial responsibility, but it did not effect a permanent solution of the problem. The Extremists of both races never accepted it in the proper spirit and the Moderates were not always able to agree on the applications of its principles to concrete cases. It is doubtful whether it would have succeeded at all if it had not been for the courtesy, good sense, and diplomatic skill of the Honorable Srinivasa Sastri, the first Indian Agent-General in South Africa (1927–29). His successor, Sir Kurma V. Reddi, was also tactful and courteous, although he was handicapped by ill health and a revival of racial prejudice. General Hertzog was inclined to follow the path of conciliation, but that was not the case with Mr. Tielmann Roos, Minister of Justice from 1924 to 1929, or with Dr. D. F. Malan, Minister of the Interior, Education, and Public Health from 1924 to 1933. The chief sources of friction were assisted emigration, the "condonation scheme," the employment of Indians on licensed premises, and the old question of Asiatic trading licenses in the Transvaal.

The voluntary repatriation of Asiatics with government

assistance had been a feature of South African policy for several years. The Cape Town Agreement, as interpreted by the Indian community, merely endorsed this policy and provided for coöperation on the part of the government of India. Emigration might be stimulated by South African money and Indian hospitality, but it would still be on a purely voluntary basis. A new plan might be devised, but it would be intended only "for those Indians in the Union who may wish to avail themselves of it." This interpretation was rejected by Dr. Malan and a large section of the European community. The agreement recognized the right of South Africa "to use all just and legitimate means for the maintenance of Western standards of life," guaranteed that Indians who were prepared to conform to those standards should be enabled to do so, and approved "a scheme of assisted emigration to India or other countries where Western standards are not required." This implied that assisted emigration was a just and legitimate means of getting rid of Indians who were not prepared to conform to Western standards and that the use of force to compel their departure was justified. If this interpretation was accepted, there would have to be a legal definition of "Western standards of life" so that the test could be applied in individual cases. Dr. Malan evidently expected a high standard to be established because he was quoted as saying that the aim of the agreement was to reduce the Indian population of South Africa to an irreducible minimum.

The new plan was put into operation in August, 1927. It provided that any Indian who wished to leave the country permanently should receive a liberal bonus in addition to the cost of transportation. In accordance with the Cape Town Agreement, he might return within three years on refunding the money advanced by the government, but he lost his domicile if he remained away more than three years. The plan worked fairly well for the first two years. Dr. Malan stated in a speech in the Assembly in August, 1929, that between 6,000 and 7,000 people had taken advantage of it and only 4 of them had returned. The bonus was the chief stimulant, but a part of the result should perhaps be attributed to the more rigid enforcement of the Color Bar Act and other racial economic legislation. There was probably very little direct pressure and no serious effort was made to apply the Western standards test. It is doubtful if the plan can ever be carried very far on a voluntary basis. The chief object is to get rid of the trading community, especially in the Transvaal, but nearly all of the emigrants have gone from the rural sections of Natal. There has also been a decline in the movement itself since the summer of 1929. The number of non-Europeans (mostly Indians) departing permanently from South Africa was 3,267 in 1927–28, 3,782 in 1928–29, and 1,450 in 1929–30, and the amount spent on Asiatic assisted emigration dropped from £83,826 in 1927–28 and £70,099 in 1928–29 to £28,474 in 1929–30.[14] There is still a net official loss from emigration, but it is more than offset by the excess of births over deaths and by the illegal immigration that has occurred in recent years.

Illegal immigration has become a serious problem. In 1927, when the Cape Town Agreement was signed, there were several thousand Indians in South Africa who had entered the country in violation of the law. Most of them had either been smuggled across the frontier from Portuguese East Africa or had been admitted on certificates of domicile purchased from Indians who had returned to India. A few had come in with false affidavits issued by European residents in South Africa stating that they had previously acquired a domicile. In 1928, the government put forward a "condonation scheme," in which it offered to condone or legitimatize the position of these people on two conditions: (1) they must give up the fraudulent papers upon which they had been admitted, and (2) the Indian community, through the South African Indian Congress, must promise not to countenance or assist the illegal entry of Indians in the future. If the conditions were accepted, the government would issue protective certificates or guarantee, in some other way, the right of the illegal entrants to remain in South Africa. Mr. Sastri urged the Indians to accept this offer, but most of those who were immediately affected were afraid that it was merely a scheme to obtain their names with a view to subsequent deportation. They also felt that an administrative guarantee was inadequate and that no action

14. *Official Year Book,* 1929–30, pp. 779, 892.

should be taken until the Union Parliament passed a bill of amnesty. As this was a political impossibility, the scheme fell through.

A liquor bill, which contained a clause prohibiting the employment of Asiatics on licensed premises, was introduced into the Assembly by Mr. Tielmann Roos in January, 1928. Although it was not retroactive, it would in time have affected about 3,000 Indian waiters and cooks in Natal and a considerable number in the other provinces. The proposal was criticized by Mr. Sastri and by some of the leaders of the South African party as a violation of the Cape Town Agreement and it was finally abandoned.

Since that time there has been no serious trouble except in the Transvaal, where the old conflict with the Indian trading community was revived in 1930.[15] Although Act No. 37 of 1919 was intended to prevent Asiatics from acquiring or occupying fixed property on the Rand after May 1, 1919, it did not fully accomplish its purpose. Licenses to trade in proclaimed areas were occasionally issued to Asiatics by the local authorities and it was assumed that they validated the occupation of the stands that were needed to carry on the business. The courts upheld this view, although the licenses were issued on the explicit condition that the grant of trading rights did not validate illegal occupation. The matter was brought before the Union Assembly early in 1930 and the Transvaal Asiatic Tenure (Amendment) Bill passed its first reading on May 14. This provided that the law should be rigidly enforced and that all Asiatics who were occupying stands illegally should be given five years to dispose of their businesses. The area affected by this type of legislation was somewhat extended and there was also more rigid provision for dealing

15. The act which provided for the enfranchisement of European women in 1930 involved a discrimination against all non-European women living in South Africa, but it did not arouse very much criticism. This was the first time that a racial qualification for the suffrage was ever imposed in Cape Colony. There was really no new discrimination in the other provinces because they had already confined the suffrage to Europeans.

with segregation and the granting of trade licenses. The Indian community was greatly alarmed, but, at the request of the government of India, the bill was postponed from time to time until after the next conference between the representatives of the Union and Indian governments.

This conference was held at Cape Town, January 12 through February 4, 1932, to consider the renewal of the Agreement of 1927. Dr. Malan was the chairman of the South African delegation and Sir Fazl-i-Husain the chairman of the Indian delegation. The main features of the agreement were continued, but it was recognized that the possibilities of repatriation to India were now exhausted partly because of the economic conditions in India and partly because 80 per cent of the Indians living in South Africa were of South African birth. The two governments were to coöperate, however, in assisting Indians to emigrate from South Africa to other countries and were to investigate the possibilities of land settlement schemes devised for that purpose. The Transvaal Asiatic Tenure Bill was considered by a subcommittee and it was agreed that certain changes should be recommended to the Select Committee of the Union Parliament which had the bill in charge. The segregation and license clauses were to be liberalized and, under certain conditions, the titles to fixed property acquired by Asiatic companies prior to May 1, 1930, were to be validated, but the South African delegates refused to recommend any change in the clause extending the area affected by anti-Asiatic legislation.

The Indians were not entirely satisfied with the results of the conference. The Tenure Bill was shorn of some of its worst provisions before its final enactment, but it increased the area subject to racial discrimination and it tried to close the gaps in the legislation of 1885, 1908, and 1919. It will be more difficult in the future for Indians or Indian companies to secure trading licenses or acquire fixed property in the Transvaal. At the same time, they were greatly relieved by the announcement that the Union government was prepared to abandon the policy of repatriation. The suggestion that Indians from South Africa might establish agricultural colonies in other countries does not sound practical, but if an attempt is ever made to carry it out, the government and people of India will insist that it shall be done on a purely voluntary basis.

In the other Dominions the Indian population is small, but there is a certain amount of differential treatment. The resolution on this subject adopted by the Imperial Conference of 1921 has already been discussed. Shortly after the conference adjourned, Mr. Sastri made a semi-official visit to Australia, New Zealand, and Canada to find out what steps were being taken to put the resolution into force.[16] In Australia he found that Indians, in common with other Asiatics, suffered a few minor disabilities. They could not vote in the Commonwealth parliamentary elections unless they were entitled by the laws of the state in which they resided to vote in the elections for the more numerous house of the state Parliament. Under this regulation they were disfranchised in Queensland and Western Australia. They were disqualified from obtaining leases of land in certain irrigated and reclaimed areas and from receiving invalid and old-age pensions. The various acts providing for the payment of bounties on goods grown or produced by white labor also constituted a discrimination. In Queensland there were laws requiring educational tests for employment in the dairy, banana, and sugar industries which were designed to exclude colored labor. In Western Australia mining rights could not be granted to Asiatics or Africans, even when they were British subjects, without special ministerial approval.

Through the efforts of Mr. Sastri, some of these restrictions were removed. The Commonwealth franchise was granted to Indians in 1925 and other acts were passed later admitting them to the benefits of invalid and old-age pension and maternity allowances. Queensland has enfranchised them and admitted them to the banana industry, and South Australia has

16. There is, of course, no British India problem in the Irish Free State. The conditions in Southern Rhodesia are similar to those that exist in the Union of South Africa and there is the same kind of differential treatment, but the Indian population is too small to constitute a serious menace.

agreed to remove the ban on the granting of lands in irrigated and reclaimed areas. They are still excluded from the state franchise in West Australia and a few of the economic restrictions are still in force.

In New Zealand, Indians have full franchise privileges. The only grievances of this domiciled community at the time of Mr. Sastri's visit was their exclusion from old-age pensions and a few technical restrictions on the granting of passports for visits to India. The New Zealand government promised to give sympathetic consideration to Indian representations when the Old-Age Pension Act came up for revision.[17] It also agreed to liberalize the passport regulations if a satisfactory method of preventing the fraudulent use of passports could be devised.

The problem in Canada is confined to the Pacific coast. In British Columbia, Indians and other Asiatics are entirely disfranchised and are ineligible for employment on public works. They were also excluded from employment on Crown-granted lands until 1922 when the law was declared unconstitutional by the Supreme Court of Canada on the ground that it was contrary to the British North America Act of 1867 and to the obligations of the Japanese Treaty of 1913. There are only a few Indians in the province and the authorities assured Mr. Sastri that they would remove all restrictions against them if it were possible to do so without extending the same privileges to the Japanese and the Chinese.

From the facts given above it is obvious that all of the Dominions have a common interest in the exclusion of Indian immigrants, but that the treatment of Indians who have already secured a legal domicile is a serious problem only in the Union of South Africa. As a matter of fact, the people of South Africa are probably unduly alarmed. Assuming that the present ban on immigration will be maintained, the European ought to be able to hold his own even if he has to abandon a few trades and industries to his Indian competitors. The native African and not the Indian is the real menace to white supremacy.

17. This promise has not been fulfilled. See *The New Zealand Year Book,* 1936, p. 477.

In East Africa, however, the conditions are different. The Indians already outnumber the Europeans by about three to one and their preponderance is increasing. The highland area available for European settlement is comparatively small and the greater part of it is unsuitable for intensive cultivation. There can be no doubt that unless Europeans are given governmental protection they will soon be eliminated. As the London *Times* expressed it in a recent article, the future of Kenya "premises a handful of wealthy men outside the Government service, a few, scarcely so opulent, within it, and for the rest—India." This it is safe to say is the fundamental cause of the bitter anti-Indian prejudice that exists today among the white people of East Africa. It is for them a question of life and death, a question of whether they will continue to live in the land of their adoption or be supplanted, as the Europeans of Mauritius have been supplanted, by a host of Asiatic immigrants. The antagonism is also strengthened by the fact that a large proportion of the settlers came originally from South Africa, where they had already acquired an antipathy to the Indian as a business competitor.

The Indians contend that they were the pioneers in East Africa and that they have done more for the development of the country than the Europeans. A member of the Legislative Council of Kenya attacked this claim in a letter to the London *Times* of August 19, 1921. He admitted that there were a few Indian traders and shopkeepers in Mombasa and Zanzibar in the early days, but he asserted that they never dared to penetrate the interior until the white man blazed the trail. Then they followed in his wake and under his protection. White men developed Kenya with their capital and their capacity to handle native races. The Uganda railway which opened up the Nairobi plateau for settlement and stimulated trade with the rich country about Lake Victoria was planned by British statesmen, financed by British capital, and constructed by British engineers.

This is the plea of the capitalist. It still has the power to influence governmental policy, but it does not arouse very much public sympathy. The white settlers, therefore, in presenting their case before the bar of public opinion in Great Britain are inclined to emphasize the fact that they and the Indians are both intruders in the black man's country and that the interest of the black man should be the paramount consideration. A good example of this is to be found in the following resolution adopted by the Convention of Associations, a European organization in Kenya, at a meeting held in November, 1921:

> The introduction of a form of Eastern control in Africa is a real and potent danger to the Empire. The Imperial Government should not prejudice the future of the African by sharing the burden of responsibility for government with a race who have no right either by conquest or peaceful penetration (except under British protection), to consider themselves entitled to rule the African. . . . European settlers are undoubtedly complementary to African advancement; Asiatics are only detrimental to it.[18]

There is possibly a note of hypocrisy in this statement, but it undoubtedly contains a large element of truth. The native may be subjected to European political control and to European economic exploitation, but there is a good climatic guarantee that he will never be seriously affected by the pressure of European colonization. There is no such protection against India. The Indian is accustomed to live under tropical conditions and experience has shown that he can live and bring up a family in the lowlands of East Africa. Mombasa is only a week's sailing from Bombay and there are millions of Indian peasants who would be glad to exchange their worn-out farms for the fertile well-watered lands of East Africa. If East Africa is thrown open to unlimited Indian immigration there can be only one result, the African will be doomed to extinction along with the European.

British East Africa includes Kenya, with 16,842 Europeans and 55,715 Asiatics; Uganda, with 1,873 Europeans and 14,002 Asiatics; Zanzibar and Pemba, with 278 Europeans and 49,000 Asiatics; and the mandated Territory of Tanganyika, with 6,900 Europeans and 23,000 Asiatics. There are about 50,000 Arabs in Zanzibar and Pemba and the

18. Quoted in the London *Times,* December 12, 1921.

coast sections of Kenya and Tanganyika, but, with this exception, the Asiatics are practically all Indians or Goanese.[19] It should also be remembered that there are about 11,500,000 native Africans, which is more than 98½ per cent of the total population. Kenya is the chief center of trouble. The European settlers in that colony are convinced that it is necessary not only to stop all further immigration from India, but also to discriminate in some measure against the local Indian community. They believe, for example, that Indians should be excluded from ownership of agricultural land in the highlands, that they should be segregated in the towns and that they should never be allowed to acquire enough political influence to endanger European supremacy.

In 1908 the Governor of the East African Protectorate (now Kenya) was informed by Lord Elgin, Secretary of State for the Colonies, that His Majesty's government was opposed in principle to the imposition of legal restrictions on any particular section of the community in regard to the acquisition of land, but that it was willing to agree, as a matter of administrative convenience, that Crown lands in the upland area should not be granted to Indians. Although this regulation was effective so far as it went, it was the general opinion among the permanent European settlers that it did not go far enough, because it did not prevent Indians from acquiring land from the original grantees. In the general exodus of British planters at the beginning of the war some of the best land in the province fell into the hands of Indians. To guard against this danger, an ordinance was sanctioned by the Colonial Office in 1915 which provided that no transfer of land in the highlands could be made by a person of one race to a person of another race without the approval of the Governor, and the Governor was instructed to refuse his assent whenever the proposed purchaser was an Indian.

All the questions at issue between the two communities were brought before Lord Milner while he was at the head of the

19. These figures are taken from *The Dominion Office and Colonial Office List* for 1932. The Goanese are really Indians, but, as Portuguese subjects, they are sometimes listed separately in the population statistics.

Colonial Office and he proposed a settlement in September, 1920, which was favorable to the Europeans. In speaking of the policy of excluding Indians from the right to acquire lands in the highlands, he said:

I do not feel that I should be justified in reversing it. It is clear that if the limited area on which the European settlers can live were thrown open to the competition of Asiatics, who are physically fitted to settle in the other areas from which Europeans are by nature excluded, there would be, taking the Protectorate as a whole, a virtual discrimination in favour of Asiatics as against European settlers.

He went on, however, to add that he was also in favor of setting aside one or more areas of adequate extent and good quality to be used exclusively for Indian agricultural colonization.[20] This would probably be the wisest solution so far as the Europeans and Indians are concerned, but there is always a danger in any scheme of racial land monopoly that there will not be enough care taken to safeguard the interests of the helpless and ignorant natives. As a matter of fact, there is already a tendency in that part of Africa to restrict the native agricultural reserves in order to compel natives to become the wage slaves of Europeans.

Local race segregation in the townships is another highly controversial issue. Practically all Europeans who live in the tropics are convinced that there are good sanitary and social reasons why they should have their own residential quarters, upon which no other race should be allowed to encroach, and they are quite willing that the privilege should be shared by other races. There is also a demand for segregation in the commercial areas, but this is primarily an economic question and the arguments in favor of it are not quite so convincing. Lord Milner accepted the principle of segregation. "It is, in my opinion," said he, "best for all races—European, Indian, or native. I desire, therefore, that this principle should be adhered to in residential areas, and wherever practicable, in commercial areas also." He then went on to say "that, as a rule, no transfer of land, either by way of ownership or mortgage, be-

20. *India,* September 2, 1920.

tween Europeans and Asiatics in townships should be allowed."[21]

These questions are of course closely associated with the problem of government. The European planters are constantly protesting against the bureaucratic methods of the Colonial Office and demanding a greater measure of local autonomy, but are not at all willing to share the responsibilities of government with the Indians. There were formerly two Indian members and one Arab member of the Provincial Council, nominated by the Governor, as against seventeen Europeans, nominated by the Governor, and eleven Europeans, elected by the European community. The only change suggested by Lord Milner was that the two Indian members should be elected on a special franchise. The Indians refused to accept this arrangement and provision was finally made for four Indian representatives. The municipal governments were also reorganized in 1920–21. In Nairobi, for example, the Municipal Council had previously consisted of four nominated official members and eight elected members, of whom five were Europeans, two were British Indians, and one was a Goanese. Under the new plan the official representation was eliminated and the elected European membership was increased to nine. In 1928, it was decided that there should be nine elected European members and seven nominated Indian members. There were to be seven of each race, all nominated, on the Council at Mombasa.

Various protests against the Milner recommendations were made by the government of India, the Indian National Congress, and the East African (Indian) National Congress; and the Joint Committee of Parliament on Indian Affairs asserted (July 23, 1921) that there was "no justification in Kenya for assigning to British Indians a status in any way inferior to that of any other class of His Majesty's subjects." This so aroused the European community that it sent a delegation to London to make it clear that it would not tamely submit to a radical revision of the Milner settlement. After nearly three years of deliberation, during which the arguments on both

21. *India,* September 2, 1920.

sides were stated and restated many times, the Colonial Office published the so-called *Kenya White Paper* in August, 1923.

The outstanding feature of this document was its assertion that "native interests must be paramount," that in dealing with East Africa the welfare of the African majority must always be the first consideration. The principle is sound, but it is vague and difficult to apply, especially in a region where there is already a large and well-established foreign population. The authorities of the Colonial Office evidently felt, however, that it could be applied immediately to the problem of immigration. There was to be no racial discrimination in the immigration laws, but there might be a general restriction on all immigration if it seemed to be for the best interest of the African people themselves. The Governors of Kenya and Uganda were to consider the question and prepare an immigration ordinance in harmony with these recommendations.

Next to immigration, the political problem was the most important. The main issue was whether there should be a common registration list, with the same qualifications for all voters, or the Indian system of communal representation, in which each community voted separately for its own representatives. The Indians preferred the former method and the Europeans the latter. The Europeans know that if there is a common voting list they will be swamped by the Indian majority. The evil day might be postponed for a time by means of educational and property tests, but ultimately it would have to come. If, on the other hand, each race is represented separately and the Europeans are guaranteed a majority in both the Provincial and Municipal Councils, regardless of population, their supremacy is assured. *The White Paper* settled the question in favor of the Europeans. In the Provincial Council, for example, they were to continue to elect eleven members, the Arabs were to elect one, and the Indians, five. But the European demand for Home Rule was rejected because it conflicted with the paramount interests of the natives. There was still to be a slight majority of nominated members who would vote as a bloc on all important questions under instructions from the Colonial Office. The township governments were to remain substantially unchanged, with the Councils under European elective control. The other questions at issue were compromised. The Europeans were to retain the highland reserves, but there was to be no legalized segregation in the townships.

The White Paper was unpopular with both communities. Although the Europeans had used the native argument against the Indians, they did not like to have it turned against themselves. They probably did not expect that responsible government would be established immediately, but they naturally resented the adoption of a principle that might be used as a pretext to put it off forever. The formation of the Labor government in England increased their alarm because the Labor party has a "sentimental" regard for backward races and was likely to be fanatical in upholding the paramount theory of native interests. In their rage and despair, they threatened secession and also appealed for aid to the Union of South Africa. In the London *Times* of April 23, 1924, the Nairobi correspondent said that there was a strong movement in Kenya to have all of the British communities in Africa unite, under the leadership of South Africa, in drawing up some sort of "Monroe Doctrine for Africa together with an agreement to resist all outside interference and all policies not in accordance with the maintenance of white prestige on the continent and the real interests of the African natives."

The Indians and their friends were almost equally vociferous. *The White Paper* was denounced by the government of India, the National Congress, and numerous other Indian organizations. They were especially suspicious of Sir Robert Coryndon, the Governor of Kenya, who would play the chief part in framing the new Immigration Ordinance. It would be possible, of course, by means of educational and property tests, to exclude practically all Indians without affecting very much the small stream of European immigration. As a matter of fact, a draft ordinance of this character was prepared, but it was rejected by the Colonial Office in February, 1924, and sent back for revision. Another feature of the plan which was very unpopular in Kenya itself was the provision for communal representation in the Provincial and Municipal Councils. The East African Indian National Congress resolved to adopt the principle of noncoöperation, boycott the elections, and refuse to pay poll taxes. This policy was soon modified through the influence of Mr. Abdul Wahid, a wealthy Indian of Kenya, but the bulk of the community still refused to participate in the elections. With one or two exceptions, the Indian representatives in the Provincial Legislative Council have all been nominated by the Governor.[22]

Since 1923 the conflict has been waged mainly along political lines. The European community has continued to agitate for the establishment of a system of responsible government with a European elective majority in the legislature, and the Imperial government has been considering the advisability of forming a British East African federation. The two questions are closely related because a responsible government in Kenya would endeavor to control the federation and secure the general adoption of its racial program. This is not the place to consider in detail the report of the Ormsby-Gore Commission in 1925, the Report of the Hilton-Young Commission in 1929, or the results of the special investigation conducted by Sir Samuel Wilson in 1929. The government of India followed the proceedings with keen interest and in April, 1929, Mr. Sastri was sent to help the local community present its case to Sir Samuel Wilson. In the report which he made on his return to India he urged the government (1) to use its good offices to secure the establishment in Kenya of a common electoral roll based on a civilization franchise, (2) to oppose the grant of responsible government to Kenya, (3) to oppose the establishment of a Central East African Council unless adequate provision was made in each province for the unofficial representation of the Indian community, and (4) to demand that the representation of natives in the Kenya Legislative Council should be by natives or by Europeans and Indians in equal proportion. The question was considered by His Majesty's government and a Joint Select Committee of Parliament and it was finally decided in August, 1932, that the time had not yet arrived for the creation of an East African federation, that

22. See W. McGregor Ross, *Kenya from Within,* pp. 428–429. Mr. Ross says that only about 200 Indians were registered on the communal roll in 1927, although about 15,000 were eligible.

the official majority in the Kenya Legislative Council should be retained, and that it would be impracticable under present conditions to adopt a common electoral roll.

The question of the future government of East Africa is still under consideration. The *status quo* will probably be maintained in Kenya for some time to come. As long as His Majesty's government adheres to the principle that native interests are paramount it probably will not sanction the establishment of full responsible government. Responsible government, with a communal electorate, would place the other communities under the control of the European planters; responsible government, without a communal electorate, would place the other communities under the control of the Indian traders. Either system would be disastrous to the natives and to one of the other groups. For this reason, the present bureaucratic system, with all its faults, is likely to be continued indefinitely. The trouble will never be very acute in Uganda because the climate forbids intensive European settlement, but the conditions in Tanganyika will gradually approximate those in Kenya as the highland areas are more fully settled. If a union or federation is formed it will be very difficult to frame a uniform racial policy. The Europeans of Kenya will not willingly give up any advantages they have gained in the last forty years and the Indians will certainly object to the extension of the Kenya system to the other provinces. The British authorities are facing a serious dilemma. They know that a European community cannot thrive in the tropics without protection from Asiatic competition, but they are precluded from treating the Indian question in East Africa as a purely local problem by the knowledge that the grievances of Indians in a Crown colony can always be used to fan the flames of racial hatred in India.

There are other tropical colonies and protectorates in which the problem assumes a different character. They have no highland areas and are entirely unsuitable for European colonization, but their natural resources are rich and well adapted to large-scale production. Their native population has neither the capital nor the skill to perform the task and it is sometimes unable or unwilling to supply the necessary amount of labor.

In these cases, the capital and the skilled labor are likely to come from Europe while the unskilled labor is imported from India or China. The Indian indenture system has already been discussed. It was abolished in 1916 and unskilled emigration of all kinds was prohibited in 1922 except to such countries and under such conditions as might be specially approved by the government of India and both houses of the Indian legislature. Under this law, special agreements were made with Ceylon and British Malaya in 1923 which contain elaborate provisions for the protection of the emigrants from mistreatment. Standard minimum wage scales for Indian laborers in Ceylon and parts of Malaya were also fixed as a result of later negotiations, although the rates have had to be revised on account of the fall in the price of rubber. An agreement made with Mauritius in 1923 for one year was not renewed because the conditions there were not regarded as entirely satisfactory. The government of Fiji has also been trying to secure a revival of unskilled emigration to that colony, but its efforts have so far been unsuccessful. British Guiana was more fortunate. After years of negotiations, an agreement was reached in 1926, but owing to the financial stringency, there was some delay in putting it into operation.

There are no serious internal conflicts in these colonies, although the racial distribution of the population has influenced to some extent the process of constitutional development. The conditions in Fiji and British Guiana are very much alike. In both cases the Europeans are greatly outnumbered by the Indians and other peoples of non-European stock.[23] If the Constitution develops along democratic lines, the Europeans will obviously be swamped by people of other races. There are, however, two other possible solutions: the Constitution may be made more autocratic, as it was in Jamaica after the great negro insurrection of 1865; or it may progress toward self-government with artificial protection for the European minority. The former solution has apparently been adopted in

23. The population of Fiji and Royuma at the close of 1934 was estimated at 197,449, of whom 4,763 were Europeans and 89,289 were East Indians. The total for British Guiana was 323,171, which included 10,585 Europeans and 136,004 East Indians.

British Guiana and the latter in Fiji. Under the old Constitution of British Guiana the elective element in the legislature had control over the finances, but the Constitution of 1928 provides for a nominated majority in the new Legislative Council and also gives the Governor and his Executive Council the power to legislate in emergencies. In Fiji, the government was formerly of the extreme Crown colony type, but in the course of time six elected European members were added to the Legislative Council. The new Constitution, promulgated in 1929, made no essential change in the system except to provide that the Indian members should be elected. The Indians refused to accept this concession because it involved a recognition of the principle of communal electorates. Their members resigned from the Council in 1929 and the vacancies were not filled.

The problem does not exist in Malaya[24] and Mauritius because their Constitutions are still based on the old autocratic principles. In Ceylon the friction is between the Indians and the Sinkalese. When the Constitution of 1931 was drafted, it was proposed that Indians who had lived in Ceylon for five years and intended to become permanent residents should have the franchise, provided they would renounce all claims to protection from the government of India. The Indian community strongly objected to this and the Colonial Office finally conceded the point and agreed that the Indians should have the right to vote and the right to appeal to India for protection.

24. The term Malaya or British Malaya is used here to include the Straits Settlements, the Federated Malay States and the non-federated states of Johore, Kelantan, Trengganu, Kedah, and Perlis.

CHAPTER X

RELIGIOUS GRIEVANCES

THE Marquess of Zetland (formerly the Earl of Ronaldshay) has written several interesting books on India. His main thesis, which he elaborates in *The Heart of Aryavarta,* is that the secret of Indian unrest is to be found in the efforts of the Hindus to save their ancient faith and culture from being submerged by the tide of Western civilization. The Moslems are fighting the same battle and they are also struggling to prevent themselves from being overwhelmed by the Hindus when the British legions are withdrawn. This explains both the Hindu-Moslem entente, which is so difficult for the British to understand, and the growing friction between the two communities, which is so difficult for the Indians themselves to understand.

The religious revival in India has already been discussed in connection with the revolt of the Asiatic against the European.[1] It is an important psychological factor in the general relations between the Indians and the British, but it would be hard to analyze it or rather to improve upon the excellent analysis already made by the Marquess of Zetland. So far as the Hindus are concerned, there are no concrete issues involved at the present time. Although suttee (sati) was abolished and thuggee (thagi)[2] was suppressed while Lord William Bentinck was Governor-General (1827–35), it has been the policy of the British authorities not to interfere with the manners and customs of the people or to take sides in religious disputes. This applies to Moslems and Sikhs as well as to Hindus, but in recent years they have both come into conflict with the government over other issues. The trouble with the Moslems originated outside India. They belong to a great inter-

1. See chap. ix.
2. The thugs were a brotherhood of Hindus who practiced robbery and murder by strangulation in the name of the Goddess Kali.

national community and are unusually sensitive about the treatment of their coreligionists in other parts of the world. The Sikhs occasionally quarrel among themselves and, as property rights are involved, it is impossible for the government to avoid being drawn into the conflict. The present chapter, therefore, will deal first with Moslem reaction to British policy in the Near East and then with the Akali movement among the Sikhs.

From the beginning of the reign of Abdul Hamid in 1876 a systematic propaganda was carried on to unite the Moslem world under the leadership of Turkey, but until about 1911 it was not very successful.[3] The French occupation of Tunis and Morocco and the British occupation of Egypt and the Sudan, the establishment of British protectorates over Zanzibar and the Malay States, the expansion of Russia in Central Asia, and the threatened Anglo-Russian partition of Persia were all apparently accepted by the followers of the Prophet in a spirit of fatalistic indifference. Although there were some local uprisings, such as the Arabi rebellion in Egypt (1882) and the Mahdist insurrection in the Sudan (1883–85), no concerted resistance was made and there is very little evidence to indicate that the general significance of the movement was ever appreciated. The Turks and the Arabs still seemed to be more interested in their own internal differences than they were in protecting Islam as a whole against European aggression.

The situation changed rapidly in the years immediately preceding the Great War. The Shuster episode in Persia, the Italian adventure in Tripoli, the formal establishment of French and Spanish protectorates in Morocco and the successful attacks of the Balkan peoples upon Turkey finally convinced the Moslem world that it must present a united front against its enemies or be destroyed. The British were held chiefly responsible for these calamities. They supported Russia in Persia and France in Morocco and there was good reason to believe that they encouraged Italy in the raid upon Tripoli.

3. Abdul Hamid was deposed in 1909, but his pan-Islamic policy was in the main continued by the Young Turks. For a general history of pan-Islamism and its influence on international politics, see Lothrop Stoddard, *The New World of Islam* (1921).

Egypt was forced by Lord Kitchener to remain neutral in the Turco-Italian conflict although it was a part of the Ottoman Empire and its army was legally subject to the Sultan's commands. The truth of the matter is that the British in their fear of Germany were compelled to sacrifice Moslem friendship on the altar of European imperialism.

The immediate object was accomplished. Germany was isolated and defeated, but, as Mr. Lloyd George admitted in a speech in the House of Commons on February 14, 1922, it was a dangerous game to play. "One of the unfortunate consequences of the war from the point of view of India," said he, "was that we were manoeuvred into a position of having to fight the greatest Islamic power in the world. It was an undoubted triumph of German diplomacy." This is true, but it is only a part of the truth. The real cause of the trouble was not that Great Britain and Turkey were on opposite sides, but the fact that Great Britain allowed the war to be used as an excuse for the extension of European political control in the Near and Middle East. Indian Moslems fought loyally by the side of British troops in Mesopotamia and throughout the war they discouraged the efforts of Hindu and Sikh agitators to stir up trouble in India itself. They expected that Turkey would be punished for giving her support to the Central Powers, but they were led to believe that the punishment would take the form of the establishment of independent Moslem states in Arabia, Syria, and Mesopotamia. Mr. Lloyd George assured them in a speech in the House of Commons on January 5, 1918, that Turkey would not be deprived "of its capital or of the rich and renowned lands of Asia Minor and Thrace which were predominately Turkish in race." When the secret agreements of 1914–18 were published and when the Treaty of Sèvres was concluded in August, 1920, they naturally felt that they had been deceived. Constantinople and the Straits were put under an international commission, a large part of Asia Minor was partitioned between France, Greece, and Italy, and nearly all of eastern Thrace, including Adrianople, was given to Greece. The British not only agreed to these terms but they opposed the efforts made later by France to have them revised in favor of the Turks.

This again is only part of the truth. In justice to Great Britain, it is necessary to consider another aspect of her policy in the Near East which is highly creditable to her sense of humanity even if it is not good politics. The British are the only people in the world who have made any serious effort in recent years to protect the Christian minorities in the Ottoman Empire. They encouraged the Greek invasion of Anatolia and Thrace partly because that seemed to be the most practical method of saving the resident Greeks from persecution and death. They supported the French and Italians in Cilicia and Anatolia partly as a means of securing additional protection for Armenians, Greeks, and other Christians who live in that part of the Ottoman dominions. Their reluctance later to agree to the Treaty of Lausanne really meant that they were unwilling to hand over two or three million Christians to the mercies of the Turks, who were now maddened by a desire for revenge.

But while the pressure of the Allies and the desire to protect Christian minorities from persecution were the chief causes of Great Britain's anti-Moslem attitude, they were by no means the only factors involved. For the first three years after the war the British government was inclined to flout Moslem opinion and to engage in a reckless campaign of imperialism on its own account. The War Office and the Admiralty, with the support of Lord Curzon and Mr. Churchill, tried to maintain a protectorate over Egypt against the advice of Lord Milner and in face of the unanimous opposition of the Egyptian people. Efforts were also made to discipline Afghanistan and to carry out a so-called forward policy in Persia and Iraq (Mesopotamia) as a means of securing fuel oil for the navy.

In recent years this program has been very much modified. The Treaty of Sèvres has been replaced by the Treaty of Lausanne. The Turks have recovered all of Asia Minor and eastern Thrace as well as large parts of Kurdistan and Armenia. The independence of Persia, Afghanistan, and Egypt has been recognized and the mandate over Iraq was given up in 1932.

The good effect of these concessions was offset by the fact that they were to a large extent secured by force and by the fact that the British Army of Occupation still remained in Egypt. Considerable feeling was also aroused over other issues, especially over the so-called Sharifian policy of Mr. Churchill and Colonel Lawrence. Sharifianism,[4] which was very effective during the war, involved the driving of a wedge between the Arabs and the Turks. It was a modified pan-Arabic movement, a movement to unite a large part of the Arabic world under the family of the Sharif of Mecca as a counterbalance to the political influence of the Turks in the Middle East. Mr. Churchill gave a general outline of the policy in a speech in the House of Commons on June 14, 1921:

> Broadly speaking, there are two policies which can be adopted towards the Arab race. One is the policy of keeping them divided. . . . The other policy . . . is an attempt to build up around the ancient capital of Bagdad, in a form friendly to Britain and her Allies, an Arab State which can receive and embody the old culture and glories of the Arab race. . . . Of these two policies we have definitely chosen the latter.
>
> If you are to endeavour to shape affairs in a sense of giving satisfaction to Arab nationality . . . the very best structure of the kind which is available, is the house and family of the Sherif of Mecca.

Through the influence of the British the Sharif Hussein became king of the Hedjas in 1916 and his sons, the Amir Feisal and the Amir Abdullah, became sovereigns of Iraq and Transjordania respectively in 1921. It was hoped that the family would acquire great prestige as guardians of the Holy Cities of Mecca, Madina, and Baghdad and that Hussein might perhaps supersede the Sultan as Caliph[5] of the Moslem world. As a matter of fact, this hope has not been realized. Although the weight of Islamic tradition might have been expected to favor Hussein as a descendant of the Prophet, there were other influences working in the opposite direction.

Constantinople had been the seat of the Caliphate[5] for more

4. Arabic Sharif, noble, even of Mohammed's line; title of Wahhabi ruler of Mecca.

5. The old spelling is used because it is more familiar to Western readers. Modern Arab scholars prefer Khalifa and the Khilafat.

than four hundred years, which is long enough to establish a tradition even in the Orient. Furthermore, the Caliph had always been regarded by Sunni Mohammedans as a temporal rather than a spiritual ruler. The Ottoman Empire had for centuries been the strongest Moslem country in the world and in spite of its feeble condition at the close of the war it still had a greater prestige than any state or confederation of states that was likely to be formed by the Sharif of Mecca. The Turks also had the martyrs' advantage. The steady encroachment of European powers upon their territories since 1911 had not only strengthened the Islamic movement, it had also made it more distinctly pro-Turkish. The Turks were loved for the enemies they had made, the Sharif of Mecca and his followers were hated because of their alliance with those enemies.

For these and possibly other reasons, the great majority of Moslems, including the 70,000,000 who live in India, repudiated Hussein's pretensions and instituted a movement to boycott the Arabian Holy Places until they were restored to Turkish control. Hussein was not even able to unite the Arabs themselves. When the British military support was withdrawn in 1925, he was defeated by Ibn Sa'ud, the Wahhabi Amir of Nejd, and compelled to abdicate. His son Ali, who succeeded him as king, was also defeated and the Holy Places of Mecca and Madina are still in the possession of the Wahhabis.

The Sharifian policy was condemned not only for its sins of commission, but also for its sins of omission, not only because it was used against the Turks, but because it was not used against the French and the Jews. After the conquest of Syria, the Amir Feisal was allowed to establish a government at Damascus and he was apparently led by General Allenby to believe that he would in a short time be recognized as king of all Syria. The French complained that this was a violation of the Sikes-Picot Agreement of 1916 and, after some negotiations between the governments of Great Britain and France, a compromise was finally reached in September, 1919. Western Syria was to be occupied by French troops and brought under direct French control, while eastern Syria was to remain under the government of Feisal, but was to be regarded as within the French zone of influence. There was friction almost immediately. Damascus was seized by a French force under General Gouraud in March, 1920, and Feisal was driven into exile. At the San Remo Conference in April the whole of Syria, with the exception of Palestine, was allocated to France under a mandate from the League of Nations. Although Feisal received compensation in the kingdom of Iraq in 1921, the Pan-Arabs of Syria are still bitterly discontented.

The Zionist movement to establish a national home for the Jews in Palestine was another obstacle to the success of the Sharifian program. In November, 1917, shortly before General Allenby's conquest of Jerusalem, Mr. Arthur J. (later Lord) Balfour made the following declaration on behalf of the British government:

> His Majesty's Government views with favour the establishment in Palestine of a national home for the Jewish people, and will use their best endeavours to facilitate the achievement of this object, it being clearly understood that nothing shall be done which may prejudice the civil and religious rights of existing non-Jewish communities or the rights and political status enjoyed by Jews in any other country.

This declaration was approved by the Allied Powers and a mandate over Palestine was allocated to Great Britain at the San Remo Conference in April, 1920. Sir Herbert Samuel was sent out a few months later as British High Commissioner to establish a civil administration and to put the declaration into practical operation.

It was apparently intended that Palestine should remain under a British mandate, with a Jewish High Commissioner, until enough Jews could be brought into the country to control the government or at least to protect themselves from persecution. The Arabs, who constituted at that time about 90 per cent of the population, were naturally very much opposed to this program and a special delegation, composed of both Christian and Moslem Arabs, was sent to England in 1921 to lay their case before the government and people of the United Kingdom. There were bad riots in Jerusalem and

Jaffa and other places in April and May, 1921, and the situation became so serious that for a time Jewish immigration had to be almost entirely suspended. The British government finally interpreted the Balfour Declaration in a manner more reassuring to the Arabs, but there were other serious conflicts in 1929 and 1936 and the trouble is still very acute.

In addition to the general question of political control there was the specific issue of the guardianship of religious shrines. Very few people seem to realize that the Holy Land is holy for Moslems as well as for Christians and Jews or take into consideration the fact that the Moslems have a vested interest in the shrines that goes back more than a thousand years. This being the case, it would be hard for them to give up their rights of guardianship and doubly hard if they suspected that their successors would be Jews. As a matter of fact their suspicions are not very well founded. They still have complete control over their own shrines and a system of nonsectarian guardianship has been devised for the shrines that are common to all three of the great religious communities.

With this summary of the problems that have grown out of the disruption of the old Ottoman Empire, we are now ready to consider their effect upon Moslem sentiment in India. There has been a certain amount of pan-Islamic propaganda in India for more than half a century. It was strengthened by the events that followed the Italian invasion of Tripoli in 1911, but it never became a really important factor until after the conclusion of the Treaty of Sèvres in 1920.

The most influential leaders in this movement were the Ali brothers, the sons of a small landowner in the state of Rampur. Shaukat Ali was for many years a subordinate official in the Opium Department of the government of India. Mohammed Ali, the younger brother, who was the real head of the movement until his death in 1931, graduated at Allahabad University in 1898, after which he went to England and made an unsuccessful attempt to pass the Indian Civil Service examinations. He received the degree of Bachelor of Arts, however, from Oxford and returned to India in 1902. He and his brother took part in the foundation of the All-India Moslem League in 1906 and also in the establishment of the *Comrade*, a weekly newspaper which became one of the most influential organs of the Moslem Extremists.[6] They were both interned during the war because of their pro-Turkish activities and refused to accept a pardon on condition that they would take an oath of allegiance to the King-Emperor. They also opposed the Afghan War and were imprisoned for disloyalty in June, 1919, but were released under the Royal Proclamation of Amnesty issued on the passage of the Government of India Act in the following December. Mohammed Ali was at once selected as the head of the Caliphate delegation which went to England in March, 1920, to intercede for Turkey in the peace negotiations.

In the meantime, Hindu and Moslem Extremists were drawing closer together and the Alis were falling more and more under the influence of Mr. Gandhi. Shortly after the conclusion of the Treaty of Sèvres on August 10, 1920, Mr. Gandhi announced that he would organize a nonviolent noncoöperation campaign to compel a modification of its terms in favor of Turkey. By this clever stroke the great majority of the Moslems were swept into the radical movement which was already popular with the Hindus because it promised revenge for the Punjab grievances and held out a prospect of the immediate acquisition of swaraj or Home Rule. The Indian National Congress, at a special meeting held at Calcutta in September, approved the policy of noncoöperation and a plan of action was drafted providing for the boycott of government-aided schools and colleges, courts of justice, and legislative councils and also for the renunciation of all honors and titles conferred upon Indians by the British authorities.

During the latter part of 1920 and the early months of 1921, Mr. Gandhi and the Ali brothers traveled over India preaching the doctrine of noncoöperation and denouncing the Turkish treaty. The Alis sometimes used language that was inconsistent with the principle of nonviolence and there were occasional riots as a result of their impassioned appeals. The situation finally became so serious that the government of India decided, in May, 1921, that they would have to be arrested.

6. The *Comrade* was started at Calcutta in 1911, but it was removed to Delhi in 1912, where it continued to be published until 1914.

Mr. Gandhi interceded with Lord Reading, however, and as a result the order of arrest was withdrawn and the brothers signed a formal statement disavowing any intention to incite to violence, apologizing for "the unnecessary heat of some of the passages" in their speeches and promising that they would not "directly or indirectly advocate violence at present or in the future, nor create an atmosphere of preparedness for violence."

This promise was repeatedly broken, but the government took no further action until after the meeting of the All-India Caliphate Conference at Karachi in July. At that conference a resolution, introduced by Mohammed Ali, was adopted which declared it unlawful in a religious sense for any Moslem to remain in the Indian Army or to enlist or to encourage others to enlist. The authorities again decided that the brothers would have to be arrested, but the decision was not carried out immediately, probably because of the fear that it might provoke a rebellion. They were, however, finally seized about the middle of September, together with Dr. Kitchlew, a prominent Mohammedan barrister of Amritsar, and all three were convicted and sent to prison.

This agitation bore fruit in two tragic episodes which brought suffering and death to thousands of innocent people, namely, the Hijrat of 1920 and the Moplah (Mappilla) rebellion of 1921–22. The Hijrat was a scheme, encouraged by the Ali brothers and other Moslem leaders, to have Indian Moslems leave their homes and emigrate to Afghanistan as a protest against the treatment of Turkey. About 18,000 peasants of Sind and the North-West Frontier took part in this absurd enterprise which resulted in an immense amount of hardship and loss of life. It must be said to the credit of those who organized the movement, however, that they soon realized their mistake and did everything possible to assist the authorities in their efforts to relieve distress and to get the victims reestablished in their homes.

The Moplah rebellion was a movement of an entirely different character, but it was produced by the same kind of appeal to religious fanaticism. It is true that the Moplahs had often rebelled in the past and that they had other grievances besides the Turkish peace treaty. At the same time, there can be no doubt that this particular uprising was the result of Caliphate propaganda. The rank and file were encouraged in the belief that they were fighting for the cause of Islam and the political organizations set up by the local leaders in the first flush of victory were called Caliphate kingdoms.

About 90 per cent of the population of South India is non-Moslem, but there are a few Moslems scattered among the general population and occasional groups who have been gathered in more or less compact bodies. One of the most important of these groups is the Moplahs, numbering about a million people, who live mainly in the Ernad and Walavanad taluks of the Malabar district of Madras. Although they are racially very closely related to their Hindu neighbors, they were converted to Islam by Arabs who traded on this coast in the Middle Ages and there is a strain of Arab blood in their veins. Cut off from their fellow Moslems in other parts of India and outnumbered about three to one by the Hindus, even in the Malabar district, they have naturally developed a strong spirit of religious fanaticism, a spirit which is still further intensified by ignorance and agrarian discontent. Their women are almost entirely illiterate and only about one male in ten can read and write in even the most elementary fashion. The Hindus and the Christians, on the other hand, have higher educational qualifications and in consequence are able to monopolize most of the subordinate government positions. The agrarian problem also has its religious aspect. Nearly all the land is held in large estates by Nambudri Brahmans and by Nayars, who were originally the military caste of the district, while the tenantry is composed of Moplahs and low-caste Hindus. The tenant rights are very precarious and the Moplahs often have difficulty in securing sites for mosques and burial grounds.

A Moplah outbreak usually begins with the assassination of a landlord, the looting of a Hindu shop, or the defiling of a Hindu temple. Until the great uprising in 1921 the most serious troubles in recent years occurred in 1873, 1885, 1894, and 1896. There were usually only one or two small gangs involved in these affairs, with perhaps less than a hundred members, but they were apt to fight with desperate fanaticism until the last man was killed. In order to be prepared for these sporadic outbreaks the government has kept a small detachment of British troops at Malappuram in the center of the Moplah country since 1873 and a special police force has been stationed there since 1885.

Early in 1921, political agitators from other parts of India came to Malabar to arouse sentiment in favor of Turkey and to organize the noncoöperation movement. The authorities soon put an end to the holding of public meetings, but they were unable to stop the secret propaganda that was carried on by local organizations. Although there were indications as early as June that the Moplahs were getting dangerously excited, the government of Madras took no decisive steps to strengthen the military and police forces. On August 21, the police, after arresting some Moplah criminals at Tirurangadi, were attacked by an armed mob and there was considerable loss of life. This seemed to be the signal for a general uprising. Thousands of men and boys, armed with guns, knives, and clubs, gathered together and in less than a week three taluks of South Malabar were in their possession. A few Europeans, mostly police and military officers, were killed, but the chief sufferers were Hindus. Their shops were looted, their temples were desecrated or destroyed, their women were raped and thousands of men, women, and children were murdered or driven into exile. There were also many cases of forcible conversion to the Moslem faith.

Martial law was proclaimed in the disaffected area as soon as the trouble began in August, 1921, and it was kept in force until February 25, 1922. Several battles were fought, including one at Podakultoor on August 26 in which 400 Moplahs were reported killed, and there was also considerable guerrilla warfare in the foothills of the Nilgiri Mountains. The total loss of life will never be known, but if we consider the number of people who died of starvation or malnutrition because they were unable to plant their crops, 10,000 would probably be a conservative estimate.

This uprising illustrates the danger as well as the absurdity of appealing to the religious bigotry of ignorant peasants with the expectation that they will act upon the principle of passive resistance. It also indicates that the Hindu-Moslem entente is a conception of the intelligentsia which has very little meaning for the lower classes of the community. It would of course be unfair to judge Indian Moslems in general by the Moplah standard, but there can be no doubt that the masses of them everywhere are ignorant and fanatical and that when they are aroused they are likely to attack Hindus even if there is no other reason than the fact that Hindus are the only people available. The following extract from a leading article in the London *Times* of September 8, 1921, is interesting in this connection.

> Mr. Gandhi preaches "non-cooperation" to the mob, the Ali brothers talk to Mohammedans about the woes of Turkey. Mr. Gandhi professes to be disconcerted when his dupes translate "non-cooperation" into terms of violence, but what has he to say when he discovers that primitive Mohammedans, when once influenced by incendiary propaganda soon forget about Turkey and start killing Hindus?

The government had a good opportunity at this time to win the support of the conservative elements in India who were opposed to the noncoöperative program. The opportunity was lost, however, through a terrible blunder which made it possible for the radical leaders to reinvigorate the Hindu-Moslem entente by an appeal to anti-European race prejudice. On November 19, 1921, 100 prisoners (97 Moplahs and 3 Hindus) were sent in a luggage van from Tirus to Coimbatore. The trip lasted several hours, the weather was intensely hot, and the wire screens that covered the ventilators had recently been painted so that they did not admit the usual amount of air. When the train reached its destination it was found that seventy of the prisoners had died of suffocation. A British police sergeant by the name of Andrews, who had charge of the escort, was told at one of the intermediate stations that the men were dying, but he failed to take any action. He said later that he did not dare open the door because he knew that he would be overpowered and the prisoners would escape.

The British have never forgotten the Black Hole of Calcutta. It is kept fresh in their memories not so much because its victims died a horrible death, but because they were British who were done to death by people of another race. The treatment of the Moplah prisoners is regarded in India in a similar manner and the British, unfortunately, were partly to blame for it. The government of India gave orders that Andrews should be prosecuted for criminal negligence. He was tried before the district magistrate of Coimbatore and acquitted in December, 1922. The decision aroused a great deal of feeling and the bitterness was intensified by the support given to Andrews by the local European community. A large sum of money was raised by the European Association to meet the cost of his defense. If this trial was fair and impartial and if Andrews' only offense was an error of judgment, then it is time to rehabilitate the character of Siraj-ud-daula.[7] There is no reason to suppose that he intended his prisoners to die of suffocation.

The Moplah affair and the imprisonment of Dr. Kitchlew and the Ali brothers did not seriously interfere with the progress of the Caliphate movement. The agitation against the Treaty of Sèvres continued and it may be said to have reached a climax about the time of the Greco-Turkish Conference at Paris on March 22, 1922. Mr. Montagu and Lord Reading were both very much alarmed by the anti-Turkish policy of the British government and Mr. Montagu decided on a bold and unusual method of procedure. He authorized Lord Reading to send him the following telegram (March 7, 1922), which was immediately given to the press:

> On the eve of the Greco-Turkish Conference we feel it our duty to lay before His Majesty's Government the intensity of feeling in India regarding the necessity for a revision of the Sèvres Treaty. The Government of India are fully alive to the complexity of the problem, but India's services in the war, in which Indian Moslem soldiers so largely participated, and the support which the Indian Moslem cause is receiving throughout India, entitles her to claim the utmost fulfilment of her just and equitable aspirations.

7. Clive's enemy at Plassey.

The Government of India particularly urge, subject to the safeguarding of the neutrality of the Straits and the security of the non-Moslem population, the following three points:—

The evacuation of Constantinople;

The Suzerainty of the Sultan over the Holy Places;

The restoration of Ottoman Thrace (including Adrianople) and Smyrna.

The fulfilment of these three points is of the greatest importance to India.

Mr. Montagu's action was a breach of cabinet etiquette and, as a result, he became involved in a dispute with Lord Curzon, the head of the Foreign Office, and was compelled to resign. His object, however, was attained. The government and people of the United Kingdom were made to realize that the Moslems of India were keenly interested in the welfare of Turkey and that it would be dangerous to disregard their wishes. There is no doubt that this was one of the factors in the change of British foreign policy although the defeat of the Greeks in Asia Minor was of course the main consideration.

This episode should be considered in connection with the tendency of the authorities in India to favor a protective tariff policy and to protest against the ill-treatment of Indians in other parts of the Empire. In the old days, Indian Nationalists were always suspicious of the government of India and inclined to look to the government and Parliament of the United Kingdom for sympathy and protection. Now the conditions were reversed. The Imperial authorities were viewed with distrust and the government of India was beginning to enjoy at least a relative amount of popularity.

The Caliphate movement in its original form is now dead, because there is no longer any valid reason for its existence. Although political conditions in parts of the old Ottoman Empire and especially in Palestine are still unsatisfactory from the point of view of the Moslems of India, the new Turkish Republic has attained a position among the powers which even the most optimistic would have thought impossible in 1920. This is not, however, the real cause of the decline of the movement. The Moslems of India would naturally rather be associated with a Turkey that is strong and self-reliant than with a Turkey that is weak and helpless. The real trouble is that the Turks have not played the game in the approved fashion. For more than a generation they worked to restore the medieval conception of the Caliphate and just as they were about to succeed they repudiated their own efforts.

Mustapha Kemal Pasha (Ataturk), the President of the Republic is a modernist and a realist who regards the Caliphate only as a symbol of reaction and a possible source of danger to republican institutions. When the Sultanate was abolished in 1922, the title of Caliph was conferred upon Abdul Mejid, a member of the old Imperial family. Although this was a severe blow to the Moslems of India, who had always contended that the Caliph must be a powerful monarch and the protector of the Holy Places of Islam, they met the rebuff in good spirit. The All-India Caliphate Conference at its annual meeting at Gaya in December–January, 1922–23, voted its approval of the new Caliph and asserted that his election was "very near the real religious and Islamic method."

The final blow fell a few months later. Sultan Abdul Mejid was deposed and sent into exile and the Caliphate was abolished. The Indian Moslem leaders were still unwilling to admit defeat. The Caliphate Committee announced early in 1924 its intention to send a delegation to Angora to discuss the situation with the Turkish government. It is unusual for a private organization in one country to try to influence the internal policy of another country. The government of India, therefore, refused to issue the necessary passports until it could consult with the Turkish authorities and find out whether the delegation would be welcome. This action was severely criticized in India, but it had the sanction of diplomatic usage and it was also justified by the event. The Turkish government refused to receive the delegation.

The Caliphate will probably never be restored on a Turkish basis. The title may in time be assumed by the King of Egypt, the King of Iraq, the King of Saudi Arabia, or some future Amir of Afghanistan, but it is doubtful whether any of them would be able to hold the allegiance of the Moslem world. There may even be a general Moslem conference to agree upon a candidate, but, without the support of the Turks, its action would be fruitless.

In saying that the Caliphate movement in its original form is dead, we do not mean to imply that the Moslems of India are no longer organized or that they are no longer interested in the problems of the Near and Middle East. They may not be very much in sympathy with the present Turkish government, but they vigorously supported it in its disputes with Iraq over the possession of Mosul. They are not especially fond of the Wahhabis of Arabia, but they rejoiced when the Wahhabis defeated their old enemy, King Hussein of the Hedjas, and wrested from him and his family the possession of the Holy Cities of Mecca and Madina. The chief issue during the last few years has been the conflict in Palestine between the Jews and the Arabs. The Moslems of India are keenly sympathetic with the Arabs and the Caliphate Conference has received a new lease of life.[8]

Second only in importance to the Moslem problem is the problem of the Akali Sikhs. The Sikhs as a separate community originated in the Punjab in the first half of the sixteenth century and they are still practically restricted to the Punjab and the Punjab States.[9] The community was founded by Nanak, a religious reformer who attacked the caste system and preached the unity of the Godhead and the obligation of leading a pure life. It was well organized and, on the disintegration of the Mogul Empire, it developed into a territorial power. Some small feudal states were established on the Sutlej river, in the eighteenth century, and, in the early part of the nineteenth century, Ranjit Singh created a great kingdom which included nearly all of north-west India. Shortly after the death of Ranjit Singh in 1839, the Sikhs came into con-

8. The All-India Caliphate Committee held a meeting at Lucknow in December, 1933, and issued a protest against the Balfour Declaration, which "converted the home of Arabs for centuries, which was sacred to the Moslem world, into a national home for Jews."

9. They constitute about 10 per cent of the population in the Punjab and about 18 per cent in the Punjab States.

flict with the British and were defeated. The greater part of the Punjab was annexed to British India and the states were brought under British control.

In order to understand the Akali movement there are three facts that should be especially emphasized. The Sikh community had its origin in a protest against the social and religious system of the Hindus, it acquired its political character because it had to defend itself against the Moslems, and it developed a strong military tradition because it was always greatly outnumbered by its opponents. As a religious sect, the Sikhs of today are alarmed at the prospect of being absorbed by the Hindus; as a political community, they are afraid that the development of Home Rule will bring them again under the domination of the Moslems. They have fostered the martial tradition and a large proportion of their men have been trained in the Indian Army. On account of their physical strength, power of endurance, and personal bravery, they are generally regarded as the best of the Indian troops. This is one of the reasons why the importance of the Sikh problem is out of proportion to the number of people who are directly involved.

The history of the Sikhs is similar to that of many other religious communities. About a century after the death of Nanak, they began to lose their original enthusiasm and, when the Moslem menace was removed, they quarreled among themselves and divided into a number of petty sects. Some of these sects lapsed into Hinduism and others came so close to it that it was difficult to draw any line of demarcation. Toward the close of the nineteenth century a puritanical reform movement was started to check this tendency and in general to eradicate the Hindu influence. The movement made very little progress up to 1914, but it was greatly stimulated by the war, and it has now become one of the most important factors in the life of the Punjab. The reformers are called Akalis, "the Deathless." They are not very numerous, but their zeal is fanatical and they represent the militant section of the community, the section that furnishes most of the recruits for the army.

The chief point at issue is the control of the gurdwaras. A gurdwara is a religious shrine and the head of it is called a mahant. Some of these shrines are heavily endowed. Like the abbeys of the Middle Ages, they often include not only a place of worship, but also houses for the custodians, large landed estates, and other valuable property. The pious and benevolent people who founded these endowments undoubtedly intended to advance the cause of the Sikh religion. They intended that the property should belong to the community as a whole and that the mahants should act merely as trustees.

These intentions were apparently carried out until the introduction into the Punjab of the British conception of a freehold estate, when some of the mahants managed to acquire a prescriptive right to the property and to have the titles registered in their own names. There would probably not have been any serious friction even then if the mahants had lived up to their religious obligations. They are supposed to be ascetics, but many of them lead luxurious and immoral lives. There was said to be a mahant a few years ago who had sixteen wives and a number of concubines, all of whom, together with their progeny, were supported by gurdwara revenues. The mahants are also distrusted because many of them have either relapsed into Hinduism or have become unduly friendly to the Hindu point of view. Hindu idols have been set up in some of the temples and Hindus and Sikhs worship together. In other words, the danger that the Sikhs will be absorbed by the Hindus is increased by the action of their own priests.

The Akalis are determined that these conditions shall be reformed. Mahants who lead scandalous and immoral lives and those who are not thoroughly in sympathy with Sikh tradition are to be removed and the shrines are to be centralized under orthodox Sikh control. An effort was made to accomplish these objects by legal methods, but it was found to be tedious, expensive, and not very effective. With the revenues derived from the gurdwaras, the mahants were able to fight the suits brought against them and to carry their cases on appeal up to the highest courts. So far as the law was concerned, they were usually in the right and the courts had to decide in their favor. The issue has been admirably summed up by Lord Olivier, formerly Secretary of State for India:

The British view is that it is the paramount duty of the ruler to maintain the law, whatever that law may happen at the moment to be. The Indian view would be that, so far as and so long as the Sikhs were acting in accordance with the prescriptions of their religion, for which the shrines had been founded and from which they had been perverted . . . the religious obligation was of higher authority than the civil property-law, and ought to have been so regarded.[10]

Having failed to accomplish anything by appealing to the law, the Akalis decided to adopt a policy of direct action. Mr. Gandhi's influence was predominant at that time and it was accordingly agreed that the action should be of a nonviolent character. This meant that a jatha, or large band of Akalis, would invade a shrine and by sheer numbers intimidate the mahant and compel him to resign. On March 5, 1921, before the government of the Punjab had fully decided how it would meet the new crisis, the terrible Nankana Sahib massacre occurred. The mahant of this shrine had a legal title to the property and he appealed to the government for police protection. No attention being paid to his appeal, he employed a force of Pathan Moslem mercenaries and made ready to protect himself. As the Sikhs came on, the Pathans fired upon them and about 130 were killed. Their bodies were heaped in a pile and burned.

Fanaticism thrives on martyrdom. The religious enthusiasm of the peasants was aroused and from this time onward the Akali movement appears to have had the support of a large majority of the Sikh community. The government was bitterly criticized for its conduct in this affair, but the critics usually failed to mention the fact that the mahant was prosecuted and sentenced to a long term of transportation and that, in the confusion which followed the massacre, the shrine was occupied by the Akalis. There has also been a tendency to ignore the Sikh Gurdwaras and Shrines Management Act of November 17, 1922, under which the places of worship were to be managed by a Sikh Board of Control, subject to certain provisions designed to safeguard the vested interests of the mahants.

10. *The Manchester Guardian Weekly,* March 20, 1925.

This was all that the Akalis had any reasonable right to expect. If they had been influenced by religious motives only, the troubles could easily have been settled. The movement had been partly political in character, however, from the beginning and that aspect of it now became dominant. The Akali Dal, the organization for the recovery of the shrines, and the Akali Fanj, the political organization, were to a large extent identical and opposition of any kind was usually denounced as religious persecution. Some of the politicians merely wished to increase the Sikh representation in the Punjab Legislative Council, but there were others of a more ambitious temperament who dreamed of a restoration of the old kingdom of Ranjit Singh. The most radical of all were those who had been connected with the Ghadr conspiracy of 1914–15 or who had suffered in one way or another under the iron rule of Sir Michael O'Dwyer. The political element was also involved in the support given to the Akalis by Hindu and Moslem Extremists, who might ultimately suffer if the Sikhs were victorious, but who were ready to encourage any movement that promised to give trouble to the British.

The Gurdwara Act was repudiated by the Akali leaders and the policy of direct action was continued. There were especially strenuous efforts made to get possession of Guru ka Bagh, a famous shrine near Amritsar. The government had to accept the challenge. It announced its intention to maintain law and order and sent large detachments of police to guard Guru ka Bagh and other shrines that were likely to be attacked. At the same time, it investigated the titles to the shrines and took steps to dispossess the mahants wherever it could be done by process of law. The police were equipped with clubs and staves and were forbidden to use firearms except in emergencies. The result was that there was very little loss of life when a shrine was rushed, but the Akalis were so anxious for martyrdom that it was sometimes necessary to break their limbs or to beat them into insensibility before the attack could be repulsed. Thousands of wounded men were taken to the hospitals for treatment and there were thousands of others ready to take their places. With a few exceptions, the pledge of nonresistance was strictly observed.

In the early part of 1924, a committee was appointed under General Sir William Birdwood to examine the problem in all of its aspects and recommend a solution. The Sikhs refused to coöperate unless the government would agree to certain conditions, including the release of Akali prisoners. The terms were not accepted and the work of the committee was a failure. The difficulties were further enhanced about this time by a judicial decision upholding the title of the mahant to the Nankana Sahib gurdwara and ordering the return of the shrine to his trustees. Fortunately, just as the situation appeared to be getting hopeless, there was a reaction in favor of the government, which was due partly to the blunder made by the Akalis in connection with the Nabha case and partly to the firm, but conciliatory, policy inaugurated by Sir Malcolm Hailey, the new Governor of the Punjab.

Nabha is the smallest of three Sikh states in the Punjab which are called the Phulkian states in honor of the common ancestor of their rulers. It has an area of 928 square miles, made up of thirteen separate pieces of territory, most of which are scattered through Patiala and Jind, the other two Phulkian states. The Maharaja Ripudaman Singh, who succeeded his father in 1911, was an orthodox Sikh and a supporter of the Akali movement, but he was hopelessly weak and incompetent. After misgoverning his own people for many years, he finally committed a series of outrages against the subjects of the Maharaja of Patiala and in July, 1923, was compelled by the government of India to resign his administrative duties and go into exile. He was allowed to retain his title and his salutes until 1928, the government of the state meanwhile being taken over by British officials until his son was made Maharaja.

The people of Nabha were satisfied with this arrangement, but it was used by politicians outside of the state as a pretext to embarrass the government. As a general rule, the Nationalists regard the princes of India as either fools or knaves and it is doubtful whether they were really prepared to make an exception in favor of the Maharaja of Nabha. It was, however, not a question of consistency, but a question of practical politics. The Maharaja could be represented as a victim of British oppression who had suffered because he was a Nationalist and had quarreled with the ruler of another state who was known to be subservient to British influence. The Sikh politicians were interested in the case not only because it could be utilized for propaganda, but also because they were naturally unwilling that a Sikh state should come directly under British bureaucratic control even for a limited period.

But while political motives were sufficient to influence the leaders, it required an appeal to religious prejudice to stir up the rank and file of the Akalis. They were told that an orthodox and zealous prince had been deposed because the British wished to desecrate Sikh shrines. There are some sacred relics of Nanak in Jaito, one of the chief towns of Nabha, and it was alleged that they were in danger of pollution. The plan of campaign was that jathas or bands of pilgrims should march to Jaito, ostensibly to hold religious meetings in the local shrine, but really for the purpose of organizing political demonstrations. The first large jatha arrived at Jaito on February 21, 1924. It consisted of about 500 Akali pilgrims and about 6,000 sympathizers, mostly peasants, who had joined them in the march across country from Amritsar. They were met at the edge of the town by the state authorities and told that they could enter the shrine provided only fifty came at a time and they would give a pledge to leave when the services were over. The terms were refused. They were then warned not to advance, but disobeyed and were fired upon by the state troops and police. According to the figures published in the newspapers, 21 were killed and 33 were wounded.

This affair aroused a feeling of bitterness all over India. The vernacular newspapers were practically unanimous in condemning the state authorities and in criticizing the government of India for permitting such things to be done. The Swarajist members withdrew from the Legislative Assembly at Delhi as a formal expression of their disapproval. They were soon persuaded to return, however, and the government agreed to appoint a commission of inquiry. Mr. Balwant Singh, a Sikh magistrate of the first class, conducted the investigation and made a report which entirely exonerated the Nabha authorities. The evidence showed that some of the pilgrims had firearms and that they fired the first shot.

There were several other jathas sent to Jaito during the next few months, but the state authorities handled the situation with a judicious combination of firmness and conciliation. The pilgrims were told that they could visit the shrines in small groups and worship for three days. They usually refused the offer and were placed under arrest. The prisons were filled, but there was not very much suffering or loss of life. The interest in the movement soon began to wane even among the Sikhs themselves. The interference in Nabha was so obviously a political maneuver that only the most ignorant and fanatical could possibly be deceived. Its ultimate result was to strengthen the hands of the British authorities.

Another factor in the situation was Sir Malcolm Hailey, who assumed the governorship of the Punjab on June 1, 1924. His predecessor, Sir E. D. Maclagen, was tactful and sympathetic and in many respects an able administrator, but he was temperamentally unfit to meet a serious emergency. The new Governor, fortunately, was not another Sir Michael O'Dwyer, but his experience in India had extended over many years and he had the reputation of being a man of strong and determined character. Shortly after he became Governor, he traveled through the important Sikh districts of the Punjab explaining what his policy was to be and encouraging the Moderate elements of the community to exert their influence. He announced that the government was always ready to enact legislation to help the Sikhs in reforming the gurdwaras, but that no section of the people would be allowed to take the law into its own hands, whether it was actuated by religious or any other motives. His policy soon began to show results. The moderate Sikhs organized a central Reform Committee and a series of local publicity committees to coöperate with the government and to counteract the propaganda of the Akalis.

In July, 1925, the provincial government enacted a new Sikh Gurdwaras and Shrines Act, under which the Sikh community acquired control of its places of worship, the hereditary tenure of the mahants was abolished, subject to financial compensation, the property and income of the gurdwaras and shrines were utilized for the purposes for which they were founded, and provision was made that the rituals and ceremonies should be conducted according to the *Granth Sahib*, the holy book of the Sikh religion. Sir Malcolm Hailey also announced that all Sikh prisoners who would agree to work the new law and abandon the policy of direct action would be released. The prisoners refused at first to comply with these terms and were applauded by the Indian National Congress, but most of them yielded in January, 1926, and were given their freedom. The settlement was finally accepted by all of the Sikh community except a few Extremists who regretted the loss of a political issue or the opportunity to pose as religious martyrs.

One of the gravest dangers of the Akali movement was its possible influence on other communities and on other parts of India. If an organized mob of Sikhs could intimidate the government, what was to prevent an organized mob of Hindus or Moslems from following their example? The danger soon passed beyond the theoretical stage. In 1924, some Hindu politicians of Bengal organized a passive resistance attack upon the temple of Siva at Tarakeswar. On the face of it they had a good cause. The priest had neglected his duties and there was reason to suppose that he had also mismanaged the valuable funds of the shrine. An effort was made to bring the temple and its revenues under the charge of a committee of Swarajists. The matter was finally compromised. The priest was compelled to withdraw, but an orthodox Brahman was appointed as receiver and steps were taken to prevent the funds from being diverted from their original purpose. If the plan had fully succeeded, the vast wealth of Hindu religious foundations all over India would gradually have fallen into the hands of a small group of politicians and been used to overthrow British authority.

The British are unwilling to interfere in these matters because it is their policy in India not to take sides in religious quarrels. The policy is sound but it cannot always be observed. When the British law of property prevents the redress of religious abuses the authorities not only have to interfere, but they have to interfere on the wrong side. The British ought to sympathize with the people of India because their own ancestors had to face a similar problem at the time of the Reformation. The sanctity of private property did not prevent Henry VIII and Thomas Cromwell from destroying the monasteries in England and transferring the control of ecclesiastical wealth from the clergy to the laity. The conditions are of course somewhat different in India because its rulers are aliens and members of an alien religious faith. At the same time, no priest—Sikh, Hindu, or Moslem—should be allowed to control ecclesiastical property if the great majority of his community thinks he is unworthy. It would not be necessary for the government to take the initiative. It could legislate to nullify existing titles and establish the principle of trusteeship and then act in concrete cases on the advice of committees representing the various communities.

CHAPTER XI

HINDU-MOSLEM RELATIONS

HINDU-MOSLEM friction is the most serious problem in India and every step in the development of responsible government increases the difficulty of finding a solution. Some of the political leaders have been trying to work out a compromise, but they have received very little encouragement from the religious leaders who have more influence with the rank and file of the people. The political leaders themselves have made some terrible blunders. At the time of the Caliphate (Khilafat) agitation, for example, Mr. Gandhi and the Ali brothers appealed to religious prejudice against Europeans, without apparently considering the fact that Moslems respect the religion of the European and despise that of the Hindu. The results have already been described. The Moplah rebellion began as a protest against British policy in Turkey and ended with a massacre of Hindus.

The feud between the two communities is a very complicated affair. The religious aspect should naturally be considered first, although it is doubtful whether religious differences are really the chief source of trouble. There are four main issues —cow-killing, the playing of music in the neighborhood of mosques, the defilement of places of worship, and the efforts to convert people from one faith to the other.

Cows are regarded by the Hindus as sacred, but they are killed by the Moslems for food and also occasionally for sacrificial purposes. The religious law of Islam requires animal sacrifices at the Id-ul-Azha or as it is called in India, the Baqarah-'Id festival. The cost of a sheep or a goat provided for this purpose is supposed to be borne by one person, but, if a cow or a camel is used, as many as ten people may share the expense. It is, therefore, less expensive to furnish cows. When the Moslems are in a majority or feel strong enough to take the risk they sometimes lead the cows in a procession through the streets to the place of slaughter. This infuriates the Hindus and is frequently the cause of a riot. The danger is especially great when the festival, which is based on the Moslem calendar, happens to coincide with one of the Hindu religious holidays.

But the provocation is not all on one side. Hindus must have music for their religious parades and it is not always convenient to cease playing when they pass a mosque. They have even been known to stop near a mosque and play more loudly than ever, an insult which the Moslems are almost certain to resent. Each community is sometimes guilty of defiling the other's place of worship. Cows were killed in the precincts of Hindu temples during the Moplah rebellion and their entrails were wrapped around the arms and necks of Hindu idols. A bad riot occurred near Calcutta in May, 1925, because the carcass of a pig, which the Moslems regard as an unclean animal, was found in a mosque.

Religious propaganda is a comparatively new source of friction because until recently it was a purely one-sided movement. Moslems and Christians regard their religions as universal and feel an obligation to win adherents from other faiths, but, in India, they usually leave each other alone and concentrate their attacks upon the Hindus. Hinduism (or Brahmanism), on the other hand, is the religion of a people who have generally shown no desire to proselytize or even to retain the loyalty of their own members by any special creed. According to an estimate made by the Simon Commission,[1] there are over 43,000,000 Indians within the reaches of "Hinduism" who cause "pollution by touch or by their approach within a certain distance." In other words about 25 per cent of the total Hindu population are condemned by their own people to suffer disabilities which usually include a denial of access to the interior of orthodox Hindu temples. Hindus forcibly converted to Islam have actually found it difficult to get back into their community, especially if they have been defiled by circumcision or other unclean rites. A description

1. *Report of the Indian Statutory Commission* (*Simon Commission*), I, 40.

of the filthy and expensive process of purification required of Hindus who were converted during the Moplah rebellion would surprise and shock the people of England or the United States, but to orthodox Hindus the real occasion for surprise was not the hardship imposed upon these innocent victims of fanaticism, but the fact that they were ever restored to their community at all.

As a result of the efforts of the Servants of India, the Arya Samaj, and other progressive organizations, this point of view is gradually changing. Orthodox Hindus are still unwilling to receive the "untouchables" into the full fellowship of their community, but they are generally inclined to sympathize with the Shuddhi movement for the conversion of Moslems and Christians. Strictly speaking, this movement is not a departure from the tribal principle, but an attempt to win back people who have strayed from the Hindu fold. The reclamation, a few years ago, of some Rajputs of the United Provinces who had been converted under pressure from their Moslem landlords is a good example. It is difficult to say whether the motive power back of the movement is primarily religious or based on a desire to strengthen the Hindu community in anticipation of self-government. Both elements are probably involved. In any case, the Moslems are very much alarmed, especially as they do not know where the line will ultimately be drawn. The great majority of their community are the descendants of Hindus who were forcibly converted at one time or another and it is a question whether they are all to be regarded as potential proselytes. To counteract the influence of the Shuddhi movement they have started a somewhat similar type of propaganda which is called the Tanzim movement.

Religious controversies impose a tremendous burden on the administrative authorities, who are expected to be just and impartial, to protect both communities in their rights and privileges and always to maintain law and order. If they forbid cows to be led in public procession at the time of the Baqarah-'Id festival, they offend the Moslems; if they try to regulate the playing of music in religious parades, they are equally sure to offend the Hindus; but, if they yield the point in either case, they have to run the risk of serious trouble. If they allow a riot to get a good start, as they did at Calcutta in 1926 and at Bombay in 1929, they are accused of timidity; but if they suppress it in its early stages, as they did at Softa in 1928, they are just as likely to be accused of brutality.

The Softa case should be considered in some detail because it illustrates not only the difficulties of the police administration, but also the serious nature of the cow-killing problem. Softa is a small Moslem village in the southern Punjab which is almost surrounded by Hindu settlements. Just before the Baqarah-'Id festival in May, 1928, the Hindus heard a rumor that the cow that was to be sacrificed had been accustomed to graze in their fields, although her owner was a Moslem. The Superintendent of Police also heard the rumor and, knowing that there might be trouble, he went to Softa with about 25 men, took possession of the cow and assured the Hindus that she would not be sacrificed. The Hindus were not satisfied. About 1,000 of them, armed with staves, spears, and pitchforks, surrounded the village and threatened to burn it unless the cow was handed over to them for safekeeping and a promise made that no cow at all would be killed. They were warned to disperse, but refused to do so, and the situation finally became so dangerous that the police were ordered to fire. The total casualties were 14 killed and 33 injured. A judicial investigation was ordered by the Punjab government and the police were exonerated. It was found that they had to act in self-defense and also to save the village from destruction. If the police had weakened and allowed the village to be burned, there would have been communal warfare all over the Punjab and possibly in other provinces and thousands of people would have suffered.[2]

Religious disputes of this character are the immediate cause of nearly all communal riots, but there is much to be said in favor of the view generally held by British officials in India that the political differences are more fundamental. The conflict, as they see it, is really a struggle for the spoils of office and the political power which the British are giving up. In other words, communal rivalry is being stimulated by "the in-

2. For a more detailed account of this episode see *Moral and Material Conditions in India in 1928–29,* chap. i.

creasing association of Indians in every branch of the administration" and by "the progressive realization of responsible government." The troubles have increased since the enactment of the Reforms and are now more acute in the Reform area (British India) than they are in the Indian States. The so-called "cow-music" disputes were usually adjusted peacefully before 1919 and, with few exceptions, that is still the case in the states, where political power and appointment to office are dependent on the whims of an hereditary ruler.

The theory is further confirmed by the growth of communal friction in the states after it was announced in 1930 that they were prepared to enter the new federation. If they are to be represented in the central legislature, it is a matter of great importance which community will control their votes. The Moslems are already in a minority and, when the states are admitted, their relative strength will be still further reduced. They constitute 25.4 per cent of the population of British India and only 13.4 per cent of the population of the states. There are only a few Moslem states and in some of them the majority of the people are Hindus. This is notably true of Hyderabad in the Deccan, the second largest state in India, where the Hindus constitute nearly 90 per cent of the population although the Nizam himself is a Moslem.

The political issue was an important factor in the recent troubles in Kashmir and Jammu. The control of this state is necessary to round out the sectional bloc which some of the Moslem leaders are trying to create on the northern and western frontiers. It is the largest state in that region; in fact, from the point of view of area, it is the largest state in India. The conditions here are almost exactly the reverse of those that exist in Hyderabad. The ruling house is Hindu, but over 75 per cent of the people are Moslems. These Moslems have a peaceful tradition and they have endured grievances for many years without making any serious complaint. There is every reason to believe that they would have continued to suffer in silence if they had not received encouragement and help from their brethren in the Punjab and the North-West Frontier. The Ahrar (free and independent) movement was organized by these outsiders partly to deal with the immediate situation, but with the ultimate intention of bringing Kashmir and Jammu under Moslem control.

The local problem was complicated. The main charges were that the Moslems were liable to heavy penalties for cattle slaughter, they had to observe Hindu fast days, their sacred buildings were used for secular purposes, the education of their children was neglected, they were discriminated against in the assessment and collection of the land revenues, and they were to a large extent excluded from the Ministry, the higher Civil Service posts, and even the local positions in their own villages. Although loud complaints were made in 1930–31, the Maharaja did practically nothing to redress the abuses and emphasized his intransigent attitude by appointing a Brahman as Prime Minister. The revolt began in 1931. Jathas or bands of pilgrims crossed the frontier from the Punjab in such large numbers that the situation soon got beyond control and the government of India and the government of the Punjab were both compelled to intervene. The jathas were held back by military force and the Maharaja was persuaded to allow a Commission of Inquiry with a British chairman (Mr. Glancy) to investigate the Moslem grievances.

The recommendations of the Glancy Commission were accepted by the Maharaja, and Lt. Col. E. J. D. Colvin of the Political Department of the government of India was appointed Prime Minister to see that they were carried out. This satisfied the great majority of the local Moslems, but the Ahrar movement is still popular in the Punjab. With some of the leaders it is still more than a mere question of the balance of power in the federal legislature. If there ever should be a communal civil war in India, the North-West will be the Moslem stronghold. They control Kashmir because they could not afford to have an enemy in the rear. There are, however, three main influences which tend to hold the Ahrar movement in restraint: the presence of the British Army, the unwillingness of the Moslems of Kashmir to be treated as pawns in a political game, and the realization of the fact that any precedents established in Kashmir may be used against the Moslems of Hyderabad.

The appointment of the Simon Commission intensified communal feelings in British India because a revision of the Constitution necessarily involved the more or less permanent settlement of problems upon which the two communities could not agree. This is the reason why the National Congress failed to secure a general boycott of the commission or a general approval of the Nehru Report. The most important of these problems were (a) the redistribution of the provinces and the extension of the Reforms to new areas, (b) the communal apportionment of the members of the various legislatures, district boards, and municipal councils and the method of their election, and (c) the recruitment policy to be followed as the Civil Services are more widely Indianized.

With the development of provincial autonomy, it is highly desirable that the population of each province should be as nearly homogeneous as possible. To accomplish this, there will have to be a ruthless partition and redistribution of the existing provincial areas and ultimately a readjustment of some of the state boundaries. The problem is primarily linguistic, but we are concerned here mainly with its religious aspects.[3]

Several schemes have been suggested for the territorial readjustment of Bengal and the Punjab. Although Lord Curzon was primarily interested in administrative efficiency, his partition of Bengal was a logical solution of the problem in that province. If his policy had been upheld, the Hindus in the western part of the province would not now be facing the prospect of Moslem domination and the political status of their brethren in eastern Bengal would at least not be any worse. It is true that Assam has remained and will continue to remain under Hindu control, but it will not offset the loss of the rich and densely populated area of Calcutta. There are curious paradoxes in the history of India, and the Bengalis themselves may soon be advocating some form of partition.

Two plans for readjustment in the Punjab were laid before the Round Table Conference in 1931. Sir Geoffrey Corbett, one of the Secretaries of the British Indian delegation, sug-

3. For some interesting examples of the need for linguistic readjustments, see G. T. Garratt, *An Indian Commentary* (London, 1929), p. 251.

gested that the United Provinces should be divided into the original units of Agra and Oudh, and that the boundaries of Agra should be extended to include the greater part of the Ambala division of the Punjab. This would be justified on linguistic grounds because most of the Ambala people speak Hindi rather than Punjabi. As they are also Hindus, their detachment from the Punjab would increase the Moslem majority in that province from 56.5 (census of 1931) to about 62 per cent and make it possible for them to maintain political control without communal representation. The Hindus would be weakened, but presumably they would rejoice over the abolition of separate electorates. As a matter of fact, neither the Hindus nor the Sikhs received the suggestion with any enthusiasm and an alternative plan was put forward by Sardar Ujjal Singh, one of the Sikh delegates. According to his plan the greater part of the western divisions of Rawalpindi and Multan would be detached from the Punjab and either erected into a separate province or joined to the North-West Frontier. The new Punjab would then be approximately 43.3 per cent Moslem, 42.3 per cent Hindu, and 14.4 per cent Sikh. The Moslems might have separate electorates, but they would no longer have any excuse for demanding a majority of the seats. Neither of these plans has so far been given any serious consideration.

Sind was an excellent example of the need for readjustment on both linguistic and religious grounds. Originally attached to the Bombay presidency in 1842 merely because it happened to be conquered by the Bombay Army, it remained in that unnatural alliance until 1936. It was entirely cut off from the presidency proper by Gujarat and Kathiawar states and there was no direct railway communication. Its people speak a different language and profess a different religion from those that prevail in other parts of the old presidency and they are also to a large extent of a different racial stock. The Simon Commission admitted that the case for separation was strong, but it was inclined to emphasize the "grave administrative objections to isolating Sind and depriving it of the powerful backing of Bombay before the future of the Sukkur Barrage" was assured. It felt also that "there would have to be a close and detailed enquiry into the financial consequences" before a final decision was reached. The Sind Subcommittee, appointed at the first session of the Round Table Conference, accepted the principle of separation and recommended that the financial aspects of the problem should be investigated by a committee of experts. Although the report of the experts was unfavorable, His Majesty's government felt that other considerations were more important and agreed that Sind should enter the new federation as a separate province. As a matter of fact, the separation was brought about in 1936, on April 1, before the new Constitution was put into operation.[4]

This was an act of simple justice to the people of Sind, but, as 75 per cent of the population are Moslems, it also marked an important stage in the development of the political influence of the Moslem community. The Moslems were likewise anxious to have the Reforms extended to the North-West Frontier Province and to British Baluchistan, where more than 90 per cent of the population were members of their community. This would give them a solid bloc of four major provinces in the north-west and the control over Hindu minorities who could be held as hostages for the good treatment of Moslems in other parts of India. The Hindus were naturally suspicious of the program. As they would themselves have expressed it, they had no desire to see their people ruled by ignorant and fanatical Pathans, and ill-treated whenever Moslems in other parts of India felt that they had a grievance. A motion to introduce the Reforms into the North-West Frontier Province was made in the Legislative Assembly shortly after the terrible communal riots of 1926 and, with the exception of Mr. Bepin Chandra Pal, it was bitterly opposed by all the Hindu leaders. The issue was brought up again in 1929 and the debate was kept in bounds only because the more radical politicians on both sides were determined not to allow internal dissension to weaken the boycott of the Simon Commission.

The question of extending the Reforms to the North-West Frontier Province was complicated not only by its poverty and

4. The creation of the new province of Orissa, also on April 1, 1936, has already been described. It had no religious significance.

the sparseness of its population, but also by its strategic military position. There was, however, a perfectly legitimate feeling among the inhabitants of the five settled districts that their interests were neglected by the government of India because they were compelled to spend so much time in dealing with the comparatively uncivilized tribesmen of the mountains. Some of their grievances were remedied after the Frontier Inquiry Committee, commonly called the Bray Committee, published its Report in 1924, but the conditions were still far from satisfactory. Three possible solutions were suggested by a Moslem delegation which testified before the Simon Commission on November 19, 1928: the Reforms might be extended to the province with financial aid from the government of India, which could be justified on Imperial grounds; the province might be annexed to the Punjab, from which most of it had been detached in 1901; or it might be joined to some of the western districts of the Punjab to form a new province large enough to be self-supporting. The Simon Commission rejected these solutions and frankly told the people that they were the victims of their geography. The tribal area could not be controlled by a local government and it could not be controlled effectively by the government of India if it were detached from the settled districts.

> There is much force in the claim put forward by witnesses from the N.W.F.P. that the virile inhabitants of this area are not less intelligent than their neighbours, and that their geographic position ought not to deprive them of a share in India's political advance . . . , but it is not possible to change the plain facts of the situation. The inherent right of a man to smoke a cigarette must necessarily be curtailed if he lives in a powder magazine.[5]

The commission agreed, however, that the province was entitled to a more progressive form of government and to the right of representation in the central legislature. There should be a Legislative Council of about forty members, half elected and half nominated, but its powers should be very much restricted.

5. Vol. II, par. 121.

These recommendations were unsatisfactory. They enraged the people who lived in the settled districts, encouraged the mountain tribes to make trouble, and greatly strengthened Abdul Ghaffar Khan and his Red Shirt movement. The government of India, in a dispatch to the Round Table Conference, published November 14, 1930, called attention to the menace of a discontented frontier and advocated more liberal treatment. The question was considered at the first two sessions of the conference and the Reforms were finally extended to the province on April 20, 1932. The Chief Commissioner was replaced by a Governor, a Legislative Council was created, and a Minister was appointed to take charge of Transferred Subjects. The Governor acts as agent to the Governor-General for the control of the tribal tracts and, with the assistance of an Executive Committee, administers the Reserved Departments.

The problem in Baluchistan is different. Only a small part of it is British territory and, even if it were possible to include the agency area, it would still be unable to support a major provincial administration.[6] Furthermore, the Baluchis already have a tribal system of self-government which is better adapted to their needs than any scheme that may be devised for the more advanced provinces. "It may be safely stated," says *The Simon Report*, "that the Baluchis have not themselves sought any alteration of the existing regime. The demand for representative institutions of a western type certainly does not come from them." The Report recommended, however, that the province should be represented in the central legislature and this was approved by His Majesty's government.[7]

Communal electorates originated with the Morley-Minto Reforms. A Moslem delegation, led by the Aga Khan, called on Lord Minto in 1906 and presented a claim for separate

6. This is, of course, also true of Sind and the North-West Frontier Province, but it is hoped that their subventions from the central government can gradually be reduced and that they will ultimately become self-supporting.

7. Vol. I, par. 366, II, pars. 126, 144, 150. See also *The India White Paper,* issued March 18, 1933.

Moslem representation. Their case is admirably summarized in the Viceroy's reply:

> The pith of your address, as I understand it, is a claim that under any system of representation, whether it affects a municipality or a district board or a legislative council, in which it is proposed to introduce or increase an electoral organization, the Mohammedan community should be represented as a community. You point out that in many cases electoral bodies as now constituted cannot be expected to return a Mohammedan candidate, and that if by chance they did so, it could only be at the sacrifice of such a candidate's views to those of a majority opposed to his community whom he would in no way represent; and you justly claim that your position should be estimated not only on your numerical strength, but in respect to the political importance of your community and the service it has rendered to the Empire.

Lord Minto and his Executive Council approved the claim and it was finally accepted, with some reluctance, by Lord Morley and His Majesty's government. The Indian Councils Act of 1909 and the rules framed thereunder made provision for separate Moslem electorates in all the major provinces, except Burma, where the communal problem does not exist, the Central Provinces and the North-West Frontier Province, where there were no Legislative Councils at that time, and the Punjab, where it was assumed that special protection was not required. Moslems were also allowed to vote in the general constituencies which were mainly composed of big landholders, members of municipal corporations and district boards, and members of chambers of commerce.

This settlement was at first bitterly criticized by the Hindus. It not only recognized the communal principle and gave a double vote to Moslems, but it was also apparently based on the idea of using Moslems and wealthy landlords as a conservative balance against Hindu barristers and pleaders and other radicals who tended to monopolize the seats for which they were eligible. As the Home Rule movement developed, however, the criticism was modified and the leaders of each community joined in the preparation of the Lucknow Pact of 1916, which was later incorporated into the Montagu-Chelmsford Reforms. The electorate under the Reforms has already been discussed.[8] The double vote for Moslems in the general constituencies was abolished, but the principle of the communal electorates was confirmed and extended to the Punjab and the Central Provinces. On the basis of population, Moslems were overrepresented in the central legislature and in the Legislative Councils of all the provinces in which they are in the minority, but they were underrepresented in Bengal and the Punjab. In Bengal, where they constituted 54.6 per cent of the population in the electorate area in 1921, they were allowed 39 communal seats, while the Hindus, with only 45 per cent of the population, had 46 seats. The situation in the Punjab was slightly better. The Moslems, with 55.2 per cent of the population, elected one half of the communal members and the Hindus and the Sikhs together, with 43.1 per cent, elected the other half. The total disproportion was greater still because the Hindus are usually more successful in the commerce, university, and other special constituencies. In Bengal, for example, although 46 per cent of the general communal seats were allotted to Moslems, only 40.5 per cent of the total number of Indian members elected in 1926 belonged to that community.

Moslems naturally felt that they should have had the full benefit of their majority position in Bengal and the Punjab, but, with that exception, they were satisfied with the system and wished to see it extended more widely to district boards, municipal councils, and other organs of local government.[9] The Hindus, on the other hand, regretted their acceptance of the Lucknow Pact. As the majority community, they preferred the ordinary type of electoral system in which there were no seats reserved for communal groups and all voters in the general constituencies were listed on a joint or common electoral roll. But they were willing to concede a temporary

8. See chap. iii.

9. Communal electorates were provided for the election of Moslems to district boards in the Bombay presidency and the United Provinces, to local boards in Assam, and to the municipal council in Calcutta. *Report of the Indian Statutory Commission* (*Simon Commission*), Vol. I, pars. 343, 346.

reservation of seats for Moslems, wherever they were in a minority, provided the Moslems would agree to a joint electorate. They were even prepared to extend the reservation to Bengal and possibly to the Punjab if a final settlement could have been assured. They were also willing to accept the principle of weightage, under which the minority would have a larger representation than its population would warrant.

This offer was rejected by the Moslems for obvious reasons. The Hindus are not only more numerous, but they are also more clever at the game of politics. They would usually be able to elect any candidate they pleased to represent their own interests and to veto the election of Moslems who had won their disapproval. A Moslem who really represented Moslem opinion would practically never be elected in a constituency where the majority of the voters are Hindus. It is a significant confession of political weakness that the Moslems are opposed to joint electorates even in the provinces where they are in a majority. The reasons are again well known. In addition to their lack of political skill, they are economically backward as compared with the Hindus and consequently find it more difficult to meet the property qualifications for the suffrage. Their population ratio in Bengal, for example, was at that time 54.6, but their voting ratio was only 45.1. The figures for the Punjab were 55.2 and 43.7. It should perhaps be added that the disproportion in the Punjab was due mainly to the high voting ratio of the Sikhs, who were helped by the granting of the suffrage to ex-soldiers. The population and voting ratios of the Sikhs in that province were respectively 11.1 and 24.1. The corresponding Hindu ratios were 45.1 and 53 in Bengal, and 33.7 and 32.2 in the Punjab.[10] An educational qualification would also bear heavily on the Moslems and universal

10. The population ratio of a community as given here is the ratio of its population to the total population living in the electoral area at the time of the census of 1921. The voting ratio is the ratio of its qualified voters to the total number of qualified voters at the election of 1926. In so far as the statistics given above relate to Hindus, it should be noted that they are based on the assumption that "non-Mohammedan" voters, excluding the Sikhs in the Punjab, are all Hindus. The exact figures would not appreciably change the results.

suffrage would be worst of all because it would increase the proportion of their voters who could be controlled by Hindu landlords and moneylenders.

The British official attitude, as reflected in *The Montagu-Chelmsford Report* in 1918, *The Report of the Simon Commission* in 1930, and *The Report of the Joint Committee* in 1934, remains unchanged. It is assumed in all of these documents that communal electorates are theoretically wrong, but as they are based upon an agreement between the two communities they can be annulled only by mutual consent. There is also a tendency to admit the Moslem contention that a pledge was made to them by the British government when the Morley-Minto Reforms were adopted. In other words, the Hindus and the British are both really committed to the present system until the Moslems see fit to release them.

The Montagu-Chelmsford Report criticized the system on the grounds that it was opposed to the teachings of history, perpetuated class divisions, stereotyped existing relations, and was a "very serious hindrance to the development of the self-governing principle." But it then went on to say: "Much as we regret the necessity, we are convinced that so far as the Mohammedans at all events are concerned the present system must be maintained until conditions alter, even at the price of slower progress towards the realization of a common citizenship." These words were quoted with approval by the authors of *The Simon Report*. They felt, however, that the faults of the system had been exaggerated by some students of Indian affairs and that it had been blamed for results which were obviously due to other causes. "In our judgment, communal representation cannot be justly regarded as the reason for the communal tension we have been describing, and there is no solid ground for supposing that if communal representation were abolished communal strife would disappear. The true cause lies deeper and arises from conditions which are far more difficult to change[11] than the mechanics of Representation."

11. *Report on Indian Constitutional Reforms* (*Montagu-Chelmsford Report*), pars. 228–231; *Report of the Indian Statutory Commission* (*Simon Commission*), Vol. I, par. 149, Vol. II, par. 69.

The later history of the question has already been discussed in connection with the Constitution of 1935.

We come now to the third politico-religious issue mentioned above, the struggle for appointments in the Public Services. This is not entirely a new factor in the development of communal rivalry. Before the Reforms, as we have already seen, there was a wide gulf between the higher Service posts, which were practically monopolized by the British, and the medium posts, which were filled by Indians, Anglo-Indians (Eurasians), and domiciled Europeans. Although the latter were poorly paid, according to European standards, they had their attractions and were the source of keen competition. Some communities seem to have a special aptitude for learning English and passing the Civil Service examinations. As a rule, Hindus are cleverer than Moslems, Brahmans than other Hindus, Bengalis than the people of other provinces. As a result of this a large proportion of the prizes went to Bengali Brahmans until the authorities began to restrict the candidates to the provinces in which the appointments were to be made. This broke the Bengali monopoly, but the Moslems were still outclassed by the Brahmans and other Hindus of their own provinces.

After the adoption of the Reforms the value of the spoils was greatly enhanced. A steadily increasing number of Indians were appointed to posts that were formerly held by the British, posts that were coveted not only because the British scale of wages was still paid, but also because the man who held it was in a position to favor his relatives and friends and the members of his own religious community. The Moslems felt that they were not getting a fair share of these jobs and they realized that their position was likely to be still further weakened if India ever attained Dominion Home Rule or became an independent nation. It is immaterial whether the appointments are based on merit or made as a reward for political services; the Hindus are better politicians as well as better students and they also have the inestimable advantage of numerical superiority.

There is abundant evidence of the anxiety of Moslems over this issue. At a meeting of the Bengal Moslem All-Parties

Convention, held in December, 1928, the President, Sir Abdur Rahim, upheld the existing system of communal electorates and, with the approval of his audience, expressed the opinion that the proportion of Moslems in the Public Services should in no case be less than the proportion of Moslems in the central and provincial legislatures. A Moslem delegation in the United Provinces complained to the Simon Commission, December 6, 1928, that Moslems could not secure appointments in their provinces under district and municipal boards controlled by Hindus, and suggested that there should not only be separate electorates for these bodies, but that the number of Moslem officials employed under each board should be proportionate to the number of Moslem members of that board. A deputation of the Madras Presidency Moslem League proposed (February 26, 1929) that 20 per cent of all Public Service posts in their province should be reserved for Moslems. One of the resolutions adopted by the All-India Moslem League at Delhi, January 1, 1929, demanded for Moslems an adequate share of appointments in the Public Services and on all statutory self-governing bodies.

The point is often made that there is more friction over this in British India than there is in the Indian States. This is true and there are good reasons for it. In British India each of the great religious communities realizes the importance of bringing pressure to bear upon the impartial authorities who are now in control of affairs and the even greater importance of securing possession of the government that will control affairs in the future. In the states, on the other hand, the ruler does not pretend to be impartial. He belongs to one of the communities himself and is expected to favor his own community, even when it is a minority, as is the case in Hyderabad and Kashmir. Very little organized pressure is ever brought to bear against these rulers.[12] The Hindus of Hyderabad may feel that they ought to have more jobs, but they know that it would be useless to complain to the Nizam and worse than useless to stir up trouble with their Moslem neighbors.[13] The

12. In the recent conflicts in Kashmir, the struggle for office was not the paramount issue and the organized pressure came from outside.

13. The Nizam does, however, have a Moslem Prime Minister.

Moslems are in the same position in Baroda, Gwalior, and other Hindu states. It should also be remembered that the rulers of these states are hereditary autocrats and that, while so-called Legislative Councils have in some instances been created, there is no immediate prospect of the development of real democratic institutions and consequently no motive for the establishment of strong communal organizations. There may be a different story to tell in the future if a democratic federal government should try to interfere in the internal affairs of the states.

The general attitude of the Hindus toward all of these politico-religious problems is that their consideration should, as far as possible, be postponed until after the attainment of swaraj, whereas the Moslems would like to have a settlement now while they are in a position to drive a bargain. This is the rock upon which the Nehru Report was destroyed. It was also the cause of the bitter conflict between Mr. Gandhi and the Moslem leaders at the second session of the Round Table Conference.

We come now to the economic aspect of communalism. In the northwest, the moneylenders and the lawyers who defend their interests are usually Hindus and the majority of the peasants are Moslems. The growing rivalry between urban and rural interests in the Punjab is very much influenced by these religious differences. In eastern Bengal, the zamindars or landlords are mainly Hindus and the tenants are Moslems. Similar conditions prevail in many other parts of India, notably on the Malabar coast of Madras, where, as already stated, they have played a part in the numerous uprisings of the Moplahs. In India as a whole, the merchants, manufacturers, moneylenders, and professional men are apt to be Hindus, Jains, or Parsees (in Bombay) while a large proportion of the urban proletariat are Moslems. The only important exceptions to this rule are the Bohras and the Khojas, the famous Moslem traders of the west coast, many of whom have recently settled in East Africa.

The riots of February, 1929, in the city of Bombay are a curious example of the economic factor in communalism. On December 7, 1928, a strike was begun in some of the plants of the large oil companies. The strikers, who were mostly Hindus, established pickets and used various other intimidating measures which the Oriental workman has learned from his Occidental brethren. Unfortunately for them, there is in Bombay a small community of Pathans, sturdy Moslem hillmen from Afghanistan and the North-West Frontier, who are willing to act as strikebreakers and who can fight their way through any ordinary cordon of pickets. For several weeks the strike leaders were unable to make much headway and they finally decided to appeal to the fanaticism of the Hindu community at large. On February 2, a rumor was started that the Pathans were kidnaping Hindu children to sacrifice them on the foundations of a bridge in Baroda.[14] The result was a general attack upon the Pathans and, although they fought with a great deal of valor, they got the worst of it until the whole Moslem community began to rally to their support. For several days the streets were a scene of carnage and by the time the authorities restored order there had been about a thousand casualties.

This episode might perhaps also be cited as an illustration of race influence on communal friction, but that is an aspect of the problem that may easily be exaggerated. It is true that the Pathans are racially different from the Hindus of Bombay, but they are equally different from the great majority of the Moslems of Bombay. It is also true that there is an Arab strain in the blood of the Moplahs, but it is very slight and probably has little or nothing to do with their fanaticism. There are real racial differences in the extreme north-west and in parts of the Punjab, but this is a sparsely settled region and it may be estimated with a reasonable degree of accuracy that over 90 per cent of all the Moslems of India are descendants of Hindu converts and consequently of the same racial stock as their immediate neighbors. Racial antagonism, therefore, is not really a factor in the communal struggle except in

14. The belief that children are sometimes sacrificed to propitiate malignant deities and thus prevent the fall of a bridge or a tower is fairly widespread in India. There was a serious riot in Calcutta in 1924 when the Moslems heard that some of their children were being sacrificed to appease the demon of a new dock.

the North-West Frontier Province and occasionally in some sections of the Punjab.

The Hindu-Moslem entente began with the promulgation of the Congress-League plan of government in 1916. Strengthened by the Amritsar troubles of 1919 and by Mr. Gandhi's adoption of the Caliphate program, it held fairly well until 1924. There were a few communal riots during that period, but with the exception of the Moplah uprising, which was a purely local movement, they were all of minor importance compared with the terrific conflicts of later years. About 1924, however, conditions began to change. There was a riot in Delhi in July of that year in which 20 people were killed and more than 100 injured. There were also serious disturbances a little later at Lucknow, Lahore, Nagpur, Moradabad, Bhagalpur, Saharanpur, Kankinarah, Allahabad, and Kohat in British India and at Gulbarga in the state of Hyderabad. At Kohat in the North-West Frontier Province there were over 150 casualties and the entire Hindu population was for a time driven into exile.

There were also other dangerous symptoms in 1923 and 1924. Separate communal organizations became more active and bitter feelings were aroused by the development of the Sangathan movement among the Hindus and the rival Tanzim movement among the Moslems. Through the efforts of Pandit Malaviya, Lala Lajpat Rai, and other leaders, the Hindus organized an All-India Mahasabha to reclaim Hindus who had been forcibly converted to Islam, to provide relief for Hindus who had suffered in communal riots, to defend Hindus in political controversies, and to advance the general interests of their community. The leaders were apparently disturbed by the widespread assumption that the Hindus, as compared with Moslems, are a nonmartial people and a special attempt was made to encourage their young men to take part in athletic exercises and semimilitary drills. The effort to carry out these objects is known as the Sangathan movement, the term Shuddhi being applied, as already mentioned, to that part of the movement which has to do with the reclamation of Hindus from other faiths. The Moslems, influenced in large measure by the spirit of retaliation, were equally active. The All-India Moslem League, which had been suspended during the years when the entente was most effective, was revived in 1924 and the Caliphate Committee broke off its alliance with Mr. Gandhi, gave up its visionary program in the Near East and began to pay more attention to purely local affairs. Although these two bodies represented slightly different points of view, they both condemned the Sangathan program, defended the Tanzim movement as a justifiable measure of retaliation, and upheld what they regarded as the fundamental religious and political rights of their community. The chief objects of the Tanzim movement are to win adherents from other creeds, to resist the reconversion of Moslems to Hinduism, and to improve the general position of the Moslem community.

The friction is apt to be most acute where the Moslems predominate or where the strength of the two communities is approximately equal. There is practically no trouble in Madras, for example, and there is not very much in Bombay. The Moplah rebellion and the riots of 1929 in the city of Bombay, described above, were isolated episodes and not at all typical of conditions in the two presidencies as a whole. Southern India has its communal problems, but they are largely confined to the Hindus, such as the rivalry between Brahmans and non-Brahmans and the treatment of the Depressed Classes. The Hindu-Moslem feeling itself is a little worse in the Central Provinces, Bihar and Orissa, and Assam; worse still in Bengal and the United Provinces; and worst of all in the Punjab, Delhi, and the North-West Frontier Province. Delhi and the North-West Frontier Province were formerly parts of the Punjab and they are both very much influenced by conditions in that province. The people of this region, Hindus as well as Moslems and Sikhs, have a martial tradition and the consequence is that petty disputes easily degenerate into riots. The situation is especially bad in the urban centers of the Frontier Province where there are large and economically influential Hindu minorities.

It was in this province, at Kohat on September 9 and 10, that the riots of 1924 reached their culmination. By that time, the leading men of both communities had begun to realize not only that the Nationalist movement was being discredited, but that the whole future of India was being seriously jeopardized. Mr. Gandhi in particular was alarmed and filled with a deep sense of grief. He assumed responsibility for the turn that affairs had taken and announced that on September 18 he would begin a penitential fast of three weeks. This brought matters to a crisis. A so-called Unity Conference was held at Delhi on the twenty-eighth, which was attended by Hindus, Moslems, Parsees, Sikhs, and Christians. A series of resolutions was adopted and the people of India were urged to abide by them. All religions were to be tolerated and there was to be complete freedom of public worship with due regard to the feelings of other people. Hindus were informed that it was impossible to prevent the sacrifice of cows, but Moslems were urged to perform their rites in a manner as little offensive to Hindus as possible, and the Moslem leaders at the conference pledged themselves to do everything in their power to reduce the number of cows that were killed. There was also a resolution disapproving the practice of disturbing other communities by the crying of prayers, the playing of music in the streets, and the like. Probably the most important work of the conference was the attempt to establish a system of conciliation and arbitration for the settlement of religious disputes. A central panchayat of fifteen members, representing all the leading communities, was to appoint local panchayats to act as boards of conciliation. Cases that could not be settled by these methods were to be taken into the courts, but in no circumstances was there to be an appeal to force.

Mr. Gandhi's fast, which was successfully completed on October 8, probably had more influence on the rank and file of the two communities than the work of the Unity Conference. There was an improvement in the situation for a few months, but the strife was resumed early in 1925 and has continued at intervals ever since. There was a riot at Howrah in Bengal in May (1925), caused by the finding of a dead pig in a mosque and trouble at Calcutta and Allahabad at the Baqarah-'Id festival on July 2. During the summer there was a series of mysterious fires in Hindu houses at Dara Ismail Khan in the

North-West Frontier Province which was believed to be part of a plot to intimidate the Hindus and drive them into exile as they had been driven from Kohat in the previous year. But bad as the conditions were in 1924 and 1925, they were still worse during the next two years. The chief trouble in 1926 was at Calcutta, where there were terrific riots from the beginning of April until nearly the end of October. There were also serious conflicts in many other places, especially in Bengal, the Punjab, and the United Provinces. In 1927, the worst troubles were at Lahore in May, at Multan in July, and at Nagpur in September. According to the official statistics, there were 65 separate communal riots in the 18 months from April 1, 1926, to October 1, 1927, in the course of which about 300 people were killed and 2,700 were injured.

The relations between the two communities were further embittered during these years by the murder of Swami Shaddhanand and by the controversy over the Rangila Rasul case. Swami was a prominent Hindu of the Punjab and a member of the rigid vegetarian branch of the Arya Samaj. He was a zealous supporter of the Shuddhi movement and was especially obnoxious to the Moslems because of his share in the reconversion of Rajputs in the United Provinces who had been forcibly converted to Islam by their landlords. He was assassinated at Delhi by Abdul Rashid, a Moslem fanatic, on December 23, 1926. The crime was denounced by the Moslem leaders, but it was freely discussed in the bazaars and the vernacular press and it undoubtedly helped to widen the gap between the rank and file of the two communities.

The Rangila Rasul case was a little more complicated. In May, 1924, a Hindu bookseller of Lahore by the name of Rajpal published a pamphlet entitled *Rangila Rasul*, which may be translated as *The Merry Prophet* or *The Debauched Prophet*. It was a foul and scurrilous attack upon the memory of Mohammed. The police were instructed by the government of the Punjab to prosecute Rajpal under Section 153A of the Indian Penal Code which penalizes actions committed with the intention of promoting or attempting to promote feelings of enmity or hatred between different classes of His Majesty's subjects. For one reason or another, the case dragged on for over two years, but Rajpal was finally convicted and sentenced to prison for 18 months and ordered to pay a fine of Rs. 1,000. There was an appeal, first to the Sessions Judge and then to the High Court of the Punjab, where the trial was held before Mr. Justice Dalip Singh, a member of a distinguished Sikh family, but by religion a Christian. The substance of his decision, given in May, 1927, was that while the attack was undoubtedly scandalous and malicious, it did not come under Section 153A of the Penal Code, which was intended to protect existing religious bodies and not to prevent adverse criticism of deceased religious leaders. The defendant was therefore acquitted.

The Moslems were surprised and enraged by this decision. A bitter attack upon the impartiality of the judge was made in the *Muslim Outlook*, a newspaper of Lahore, and the editor and the printer were fined and imprisoned for contempt of court. The police were able to prevent any serious outbreaks in the Punjab and the settled districts of the North-West Frontier Province, but the Moslems in the tribal area attacked the Hindus in their midst and drove about 450 of them into more or less permanent exile. This is a good illustration of the tendency of frontier Moslems to look upon their Hindu minorities as hostages for the settlement of Moslem grievances in other provinces, a tendency which has already been mentioned in connection with the Hindu opposition to the extension of the Reforms to the Frontier Province and to Baluchistan.

The decision of the court was offensive to the Moslems for two reasons: in the first place, no legal penalty could be inflicted upon Rajpal and, in the second place, there was apparently no guarantee against similar attacks upon the life and character of Mohammed in the future. A small group of fanatics made it their business to settle the first grievance themselves. After several unsuccessful attempts upon Rajpal's life, he was finally assassinated at his shop in Lahore on April 6, 1929. The second grievance was remedied by legal methods. A few days after the decision in the Rangila Rasul case, another venomous attack on the memory of the Prophet was made in the *Risala Vartman*, a monthly journal published at Amritsar. There was great excitement among the Moslems, which was intensified by the fact that the men responsible for the publication were members of the Arya Samaj and advocates of the Sangathan movement and it was assumed that their conduct was approved by the Hindu Mahasabha. A prosecution was ordered and their trial was held before a Division Bench of the High Court at Lahore. In its decision, delivered by Mr. Acting Chief Justice Broadway on August 6, 1927, the court ruled that a foul and scurrilous attack on the founder of Islam was covered by Section 153A of the Penal Code and the defendants were accordingly convicted, fined, and imprisoned. This decision and a similar one made by the High Court of Allahabad were, of course, in direct conflict with the judgment in the Rangila Rasul case. In order to remove all doubt about the interpretation of the Code and to make it absolutely clear that the authorities would have power to act in such emergencies in the future, the government of India introduced a Criminal Law Amendment Bill in the Legislative Assembly which provided for the insertion of a new section (295A) in the Penal Code and the addition of the necessary amendments in the Code of Criminal Procedure. This measure, which was passed in September, 1927, received the unanimous support of the Moslem members of the Assembly, but it was vigorously opposed by the majority of the Hindus. Some of the Hindu leaders, however, voted for it, apparently for political reasons, to prevent the Moslems from being forced out of the Congress party.[15]

After the Unity Conference of 1924 there was no serious effort made to compromise the differences between the two communities for nearly three years. On the contrary, the tendency was for each side to strengthen its own organization and to emphasize its own point of view. The meetings of the Hindu Mahasabha and the Moslem League were well attended and

15. The first important case to arise under the new legislation was that of the Swami Chiddanand, editor of the *Shuddhi Samachar*, the organ of the All-India Shuddhi Sabha, who was convicted at Delhi, July 23, 1929, and sentenced to six months rigorous imprisonment and fined Rs. 300.

extravagant speeches and resolutions were received with enthusiastic approval.[16] But for the mediation of Lord Irwin, this situation might have lasted indefinitely. In his first important speech in India, delivered at the Chelmsford Club banquet at Simla in July, 1926, the new Viceroy painted a dark picture of the recent disturbances at Calcutta and elsewhere and appealed to the leaders of both creeds to work for conciliation. As nothing was done, he brought up the subject again in his speech at the opening of the Simla session of the Indian legislature on August 29, 1927, and offered to preside over a conference to discuss the problem if the leaders thought that it would be of any use.

This speech brought action, although the results were disappointing. A second Unity Conference, composed largely of Hindu and Moslem members of the Legislative Assembly, met at Simla early in September. Finding that the political differences were too controversial to be discussed, the conference devoted its attention mainly to the "cow-music" problem, but that too proved incapable of solution. The All-India Congress Committee then intervened and issued a call for a third Unity Conference, to be held at Calcutta on October 27. This body also ignored the political issues, but it reached an agreement on the "cow-music" problem and the problem of conversion from one creed to another. Moslems might slaughter cows for food or for sacrificial purposes, provided they were not led to the place of sacrifice in a festival procession and were not killed in the vicinity of a Hindu temple or a place open to the gaze of Hindus; Hindus might play music in passing a mosque, provided they did not stop in front of it or play music of an offensive character; persons over eighteen years of age might be freely converted or reconverted, provided it was done by argument or persuasion and not by force. Although this settlement was not very widely accepted at the time—the

16. The presidential address of Lala Lajput Rai at the Calcutta meeting of the Mahasabha on April 11, 1925, and that of Sir Abdur Rahim at the Aligarh meeting of the Moslem League in December are good examples. The former was a eulogy of the Mahasabha and all its works and the latter was a statement of the Moslem position which was too extreme for any kind of compromise.

Hindu Mahasabha and the Moslem League not being represented at the conference—it has influenced all subsequent compromise proposals and will probably be embodied in the final agreement, if one is ever made.

The next step was taken by the National Congress at its annual meeting in December (1927), when, for the first time, a serious effort was made to deal with political issues. It was resolved that communal electorates should be superseded by joint electorates, with a reservation of seats and with special provision for a weighted representation of minorities. This meant that seats would still be reserved for Moslems even when they were in a majority, as in Bengal and the Punjab, and also that minorities, whether Hindu, Sikh, or Moslem, would have a representation somewhat in excess of that to which they would be entitled on the basis of population. That is to say, communal electorates were to be abolished, but the communal allotment of seats was to remain unchanged. There were also resolutions stating that the Reforms should be extended to the North-West Frontier Province and Baluchistan when their judicial administrations were brought up to the level of the major provinces; that there should be a redistribution on a linguistic basis of those provinces where such a change was desired and that, as a beginning, Andhra, Sind, and the Karnatic should be made into separate provinces; that matters declared to be intercommunal should not be moved or discussed in any legislative body if three fourths of the members of the community affected were opposed; and that a decision as to what constituted an intercommunal matter should be left to a standing committee of Hindus and Moslems in each legislative body, elected at the beginning of each session. The resolution of the Calcutta Unity Conference dealing with conversions was reaffirmed and Hindus and Moslems were both urged not to resist by force the right claimed by one community to use music in its processions or the right claimed by the other to slaughter cows.

The Moslems were badly divided at this time. The majority were conservative and rejected both the unity resolutions and the proposal to boycott the Simon Commission. They were strong in the Punjab, Sind, and the North-West Frontier

Province. Bengal might also be added to the list because the Moslem representatives in the Provincial Legislative Council, after wavering for a time, finally voted to coöperate with the Simon Commission. Their most influential leader was Sir Mohammed Shafi of Lahore, an ex-member of the Viceroy's Executive Council. The Left-Wing minority was composed of two factions, the Caliphate group, which followed the Ali brothers, and the Jinnah group, which drew its inspiration mainly from Mr. Mohammed Ali Jinnah, the leader of the Independent party in the Legislative Assembly. The former had declined in strength after the abolition of the Caliphate in 1924, but Mr. Jinnah had a large following, especially in Bombay, Madras, and other provinces in which the Moslems are in a minority. This may be an illustration of the maxim that discretion is the better part of valor; a willingness to coöperate with Hindus now may turn away wrath in the future when the local governments are brought more exclusively under Hindu control. In any case, Mr. Jinnah and his followers were willing to accept the unity resolutions and were especially anxious to consolidate the opposition to the Simon Commission.

These divisions were reflected in a split in the Moslem League at the annual meeting in December, 1927. The conservatives met in Lahore under the presidency of Sir Mohammed Shafi, while the radicals met in Calcutta under Maulvi Mohammed Yakub, deputy president of the Legislative Assembly and a follower of Mr. Jinnah. The conservatives adopted the usual resolutions in favor of communal electorates, the separation of Sind from Bombay and the extensions of the Reforms to the North-West Frontier Province and Baluchistan. The radicals approved the unity resolutions, but with the proviso that communal electorates should be abandoned only on condition that the Moslem program was carried out in Sind, the Frontier Province, and Baluchistan. A resolution to boycott the Simon Commission was also adopted.

For more than a year after these meetings it was an open question whether Mr. Jinnah and his adherents would form a more or less permanent alliance with the Hindus or would reunite with the majority of their own community. As long as a negative attitude toward the Statutory Commission was the dominant issue the former alternative seemed more likely, but when the positive task of preparing a constitution was undertaken the situation rapidly changed. The All-Parties Conference and the Nehru Report are discussed in another chapter. Here, it will be sufficient to say that the conference made a new effort to devise a religious settlement, acceptable to the majorities of both communities, and that the results were embodied in a series of resolutions adopted at the Lucknow meeting on August 28, 1928. The first resolution followed the line of least resistance and, with one exception, postponed the consideration of the question of communal electorates for a period of ten years. The exception, however, was very important and probably the result of pressure brought to bear by the Hindu Mahasabha. Communal electorates and the reservation of seats were both to be abolished in the Punjab as soon as the new plan of government went into operation. The next most difficult problem was that of Sind and the resolution dealing with it was long and complicated. It provided, in substance, that "simultaneously with the establishment of government in accordance with the Nehru Committee Report," Sind should become a separate province, on condition (a) that it was financially self-supporting or the majority of its inhabitants expressed their readiness to bear the financial burdens, (b) that the form of government was the same as that in other provinces under the Nehru Constitution, and (c) that, in the matter of representation in the central and provincial legislatures, the Hindu minority was treated in the same way that Moslem minorities were treated in Hindu provinces. There was also a resolution providing for the extension of the Nehru form of provincial government to the North-West Frontier Province and Baluchistan.

This scheme was generally regarded by Moslems as less favorable than the unity resolutions, which the majority of the community had already repudiated. It abolished the reservation of seats in the Punjab along with the communal electorates and postponed the separation of Sind from Bombay until some problematical date in the future when the British might accept the Nehru Report. These defects were partially offset by the decision to continue the general system of communal electorates for ten more years. But even that was a concession only to the radicals. The conservatives, as well as the radicals, are convinced that Dominion Home Rule or independence will come within less than ten years and they would like to see the electoral problem settled permanently in their favor and the result embodied in some kind of unamendable Constitution before the British influence is withdrawn.

Among the critics, there were not only conservatives, like Sir Mohammed Shafi and Sir Zulfikar Ali Khan in the Punjab and Sir Abdul Karim Ghaznavi in Bengal, but also radicals, like Mr. Shaukat Ali, the Caliphate leader, and Maulvi Mohammed Yakub, who, as we have seen, was one of Mr. Jinnah's followers and president of his section of the Moslem League. Mr. Jinnah himself refused to join in the chorus of disapproval and made another effort to bring about a really satisfactory compromise. With a few of his followers, he attended a meeting of the All-Parties Conference, held at Calcutta on December 22 (1928), and offered a series of amendments to a resolution approving the Nehru Report. One of them provided for the reservation of seats for Moslems in Bengal and the Punjab, if adult suffrage were established, and another provided that the separation of Sind from Bombay should not be contingent on the establishment of the Nehru Constitution. In the discussion that followed, bitter feelings were aroused and, after a passionate speech by Mr. M. R. Jayakar, deputy leader of the Nationalist party in the Legislative Assembly, the amendments were rejected. Mr. Jinnah and his friends then withdrew and the All-Parties Conference became practically a purely Hindu organization.

As the rift between the two communities widened, Sir Mohammed Shafi and a few other leaders started a movement to reunite the Moslems on a common platform. The Aga Khan was asked to act as mediator and he presided over an All-India Moslem All-Parties Conference which met at Delhi, December 31, 1928–January 1, 1929. The chief work of this conference was the adoption of a long resolution summarizing the constitutional demands of the Moslem community. They wanted a federal system of government with complete provincial autonomy, the powers of the central government to be enumerated and all residuary powers to be vested in the provinces; separate communal electorates with a reservation of seats in all legislatures and other statutory self-governing bodies; the enjoyment of a majority position in the provinces in which they constitute a majority of the population and a representation in the other provinces which shall in no case be "less than that enjoyed by them under the existing law"; 33 per cent of the representation in the Legislative Assembly; a due share of all posts in the central and provincial Ministries; a guarantee that no bill, resolution, or motion regarding intercommunal matters shall be moved, discussed, or passed by any legislature if it is opposed by three fourths of the Hindu or Moslem members; the separation of Sind from Bombay as an autonomous province and the extension of the Reforms to the North-West Frontier Province and Baluchistan, with a representation of Hindu minorities as liberal as that enjoyed by Moslems in the Hindu provinces; an adequate share of appointments in the Public Services; adequate safeguards for the protection and promotion of the religious, charitable, and educational interests of Moslems, and a guarantee that "no change in the Indian constitution shall, after its inauguration, be made by the Central Legislature except with the concurrence of all the States constituting the Indian federation." The resolution closed with an ultimatum to the effect that no constitution, by whomsoever proposed or devised, would be acceptable to Indian Moslems if it did not comply with these principles.[17]

Although the conference was attended by a majority of the Moslem members of the central and provincial legislatures, its personnel was largely conservative and its right to speak for the whole community would ordinarily have been seriously questioned. It put forward its program, however, at exactly the right moment. Mr. Jinnah had just been snubbed by the All-Parties Conference at Calcutta and it was obvious that Hindu policy was being more and more influenced by the Mahasabha. In the Moslem reaction that followed, no plat-

17. For the text of the resolution see *The Simon Report,* II, 84–85.

form could have been too extreme for popular approval. The All-Parties Conference and all of its works were rejected and there was even a tendency to repudiate the National Congress itself because it supported the Nehru Report. This was shown in the budget debate in the National Assembly on March 11, 1929, when the Nehru Report was criticized not only by conservatives, but by men like Mr. Jinnah and Maulvi Mohammed Shafi Daudi who were usually inclined to coöperate with their Hindu colleagues. It was also reflected in a manifesto signed by twenty-three prominent Moslems early in March, suggesting "that as long as present conditions in India continue to exist no Moslem should take part directly or indirectly in any of the processions or meetings which are being organized under the auspices of the Indian National Congress from March 10th onwards, as we firmly believe they are propaganda in support of the Nehru Report, which is not acceptable to Moslems."

Mr. Jinnah did not attend the All-India Moslem All-Parties Conference, but most of the members of his Independent party in the Legislative Assembly were present and he subsequently took part in a series of informal discussions at Delhi and agreed to accept the conference resolution. He also tried to heal the schism in the Moslem League by making an arrangement with Sir Mohammed Shafi that the two wings should hold simultaneous meetings at Delhi and vote to amalgamate. Mr. Jinnah was to preside over his own section and presumably over the whole League after the reunion had been accomplished.

The scheme failed. The majority of both factions were agreed as to general policy, but there was too much jealousy and personal antagonism. Sir Mohammed Shafi fell ill and his adherents refused to carry out their part of the program on the ground that certain conditions upon which they had consented to the reunion had not been fulfilled. The trouble may have been due, in some measure, to the fact that Mr. Jinnah came to the meeting with an elaborate statement of the Moslem platform, which, from the point of view of the Shafi group, was unnecessary because the field had already been adequately covered in the conference resolution. There was also friction in Mr. Jinnah's own camp. The majority were prepared to follow his advice and scrap the Nehru Report, but there was an active minority who believed that the Report should be approved, subject to the adjustment of certain differences with the Hindus. When his section of the League met on March 28 (1929), Mr. Jinnah was in conference with the Ali brothers trying to persuade them and their followers to come into the union movement. Taking advantage of his absence, the Extremists organized the meeting and elected a temporary presiding officer. A motion to approve the Nehru Report was then submitted and, amid loud protests, was declared to be adopted. Mr. Jinnah arrived while the pandemonium was at its height and adjourned the meeting sine die.

The schism was now worse. A new faction was created and the old factions were unable to unite. The Extremists broke away from Mr. Jinnah's leadership and organized the All-India Nationalist Moslem party at Allahabad on July 29, 1929. The declared objects of the new party were to counteract the "reactionary activities of the so-called All-Parties Moslem Conference," to promote a spirit of nationalism among Moslems, to develop a mentality opposed to communalism, and to induce Moslems and Hindus to treat one another in a spirit of broad-minded patriotism. The leaders in the movement were Mr. A. K. Azad, Dr. Ansari, and Dr. Mohammed Alam. The other factions were drawn closer together by this secession, but they were still unable to effect a complete reunion. The chief obstacle apparently was the tendency of the Shafi group to regard the conference resolution as sacrosanct and unalterable, an attitude that offended the pride of Mr. Jinnah and his followers, and also closed the door against any future compromise with the Hindus.

The internal history of the Moslem community since 1929 is somewhat complicated, but the essential facts may be summarized in a few words. The All-India Moslem Conference still represents the extreme Right Wing, the group that insists on the adoption of all the Moslem demands and refuses to make any concessions to the Hindus. The All-India Moslem League, rehabilitated in 1934 through the efforts of the Aga Khan, is more advanced in its political views and somewhat more conciliatory in its attitude toward the Hindus. The outstanding leader is Mr. Jinnah, whose platform, the Fourteen Points, is a slightly modified version of the Delhi resolutions of 1929. The Caliphate Conference was weakened and almost destroyed by the abolition of the Caliphate, but it has been revitalized by the Moslem-Jewish conflict in Palestine. The bond between the Arabs and the Moslems of India was especially strengthened by the burial of Mohammed Ali in the Mosque of Omar in Jerusalem (1931). Shaukat Ali was at one time the most influential member of the conference group.

These three organizations—the Conference, the League, and the Caliphate Conference—represent the bulk of the Moslem community. Their policies are very much alike, but the efforts of the Aga Khan, Shaukat Ali, and other leaders to bring about an amalgamation have so far been unsuccessful. There is also a small group of Moslem Nationalists who have no definite organization of their own because they prefer to work through the Indian National Congress. It is this group, flattered and cajoled by Mr. Gandhi, which pretends to represent Moslem public opinion. Its leaders have already been mentioned, Dr. Ansari, Mr. A. K. Azad, and Dr. Mohammed Alam.

The majority of the Hindus are Nationalists, but they also have an intransigent element. At the annual meeting of the Mahasabha, held at Jubbulpore in April, 1928, Dr. Moonje criticized the Congress unity resolutions dealing with Sind, the Frontier Province, and Baluchistan and argued that communal provinces were as great an evil as communal electorates. He was somewhat appeased by the Sind-Punjab resolutions of the All-Parties Conference of August 28, but was again exasperated by the refusal of the Moslems to accept the Nehru Report. At the Surat meeting of the Mahasabha on March 30, 1929, he offered a resolution stating that, in view of the Moslem rejection of the Report, the Mahasabha would return to its original policy of opposing the special treatment of any community in any circumstances whatever. This was amplified by a second resolution which demanded that there should be a uniform franchise, mixed electorates, no reservation of communal seats, and no communal representation in the Public Services. There was also a resolution opposing the separation of Sind from Bombay. Dr. Moonje was inclined to blame Mr. Jinnah for the failure of the compromise program and he even went so far as to say that he would withdraw his resolutions if Mr. Jinnah would approve the Nehru Report. Needless to say, this was not done and the resolutions were approved by acclamation.

There is a curious paradox in the relations between the two communities in the last few years. Political rivalry, which is supposed to be the chief source of friction, has grown more acute, but mob violence has gradually declined. Since the Pathan troubles in Bombay in February, 1929, there have been very few communal conflicts and most of them have been on a minor scale. The riot at Cawnpore, however, in March, 1931, was one of the worst in the history of India. There had been bad feeling between the Hindus and the Moslems at Cawnpore for many years, but the immediate cause of the riot was a hartal which followed the execution of Bhagat Singh at Lahore. The story of Bhagat Singh is told elsewhere. He was a young Punjabi enthusiast who gained notoriety in April, 1929, when he and an accomplice threw some bombs from the gallery into the chamber of the Legislative Assembly at Delhi. It was discovered later that he had also been involved in a revolutionary conspiracy and was implicated in the murder of two police officers at Lahore in December, 1928. He was the central figure in the famous Lahore Conspiracy Case and a popular hero, especially among those who believed that the police officers deserved to be killed in retaliation for the death of Lajpat Rai.[18]

After a prolonged trial, he and two of his accomplices were convicted on the murder charge and were executed on the evening of March 23, 1931. The news of the execution spread rapidly and a so-called universal hartal was observed on the following day. The Moslems were not very much interested,

18. According to the official records, Lajpat Rai died of heart disease, November 17, 1928, but there was a general belief among the Indians that his death was due to injuries received at the hands of the police while he was leading a demonstration against the Simon Commission at Lahore, on October 30.

however, and as a general rule they did not participate. This was particularly the case in Cawnpore, where there had been a series of hartals, processions, and other political activities going on for several months. But Bhagat Singh was the special hero of the younger element among the Hindus and they were determined that the hartal should be strictly enforced. No conveyances were allowed in the streets and it was alleged that Moslem women were compelled to leave their tongas and walk. Moslem shops were forcibly closed or their windows were broken and they were otherwise badly damaged. The Moslems fought back and for three days there was a riot of murder, arson, and looting. After that the excitement gradually subsided and order was finally restored. The loss of life and property was heavy. There were four or five hundred people killed and more than a thousand injured. A number of temples and mosques were desecrated or destroyed and a great many houses were pillaged and burned.[19]

This was a terrible episode, but fortunately it was not symptomatic and the record since 1929 has otherwise been fairly satisfactory.[20] The chief reason for the improvement has probably been the concentration of attention on constitutional issues. An effort on the part of the British to revise the Indian Constitution was bound to emphasize the differences between them and the Indians and to minimize the internal differences among the Indians themselves. In this case, the tendency was strengthened by the selection of a purely British investigating commission, which offended the race pride of Moslems as well as Hindus and of conservatives as well as radicals. Popular energy was naturally turned into anti-British channels and there was a cessation of communal warfare just as there had been under similar conditions in the period from 1919 to 1923. There is also another reason. The autocratic powers used to suppress political disorders since 1930 are equally efficacious in dealing with communal disor-

19. For a more detailed account see *East India (Cawnpore Riots). Report of the Commission of Inquiry and Resolution of the Government of the United Provinces*, Cd. 3891 (London, 1931).

20. The troubles in Kashmir and Jammu have already been discussed.

ders. The Indians themselves were inclined to blame the authorities for not using those powers more firmly at Cawnpore.

The Simon Report in 1930 dealt with the communal problem in considerable detail, but most of its conclusions have already been discussed. The recommendations with regard to Sind, the North-West Frontier Province, and Baluchistan were adverse to the Moslem claims. The system of communal electorates was accepted as a necessary evil, to be maintained in each province until a substantial majority of the Moslem representatives in the provincial legislature should ask to have it abolished. Members of the central legislature were to be elected by the provincial legislatures under a form of proportional representation which would give the Moslems an opportunity to choose their own representatives. There was no definite recommendation dealing with the allocation of seats in the provincial legislatures. As both communities are dissatisfied with the present arrangement, the commission urged them to get together and make a new agreement and warned them that, if they failed to do so, the question would have to be settled for them by the British authorities.[21] The only concrete suggestion was that the Moslems should be allowed to retain their present weightage in the minority provinces if they would abandon the separate electorates in Bengal and the Punjab or give up their claims to representation in those provinces on the basis of population.

Two methods have been proposed to abolish separate communal electorates in the provinces without giving up the principle of communal representation. The plan generally advocated by the Hindus provides for a reservation of seats in a joint electorate, which means that a seat would ordinarily be reserved for the minority community in a multiple-member constituency. The authors of the Report agree with the Moslems that in such an election the successful candidate would usually be one who was "more concerned to keep the favour

21. After an unsuccessful effort was made to reach a settlement at the Round Table Conference, His Majesty's government devised a provisional scheme for the provincial legislatures in August, 1932. See also *East India (Constitutional Reforms), Communal Decision*, Cd. 4147.

of the non-Moslem majority of voters than to represent Mohammedan interests." The other plan is based on the idea of a communal primary. Moslems and other minorities, voting by themselves, would select a panel of candidates, from amongst whom the seat or seats reserved for the community would be filled by the vote of a joint electorate. The plan was discussed in some detail in the Report and also in an appendix, where its advantages and disadvantages were summarized. The commission did not recommend its adoption, but it suggested that "it should be further considered by both communities chiefly concerned to see if it provides a basis of agreement."[22] The plan was accepted in the Poona Pact of 1932 as the method of electing the representatives of the Depressed Classes.

It is difficult to find out what the people of India thought about these recommendations, because the boycott and the civil disobedience movement prevented the Report from being judged according to its merits. The Hindus, having decided to condemn and ridicule the whole document before it was even published, could not consistently discuss any of its details. If they had been free to express an opinion and had not been afraid of alienating the small group of Moslems who were still working with them, they would probably have criticized the proposal to continue the system of communal representation and communal electorates. As a rule, the Moslem leaders were less obdurate. They accepted the Report as a document that should be read and carefully considered, although they disagreed with many of its most important conclusions. The Executive Board of the All-India Moslem Conference, at a meeting held at Simla, July 6, 1930, approved the proposal that the Constitution should be on a federal basis and that the sys-

22. *Idem,* II, 61, 86–87. The general system of reserved seats in joint electorates has already been discussed in connection with the non-Brahmans in Madras and the Marathas in Bombay. To avoid confusion, it should always be remembered that their cases are not analogous to that of the Moslems because they are both majority communities while the Moslems are nearly everywhere in the minority. *The Simon Report* recommended that the reservations should be abolished in the case of the non-Brahmans of Madras, but that it should be continued for the present in the case of the Marathas.

tem of separate electorates should be maintained, but declared that it was "emphatically of the opinion that the minimum demands of Mussalmans of India have not been met by the Commission." Coming down to details, it criticized the scheme of proportional representation and insisted that Moslems should have a minimum of one third of the seats in each house of the central legislature. They should also be guaranteed a majority in the legislatures of Bengal and the Punjab and given an adequate representation in the Public Services. Sind should be separate from Bombay, the Reforms should be extended to the North-West Frontier Province, and Baluchistan should be granted full provincial autonomy. The general Moslem point of view was well expressed in the following resolution which was unanimously adopted by the Moslem Conference of the United Provinces, held at Lucknow on July 10, 1930:

> This conference while appreciating the principle of a federal system of government and the retention of separate electorates for the Moslem minority, records its dissatisfaction at, and disappointment with, the Simon Commission Report, as it fails to concede most of the demands formulated by Moslems of all shades of opinion assembled at Delhi on January 1, 1929, under the presidency of his Highness the Aga Khan, and as, instead of advancing the present constitution toward self-government, it sets it back in certain respects.

Some of the Moslem leaders believe that it does not pay to be friendly with the British because it has been proved by experience, in India as well as in Ireland, that obstruction is more profitable than coöperation. *The Report of the Simon Commission* apparently justified this belief. The majority of the Moslems supported the commission after they had recovered from their initial disappointment over its purely British personnel, while most of the Hindus adhered to the original policy of the boycott. What was the result? The issue of communal electorates was decided in their favor, but they were told somewhat ungraciously that it was only because they insisted on the fulfilment of a pledge and that they were really obstructing the progress of responsible government. All other issues were either ignored or decided against them. It is true that the commission approved a federal system of government, but the recommendation on that subject was based on a variety of considerations and cannot be considered as a special consideration to any community. The balance was redressed to some extent by His Majesty's government. It rejected the recommendations of the commission in regard to Sind and the North-West Frontier Province, and it also adopted a more favorable policy toward the Moslems on the subject of representation in the provincial legislatures. The recent history of the problem, including the Communal Award of 1932, is closely associated with the framing of the new Constitution, and has already been considered in that connection.

CHAPTER XII

THE REPORT OF THE STATUTORY COMMISSION

THE Montagu-Chelmsford Reforms were adopted by Parliament on the condition that they should remain in force for ten years without any substantial change. At the end of that period a commission was to be appointed to inquire into the working of the system and report whether and to what extent it was desirable to establish the principle of responsible government or to extend, modify, or restrict the degree of responsible government already in existence.[1] No political party of any standing in India was ever willing to accept this limitation and resolutions asking for an immediate revision of the Constitution were frequently passed by the Legislative Assembly. A resolution was moved in 1924 requesting the establishment of Dominion Home Rule with full responsible government in the provinces. Pandit Motilal Nehru offered an amendment providing that a Round Table Conference should be summoned to prepare the draft of a new Constitution.

The amendment was passed with a large majority, but it was more than six years before the conference was held and then it was boycotted by the very people who had been its original advocates. The new Labor government in Great Britain had already decided, however, on a gesture of conciliation. Lord Reading was authorized to appoint a committee to inquire into the working of the Government of India Act of 1919 and "to investigate the feasibility and the desirability of securing remedies consistent with the structure, policy and purposes of the Act." This body was known as the Reforms Inquiry Committee or the Muddiman Committee, from the name of its chairman, Sir Alexander Muddiman, the head of

1. Section 84A, Government of India Act, 1919.

the Home Department of the government of India. There were three British and six Indian members, but Mr. Nehru, who was asked to serve as one of the nonofficial Indian representatives, refused to do so because he felt that the scope of the inquiry was too limited. The British members and two of the Indians followed closely the terms of reference. Among the difficulties that had arisen in the working of the Reforms, they emphasized the financial handicap imposed upon the provincial governments by the Meston Settlement, the communal friction between Hindus and Moslems, the illiteracy of the electorate, and the lack of linguistic unity in some of the provinces. A few remedies were proposed, but, owing to the restrictions under which the committee was compelled to work, they were not very helpful. The Minority Report, signed by four of the Indian members, was mainly a criticism of the terms of reference and an effort to prove that the Reforms should be scrapped and not repaired.

Some of the committee's recommendations were adopted by the government, but so far as any beneficial effects on Indian public opinion were concerned its work was a failure. If it had any effect at all, it merely strengthened the demand for a new Constitution for India as a self-governing Dominion. A nonofficial effort to meet this demand had in fact just been made by Mrs. Besant and a few of her Indian friends. Most of the leaders were rather cool toward her project, but it was somewhat revised by a so-called All-Parties Conference which met at Delhi in January–February, 1925, and was formally approved by a convention held at Cawnpore in April. It was drafted as a statute and introduced in the House of Commons by Mr. George Lansbury, December 9, 1925, under the title, "The Commonwealth of India Bill." The bill proposed to confer upon India at once the full status of a Dominion, subject to certain temporary reservations. The Viceroy, as the representative of the King-Emperor, was to have complete charge of military and naval forces and foreign relations until the Indian Parliament by its own act should signify its readiness to assume control. Any step taken by the Indian Parliament concerning the Indian States must have the previous approval of the Viceroy. There was a Bill of Rights which included, among other things, guarantees of personal liberty, freedom of conscience, freedom of speech, and equality of sex.

This scheme did not arouse any popular enthusiasm, partly perhaps because it was not really an Indian product, but mainly because of the negative character of the Nationalist movement. The leaders were more interested in opposing the existing system than they were in preparing a constructive alternative. There were two things which finally aroused them from their lethargy. Lord Birkenhead, the Secretary of State for India, made a speech in the House of Lords in which he challenged the Indians to draft a Constitution of their own and implied that they could not produce one that would meet with popular approval. The second factor was the appointment, in November, 1927, of an All-British Statutory Commission which aroused a strong spirit of race consciousness and convinced at least some of the leaders that Lord Birkenhead's challenge would have to be accepted. When the Congress met in Madras at the end of the year, it voted to boycott the commission, proclaimed independence as the goal of the Indian people and resolved that a draft Constitution should be prepared and placed before a special convention to be held in the early spring. The preliminary work on the Constitution was begun at Delhi in February, 1928, by a body called the All-Parties Conference, which was composed mainly of members of the central legislature. At the close of the legislative session, the conference adjourned to meet in Bombay about the end of May to consider the reports of the various subcommittees that had been appointed. The Bombay meeting was short, but a committee was chosen to complete the work and Pandit Motilal Nehru was named as chairman. Its Report was soon finished and was approved at another meeting of the All-Parties Conference held at Lucknow in August.

The document that finally emerged was mainly the work of Mr. Nehru and it was commonly called the Nehru Report. For some reason, the Congress resolution in favor of independence was disregarded and the Report was based on the theory that India was to remain in the Empire as a self-governing Dominion. It contained a Bill of Rights, a description of the machinery of government, a proposal for the creation of a

Supreme Court, a suggestion that the provinces should be redistributed on a linguistic basis, a discussion of the relations between the Dominion and the Indian States, and various other provisions that need not be considered here.

The controversy over this Report tended to justify Lord Birkenhead's cynical attitude. There were two main elements in the opposition, the advocates of independence and the majority of the Moslem community. At the Lucknow Conference, Mr. Nehru tried to placate the former group by accepting a proviso that the approval of Dominion status should not be held to restrict "the liberty of action of those political parties whose goal is complete independence." This was not entirely satisfactory to Mr. Srinivasa Iyengar, Mr. Subhas Bose, and other leaders of the independence movement and the fight was carried into the National Congress at the annual meeting at Calcutta in December, 1928. The question was considered first in the Working Committee, where Mr. Gandhi acted as peacemaker. After a long controversy, the committee finally recommended that the Report should be approved on the condition that if the British Parliament failed to grant Dominion status by the end of 1930, a Declaration of Independence would be adopted. This was opposed by Mr. Iyengar on the floor of Congress and it was finally voted that the date for the expiration of the ultimatum should be moved forward to the end of 1929. The radical element was still disappointed and an amendment in favor of immediate independence was offered by Mr. Bose, but, through Mr. Gandhi's influence, it was rejected by a vote of 1,350 to 973.

With the exception of a small group led by Dr. Ansari and Mr. Azad, the Moslems were solidly opposed to the electoral provisions and to the efforts which they felt were being made to postpone the separation of Sind from Bombay. It was fortunate from the Nationalist point of view that Parliament ignored the Congress ultimatum because it gave a logical excuse to scrap the Report and revert to the old policy of uniting the Hindus and the Moslems on a negative platform. The communal issue remained unsettled, however, and it is still a serious obstacle to constitutional reform.

The first official step in making the new Constitution was

taken when His Majesty's government decided that it would not wait until 1929 to appoint the commission provided for in the Government of India Act, 1919. The act was amended to make this possible and the appointment of an Indian Statutory Commission, commonly known as the Simon Commission, was announced in the House of Commons on November 8, 1927. The commission was composed of Sir John Simon (chairman), Lord Burnham, Lord Strathcona and Mount Royal, Mr. Edward Cadogan, Mr. Vernon Hartshorn, Col. G. R. Lane Fox, and Major C. R. Attlee. They were all British and all members of Parliament. Three were Conservatives, two were Liberals, and two belonged to the Labor party. It was a tragic blunder and contrary to precedent for many years to select a body of this kind without a single Indian representative. The arguments advanced to justify the discrimination are not convincing and they do not have the ring of sincerity. It was said, for example, that it was a Statutory or Legislative Advisory Commission and as such was naturally chosen from members of Parliament. There were two Indians in Parliament at that time, Lord Sinha, who was disqualified by ill health, and Mr. Saklatvala, who, as a Communist, would have found it difficult to coöperate with a "capitalist" commission. The fallacy of the argument lies in the assumption that the choice had to be restricted to members of Parliament. If that was the correct interpretation of Section 84A of the Act of 1919, the Section could easily have been amended when the date for the appointment of the commission was moved forward. Another argument which was somewhat more plausible was that efficiency required a small body made up of members who had the same fundamental conception of the duties imposed upon them by the Act of 1919. A mixed commission representing all the diverse interests in India would have been large and unwieldy and there would have been no reasonable chance of arriving at an agreement. This may have been good technique but it was certainly bad politics. If Lord Birkenhead and his associates did not deliberately intend to insult and humiliate the people of India they were woefully ignorant of racial psychology.

As a result of this blunder, the commission was compelled

to work under a heavy handicap. Its labors were never fully appreciated and it too was finally insulted and humiliated in order to placate the Indian Liberals and persuade them to take part in the Round Table Conference. Several attempts were made to mitigate the effects of the original blunder, but they were not very successful. When Mr. Baldwin announced the decision that the commission was to be appointed he stated that His Majesty's government felt that it would be wise "to invite the Central Legislature to appoint a Joint Select Committee chosen from its elected and nominated unofficial members which would draw up its views and proposals in writing and lay them before the Commission for examination in such manner as the latter may decide." The committee might then remain in existence to be consulted by the commission at later stages of the inquiry. It was further suggested that a similar procedure should be adopted with the provincial legislatures. Mr. Baldwin also said that it was not the intention of the government to ask Parliament to adopt the proposals of the commission until a full opportunity had been given for Indians of all schools of opinion to lay their views before a Joint Select Committee of Parliament.[2]

The reactions of the Congress and the Moslem League to the appointment of the commission will be discussed more fully in a later chapter. The Congress passed a resolution advising the people of India to boycott the commission and all its works, declared itself in favor of independence, and initiated the movement that led to the preparation of the Nehru Report. The League was split. The boycott was supported by Mr. Jinnah's faction, but it was rejected by the more conservative group who followed the leadership of Sir Mohammed Shafi.[3] The latter was not enthusiastic over the personnel of the commission, but distrusted the Hindus and was convinced that the Moslems, as a minority community, had more to gain by cooperating with the British. The only other important All-India organization, the National Liberal Federation, met at

2. The institution of the Round Table Conference will be noted later. The Indians were really given three separate opportunities to express their views after *The Simon Report* was published.

3. See chap. xi, "Hindu-Moslem Relations."

Bombay on December 27 and endorsed the boycott policy. A conference of all the opposition groups was then assembled at Benares, January 16, 1928, and resolutions were passed to observe a general hartal and hold meetings of protest on the day when the commission was due to arrive in Bombay.

Sir John Simon made heroic efforts to overcome this opposition. On February 6, three days after his arrival in India, he wrote an open letter to the Viceroy proposing a method of procedure by "Joint Free Conference." The two houses of the central legislature would be invited to choose from their non-official members a Joint Committee, "which might conveniently be seven in number," and each local Legislative Council would be asked to constitute a similar body. "The Indian side of the Conference would consist, when Central subjects were being dealt with, of those first named; in a Province, the Indian wing would primarily consist of the Provincial members," but it was hoped that some or all of the Central Committee would also find it possible to attend the provincial sittings. The two sides would collaborate "on equal and honourable terms," but the commission reserved the right to hold separate sittings for the examination of witnesses and documents if it seemed necessary to avoid intimidation. The commission would also have the sole responsibility for the Report that would be presented to Parliament, although the Indian Joint Committee might submit a Report of its own to the central legislature which could be "forwarded to and made available for the British Parliament."

The commission paid two visits to India, the first lasting from February 3 to March 31, 1928, and the second from October 11, 1928, to April 13, 1929. The object of the first visit was to make a preliminary survey. Numerous deputations were received, but no final evidence was taken and the time "was mainly devoted to attempting to master the elements of the situation and to visiting more of the country districts [particularly in the Madras presidency and the Punjab] than was possible on the second visit." This object was emphasized by Sir John Simon in the letter mentioned above and he made it clear that the Joint Free Conference would not begin its work until October. In other words, the various legislative bodies in India had about eight months to decide whether they would take part in the conference. The first test came in the Legislative Assembly on February 18, when a motion by Lala Lajpat Rai refusing to coöperate with the commission at any stage or in any form was carried by a vote of 68 to 62. The Council of State, however, voted in favor of coöperation and elected three of its members to participate in the conference. When it became evident that the Assembly would remain obdurate, the Viceroy appointed a Central Committee made up of five members of the Assembly and four members of the Council of State, including the three who had already been elected and a fourth to represent the Sikhs. The chairman was Sir Sankaran Nair.

The first Provincial Committee was elected in the Punjab, but it agreed to serve only on condition that its members were allowed to attend all meetings when evidence was taken relating to their province. This involved the commission in a serious dilemma. If the concession were granted, it would have to be extended to the other Provincial Committees and also to the Central Committee, although it was well known that in some cases witnesses would not testify freely before a conference that contained Brahman members. On the other hand, if the concession were refused, it was not likely that very many of the provinces would coöperate. The commission finally chose what it regarded as the lesser evil and the condition was accepted. This weakened the boycott and by December, 1928, all of the local legislatures, except that of the United Provinces, agreed to collaborate. The opposition was still formidable, however, and the vote of the official bloc was usually required to secure a majority. In the North-West Frontier Province, where there was no legislature at that time, four of the leading residents were invited to sit with the conference.

During its second visit to India the commission traveled about 14,000 miles and evidence was taken in Delhi and all of the major provinces. The Indian Central Committee then went to England and the joint sittings were continued in London from June 19 to July 30, 1929. After that the two groups separated and each prepared its own Report. The Central Committee presented its Report to the Viceroy on October 18, with a request that it should be made available for Parliament, and it was published in London on December 24. The Provincial Committees published the results of their labors at various times and they were subsequently collected and reprinted in Volume III of the *Report of the Statutory Commission.* The latter body worked more slowly and more thoroughly and its Report was not published until June, 1930.

The Central Committee was unable to reach any substantial measure of agreement. Its Report covers only 82 pages, but one of the members presented a separate Report of 40 pages and there are 242 pages devoted to minutes of dissent and explanatory memoranda. It was generally agreed, however: (a) that Parliament should make an explicit declaration that full Dominion status was the goal to be attained in India, (b) that a liberal and substantial step should be taken in that direction at once by establishing provincial autonomy and a system of dyarchy in the central government, and (c) that provision should be made for the attainment of the ultimate goal without further inquiry by a Statutory Commission or any other agency. The communal issue was, as usual, the chief obstacle to harmony. The majority argued that communal electorates were vicious in principle and should be retained only in exceptional cases,[4] but they were willing that a certain number of seats should be reserved for Moslems in the provinces where they constituted a minority of the population. The two Moslem members of the committee vigorously dissented from this conclusion and they also objected to any weakening of the central government until the position of the Moslem community was definitely assured.

As the commission proceeded with its work it became convinced that the scope of the inquiry should be enlarged and the procedure outlined by the Prime Minister in 1927 should be revised. To quote its own words, it was "increasingly impressed by the impossibility of considering the constitutional problems of British India without taking into account the relations between British India and the Indian States." A body called

4. Among the exceptional cases mentioned there were (a) Anglo-Indians and the Depressed Classes in Madras, (b) Karens and Indians in Burma, and (c) Europeans in all of the provinces.

the Butler Committee or the India States Committee had been appointed in December, 1927, to consider these relations, but the terms of reference did not cover the whole ground and the commission wished to make a more thorough investigation. If this were done, the general scheme of procedure would have to be revised.

It seems to us that what would be required would be the setting up of some sort of conference after the Reports of the Statutory Commission and the Indian Central Committee have been made, considered and published and their work completed, and that in this conference His Majesty's Government would meet both representatives of British India and representatives of the States . . . for the purpose of seeking the greatest possible measure of agreement for the final proposals which it would later be the duty of His Majesty's Government to submit to Parliament.

This was the origin of the Round Table Conference. After consulting with the leaders of the Conservative and Liberal parties, Mr. MacDonald informed Sir John Simon on October 25, 1929, that His Majesty's government had approved the commission's recommendations.

They were also approved by Lord Irwin, who had spent the summer at home and had held frequent conferences with the Prime Minister on Indian affairs. He believed, however, that the government should go further and clear the atmosphere for the conference by making an official announcement that Dominion status was the goal of British policy in India. Mr. MacDonald concurred in this suggestion and tried to secure the approval of Mr. Baldwin, who was spending his vacation in France. Mr. Baldwin replied that he was unable to consult his colleagues in the Conservative party, but, speaking for himself only, he would approve the action to be taken, provided it had the support of His Majesty's government, the government of India, and the Simon Commission. When he discovered on October 23 that the Simon Commission had not given its approval, he consulted the party leaders and informed the Acting Prime Minister[5] that he and his party

5. Mr. MacDonald was at that time absent on a visit to the United States.

would not support the announcement. The Liberal leaders were also cold to the idea, but Lord Irwin stood his ground, and with the backing of the government, published his famous announcement in a *Gazette of India Extraordinary* on October 31, 1929. The essence of the document is contained in the following sentence:

> But in view of the doubts which have been expressed both in Great Britain and India regarding the interpretation to be placed on the intentions of the British Government in enacting the Statute of 1919, I am authorized on behalf of His Majesty's Government to state clearly that in their judgment it is implicit in the Declaration of 1917 that the natural issue of India's constitutional progress, as there contemplated, is the attainment of Dominion Status.

This announcement was severely criticized in England by both Liberals and Conservatives. It was dubious and likely to mislead the people of India, it tended to undermine the influence of the Statutory Commission, and it might even be regarded as an attempt to force the hand of Parliament and commit it in advance to a new line of policy. The Labor leaders, on the other hand, attempted to show that Lord Irwin had merely restated the traditional British policy since 1917 in order to reassure the people of India against the reactionary group that was prepared to repudiate the Montagu pledge. In the *Times* for November 5, 1929, ten quotations were cited, covering the period from 1917 to 1927, in which the word Dominion was used in connection with the goal of British policy in India. Several of these were taken from the speeches of Liberal and Conservative leaders. Lord Birkenhead, for example, spoke on March 18, 1927, of the "precious promise of a Constitution which might . . . bring India . . . on equal terms as an honoured partner into the free community of British Dominions." A few weeks later, Mr. Baldwin said that "in the fulness of time we look forward to seeing her [India] in equal partnership with the *Dominions*." This was the substance of Lord Irwin's announcement. There was no time limit. His Majesty's government would honor its pledge and "in the fulness of time" Dominion status would be attained.

The radicals in India were well aware of this fact. The President of the Tamil Congress party in Madras condemned the announcement "as not in compliance with the Calcutta Congress resolutions, as it contains no promise of immediate Dominion status." The President of the Andhra Conference also wished to know why the Indians should be elated over the prospect of a Round Table Conference. "No time limit is fixed for Dominion status." There was, however, a small group who indulged in what the *Times* correspondent called "a cheerful excursion in the art of bluff." In a meeting held at Mr. Patel's house in Delhi a letter to the Viceroy was drafted in which the following statement occurred: "We understand, however, that the [Round Table] Conference is to meet, not to discuss when Dominion status shall be established, but to frame a scheme of Dominion Constitution for India."[6] Lord Irwin patiently corrected this mistake, but it was revived from time to time, and was used with good effect by the die-hards in England to strengthen their position. It would be hard to imagine a better example of a combination between the extreme Right and the extreme Left to prevent the Center from carrying out a program of reform.

Lord Irwin was discouraged but he continued his efforts to prepare the way for the Round Table Conference. On December 23, 1929, while he was on his way to New Delhi to confer with Mr. Gandhi, Pandit Motilal Nehru, and other Indian leaders, his train was bombed and he narrowly escaped assassination. He attended the meeting, however, and Mr. Gandhi presented an ultimatum on behalf of the Congress party. It would take part in the conference only on condition that His Majesty's government would give assurance that its purpose was to draft a Dominion Constitution. The Viceroy could only reply that it would be impossible for His Majesty's government to prejudge the action of the conference or restrict the liberty of Parliament. This happened just before the annual meeting of the Congress and it strengthened the Bose-Iyengar faction that was working for an immediate declaration of independence. Its position, however, was already impregnable because the year of grace prescribed at the previous meeting

6. The London *Times,* November 4, 1929.

at Calcutta was about to expire and the British government was still obdurate. A resolution was passed in favor of independence and against participation in the Round Table Conference. It is difficult to say whether Mr. Gandhi supported this movement voluntarily or was forced into it to retain his leadership. There can be no doubt that he did retain the leadership because he carried through a resolution to boycott the legislative bodies, which was very unpopular with the conservatives, and a resolution condemning the attempt to murder the Viceroy,[7] which was equally unpopular with the radicals. A resolution was also passed authorizing him, at his discretion, to inaugurate a campaign of nonviolent civil disobedience.

This was a severe blow to the Viceroy and a source of encouragement to his critics in England. The civil disobedience campaign was begun on April 6, 1930, Mr. Gandhi was arrested and imprisoned a few weeks later, and the government was forced to issue a series of ordinances to deal with the widespread reign of violence. There is no reason to suppose, however, that Lord Irwin's policy was wrong or that it failed to accomplish useful results. It would probably be safe to say that it conciliated a large majority of the Indian Moderates, limited the scope of the civil disobedience movement, and kept open the door for advance along constitutional lines. If he had been supported by Sir John Simon, *The Report of the Statutory Commission* would have been more favorably received in India and the Congress party would probably have participated in the first session of the Round Table Conference.

The Report of the commission was published in two volumes in June, 1930.[8] Volume I, entitled *Survey*, deals with the first part of the commission's task, which was to "enquire into the working of the system of government, the growth of education, and the development of representative institutions in British India, and matters connected therewith." Volume II,

7. This resolution was carried by a vote of 897 to 816.

8. There were fifteen auxiliary volumes published later, containing the Reports of the Provincial Committees that participated in the Joint Free Conference, memoranda furnished by the government of India and the provincial governments, and material laid before the commission by nonofficial individuals and representative associations.

entitled *Recommendations*, looks to the future and presents the conclusions and recommendations. The first volume is divided into seven parts, dealing with the "Conditions of the Problem," "The Existing Constitutional Structure," "The Working of the Reformed Constitution," "The Administrative and Judicial Systems," "The System of Public Finance," "The Growth of Education in British India," and "Public Opinion in India." At the request of the commission, this volume was published a fortnight before Volume II. To quote its own words: "The problems connected with the future constitutional development of India are of such complexity and importance that we are unwilling to see our proposals for their treatment thrown into the arena of discussion and controversy before there has been time to examine and digest the survey of the present positions on which our recommendations are based, and in the light of which we believe them to be justified." It is impossible here to go into the details of this volume, but it is a mine of valuable information which will be useful to the student of Indian affairs long after the second volume has been forgotten. The following summary taken from the Report itself will give a good idea of the general point of view:

First of all, we have endeavoured to bring before those whose duty it is to provide for India's constitutional future a realisation of the facts of the situation, those stubborn facts which no amount of rhetoric or appeal to abstract principles can alter. The immense area and population of India, the diversities of race, creed and caste, the existence of the Indian States, the predominance in numbers of the rural population, the high percentage of illiteracy, and the standing menace of the North-West Frontier, are all facts which no person, British or Indian, who has to deal with the constitutional problem of India can possibly ignore.

These facts must be faced. Their existence cannot in any way be allowed to invalidate the solemn pledge of the British people with regard to the progressive realisation of responsible government in British India. They may be compared to the physical features of a site for a city, which do not prevent the city from being built, though they condition its plan and the length of time which must elapse before its completion.[9]

9. I, 8–9; II, 3.

The second volume begins with a discussion of the evils of a temporary constitution and a recommendation that the new organic law should, as far as possible, be so framed that it will not have to be revised at stipulated intervals, but will provide opportunities for natural development. It then goes on to consider the possibility of establishing an All-India federation which will include the states as well as the provinces. The states would not be compelled to enter the federation, but it was hoped that their rulers would "recognize more and more the need for adjusting their future relationship to the rest of India" and would "be ready to come into the larger whole" when they could see that their rights and position were safeguarded. The commission believed that it would take some time to reach this goal, but it proposed that steps should be taken immediately to set up "a standing consultative body containing representatives both from British India and the Indian States" to discuss and record deliberative results on "matters of common concern."

Although the federation was to expand until it included the whole of India, the area of India itself was to be reduced by the loss of Burma. It is well known that Burma is cut off from India proper by sea, mountain, and jungle. "The people . . . are entirely different from the peoples of India. They come from a different stock and have a different history. Their religion, languages, social system, manners and customs, and national dress are different, and they have a divergent outlook on life."[10] They are two thousand miles from Delhi, their representation in the central legislature is small and they are convinced that their welfare is neglected by the central authorities. On the other hand, they have been united with the people of India for many years and there are a number of financial, economic, and military questions in which they have a common interest. The commission came to the conclusion that Burmese sentiment was strongly in favor of separation and agreed that that was sufficient to override all other considerations. It is assumed, therefore, throughout the Report that it deals only with India and that Burma will be handled as a separate problem.

10. I, 77–78.

There were a few other geographical recommendations dealing with the redistribution of provinces and the possible extension of the area subject to the Reforms. The commission suggested that the government of India should set up a Boundaries Commission "which would investigate the main cases in which provincial readjustment seems called for and should endeavour to work out schemes with a view to seeing how far agreement is possible." The two outstanding cases were those of Sind and Orissa. The commission was inclined to oppose the separation of Sind from Bombay, but a subcommittee reported in favor of the amalgamation of the Oriya tracts to form a new province. For reasons that will be given later, the commission also opposed the extension of the Reforms to the North-West Frontier Province and British Baluchistan. His Majesty's government subsequently decided that Sind and Orissa should be organized as separate provinces and that the Reforms should be extended to the North-West Frontier Province. The federation, therefore, will include eleven Governor's provinces—Madras, Bombay, Bengal, the United Provinces, the Punjab, Bihar, the Central Provinces and Berar, Assam, the North-West Frontier Province, Sind, and Orissa. Partly outside of this area and directly subject to the control of the central government, will be six minor provinces—Delhi, Ajmer-Merwara, British Baluchistan, Coorg, the Andaman and Nicobar Islands, and Panth Piploda. The Backward Tracts, now called Excluded Areas, constitute still another problem. These tracts are scattered over five provinces (excluding Burma) and their total area is about 120,000 square miles. Under the present Constitution they are administered in one way or another by the provincial governments, but the commission proposed that the control should in general be handed over to the central authorities, who would use the Governors as their agents. In performing these services, the Governors would not be required to consult their Ministers or be held responsible to the local legislatures.[11]

The central feature of the Report is the criticism of dyarchy

11. Under Section 92 of the Government of India Act of 1935 the Governor will administer these areas, but their Regulations will require the previous sanction of the Governor-General.

and the defense of the principle of unitary cabinet responsibility. In attempting to follow this principle to its logical conclusion the commission became involved in a serious dilemma. It acted on the assumption that if dyarchy is bad for the provincial administration it must also be bad for the central administration and proposed that unity should be secured by transferring all subjects in one case and none at all in the other. The provincial executive would be responsible to the provincial legislature while the central executive would continue to be responsible to the Secretary of State and the British Parliament. The premise was accepted in India but the conclusion, so far as it affected the central government, was rejected by unanimous agreement. It was difficult for Indians to appreciate the type of logic that would exclude them from a responsible share in the central administration merely because they were not yet prepared to assume full control over the army and one or two other departments.

The conservative elements in England were also dissatisfied. The recommendation in regard to the government of India met their approval, of course, but they could see no reason why all of the provincial administrative departments should be turned over to the Indians merely to satisfy the commission's predilection for unity. They were especially worried about the transfer of Law and Order or the control of the Police and the Administration of Justice. They felt that, if India was to progress along peaceful lines, she must have an impartial police force which knows that it will be supported in the discharge of its duties and will not be sacrificed to popular clamor or political intrigue. "An Indian Minister, highly susceptible as he is bound to be to criticism and exposed to political pressure, especially from his own community and his own friends, may not be able to supply the conditions upon which impartial police action depends." His attitude would necessarily affect the individual members of the force. "If, for example, a policeman believes that his actions in suppressing a riot would be differently judged according to the community to which the Minister belongs, impartiality in police action is destroyed." The commission admitted the force of this argument, but it was convinced that there were still more serious objections to the continuation of dyarchy or the transfer of police administration to the central government.

To prevent danger along this line and to avoid other periods of a weak administration during the period of transition an elaborate system of safeguards was recommended. The principle was laid down that "there must be full provision made for the maintenance and efficiency of the fundamentals of government," including the defense of the frontier, the preservation of internal security, and the protection of minorities. These objects were to be achieved partly by keeping the army under British control and partly by retaining and even increasing the authority of the chief executive. The recommendations in regard to the army will be discussed in a later chapter. As for the executive, the Governor-General would continue to be "the actual and active head of the Government" and in some cases responsibility would "be placed on his shoulders which is at present constitutionally discharged by the Governor-General in Council." The Provincial Governor would have the power to act contrary to the advice of his Ministers, if, in his opinion, it was necessary "to preserve the safety and tranquility of the province or to prevent serious prejudice to one or more sections of the community as compared with other sections." He might also proclaim a state of emergency, during which he would be authorized to exercise all powers normally vested in him and his Ministry, to restore rejected demands for grants and to certify legislation which he considers essential. In all of these cases, his action would be subject to the superintendence, direction, and control of the Governor-General and they would both be responsible to the Secretary of State and the British Parliament.

The proposals dealing with the machinery of government may be summarized very briefly. The central legislature would at first be restricted to British India[12] and it would continue to be bicameral. The lower house would be called the Federal Assembly and most of its members would be elected by the Provincial Councils according to a proportional system which would ensure representation for minority communities. The

12. The rulers of the states had not decided at that time to come into the federation.

upper house would still be called the Council of State and its elective members would be chosen by the Provincial Councils or by the second chambers in the provinces that adopted the bicameral system. There would be a few official and a few nominated nonofficial members in each house.[13] The Governor-General in Council would still be the central executive, but, as has already been implied, the tendency would be to emphasize the Governor-General's position as Viceroy and increase the powers that he would exercise on his own responsibility. There were also several recommendations relating to the Executive Council which were intended to facilitate the progress of constitutional development. The members of the Council would be selected and appointed by the Governor-General and a statutory rule would replace the constitutional requirement that a certain number of them "must be persons who have been for at least ten years in the service of the Crown in India." One of the members, presumably an Indian, would be relieved of departmental burdens and would devote his whole time to the leadership of the Federal Assembly. The Commander in Chief would cease to belong to either the Executive or the Legislative branch of the government.

The provincial governments were discussed in greater detail because the changes proposed were more revolutionary and there were more subjects of controversy. The commission was unable to agree as to the general composition of the legislature. One group favored the creation of a bicameral system partly for traditional reasons and partly because a second chamber would tend to check the radical proclivities of the lower house, protect minority communities and strengthen the Governor in the exercise of his special powers. The other members felt that the system would be complex and undemo-

13. The British government subsequently decided to eliminate the official element, although the executive councilors, of whom there would be not more than three, would be *ex officio* members of both houses without the right to vote. *The White Paper* of 1933 proposed that the Governor-General should be empowered to nominate not more than ten nonofficial members of the Council of State to provide a group of the elder-statesman type, but the number was reduced to six in the first Schedule to the Government of India Act, 1935.

cratic and that there would be a ceaseless conflict between the two houses. It is interesting to note that there was a similar difference of opinion in the Indian Central Committee and the Provincial Committees that collaborated in the Joint Free Conference. The government *White Paper* of 1933 proposed that each province should settle the question for itself and assumed that Bengal, Bihar, and the United Provinces had already accepted the bicameral principle. Bombay and Madras were added to the list by the Joint Select Committee of Parliament in 1934 and Assam was added during the passage of the bill through Parliament in 1935.

The representation of communities and special interests was another complicated and controversial problem which was, as we have seen, avoided to a large extent in the case of the central government by recommending a system of indirect elections. The commission proposed that communal electorates for Moslems should be retained in the provinces until a two-thirds majority of the Moslem members of the legislature should agree to have them abolished. The allocation of seats under the Montagu-Chelmsford plan is discussed elsewhere.[14] It is based on the Lucknow Pact of 1916 which gave the Moslems a weighted representation[15] in the six provinces where they constitute a minority of the population, but denied them the advantage of their majorities in Bengal and the Punjab. As both communities are now dissatisfied with this arrangement, the Report urged them to make a new agreement and intimated that if they failed to do so a settlement would be imposed upon them by the British government. The commission did not itself offer any solution of the problem, although it expressed its opinion that the demand of the Moslems for representation in Bengal and the Punjab on a population basis was incompatible with the retention of weightage in other provinces.

Separate electorates were also to be retained for Europeans and Anglo-Indians and for the Sikhs in the Punjab, but

14. See chap. iii, "The Montagu-Chelmsford Reforms (1917–21)," and chap. xi, "Hindu-Moslem Relations."

15. Representation is weighted when a community is allotted more members than it is entitled to have on the basis of population.

a reservation of seats in joint electorates was proposed for Indian Christians and the Depressed Classes of the Hindu community.[16] The position of the Marathas in Bombay and the non-Brahman Hindus in Madras is somewhat different. They are majority communities, but the Act of 1919 provided that seats should be reserved for them in joint electorates because it was believed that they would find it difficult to cope with the political strategy of the Brahmans. The commission made a careful study of the election returns and came to the conclusion that the system should be retained for the Marathas, but that it was unnecessary for the non-Brahmans of Madras.

Passing from the general to the special constituencies, the commission dealt first with the question of the continuance of university representation. It agreed "with considerable hesitation" that these seats should be preserved, but that the numbers should not be increased.[17] The representation of commerce and industry, both European and Indian, was to be maintained in approximately its present proportions. This also applied to mining and planting associations, with a somewhat larger quota for the European tea industry in Assam. The commission felt that the labor representation should be increased, although it admitted the difficulty of devising a system that would procure the right kind of representatives. The question would be left largely to the discretion of the Governor, but if he "finds that for the present he must still resort to nomination, he should consider whether there are suitable labour organizations which he might consult before making his choice." It was agreed that the ultimate solution would be found in a lowering of the franchise that would make special representation unnecessary. The great landholders have special constituencies which send 32 members to the various Provincial Legislative Councils, but in the election of 1926 there

16. The government subsequently decided that the Indian Christians should also have separate electorates, but there has been a bitter quarrel over the representation of the Depressed Classes which is discussed in a later chapter.

17. As the legislative bodies are to be considerably enlarged, this would mean a relative decrease in the strength of university representation.

were 108 other persons qualified for these special constituencies who were elected in the general constituencies. The commission agreed that the protection could now safely be withdrawn, but it suggested that if the number elected in any province should fall below the present special quota, the Governor should have the power to fill the quota by nomination.

In dealing with the franchise, the commission made three valuable suggestions: it should be widely extended, an educational qualification should be provided as an alternative to the property tests, and there should be a substantial increase in the ratio of women to men voters. It recognized the practical difficulties in extending the franchise and was opposed to the recommendation of the Nehru Report in favor of the immediate establishment of universal suffrage, but it was convinced that the present system "is too limited in its scope to provide the material from which to build any adequate scheme of representative government." There were at that time about 6½ million registered voters in the electoral area (excluding Burma), which was approximately 2.8 per cent of the total population. It was proposed that a new Franchise Committee should be appointed with instructions to frame schemes that would enfranchise about 10 per cent of the total population or about 20 per cent of the adult population. It should also endeavor to secure the same proportion of voters in the different communities without imposing differential qualifications. Some figures were quoted from Madras and Bengal to illustrate this difficulty and to show how it might be solved. The Moslems in Madras were 6.7 per cent of the population and 4.7 per cent of the voters; the Depressed Classes, 15.5 per cent of the population and 4.1 per cent of the voters; while the Caste Hindus were 74.6 of the population and 89.4 per cent of the voters. The commission felt that these discrepancies were due to the greater poverty of the Moslems and the Depressed Classes and that they could be largely eliminated by reducing the property qualifications. The Bengal figures support this argument. The Moslem voting percentage was 48.8 in the rural constituencies of the Legislative Council, but it was 57.7 in the same constituencies of the Union Boards where the qualification was only half as large. So far as the educational test was concerned, the proposal put forward for the benefit of the Franchise Committee was that all adults who held certificates showing that they had reached the standard of the fifth class should be enfranchised. This would also weight the balance in favor of the Hindus because they are the leaders in education as well as in material progress.

These changes would increase the number of women voters, but would probably not increase their percentage in the total electorate. In order to do that, the commission proposed two additional qualifications, "viz. (1) being the wife, over 25 years of age, of a man who has a property qualification to vote and (2) being a widow over that age, whose husband at the time of his death was so qualified." The problem of securing the election of women to the provincial legislatures is considered in another part of the Report. Several schemes were proposed, but the commission found them all defective and merely suggested that women candidates should be left "a fair field and no favours." The Governor in using his limited powers of nomination might, however, be instructed to "have special regard to the extent to which women have been returned as members from general constituencies, with a view to supplementing their numbers if he thinks this should be done."[18]

The section of the Report dealing with Finance was prepared by Sir (then Mr.) Walter Layton, the financial assessor to the commission. His scheme for regulating the financial relations between the central and local governments is somewhat complicated, but its essential features may be explained in a few sentences. The revenues are now divided into two sharply defined classes: (a) those collected and spent by the central government, and (b) those collected and spent by the provincial governments. The allocation is favorable to the central government. Its revenues are expansive and should increase rapidly as prosperity returns, but the expenditures under the new Constitution ought to remain comparatively stationary. With the provinces, it is exactly the reverse. Their revenues are not capable of very much expansion, but educa-

18. The methods proposed by the British government for dealing with these problems will be considered later in connection with the Communal Decision of 1932 and *The White Paper* of 1933.

tion, sanitation, and other "nation building" services will demand a steady growth of expenditure. It is practically impossible to solve the problem by transferring central sources of revenue to the provinces because they are nearly all of a nature that requires a uniform system of administration. This is especially true of the tariff which is the most important source of central revenue. It would obviously be unfair to allow Bengal and Bombay to retain duties collected in their ports on goods consumed in other parts of India. Sir Walter's proposal involves the creation of two additional classes of revenue: (c) revenue collected by the central government and distributed to the provinces on the basis of origin, and (d) revenue collected by the central government and distributed to the provinces on the basis of population.

The central authorities would continue to administer the income tax, but 50 per cent of the yield from personal incomes and all of the yield from a new tax to be imposed on agricultural incomes[19] would be allocated to the provinces in which they are collected. In addition to this, the provinces would be empowered to levy surcharges of not more than 25 per cent on personal income taxes, which would be collected for them by the central authorities. New excise taxes on matches and cigarettes would constitute the nucleus of a Provincial Fund, which would be augmented by the proceeds of the salt duty, when they could be spared by the central budget. This fund would come under class (d), that is, it would be distributed among the provinces on a basis of population. It was also proposed that the provinces should be given power to impose terminal taxes, which means taxes "generally levied at a railway station and collected by the railway administration on all goods imported or exported from the station." If all of these sources are utilized, Sir Walter estimates that the provincial revenues (excluding Burma) will increase from Rs. 78 crores in 1929–30 to Rs. 114 crores at the end of ten years.[20]

19. Sir Walter does not accept the argument "that land revenue is the counterpart of income tax in other countries, and that to impose income tax as well upon the incomes of the zamindars would be a form of double taxation." *Report of the Simon Commission,* II, 239–241.

20. At the present rate of exchange, this would mean an increase from £58,500,000 to £85,500,000 sterling.

"The scheme would . . . greatly help those provinces which have most to complain of under the present system, without either introducing a system of doles or making the provinces too greatly dependent upon financial policy determined outside their borders." Bengal would be the chief beneficiary. Her government has been starved since 1920, although her people pay nearly half of the income taxes (excluding Burma) and she has a large and wealthy class of landlords whose incomes are not taxed at all. Next to Bengal, the province of Bombay would receive the greatest benefit from the allocation of a part of the income tax and the opportunity to impose a surcharge. The taxation of agricultural incomes would tend to distribute the financial burden more equitably, not only in the Permanent Settlement area, but in all of the provinces where the landlord system prevails.

Sir Walter's account of the financial relations of the Indian States is based mainly on the report of the Butler Committee. He believes that protection imposes a burden on the inhabitants of the states which will grow heavier as the tariff becomes more and more the mainstay of the central budget, but he also emphasizes the fact that the states have so far contributed very little to the support of the army. As the problem requires a more detailed study, he approves the recommendation of the Butler Committee that a body of experts should be appointed to inquire into (1) the claims of the various states to a share in the customs revenue and (2) the adequacy of their contribution to Imperial burdens. The creation of a federal system, embracing both the states and the provinces, will not solve the problem, although it will change its character to a considerable extent. It will become an internal political issue in the struggle between industrial and agrarian interests, with a majority of the states on the agrarian side.

Most of the recommendations relating to the Civil Services have already been discussed. Although Law and Order is to be a Transferred Subject, the Security Services would continue to be recruited by the Secretary of State and the personnel would continue to be predominantly British until 1939 in the case of the Indian Civil Service and 1949 in the case of the Indian Police Service. Provision would also be made for safeguarding their rights as well as those "of existing members of any All-India services for which no further recruitment will be made." The commission discussed the value of Public Service Commissions, commended the Central Commission established in 1926, and proposed that similar bodies should be created in every province.[21]

The defense of India would be treated "as a matter which should fall within the responsibilities of the Governor-General, advised by the Commander-in-Chief, as representing the Imperial authorities, instead of being part of the responsibilities of the Government of India in relation to the Central Legislature." The financial burden would be shared by India and the Imperial government, although the Indian contribution would presumably be much larger than that made by the United Kingdom. It was hoped that friction could be avoided by stabilizing India's contribution for a period of years and providing some form of arbitration for the adjustment of minor disputes. "In the case of extraordinary or war expenditure, there is a broad distinction between the cost of expeditions or operations which are the result of tribal activities . . . and exceptional expenditures rendered necessary by the organized attack of a foreign power." In the former case, the charges would fall entirely on the revenues of India, but "the circumstances may be such in the latter instance as to make a case for spreading the financial burden more widely." The army would still be used occasionally to maintain internal security, but, except in extreme emergencies, this would be done only at the request of the Governor of the province in which the disturbance occurs. It was suggested that the province might be asked to contribute a part of the cost of intervention in order to prevent the excessive use of troops as a substitute for the police.[22]

One of the most interesting sections of the Report from the constitutional point of view is that which deals with the relations between the Home government and the Indian govern-

21. For a further discussion of this subject, see chap. vii, "Political Grievances: the Services."

22. The problem of Indianization and the proposal to create a new military force composed entirely of Indians have already been discussed.

ments. The Secretary of State would be kept informed about provincial affairs, but his control would be restricted to supporting and directing the Governor in the exercise of his special functions or in the administration of the government when a state of emergency had been proclaimed. The government of India, on the other hand, would remain in a state of constitutional subordination to the Secretary of State, although it was hoped that in practice there would be a wide delegation of powers. The commission was inclined, however, to oppose the form of delegation represented by the Fiscal Convention of 1919, under which the Secretary of State binds himself not to interfere if the government of India and the Assembly agree upon a particular policy.[23] Its argument was that the government of India will inevitably become more and more responsive to the views of the legislature and will not be able to arrive at an independent conclusion. In connection with the machinery of the India Office, the old controversy over the Council of India was discussed and a compromise was proposed which leans toward the conservative side. The Council would be reduced in size and would in general be a purely advisory body which the Secretary of State could consult at his discretion. But it would still contain some retired Civil Service officials and would still be vested with its old powers to protect the rights and privileges of the Services and to veto nonvotable expenditures of the central government. The control over military expenditures would, however, tend to disappear if the suggestion is accepted that the Imperial government should "undertake the responsibility for the defense of India in return for an annual payment by India fixed for a term of years." The High Commissioner for India would still exercise his present functions, which are concerned mainly with the purchase of government stores and the recruitment of such personnel as the provincial governments draw from Great Britain.

23. Two conventions of this type have already been adopted: the Fiscal Convention itself, which gives the government and legislature of India a wide control over tariff policy; and a later convention which permits the central and provincial governments and legislatures to buy nonmilitary stores wherever they please.

The last chapter of the Report is a general survey and conclusion. After emphasizing the fact that success can be achieved only by sustained good will and coöperation between the communities in India, as well as between India and Great Britain, it ends on the following note:

We have grown to understand something of the ideals which are inspiring the Indian national movement, and no man who has taken part in working the representative institutions of Britain can fail to sympathize with the desire of others to secure for their own land a similar development. But a constitution is something more than a generalization: it has to present a constructive scheme. We submit our Report in the hope that it may furnish materials and suggest a plan by means of which Indian constitutional reconstruction may be peacefully and surely promoted.

CHAPTER XIII

THE ROUND TABLE CONFERENCE

AFTER the publication of the *Report of the Statutory Commission* in 1930 there were four main stages in the evolution of the new Constitution. During the period from November, 1930, to December, 1933, three sessions of a Round Table Conference were held in London between representatives of the United Kingdom, British India, and the Indian States. His Majesty's government informed the conference that it was its policy to convert "the present system of government in India into a responsibly governed Federation of States and Provinces, on the understanding that the responsible Government so established must during the period of transition be qualified by limitations in certain directions." That policy was approved by both houses of Parliament in December, 1931, and the government then pursued further inquiries and discussions which culminated in March, 1933, in the publication of a *White Paper* entitled "Proposals for Indian Constitutional Reform." Those proposals were considered by a Joint Select Committee of Parliament, in consultation with representatives from India, and their Report was published on November 21, 1934. The final stage was the discussion in Parliament of this document and the passage of the Government of India Act, 1935, which implemented its recommendations.

The *Report of the Statutory Commission* was damned in India by universal consent. Even the Moderates, who kept an open mind, were disappointed and disillusioned. They were especially annoyed by the failure to mention Dominion status as the ultimate goal and by the autocratic character of the proposals relating to the central government. Mr. MacDonald was placed in an embarrassing position. He had to win the support of Indian Moderates for the Round Table Conference without antagonizing British Liberals and Left-Wing Conservatives whose coöperation was also essential. Three major concessions were offered to the Indians. An official announcement was made that the Report would not be used as the basis for discussion in the conference and that no members of the commission would be included in the British delegation. Lord Irwin was authorized to repeat his assurance to the Indian Legislative Assembly that "the attainment of Dominion status is the natural completion of India's constitutional growth." Finally, the government of India wrote a long dispatch on the Report which was intended to mitigate some of its most objectionable features.[1] The central executive, for example, would not be formally responsible to the legislature, but it would "include an appreciable popular element consisting of elected members of the Legislature." This would not be dyarchy, although it would imply "a form of dualism within the Government." The dispatch also rejected the proposal to put the military forces of India under Imperial control and it favored a more liberal treatment of Sind and the North-West Frontier Province.

Thanks to these concessions and the Viceroy's tactful diplomacy, the Moderates were reconciled and an effort was made by their leaders to persuade the Congress party to participate in the conference. In the spring of 1930, Mr. Gandhi had initiated a civil disobedience campaign, with the result that he was now imprisoned at Poona and his associates, Pandits Motilal Nehru and Jawaharlal Nehru, were in the jail at Allahabad. In August, they were visited by Sir Tej Bahadur Sapru, the well-known Liberal leader, and Mr. Jayakar of the Responsivist group and an attempt was made to reach an agreement which would be acceptable to the Viceroy. The negotiations were unsuccessful. Mr. Gandhi and the Nehrus adopted an intransigent attitude and made demands which Lord Irwin could not possibly accept. The essence of their ultimatum was that they would modify the civil disobedience movement and take part in the conference, if the Viceroy would guarantee that its sole object was to frame a Dominion

1. The dispatch, which was dated September 20, 1930, was printed in London and laid before the delegates to the conference on November 14, Cd. 3700.

Constitution. They also insisted that the right of secession should be recognized, the defense forces should be placed under complete Indian control, and all British claims and concessions in India, including the public debt, which seemed "unjust" should be submitted to arbitration.

The first session of the Round Table Conference was held in London from November 12, 1930, to January 19, 1931. It was attended by 16 delegates from the United Kingdom, 16 from the Indian States and 57 from British India (including Burma). The most active members were Mr. MacDonald, Lord Sankey, Lord Reading, Lord Peel, and Sir Samuel Hoare, representing Great Britain; Sir Muhammed Akbar Hydari, Sir Mirza Ismail, and the Maharaja of Bikaner, representing the Indian States; and Mr. Sastri, Sir Tej Bahadur Sapru, Mr. M. A. Jinnah, and the Aga Khan, representing British India. The Depressed Classes were represented by Dr. Ambedkar, the Anglo-Indians by Lieutenant-Colonel Gidney, and the domiciled Europeans by Sir Hubert Carr and Mr. Gavin Jones. There were also special representatives of the Sikhs, the Indian Christians, and a few other minor groups.

After a ceremonial opening by the King-Emperor, the conference devoted five days to speech making and a formal debate on the general character of the future Constitution of India. It then resolved itself into a Committee of the Whole Conference and set up nine subcommittees to report on special problems. The high lights of the session were the announcement made by the Maharaja of Bikaner that the rulers of the Indian States were prepared to join an All-Indian federation and a speech by Lord Reading which pledged the Liberal party to support Mr. MacDonald in extending the principle of responsibility to the Indian central government. These two ideas were closely associated. The princes would not enter an autocratic federation[2] and His Majesty's government would probably not have conceded responsibility at the center if it

2. "We have made it clear," said the Maharaja of Bhopal, "that we can only federate with a self-governing and federated British India and that if British India is not self-governed, any federation with the present Government of India will, it is evident, be to our disadvantage."

had been dealing exclusively with British India. The belief that the princes would exercise a stabilizing influence and oppose secession or revolution undoubtedly made it easier for the Conservative party to support the government's policy.

The Indian delegates had no illusions about the measure of self-government that was to be conceded. They were clearly informed both by the Prime Minister and by Lord Reading that, during a period of transition, responsible government would be subject to certain limitations or safeguards of the type mentioned in *The Simon Report*. The safeguards actually discussed by Mr. MacDonald may be divided into four categories. A modified system of dyarchy would be established in the federal government, with the control of defense and foreign affairs reserved to the Viceroy; the legitimate interests of minorities would be protected; the sanctity of contracts and other vested rights, especially those relating to Finance and the Public Services, would be fully guaranteed; and, finally, the Viceroy and the Provincial Governors would be given adequate emergency powers to take charge of the administration in the event of a breakdown of the ordinary normal operations of government.

Lord Sankey's Subcommittee on Federal Structure drafted a general outline of the federation and sketched in a few of its details. It was to include "the federating Provinces of British India" and such states as might desire to become members. The legislature should consist of two chambers, each containing representatives of both British India and the states. The upper chamber—which might be called the Senate or Council of State—should have from 100 to 150 members and the lower chamber 250 members. It was unanimously agreed that there should be some "weightage"[3] in favor of the states in the distribution of seats in the upper house, but the representatives from British India were unwilling to extend this concession to the lower house. In both houses, the seats allocated to British India should be distributed among the provinces on the basis

3. This means that the states would have a representation somewhat in excess of that to which they would be entitled on the basis of population.

of population. The distribution among the states was left for future consideration, with the suggestion that, so far as the upper house was concerned, "this must clearly be a matter for agreement by their Rulers in consultation between themselves and, if necessary, with the Viceroy." A number of other questions relating to the legislature were considered and a study was made of the federal executive, with especial reference to the extension of the principle of responsibility to the central government. A classification of central and provincial subjects was also prepared in collaboration with the Subcommittee on Provincial Constitutions.[4]

The communal distribution of seats in the federal and provincial legislatures was the most difficult problem that came before the conference. The tendency of the Moslems to insist on certain safeguards and privileges was strengthened by the decision to form an All-Indian federation because of their weakness in the states as compared with British India.[5] They were determined to have separate communal electorates with weighted representation in the central legislature and the minority provinces, and majorities in Bengal and the Punjab. Dr. Ambedkar also insisted on separate electorates for the Depressed Classes, at least until the franchise was based on adult suffrage. As the Hindus and especially the Mahasabha group were unwilling to make these concessions, the Subcommittee on Minorities was forced to report its inability to reach an agreement.

Other problems were considered with more favorable results. The Subcommittee on Burma asked that a public announcement should be made accepting the principle of separa-

4. Mr. Arthur Henderson was the chairman of this subcommittee which dealt with the powers of the provincial legislatures and the constitution, character, powers, and responsibilities of the provincial executives. Their Report covered very little ground and in general followed the path marked out by the Simon Commission.

5. In 1931, they constituted 25.4 per cent of the population in British India and only 13.4 per cent in the states. Considering the fact that the states' representatives will be chosen by the princes, it is perhaps more significant to note that nearly all of the influential rulers, except the Nizam of Hyderabad, are non-Moslems.

tion, without prejudice to Burma's prospects of constitutional advancement. His Majesty's government agreed to this and, on the recommendation of other subcommittees, also promised that the existing Reforms should be extended to the North-West Frontier Province and that both the Frontier Province and Sind, which was to be separated from Bombay, should rank as Governor's provinces under the new Constitution. The Subcommittee on Defense urged that immediate steps, including the establishment of a military training college, should be taken to increase substantially the rate of Indianization in the Indian Army. The Prime Minister promised to take up this question with the authorities in India and, although there has so far been very little advance in the rate of Indianization, the Indian Military Academy was opened at Dehra Dun on December 10, 1932.[6]

During the interval between the first two sessions of the conference (January 19–September 14, 1931), there were three main factors that influenced the progress of events. In the first place, the Irwin-Gandhi Agreement was concluded at Delhi on March 4 and approved by the Congress at Karachi on the thirtieth. Lord Irwin agreed to release political prisoners and to make a few other minor concessions, while Mr. Gandhi promised to call off the civil disobedience movement and to participate in the Round Table Conference. The second factor was the tendency on the part of some of the princes to emasculate the plans for a federal Constitution. The Maharaja of Patiala proposed an alternative scheme, based on the idea of a confederation which would represent the interests of the states as a whole against the government of British India. Efforts were made to minimize the significance of this revolt, but it soon became obvious that a number of states would refuse to coöperate and that others would have to be conciliated by political and financial concessions. It would also be necessary to decide how large and how strong the initial state membership must be before the federation would be established. The third factor was the recrudescence of the Hindu-Moslem feud. There was trouble in Kashmir and Jammu and a series of riots in the United Provinces, beginning at Benares on February

6. See chap. vii.

12 and culminating in the terrible massacre at Cawnpore in the latter part of March.[7] As the tension increased, both communities became more aggressive and more obstinate in their political demands. The Hindu Mahasabha and the Working Committee of Congress clamored loudly for joint electorates, while the various Moslem organizations insisted upon a separate communal representation in all of the legislative bodies, with Moslem majorities in Bengal and the Punjab.

The second session of the conference was held between September 14 and December 1, 1931, during a very critical period in the history of the United Kingdom. The National government had been formed on August 24, the gold standard was suspended on September 21, and the general election occurred on October 27. The conference was not very active until after the election, although it was kept alive by Lord Sankey and other delegates from the House of Lords who did not have to take part in the campaign. There was also some uncertainty about the policy of the National government. Sir Samuel Hoare, the new Secretary of State for India, was a Conservative and the election proved to be a Conservative landslide. The question was finally settled by Mr. Baldwin's pledge that he and presumably the majority of his party would support Mr. MacDonald's program.

Most of the work was done by two committees which were carried over from the previous session. The Federal Structures Committee was chiefly concerned with safeguards and the terms under which the states would enter the federation, while the Minorities Committee struggled with the problem of minority representation in the new legislatures. Mr. Gandhi, who was an active member of both of these bodies, was anxious to settle the communal problem immediately or to postpone it for future consideration so that a concentrated drive could be made to whittle down the safeguards and to establish real self-government. His efforts were unsuccessful because the minimum demands of the various committees were incompatible and Moslem delegates had been instructed by the All-India Moslem Conference not to participate in the general constitu-

7. These troubles are discussed in chap. xi, "Hindu-Moslem Relations."

tional discussions until all of their demands were conceded. He also damaged his own cause by adopting a domineering attitude toward the Depressed Classes, the Indian Christians, the Anglo-Indians, and the Europeans, which forced them into an alliance with the Moslems.

The Moslem demands have already been discussed. After some debate and a great deal of recrimination, Mr. Gandhi agreed to concede practically all of them, on condition that the Moslems would abandon the other minority groups and vote against giving them separate representation.[8] His offer was rejected and the allies held a separate meeting and drafted a long list of demands, to which they pledged their united support.[9] The Mahatma then added fresh fuel to the flames by making an open charge that they were not properly representing their communities.[10] At this stage of the proceedings, the Minorities Committee gave up in despair and reported to the conference that it was unable to reach an agreement.

The failure to settle the communal problem seriously hampered the work of the Federal Structures Committee. For a time, the Moslem delegates felt bound by their instructions to boycott the committee, but they finally agreed to coöperate, on the understanding that the Constitution would not be acceptable to the Moslem community until it incorporated all of their demands and safeguards. They also widened the breach between themselves and the Hindus by supporting the policy of the half-way house, which involved the immediate establishment of provincial autonomy, leaving the problem of federa-

8. If this offer had been accepted, Mr. Gandhi would have found it difficult to carry out his part of the bargain, especially the promise that the Moslems should have legislative majorities in Bengal and the Punjab.

9. Published in the London *Times,* November 13, 1931. The Sikhs and one of the Indian Christian delegates refused to take part in the revolt.

10. Mr. Gandhi distrusted Dr. Ambedkar as the spokesman of the Depressed Classes and was also annoyed because Dr. Ansari, the well-known Nationalist leader, was not included among the Moslem delegates. So far as Dr. Ansari was concerned, he could have been chosen as a delegate of the Congress, if the Mahatma had not insisted on being their sole representative.

tion and responsibility at the center for future consideration. This did not mean that they were opposed to Dominion Home Rule, but simply that they were unwilling to take such a long step in that direction until some infallible method had been devised for protecting their rights and privileges. They could see no reason why provincial reform should be delayed until this was accomplished, especially as they would control four provinces and would probably never be able to exercise very much influence over the federal government.

The Hindus, on the other hand, were anxious that all constitutional issues should be settled together, even though it meant a delay in the attainment of provincial autonomy. Their point of view can easily be explained. If the Moslems were conciliated and their pressure on the British was withdrawn, the zeal for reform would cool and the half-way house would tend to become a permanent habitation. Furthermore, the Hindus, being the majority community and the traditional exponents of national unity, were not very much interested in provincial rights. The Sikhs were generally inclined to support the Hindus, partly because they must coöperate with the Hindus against the Moslem majority in the Punjab and partly because Mr. Gandhi had agreed to help them retain their separate electorates.[11] By the same token, it was his refusal to concede separate electorates to the other minority communities that led to their alliance with the Moslems.

In spite of this rather barren record, the conference was not a total failure. Several problems not directly involved in the communal controversy were discussed and constructive suggestions were made by Sir Tej Bahadur Sapru, Sir Akbar Hydari, and other delegates who were overshadowed in the press notices by Mr. Gandhi. The problem of federal finance was examined by a subcommittee of the Federal Structures Committee under the chairmanship of Lord Peel. In its report, it explained the general character of the question and recommended that two committees should be appointed to continue the investigation in India and collect the data that would be

11. The Sikhs are in favor of the abolition of separate electorates in the Punjab, but until that is done they are unwilling to compete with Hindus in the general constituencies.

needed for a final settlement. This was approved and it was decided that a third committee should also be constituted to examine the revision of the franchise.

On December 1, the last day of the session, the Prime Minister made a formal statement of the government's Indian policy. In spite of political changes, it was still committed to the establishment of responsible government, both central and provincial, with statutory safeguards for a transitional period. There was no intention to introduce provincial autonomy as an ad interim measure, but, if opinion and circumstances in India should change, this decision was not to be regarded as irrevocable. It was hoped that the Indians themselves would soon reach an agreement on the communal problem, but, if they failed to do so, His Majesty's government would be compelled to impose a provisional settlement. The three committees recommended by the conference would be appointed immediately and a small Working Committee would be set up in India to carry on until the next meeting of the conference. "In the end," said Mr. MacDonald, "we shall have to meet again for a final review of the whole scheme."

This statement was at once submitted to Parliament and approved by both houses, Mr. Churchill's adverse amendment in the House of Commons being rejected by a majority of 369 to 43. The appointment of the investigating committees was announced on December 24. Lord Lothian was selected as the chairman of the Franchise Committee, Lord Eustace Percy of the Federal Finance Committee, and Mr. J. C. C. Davidson, M.P., of the Federal States Inquiry Committee (Financial). The Working Committee or, as it came to be called later, the Consultative Committee of the conference was composed of nineteen members under the chairmanship of the Viceroy.

The Report of the Federal Finance Committee was published on May 7 and that of the Federal States Inquiry Committee (Financial) on July 29, 1932. They are full of technical details, but their essential features may be described in a few words. The Percy Committee considered two very difficult problems, the allocation of revenue from the income tax and the question whether the federation should assume the whole of the prefederation debt. It was assumed that the federal income tax would be collected only in British India and a suggestion had been made that the proceeds should be turned over to the provinces, leaving the deficit in the federal budget to be covered by provincial contributions. The committee rejected this suggestion and proposed instead an intricate scheme for distributing a part of the income tax revenue among the provinces, but not enough to cripple the federal government or to require the re-introduction of the system of provincial contributions which had worked badly in the early days of the Montagu-Chelmsford Constitution. The other problem affected more directly the interests of the states. Should they, as members of the new federation, assume part of the responsibility for a public debt that had been contracted by British India alone? The committee assumed an optimistic view and reported that the assets exceeded the liabilities. In other words, the states would become coproprietors of railways, irrigation works, and other public properties that would bring in more than enough revenue to service the debt. The Davidson Committee dealt with a few complicated problems affecting the financial relations of the federation with certain states. It recommended that tributes paid to the Crown should gradually be remitted, that credit should be given to those states that had ceded territory in lieu of tribute and that there should be an adjustment of immunities which some of the states now enjoy in regard to tariffs, salt, posts, and telegraphs. The settlement as a whole would be favorable to the states, but this is a part of the price which must be paid to induce them to enter the federation.

The Lothian (Franchise) Committee issued its Report on June 2. Owing to administrative difficulties and the high percentage of illiteracy, the committee said that it would be impossible to establish adult suffrage immediately. It recommended, however, an increase in the provincial electorate from about 7,000,000 to 36,000,000, or from 3 to 14 per cent of the population, by reducing the property qualifications and creating an alternative educational test based on an upper primary standard. It also proposed the adoption of differential tests to secure a more effective representation for various groups that are now largely disfranchised. The present ratio of women to men electors is about 1:20. This would be raised to 1:4.5 and the number of women voters increased from 315,000 to about 6,000,000 by extending the franchise to all women (1) who are literate, (2) who have a property qualification in their own right, or (3) who are the wives or widows of men with the property qualifications for the present provincial legislatures. There would be a somewhat similar increase in the Labor vote and the number of seats allotted to Labor would be raised from 9 to 38, which would considerably reduce the present disparity between the representation of Labor and that of Commerce and Industry. These seats would be filled on a noncommunal basis, partly by trade unions and partly by special Labor constituencies. A differential test would also be applied to the Depressed Classes, but the committee was not authorized in their case to deal with the method of representation. So far as the federal legislature was concerned, it was proposed that the Assembly should consist of 300 members, instead of the 200 suggested by the Federal Structures Subcommittee, that the area of the territorial constituencies should be proportionally reduced, and that the electorate should be increased from about 1,250,000 to 8,500,000.

The next step toward the solution of the franchise problem was the publication of the Communal Decision or Communal Award on August 16, 1932. This was a provisional settlement, devised by His Majesty's government in accordance with its warning of December 1 that it would take such action if the communities themselves failed to reach an agreement in time to prevent delay in the framing of the Constitution. It was confined to the provincial legislatures, with a proviso that when the composition of the federal legislature was considered, full regard would be paid to the claims of all communities for adequate representation. The government announced that it would not take part in negotiations to revise the Award, but if, at any time before the Constitution was completed, the communities affected could reach a mutual agreement on a practical alternative scheme, either in respect of a part or the whole of British India, Parliament would be asked to accept it as a substitute. At the end of ten years, the plan might be revised with the assent of the communities affected and, at the end of twenty years, the separate electorates for the Depressed Classes would be abolished, if they had not previously been given up by voluntary agreement.

All of the seats in the Provincial Assemblies were allocated and a statement was made that in the bicameral provinces the composition of the Council or upper house "should be such as not to disturb in any essential the balance between the communities resulting from the composition of the Lower House." There would be separate communal electorates for Moslems, Sikhs, and Europeans covering between them the whole area of the province (except Backward Tracts). It was hoped that, by the use of postal ballots, the whole area might also be covered by the Anglo-Indian electorates. The Indian-Christian problem is more difficult. Except possibly in Madras, their constituencies would not cover the entire province, but would be formed in a few selected areas. All qualified electors, who are not voters in a Moslem, Sikh, European, Anglo-Indian, or Indian-Christian constituency, would be entitled to vote in a general constituency. The general constituencies would, therefore, be composed mainly of Caste Hindus and the Depressed Classes, but they would also include members of other communities who live in provinces or parts of provinces where they do not have their own separate electorates. Sikhs, for example, who live outside of the Punjab and the North-West Frontier Province would vote in the general constituencies. Seven seats would be reserved for Mahrattas in plural member general constituencies in Bombay. Seats would also be reserved for women in all of the provinces except the North-West Frontier. They would be filled on a communal basis, except in Assam, where one woman member would be chosen in a noncommunal constituency at Shillong.[12]

The special electorates would continue to be noncommunal, although in practice most of them would be controlled by

12. The Communal Award provided that 39 seats in all should be reserved for women and 2 more were added later when it was decided to create the new province of Orissa. In addition to the noncommunal members in Assam, there will be 27 Hindus (chosen in general constituencies), 10 Moslems, 1 Sikh (Punjab), 1 Indian Christian (Madras), and 1 Anglo-Indian (Bengal).

Europeans and Hindus. The Franchise Committee's allotment of 38 seats to Labor was approved, but the number given to Commerce and Industry, Mining and Planting was increased from 46 to 55. There were at that time 32 seats allotted to the great landholders. The Award proposed to retain this system and increase the number to 36, in spite of the evidence given by the Simon Commission that such representation is unnecessary. Eight seats were to be filled from the University constituencies. The creation of the province of Orissa will add one seat to each of the privileged groups, but the Labor and University representation will remain unchanged. The 56 seats allotted to Commerce and Industry, Mining and Planting would be filled by election through chambers of commerce and other associations. As these bodies are either predominantly European or predominantly Indian, the racial distribution of seats can easily be calculated. Thirty-six will be held by Europeans[13] and 20 by Indians. The other special seats—37 Landholder, 38 Labor, and 8 University—will all be filled by Indians. It is impossible to say exactly what proportion of the Indian seats will be secured by the Hindus, but they will undoubtedly get the lion's share. In view of this fact, there is a movement among the Moslems to have all of the special seats filled on a communal basis.

The two most difficult problems were (a) to devise an equitable method of representation for the Depressed Classes and (b) to allocate the communal seats with a minimum amount of friction. The solution of the former question involved the use of differential voting qualifications which would enfranchise about 10 per cent of the total population of the Depressed Classes. It was also based on the principle of the dual vote, a complicated form of procedure for such a backward section of the population. They would vote in general constituencies, but as this would not at present secure an adequate representation, a number of seats would be set aside to be filled on a communal

13. The Europeans will have 14 of these special seats in Bengal in addition to 11 communal seats. They will have 8 special seats in Assam, where the tea industry is concentrated, 4 each in Madras and Bombay, and a few scattered seats in other provinces, except in the Punjab and the North-West Frontier.

basis. These separate electorates would be formed in selected areas which, except in Madras, would not cover the whole province. One or two examples will show how the plan was intended to work. In Madras, the Depressed Classes would participate in the election of 134 members in the general constituencies and would also choose 18 members to represent their own community. The figures for Bombay (excluding Sind) were 107 and 10; for the United Provinces, 132 and 12; and for the Central Provinces and Berar, 77 and 10. All of these members, those elected in the communal as well as those elected in the general constituencies, would count as Hindus in the general allocation of seats.

On the main issue, the Award leaned toward the Moslems, although it did not concede their maximum demands. The principle of weightage, under which certain minorities are given representation in excess of their population ratio, was approved and extended to all the provinces. It applies especially to Europeans in Bengal and Assam, to Sikhs in the Punjab and the North-West Frontier, to Hindus in Sind and the North-West Frontier, and to Moslems in the seven provinces where they are in the minority. The chief difficulty was the distribution of seats in Bengal and the Punjab. The Moslems were allotted 119 communal members in Bengal out of a total membership of 250. As they are not likely to be very successful in contesting the special seats, they would be unable to form a government without support from other communities. It was obviously intended that the 25 European members should hold the balance of power.[14] In the Punjab the Moslems will have 86 communal seats and will probably win 2 of the special Landholder seats, which will give them a majority of 1 in an Assembly of 175. Their representation in both of these provinces will be well below the population ratio because of the heavy weightage in favor of Europeans in Bengal and of Sikhs in the Punjab.

The Award was received unfavorably in India. The real

14. If the Hindus (including the Depressed Classes) should win all of the special seats which are not earmarked for Europeans, they would have only 100 members. There will also be 2 seats reserved for Indian Christians and 4 for Anglo-Indians.

Nationalists, the little group of intellectuals who are able to rise above communal considerations, felt that it was a long step backward. They realized that separate electorates could not be abolished immediately, but they resented the extension of the principle into new fields and its adoption as a more or less permanent part of the Constitution. Most of these people are Hindus and it is impossible to draw a line between them and the bulk of the Hindu community because the majority would naturally oppose separate electorates. Shortly after the Award was published, the Working Committee of the Mahasabha, which represents the Caste Hindu point of view, denounced it mainly on the grounds that it gave the Moslems control of Bengal and the Punjab, that it denied to the Hindus in those provinces representation in proportion to their population, that it granted too much weightage to Moslems in Hindu provinces and that it implied the formation of Sind as a separate province. The Award was also criticized by the larger minority groups. The Moslems were perhaps influenced to some extent by tactical considerations, but they were undoubtedly convinced that they were entitled to statutory majorities in the legislatures of Bengal and the Punjab, especially as the Hindus were given complete control in their majority provinces. The Sikhs were embittered by the Punjab settlement, although it confirmed their claims to weightage,[15] because it did not give them and the Hindus together a majority of the seats. So far as the Depressed Classes were concerned, the Ambedkar faction complained that its representation was inadequate, while the rival group, led by Mr. Rajah, lamented its treatment as a separate community. The principle of separate electorates was also denounced by a small Nationalist element among the Indian-Christians. The only people apparently who were entirely satisfied were the Europeans and the Anglo-Indians.[16]

In spite of this widespread dissatisfaction, the communities

15. The Sikhs constitute about 13 per cent of the population of the Punjab, but they were allotted approximately 19 per cent of the seats in the Provincial Assembly.

16. An excellent account of the reaction to the Award in India will be found in *The Round Table* for December, 1932, XXIII, 142–161.

were still unable to devise an alternative plan. The only change made by mutual consent was that embodied in the Poona Pact, an agreement between the two sections of the Hindu community, signed at Poona on September 25, 1932.[17] It will be recalled that Mr. Gandhi, at the second session of the Round Table Conference, had bitterly opposed the creation of separate electorates for the Depressed Classes. His motives were partly Nationalistic and partly communal, but he was primarily concerned with the probable effects of the change on the Depressed Classes themselves. If they were treated as a separate political group, the gulf between them and the Caste Hindus would be widened and the evils of untouchability would be harder to eradicate. The element of prestige was now also involved. Having fought so strongly against separation in London, he had to continue the battle or admit that he was no longer a leader even among the Hindus.

His plan of action was characteristic. He announced that he would "fast unto death" unless the representatives of the two sections could reach an agreement involving the abolition of separate electorates. The negotiations were, therefore, conducted with frantic speed and under a severe emotional strain. Even in these circumstances, a compromise would have been impossible, if the Mahatma had not partially reversed the attitude he had taken at the Round Table Conference and agreed that seats might be reserved for the Depressed Classes in the general constituencies. Dr. Ambedkar drove a hard bargain with the Caste Hindu representatives. The Pact provided that the Depressed Classes should give up their separate electorates, but the number of seats reserved for them was increased from 71 to 148 and they were allowed, under certain restrictions, to nominate their own candidates.

All members of the Depressed Classes who are registered on the general electoral roll of certain constituencies will elect a panel of four candidates belonging to their own body, and the four persons who receive the highest number of votes in this primary elec-

17. The negotiations were held at the Yeravda jail in Poona, where Mr. Gandhi had again been imprisoned for renewing the civil disobedience campaign.

tion will be the only candidates for election to the reserved seat; but the candidate finally elected to the reserved seat will be elected by the general electorate, that is to say, by caste Hindus and by members of the Depressed Classes alike.[18]

There were also several other concessions. Going beyond the field covered by the Award, the Pact provided that the Depressed Classes should have 18 per cent of the general seats in the central legislature, that every endeavor should be made to secure adequate representation for them in local bodies and in the Public Services, and that they should have a fair share of public money spent for educational purposes. Finally, the Caste Hindus who took part in the negotiations passed a resolution urging the removal of the social and religious disabilities of the untouchables and appointed a committee to raise funds to educate the public on this issue.

After the Mahatma's fast was broken, both parties had time to study the agreement more carefully and to consider how it would affect their position. Dr. Ambedkar soon came to the conclusion that the panel primary was a complicated and expensive device which could probably be manipulated by Hindu politicians. He had an interview with Mr. Gandhi and suggested that the Pact should be modified to provide for only one election, with the understanding that a Depressed Class candidate could not be elected unless he secured a certain fixed proportion of the votes of his own community. The suggestion was rejected and he retaliated by opposing all changes that were desired by the other side. The Caste Hindus realized that they had to make concessions at Poona to save the Mahatma's life, but they soon began to feel that the sacrifice was excessive and should be at least partially remitted. The chief trouble was in Bengal, where they constitute the bulk of the educated and wealthy classes. From their point of view, the Award was bad enough, but the Pact made it infinitely worse. There are 80 general seats, of which 30 are reserved for the Depressed Classes, so that the Caste Hindus might win all of the non-European special seats and still have only 70 members in a

18. *Joint Committee on Indian Constitutional Reforms,* Vol. I (Part I), *Report* (1934), p. 66.

total membership of 250. They contend that, under a reasonable interpretation of the terms, the Depressed Classes are not very numerous in Bengal and there is no reason why they should have a representation in excess of their population ratio. The situation in the Punjab is somewhat similar. The Award made no provision for the Depressed Classes, but the Pact reserved for them 8 of the 43 general seats. As the Caste Hindus cannot win more than 8 of the special seats, their maximum membership will be less than one fourth of the total of 175.

While these issues were under discussion, preparations were also being made for the third and final session of the Round Table Conference. In order to save time, His Majesty's government suggested early in the summer (1932) that this meeting should be abandoned and the Joint Select Committee of Parliament on Indian Constitutional Reform appointed immediately, with powers to invite Indian delegates to attend their deliberations. The suggestion was received unfavorably in India, however, and the original plan was finally carried out. The conference was in session from November 17 to December 24, 1932. The Congress party and the British Labor party refused to participate, the former because it had reverted to its old policy of noncoöperation, and the latter because it felt that the agenda was too conservative. The personnel was otherwise very much the same as it had been in the previous sessions. Three main problems were considered at this meeting—safeguards, the terms under which the states would enter the federation, and the allocation of residuary legislative powers.

The term safeguards covers a wide field, including the Reserved Departments of the central government; the special responsibilities[19] of the Governor-General and the Provincial Governors; the control of finance, currency, and exchange; and the prevention of discrimination against British interests. These were controversial issues and there was a vigorous debate, but it had very little effect on the final result. The British

19. When the chief executive is vested with a special responsibility he may disregard the advice of his Ministers and override the legislature.

authorities laid down the law and refused to make any major concessions. The list of Reserved Subjects, which already included Defense and External Affairs, was extended to cover the Ecclesiastical Department. The army was to be kept entirely under executive control. The Governor-General would not be required to select a member of the legislature as the head of the Defense Department, there would be no statutory Defense Committee, no guarantee would be given that Indian troops should never be used outside of India without the consent of the Indian legislature. Every effort would be made to economize military expenditures and to continue the program of Indianization, but there could be no definite commitment on either of these subjects. The Governor-General and the Provincial Governors would have special responsibilities to prevent any grave menace to the peace and tranquility of India or any part thereof, to protect minorities, to safeguard the rights of the Public Services and to deal with a number of other subjects. The Governor-General would be given full powers to safeguard the financial stability and credit of the federation and a Reserve Bank, free from political influences, would be created as soon as possible to manage the problems of currency and exchange. British commercial interests would be protected against legislative discrimination by extending the special responsibilities of the Governor-General.

The state would be admitted into the federation on a voluntary basis. Any ruler who wished to participate would make an agreement with the Crown, styled the Instrument of Accession, in which he would indicate the subjects acceptable to him as federal in character. This meant that the powers of the federation would vary from one state to another and would be less extensive in the states as a whole than they would be in British India; applications for admission might of course be rejected by the Crown, if the terms were incompatible with the objects of the federation, but the conference did not attempt to define the minimum requirements. The discussion of federal finance was equally barren. So far as the states were concerned, the main fact that emerged was that they would not submit to direct taxation and would not surrender their special privileges without adequate compensation.

The allocation of residuary legislative power is primarily a British Indian problem. It was generally agreed that the present system should be followed in so far as it provides separate lists of central and provincial subjects. This is not a final solution, however, because it is inevitable that some subjects will be overlooked and that others will develop in the future. The residue may be small, but its allocation is likely to influence the character of the federation for many years to come. This is largely a communal issue. The Hindus would like to have the residuary powers delegated to the central legislature, but as they are now, while the Moslems would prefer to hand them over to the provinces. As no agreement could be reached, the question was left to His Majesty's government for settlement. Canada has one system and the United States has another and, if we may judge from their experience, it will not make much difference in the long run which solution is adopted.

The franchise, the judiciary, and a number of other topics were discussed with the same futile results. An effort was also made by delegates from British India to follow American precedents and have a Bill of Rights incorporated in the Constitution, but it was vetoed by the British authorities. His Majesty's government was hampered by the political situation. It was compelled to bid against Mr. Churchill for the support of the Tory party in the United Kingdom and, in doing so, it lost the support of the moderate element in India. At a meeting of the Central Council of the Unionist associations, held in London on February 28, 1933, a resolution condemning the government's Indian policy was rejected by a vote of 189 to 165. This was a victory, but the margin was close enough to accentuate the movement toward the Right. There was no other course possible. It would have been a waste of time and a disservice to India to draft a bill which Parliament would refuse to pass. From this time onward, the tendency was to emphasize the system of safeguards and treat it as a more or less permanent part of the Constitution and to say very little about the really broad powers and responsibilities that were being transferred to the people of India.

CHAPTER XIV

THE CONSTITUTION OF 1935

THE government's *Proposals for Indian Constitutional Reform*,[1] commonly called *The White Paper*, was issued on March 18, 1933. In analyzing this document, it will avoid confusion if we mention the additions and amendments subsequently recommended by the Joint Committee of Parliament and also consider the more important changes that were made during the progress of the Government of India Bill through Parliament. The Joint Committee was appointed in April, 1933, and was reorganized at the beginning of the new session of Parliament in the following November. It was composed of 32 members, 16 from each house, with the Marquis of Linlithgow as chairman. Seven delegates from the Indian States, 21 from Continental British India and 12 from Burma were invited to attend their deliberations. The meetings were held over a period of several months, hundreds of witnesses were examined, and Sir Samuel Hoare explained the intricate details of *The White Paper* proposals. The Report was published in November, 1934. The point of view of the Labor members of the committee was set forth in a Draft Report presented by Mr. Attlee, and a statement representing the minority recommendations of the Right-Wing Tories was published separately. There was also a Joint Memorandum prepared by the British Indian delegation.

A resolution accepting the recommendations of the Report

1. *Joint Committee on Indian Constitutional Reform* (Session 1933–34), Vol. I (Part I) *Report,* (Part II) *Proceedings;* Vol. II, *Records* (London, 1934). Mr. Attlee's Draft Report is printed in Vol. I (Part II) *Proceedings,* pp. 253–287. See also *Statement Representing the Minority Recommendations of the Marquis of Salisbury, K.G., Lord Middleton, M.C. . . . being Conservative Members of the Indian Committee opposed to the White Paper and the Majority Report* (London, 1934).

was approved by both houses and the Government of India Bill was introduced in the House of Commons on February 19, 1935. After a prolonged debate, the bill was finally passed and was signed by the King on August 2. The opposition was divided. The Right-Wing Tories felt that the bill went too far, while the Labor party and a small group of Liberals felt that it did not go far enough in the direction of Dominion Home Rule. The former were more successful. Although they were unable to defeat the bill, they forced the government to accept a series of amendments which emphasized its autocratic character. Other reactionary changes were also made in an effort to conciliate the rulers of the states who were becoming more lukewarm in their attitude toward the federation.

Although *The White Paper* is based on *The Simon Report*, the proceedings of the Round Table Conference, the Lothian Report, and a mass of other material, it is itself a masterpiece of brevity. The intention of the government was not to justify the proposals, but "to explain their exact nature and intended effect." This method has a serious disadvantage. The proposals relating to responsible government can be explained in a few words because the basic conception is familiar, but it takes considerable space to clarify the details of a system of safeguards which is an innovation in public law. The result is that a document which contains some very liberal features was made to appear even more reactionary than the political situation in the United Kingdom required. The authors seemed to ignore the fact that it would have a wide circulation in India.

The first proposal or rather the first assumption is that the present organic law of British India, which is a consolidation of statutes going back in some cases to the eighteenth century, would be repealed *in toto* and replaced by a new statute, to be called the Constitution Act. This act would be supplemented and made more flexible by Instruments of Instructions given to the Governor-General and the Governors of the provinces. As the Instruments, to all intents and purposes, will be a part of the Constitution, it was proposed that Parliament should have an opportunity to pass upon them before they are finally issued by the Crown. The Joint Committee approved this proposal and suggested as the appropriate procedure that the

Secretary of State should communicate to Parliament a draft of the proposed Instrument or of any subsequent amendments and that Parliament, if it sees fit, may present an address praying that the Instrument should issue in the form of the draft with such modifications as may be agreed upon by both houses.[2]

The federation will be composed of two classes of units, the provinces and the federated states. The provinces will come into the new system as a matter of course, there will be no right of secession[3] and, so far as the Governor's provinces are concerned, they will occupy the same constitutional position in relation to the federal government. The states, on the other hand, will enter at their own discretion and, if the fundamental character of the federation should ever be changed, they would presumably have a right to withdraw.[4] Those that do enter will not all be on an equal footing because the rulers will not be required to accept the same list of federal subjects.

The federal authority will, therefore, extend to the whole of

2. *The White Paper*, pp. 40, 54; *The Report of the Joint Committee*, p. 43; The Government of India Act, 1935, Section 13. This unprecedented concession to parliamentary control was perhaps partly designed to tie the hands of a future Labor government. The House of Lords will be able to prevent any radical alterations in the Instruments of Instructions.

3. The question of secession was involved in the discussion of the political future of Burma. Some of the Burmese politicians believed that Burma would reach her constitutional goal more quickly if she acquired provincial autonomy as a member of the federation and then seceded. The Joint Committee denounced this idea as "wholly impracticable" and affirmed that the British Indian delegation had ruled it out as "incompatible with the conception of Federation." *The Report*, p. 249.

4. It is possible, however, that the right of secession is barred by Section 6 (3) of the Government of India Act, 1935, which states that "A Ruler may, by a supplementary Instrument executed by him and accepted by His Majesty, vary the Instrument of Accession of his State by extending the functions which by virtue of that Instrument are exercisable by His Majesty or any Federal Authority in relation to his State." This may imply that he cannot restrict or withdraw altogether the functions that have already been granted.

British India and to the states which have acceded to the federation, in respect to those subjects which their rulers have agreed to accept as federal. The present territorial limits of India will, however, be reduced by the loss of Burma and the settlement of Aden. The problem of Burma will be considered later. The Joint Committee recommended and Parliament approved its separation from India before the federation is established. The settlement of Aden—the town and a small tract of adjacent territory—was formerly a part of the presidency of Bombay, but in 1932 it was brought under the direct control of the government of India as a Chief Commissioner's province. His Majesty's government has been responsible for its political and military affairs since 1917 and it is now proposed that it should also take charge of its civil administration. This is a logical arrangement because it unifies the administration of the settlement and brings it into harmony with the administration of the protectorate, which was already completely under the control of His Majesty's government. The local Indian community is opposed to the change, but it is popular with the Arab majority and Parliament has voted that it shall be carried out "on such date as His Majesty may by Order in Council appoint."

The date and the conditions for the inauguration of the new regime were discussed in both *The White Paper* and *The Report of the Joint Committee*. It was recognized that a considerable amount of preparatory work would have to be done after the Constitution Act was put on the Statute Book. It would be necessary, for example, to prepare the new electoral rolls, to delimit the new constituencies and to discuss with the princes their Instruments of Accession. The government still adhered to the policy announced at the close of the first session of the Round Table Conference that the accession of the states is an essential condition to the establishment of federation and the transfer of responsibility at the center. The time had now come to express this in a more definite form, especially as the princes had begun to lose some of their original enthusiasm for federation. It was therefore proposed that the federal system should not be put into operation until the rulers of states representing not less than half the aggregate population of the states and entitled to not less than half the seats to be allotted to the states in the federal upper chamber should have executed Instruments of Accession. A few financial prerequisites were also recommended. There must be a general condition of financial stability,[5] and a Reserve Bank, free from political influence, must have been set up by Indian legislation and be already in successful operation before the first Ministry is appointed.[6] If other requirements are satisfied and the financial and economic situation in the world at large should make it impossible to meet these conditions, His Majesty's government would reconsider the position, in consultation with the representatives of Indian opinion, and "determine in the light of the then circumstances what course should be pursued." The federation will be inaugurated by Royal Proclamation, but not until both houses of Parliament have presented an address to His Majesty with a prayer for its promulgation, a method of procedure that will enable Parliament to satisfy itself that all of the requirements have been fulfilled.

So far as British India is concerned, the first step in the establishment of the federation will be the creation of autonomous Governor's provinces and the assignment to them of a definite and exclusive field of governmental activity. Their

5. Under the Reserve Bank of India Act, passed by the Indian legislature in 1934, the control of the Bank was vested in a Central Board of Directors, consisting of a governor, two deputy-governors, a government official and four directors, all appointed by the Governor-General in Council, and eight directors elected by the shareholders. Sections 152 and 153 of the Government of India Act of 1935 provide that the appointments which were to be made by the Governor-General in Council shall be made by the Governor-General at his discretion and that no bill or amendment which affects the coinage or currency of the federation or the constitution or functions of the bank may be introduced into the legislature without his previous sanction.

6. The Report of the Committee of the third Round Table Conference on Financial Safeguards laid down the following specific conditions: "That the Indian Budgetary position should be assured, that the existing short-term debt both in London and in India should be substantially reduced, that adequate reserves should have been accumulated, and that India's normal export surplus should have been restored."

powers will no longer be derived by devolution from the central government, but will be based on a direct grant from the Crown. All of the rights, authority, and jurisdiction of the Crown in British India will be resumed and redistributed between the provinces and the federation. The problem of distributing legislative powers will be solved by preparing three lists of subjects, federal, provincial and concurrent, and making "appropriate provisions for resolving conflicts of laws." The need for a concurrent list was explained by the Joint Committee as follows:

> Experience has shown, both in India and elsewhere, that there are certain matters which cannot be allocated exclusively to a Central or to a Provincial Legislature, and for which, though it is often desirable that provincial legislation should make provision, it is equally necessary that the Central Legislature should also have a legislative jurisdiction, to enable it in some cases to secure uniformity in the main principles of law throughout the country, in others to guide and encourage provincial effort, and in others again to provide remedies for mischiefs arising in the provincial sphere but extending or liable to extend beyond the boundaries of a single Province. Instances of the first are provided by the subject matter of the great Indian Codes, of the second by such matters as labour legislation, and of the third by legislation for the prevention and control of epidemic disease.[7]

When there is a conflict in the concurrent field, the central legislation will prevail unless the provincial law is more recent and "having been reserved for the consideration of the Governor-General or for the signification of His Majesty's pleasure, has received the assent of the Governor-General or of His Majesty." In a case of this kind, a bill or amendment overriding the provincial statute cannot be introduced in the federal legislature without the previous sanction of the Governor-General in his discretion. Residuary powers will be allocated by the Governor-General, which means that whenever there is need for legislation on a subject not included on any of the lists, he will decide the question of jurisdiction. As this involves the power to determine whether a given legislative

7. *The Report,* pp. 30–31.

project is covered by the enumeration as it stands, the Joint Committee assumed that in practice the Governor-General would seek an advisory opinion from the Federal Court.

Owing to the uncertain attitude of the princes, the government admitted that provincial autonomy might have to be introduced before the establishment of the federation. Therefore, a transitional arrangement was proposed under which the central government as it now exists would remain substantially unchanged, although it would necessarily be deprived of much of its range of authority in the province. In accepting this proposal, the Joint Committee suggested three important modifications: first, the statutory distribution of legislative powers and financial powers and resources should be the same as that contemplated under the federation; second, in order to settle legislative and financial disputes arising between the center and the provinces, a court should be established with the same powers in this sphere as it was proposed to confer on the Federal Court; and finally, the Governor-General in person should exercise the same control over the Provincial Governors that will be vested in him when the federation is fully established.[8]

The description of the federal center in *The White Paper* is a marvel of condensation:

It is proposed to set up a Federal Legislature, consisting of elected representatives of British India and of representatives of Indian States to be appointed by their Rulers, and a Federal Executive consisting of the Governor-General representing the Crown, aided and advised by a Council of Ministers, who will be responsible (subject to the qualifications to be explained later) to the Legislature so composed, and to endow these authorities with powers and functions in relation to British India and with such powers and functions in relation to the States as the States-

8. *The Report,* pp. 242–244. These recommendations and a few other transitory provisions were incorporated in Part XIII of the Government of India Act, 1935. The Federal Court, the Federal Public Service Commission, and the Federal Railway Authority are to be organized under those names and are to perform in relation to British India the functions which, by or under the act, they will perform in relation to the federation when it is finally established.

members of the Federation will formally accept as being of full force and effect within their territories. Full liberty will of course be reserved to the Crown to refuse to accept the accession of any State to the Federation if it is sought on terms incompatible with the scheme of Federation embodied in the Constitution Act.

All powers now "appertaining and incidental to the government of British India will vest in the Crown" and will be exercised on behalf of the Crown by the Governor-General, the Provincial Governors and other authorities established under the new Constitution.

The powers vested in the Crown in relation to the States, and now exercisable through the Governor-General of India in Council, except in so far as they are requisite for Federal purposes and the Rulers have assented to their transfer to the appropriate Federal authority for those purposes, will be exercised by the Crown's representative in his capacity of Viceroy, and these powers will be outside of the scope of the Federal Constitution.

In other words, *The White Paper* proposed that the chief representative of the Crown should occupy a dual position, serving under the Constitution as Governor-General and outside it as Viceroy. The Joint Committee approved the substance of this recommendation, but because the two offices would be held by the same person, it thought "that the title of Viceroy should attach to him in his double capacity." The Government of India Act, 1935, follows the usual parliamentary tradition and ignores the title of Viceroy altogether. There will be two distinct offices, one filled by the Governor-General and the other by His Majesty's representative for the exercise of the functions of the Crown in its relation with Indian States, but "it shall be lawful for His Majesty to appoint one person to fill both the said offices."

The central executive will be a dyarchy, although a certain amount of unity will be secured through the concentration of activity in the hands of the Governor-General. He will have supreme command of the military, naval, and air forces in India, "subject to the power of His Majesty to appoint a Commander-in-Chief to exercise in relation to those forces such functions as may be assigned to him." He will be personally responsible to His Majesty's government and ultimately to Parliament for the exercise of powers relating to Reserved Subjects, to the administration of British Baluchistan, and to a wide range of matters left by the act to his discretion. To assist in the administration of Reserved Subjects, he will be authorized to appoint at his discretion not more than three Councilors, whose salaries and conditions of service will be determined by His Majesty's government. They will be *ex officio* members of both houses of the legislature, but will not have the right to vote. They will be encouraged to consult and coöperate with the Ministers, but they will not belong to the Ministry and will not share its responsibility to the legislature.

There will be three Reserved Departments—Defense, External Affairs, and Ecclesiastical Affairs. They will be controlled by the Governor-General and their expenditures will not be submitted to the vote of the legislature. The Department of Defense will be the most important and its administration will probably be the chief source of friction. The British Indian delegation, in its Joint Memorandum, called attention to the fact that "the reservation of the Department of Defense to the Governor-General will have the effect of depriving Ministers of the influence over Army policy which at the present time Indian Members of the Governor-General's Council are able to exert." It suggested therefore (1) that the Councilor in charge of the department should always be a nonofficial Indian, and preferably a member of the legislature; (2) that the control now exercised by the Finance Member and the Finance Department should be continued; and (3) that all questions relating to army policy and the army budget should be reconsidered by the Councilor and the Ministers, although the final decision would rest with the Governor-General. The Joint Committee rejected the first two suggestions and specifically recommended that the Subdepartment of Military Finance and Military Accounts should be removed from the Finance Department to the Department of Defense. It agreed that the Ministry should be consulted before the army budget is laid before the legislature, but insisted that the personal responsibility of the Governor-General must remain unimpaired.

The Joint Committee also considered the relations between the Department of Defense and other government agencies, the Indianization of the army and the problem of lending Indian troops to His Majesty's government for service abroad. The Department of Defense, especially in times of emergency, may have to take charge of transportation facilities, control the movement of persons and goods, and assume a variety of functions that will encroach upon the work of other departments. "In all matters of this kind where there is a difference of opinion with other authorities, the final responsibility for a decision, if defense policy is concerned, must rest with the Governor-General, his views must prevail, and he must have adequate means of giving effect to them."[9] As for the Indianization of the army, the Joint Committee agreed that the scheme introduced in 1931 should be given a thorough trial, but it rejected the suggestion of the British-Indian delegation that the program should be completed within a time-limit of twenty to twenty-five years. "It is in our judgment impossible to include in the Constitution Act or in any other statute a provision for the complete Indianization of the army within a specified period of time." Its recommendation in regard to the employment of Indian troops outside of India was even more conservative. If the Governor-General decides that the troops can be spared and that the occasion involves the defense of India in the widest sense of the word, he will act on his own responsibility. If he believes that the defense of India is not involved, he will submit the request for troops to his Ministry and will give "the greatest weight" to their advice before reaching his final decision. This would seem to indicate that he will still have the power to lend Indian troops to His Majesty's government for service anywhere in the world without securing the approval of the Indian legislature.

9. *The Report,* p. 97. If the conflict arises with a Federal Department, the Governor-General will act under the special responsibility conferred upon him in respect to any matter affecting the administration of a Reserved Department. If the trouble is local, he will avail himself of his power "to give direction as to the manner in which the executive authority in the Provinces is to be exercised in relation to any matter affecting the administration of a Federal subject."

The Department of External Affairs will deal with the foreign countries and the frontier trade of India, but not with the British Dominions or with the Indian States in matters in which they have not agreed to federate. The relations with the Dominions will be subject to ministerial and legislative control; the nonfederal relations with the states will be handled outside of the Constitution Act altogether by the Governor-General in his capacity as His Majesty's representative for the exercise of the functions of the Crown in its relations with the Indian States. The Joint Committee considered a suggestion that trade with foreign countries should be made by the Minister of Commerce, but it decided that all negotiations with foreign countries should be conducted by the Foreign Office or Department of External Affairs as they are in the United Kingdom. In concluding agreements of this character, the Foreign Secretary always consults the Board of Trade and it was assumed that the Governor-General would in like manner consult the Minister of Commerce in India. This may be true, but the analogy itself is false. In the United Kingdom, both departments are subject to the same legislative control, whereas in India one is responsible to the federal legislature and the other to the Imperial Parliament.

The Ecclesiastical Department is an outgrowth of the obligation imposed by the charters of the East India Company to supply chaplains and houses of worship for the employees. When the Company was dissolved in 1858 it became the duty of the government of India to provide out of the Indian revenues "for the spiritual needs of British troops stationed in India and, so far as circumstances admit, of the European members of the Civil Services." The Anglican Church in India, which became an autonomous body in 1927, also receives a certain amount of financial support. The Labor members of the Joint Committee were strongly opposed to the continuation of this system and especially to the proposal in *The White Paper* that the Ecclesiastical Department should be Reserved.

We think it would be very much better to abolish this Department and include religious ministrations as an integral part of the Army administration. We would go further and propose that so long as we have an Army and Services in India whose spiritual needs are entirely different from those of the peoples amongst whom they serve, it would be a gracious act on our part if the necessary expenses were placed on British instead of Indian revenues. We are in any event entirely opposed to their being included as a Reserved Department of the Government of India.[10]

The Joint Committee did not accept this suggestion, although it recommended that the Constitution Act should specify the maximum annual limit for ecclesiastical expenditures. The limit has been fixed at 42 lakhs of rupees (£315,000), but this does not include pensions paid to retired members of the Ecclesiastical Service.

British Baluchistan will be administered by the Governor-General acting through the agency of the Chief Commissioners. Its position will be the same as the Chief Commissioners' other provinces except that the Governor-General will act in his discretion and not on the advice of his ministers. No act of the federal legislature will apply to British Baluchistan unless the Governor-General in his discretion by public notification so directs, and in giving such directions he may make any exception or modifications that he thinks fit. He will also have powers to issue Regulations which, in case of conflict, will supersede any act of the federal legislature or any existing Indian law which is for the time being applicable to the province.[11]

In all other fields of federal activity, the principle of responsible government will be applied with certain restrictions. A Council of Ministers, not exceeding ten in number, will be appointed by the Governor-General, who will be enjoined in his Instrument of Instructions (a) to select those persons who will be best qualified collectively to command the confidence of the legislature and (b) to include in the Ministry so far as possible members of important minority communities and representatives of the states. The Ministers must be members or must, within six months, become members of one or the other of the federal legislative chambers. They will be encouraged to

10. Vol. I (Part II), *Proceedings,* p. 275. Minority Report.

11. The Government of India Act, 1935, Sec. 95.

consult and coöperate with the Governor-General's Councilors, but they alone will be responsible to the legislature.

In dealing with Transferred Subjects, the Governor-General will be guided by the advice of his Ministers "unless so to be guided would in his judgment be inconsistent with the fulfilment of any of the purposes" for which he is declared by the Constitution Act to be charged with a special responsibility. In other words, he will be required to safeguard certain essential interests against ministerial encroachment. This will usually be done simply by refusing to accept the advice of the Ministers, but, as we have already seen, in discussing the Department of Defense, positive action may be necessary in a matter affecting a Reserved Department. The special responsibilities are enumerated as follows: (a) the prevention of any grave menace to the peace or tranquility of India, or any part thereof; (b) the safeguarding of the financial stability and credit of the federation; (c) the safeguarding of the legitimate interests of minorities; (d) "the securing to, and to the dependents of, persons who are or have been members of the Public Services of any rights provided or preserved for them by or under this Act and the safeguarding of their legitimate interests"; (e) the enforcement in the executive field of the provisions made in another part of the act to prevent legislative discrimination against certain British and Burmese interests; (f) the prevention of actions which would subject goods imported from the United Kingdom or Burma to discriminatory or penal treatment; (g) the protection of the rights of any Indian state and the rights and dignity of its ruler; and (h) "the securing that the due discharge of his functions with respect to matters with respect to which he is by or under this Act required to act in his discretion, or to exercise his individual judgment, is not prejudiced or impeded by any course of action taken with respect to any other matter."[12]

This is a long list and some of the items are expressed in very broad terms. It should also be observed that if any question arises whether any matter is or is not a matter as respects which the Governor-General is required to act in his discretion or to exercise his individual judgment, his decision is final and

12. *Idem,* Sec. 12.

the validity of anything that he does cannot be called in question on that ground.[13] The British Indian delegation especially objected to (a) and asked that it should be defined more clearly, but the Joint Committee held that the Governor-General, as the authority responsible for the defense of India, must be free to act, according to his own judgment, in dealing with any matter that threatens to affect the peace or tranquility of the country. The delegation was also disturbed by the proposal that the Governor-General should appoint a Financial Adviser to assist him in the discharge of his responsibility for safeguarding the financial stability and credit of the federal government. It was, however, made clear that the Financial Adviser would not interfere in the day-to-day administration of financial business and would not give advice to the Ministers except at their request. The Governor-General will appoint the Financial Adviser at his discretion, but, after the first appointment, he will be required to consult his Ministers as to the person to be selected. In connection with (c) there was some doubt expressed as to what minorities were affected and what exactly were their legitimate interests. The government refused to change the phraseology or to give it a statutory "definition," but it indicated in the course of the debates in Parliament that the intention was to include the ordinary racial and religious minorities and to safeguard interests of a reasonable character. In other words, the protection is not confined to purely legal rights and it does not cover political minorities. There are many other obscurities which will probably be clarified in time by the precedents established by the Governor-General and the Provincial Governors[14] in dealing with specific cases.

In addition to his functions in dealing with Reserved Subjects and British Baluchistan and the exercise of his special responsibilities, the Governor-General has a wide range of ordinary legislative powers and a few special emergency pow-

13. *Idem,* Sec. 9 (3).

14. With the exceptions of (b) and (f), which deal exclusively with federal problems, all of the special responsibilities conferred on the Governor-General are also conferred on the Governors of the provinces.

ers. The special powers are also mainly legislative in character, but there is one fundamental safeguard which covers the whole field of governmental activity. If any situation arises in which the government of the federation cannot be carried on in accordance with the Constitution Act, the Governor-General may by proclamation "(a) declare that his functions shall to such extent as may be specified in the Proclamation be exercised by him in his discretion; (b) assume to himself all or any of the powers vested in or exercisable by any Federal body or authority," and do practically anything which he regards as necessary or desirable for giving effect to the objects of the proclamation. He is forbidden, however, "to assume to himself any of the powers vested in or exercisable by the Federal Court or to suspend, either in whole or in part, the operation of any provision of this Act relating to the Federal Court." The proclamation will ordinarily expire in six months, but it may be extended by resolutions of both houses of Parliament for a maximum period of three years. At the end of that period, the proclamation will cease to operate and the government will again be carried on in accordance with the other provisions of the Constitution Act. The act may of course be amended to meet the emergency, but no amendment will be valid if it alters the conditions under which the rulers of the states have acceded to the federation. This would seem to indicate that if obstructive tactics are employed for three years the government will have to yield because it cannot take effective action without violating a contract with the rulers of the member states. The term "continuous period of three years" may perhaps be utilized, however, as authority to issue a new proclamation within decent interval after the old one has expired.

In view of the enormous powers and responsibilities which the Governor-General must exercise in his discretion or according to his individual judgment, it is obvious that he is expected to be a kind of superman. He must have tact, courage, and ability and be endowed with an infinite capacity for hard work. "We have put into this Bill many safeguards," said Sir Robert Horne in a speech in the House of Commons on February 19, 1935, "but all of those safeguards revolve about a single individual, and that is the Viceroy. He is the linch-pin of the whole system. He is the keystone of all this mighty fabric. If the Viceroy fails, nothing can save the system you have set up." This speech reflected the point of view of the die-hard Tories who were horrified by the prospect that some day there might be a Viceroy appointed by a Labor government. Two methods of averting this calamity were proposed. One provided that the Governor-General and the Governors of the provinces should be selected by an Indian Advisory Committee, composed of the Prime Minister, the Secretary of State, and the former Viceroys. The other would have given the Governor-General a kind of judicial tenure by providing that he should be removed from office only by a vote of both houses of Parliament. These suggestions were not accepted by the government and were defeated in the House of Commons.

The central legislature will be composed of the Crown, represented by the Governor-General, and two chambers, to be called the Council of State and the Federal Assembly. *The White Paper* proposed that the Council of State should have a maximum of 260 members, of whom 150 should be elected in British India, not more than 100 should be appointed by the rulers of the state-members of the federation and not more than 10 (nonofficials) should be nominated by the Governor-General. The Federal Assembly should have a maximum membership of 375: 250 elected in British India and not more than 125 appointed by the rulers. These proposals were approved by the Joint Committee with one slight modification. In order that the states might have a better representation in the upper house, the committee recommended that the Governor-General should nominate only 6 members (all from British India) and that the 4 seats thus released should be allotted to the states, which would give them 104 seats or 40 per cent of the total membership.

The White Paper proposed that the British Indian elective seats in the Council of State should be allotted on the following basis: 18 to each of the 6 largest provinces (Bengal, the United Provinces, Madras, Bihar, the Punjab, and Bombay); 8 to the Central Provinces and Berar; 5 each to Assam, Orissa, Sind, and the Frontier Province; 1 each to Delhi, Coorg,

Ajmer-Merwara, and British Baluchistan; and 10 to be chosen on a nonprovincial basis. Theoretically, the provincial seats were noncommunal, but a method of elections was proposed which was intended to give the Moslems one third of the total number of British Indian seats and to secure adequate representation for the Sikhs. Two of the nonprovincial seats were allocated to Indian-Christians, 1 to Anglo-Indians, and 7 to Europeans. Of the Assembly seats, 37 each were allotted to Bengal (50.1), Madras (45.6), and the United Provinces (48.4); 30 each to Bombay (18.0), Bihar (32.4), and the Punjab (23.6); 15 to the Central Provinces and Berar (15.5); 10 to Assam (8.6); 5 each to Orissa (6.7), Sind (3.9), and the North-West Frontier Province (2.4); 2 to Delhi (0.6); 1 each to Ajmer-Merwara (0.6), Coorg (0.2), and British Baluchistan (0.5); and 4 were nonprovincial.[15] There were 105 general (Hindu) seats, of which 19 were reserved for the Scheduled Castes or Depressed Classes. Eighty-two seats were allotted to the Moslems, 6 to the Sikhs in the Punjab, 8 to the Indian Christians, 4 to the Anglo-Indians, and 8 to the Europeans. There were 9 special seats for women, 11 for Commerce and Industry,[16] 7 for Landholders, and 10 for Labor. So far as the states were concerned, the government was not at that time prepared to make specific proposals, but it suggested that the apportionment for the Council of State should be based on the rank and importance of the states as indicated by the dynastic salute and other factors and that the apportionment for the Assembly should be based mainly on population.

These proposals were accepted by Parliament, with one alteration, and were incorporated in the First Schedule of the Constitution Act. On the recommendation of the Joint Committee, the six large provinces were divided into two groups for purposes of representation in the Council of State, 20 members each being allotted to Bengal, Madras, and the United

15. The population of each province in millions is given in parentheses. The nonprovincial seats were in the special group, three being allotted to Commerce and Industry and one to Labor.

16. On the basis of the present membership of the bodies that elect these members, it is expected that 6 will be Europeans and 5 Indians.

Provinces, and 16 each to Bombay, Bihar, and the Punjab. It was necessary to allocate the seats in the Council of State on a communal basis when Parliament decided in favor of direct elections. While this was being done, the failure of *The White Paper* and *The Report of the Joint Committee* to provide for the representation of women in the Council of State was also rectified. Of the 140 provincial elective seats, 75 were allotted to Caste Hindus (general seats), 6 to the Scheduled Castes,[17] 49 to the Moslems, 4 to the Sikhs and 6 to women. The allocation of the 10 nonprovincial seats—2 to Indian-Christians, 1 to Anglo-Indians and 7 to Europeans—has already been mentioned.

The allocation is unfair to the large provinces and also to the Hindus. A member of the Council of State will represent 200,000 people in Coorg, 600,000 in Delhi, 1,125,000 in Bombay, and 2,500,000 in Bengal. The corresponding figures for the Assembly will be 200,000 in Coorg, 300,000 in Delhi, 600,000 in Bombay, and 1,350,000 in Bengal. The Hindus will be underrepresented in nearly all of the provinces, but their position will be especially bad in the Punjab, where they will have 6 representatives in a Federal Assembly delegation of 30, and in Bengal, where they will have 10 in a delegation of 37. In British India as a whole, they are allotted 105 communal (general) seats, of which 19 are reserved for the Scheduled Castes. This means that Caste Hindus, who constitute about 60 per cent of the population of India (excluding Burma), will elect from their own ranks only 34.4 per cent of the British Indian membership and less than 23 per cent of the total membership of the Federal Assembly. It should be noted, however, that they will win most of the special seats, that they will probably dominate the Scheduled Caste members, and that, on communal issues, they are likely to be supported by the representatives from the Hindu states.

The method of electing the members of the central legislature has been a subject of controversy since 1919 when Parliament rejected the recommendations of the Southborough

17. In the Assembly the seats reserved for the Scheduled Castes are included in the general allotment; in the Council of State they are separate.

Committee and established a system of direct elections for both houses. This system has been in effect now for nearly two decades and it is strongly supported by Indian public opinion. The other side of the question was, however, very ably presented by the Simon Commission and it would probably be safe to conclude that some form of indirect election would be preferable from the point of view of constitutional efficiency. But it is doubtful whether the advantages are sufficient to warrant the risk of forcing upon the people of India a system to which they are bitterly opposed. It is the old question which has come up many times before, is it better to give the Indians what they want or what the British think they ought to have? It might also be asked whether it is wise to impose an unnecessary handicap upon a Constitution which can succeed only if it wins a measure of popular support.

The White Paper proposed a system of indirect elections for the Council of State and direct elections for the Assembly, but the Joint Committee recommended the indirect method for both houses. Parliament approved the spirit, though not the form, of *The White Paper* proposal and the plan finally adopted provides for direct elections for most of the members of the Council of State and indirect elections for the Assembly. The Council of State will be a permanent body not subject to dissolution, but the term of service will be nine years and as near as may be one third of the members will retire every three years. Every Federal Assembly will continue for five years unless it is dissolved before the expiration of that period.

The general, Sikh, and Moslem seats in the Council of State will be filled by direct election in communal territorial constituencies. The other elective seats will all be filled by indirect methods of one kind or another. In any province in which a seat is reserved for a woman, she will be chosen by the members, both men and women, of the provincial legislature. In any province in which a seat is allotted to a representative of the Scheduled Castes, he or she will be chosen by the Scheduled Caste members of the provincial legislature. Persons to fill seats allotted to Anglo-Indians, Europeans, and Indian Christian communities will be chosen by "Electoral Colleges, consisting of such Anglo-Indians, Europeans and Indian Christians, as the case may be, as are members of the Legislative Council of any Governor's Province or of the Legislative Assembly of any Governor's Province." The member from British Baluchistan will be chosen "in such manner as may be prescribed." The six British Indian members appointed by the Governor-General to constitute "a small group of the elder statesmen type" will be chosen by him in his discretion, apparently without any communal or geographical restrictions.

The seats in the Federal Assembly allotted to a Governor's province as general, Sikh, or Moslem seats will be filled by the votes of those who hold respectively general, Sikh, or Moslem seats in the Provincial Assembly. This is subject to the proviso that in the North-West Frontier Province the holders of Sikh seats, and in any province in which seats are reserved for representatives of backward areas or backward tribes the holders of those seats shall, for the purposes of this election, be deemed to hold general seats. The general seats reserved for the Scheduled Castes will be filled in accordance with the Poona Pact, under which four candidates will be nominated for each seat so reserved and the final choice will be confined to that list. The primary for this purpose will consist of the successful candidates at the last primary election held for the purpose of selecting candidates for the seats in the Provincial Assembly reserved for the members of the Scheduled Castes.[18]

The nine special seats for women will be filled by the vote of an electoral college composed of the women members of the Legislative Assemblies of the Governor's provinces.[19] At least two of these seats must be filled by Moslems and one by an In-

18. This complicated arrangement may be clarified by taking a concrete example. There will be seven Scheduled Caste seats in the Provincial Assembly of Assam. For each of these seats four candidates will be nominated, making a total panel of twenty-eight. Only seven of them can be elected, but the entire number will constitute a primary to nominate candidates from whom the Assam Scheduled Caste members of the Federal Assembly will be made by the forty-seven members who hold general seats in the Assam Assembly.

19. There will be at least forty-one members of this electoral college because that is the number of seats reserved for women in the various Provincial Assemblies.

dian-Christian. The Anglo-Indian, European, and Indian-Christian seats will be filled by the votes of electoral colleges consisting respectively of such persons as hold Anglo-Indian, European, or Indian-Christian seats in the Legislative Assemblies of the Governor's provinces.[20] The Indian-Christian electoral college will use the single transferable vote in choosing its two representatives from Madras in order to secure representation for both Catholics and Protestants. The Commerce and Industry members will be chosen by the Chambers of Commerce and other similar associations, the Landholder members by special landholding constituencies and the Labor members "by such organizations, or in such constituencies and in accordance with such manner of voting as may be prescribed." The Joint Committee believed that the Labor seats "should be allocated in part to special labour constituencies," and this will probably be done. The representative from Coorg will be chosen by the local Legislative Council and the representatives from the Chief Commissioners' other provinces "in such manner as may be prescribed."

The distribution of the seats in the federal legislature allotted to the states is based on a plan prepared by the Governor-General in 1934. The principle followed is that laid down in *The White Paper*, namely, that, in the case of the Council of State, the allocation should take account of the relative rank and importance of the states as indicated by the dynastic salute and other factors, and, in the case of the Assembly, it should be based mainly on population. The general results obtained by these tests are much alike, but there are a few striking differences. Although 34 states will have continuous sepa-

20. The difference between these bodies and those described above in connection with the elections to the Council of State may be illustrated by taking the European community as an example. The European electoral college for the Federal Assembly will consist only of the European *communal* members of the Provincial Legislative Assemblies. The college for the Council of State will include in addition (a) other European members of the Provincial Legislative Assemblies (those representing Commerce and Industry, Mining and Planting, for example) and (b) all European members of the Legislative Councils in the bicameral provinces.

rate representation in both houses, 10 others will have it only in the Council of State and 10 will have it only in the Assembly. Five states—Kalat, Bikaner, Bhopal, Cochin, and Kholapur—will each have two seats in the Council of State and only one in the Assembly. Kalat, with a population of 342,101 (1931) will have a representation in the Council of State equal to that of Travancore, which has a population of 5,095,973.

The 104 seats in the Council of State will be divided into three categories: (a) those to be filled continuously by one state, (b) those to be filled in alternation by the representatives of groups of minor states and (c) those to be filled by representatives of groups of minor states. In category (a) there will be 69 seats distributed among 44 states. Of the states whose rulers are entitled to a salute of 21 guns, Hyderabad will have 5 seats, and Mysore, Kashmir, Gwalior, and Baroda will each have 3. The six 19-gun states and the 7 largest 17-gun states will each have 2 seats while 26 states in the 13-, 15-, and 17-gun class will each have 1 seat. For the purpose of filling the seats in category (b) a number of small states will be divided into groups of 2, 3, 4, or 5 members and the rulers in each group will alternate annually in appointing the group representative. The rulers may, however, with the approval of the Governor-General in his discretion, make a joint appointment for a period of three years. Category (c) will include 2 seats to be filled by persons chosen by the rulers of a large number of very small states scattered all over India.

The 125 state seats in the Assembly will be divided along similar lines. In category (a) 16 seats will be allotted to Hyderabad, 7 to Mysore, 5 to Travancore, 4 each to Kashmir and Gwalior, 3 each to Baroda and Jaipur, 2 each to Udaipur, Jodhpur, Indore, Rewa, and Patiala, and 1 each to 32 other states. In category (b) the rulers will make joint appointments for the duration of the Assembly instead of following the principle of annual rotation. There will be 11 seats in category (c), 3 to be filled by a group of states in Orissa, 3 by a group in the Central Provinces, and 5 by the group mentioned in category (c) of the Council of State, which for this purpose will be divided into 5 subgroups.

When the federation is first organized there will be vacant

seats in both houses because of the nonaccession of the states to which they are allotted. If they remain unfilled the position of the acceding states will be prejudiced in relation to the British Indian side of the legislature and there will also be a diminution of the conservative influence which the states are supposed to exert. The Joint Committee considered this problem and, on its recommendation, it was provided that the representatives of the acceding states should be authorized to elect additional representatives in both houses up to half the number of state seats which remain unfilled. This privilege will expire at the end of twenty years or earlier, if, as the result of additional accessions, 90 per cent of the seats allotted to the states are filled.

So far as the essential facts are concerned, the procedure in the federal legislature and the relations between the chambers and the Governor-General may be described in a few sentences. All bills, except those relating to finance, may originate in either chamber. When the chambers disagree over the enactment of a bill, the Governor-General may summon them to meet in a joint session and the bill may then be passed by a majority of the total number of members of both chambers present and voting. The previous sanction of the Governor-General will still be required for the introduction of certain legislative proposals. The list as given in Section 108 (1) includes any bill or amendment which (a) repeals, amends, or is repugnant to any provision of any Act of Parliament extending to British India; or (b) repeals, amends, or is repugnant to any Governor-General's or Governor's act or any ordinance promulgated in his discretion by the Governor-General or a Governor; or (c) affects matters as respects which the Governor-General is required to act in his discretion; or (d) repeals, amends, or affects any act relating to any police force; or (e) affects the procedure for criminal proceedings in which European British subjects are concerned; or (f) subjects persons not resident in British India to greater taxation than persons resident in British India or subjects companies not wholly controlled and managed in British India to greater taxation than companies wholly controlled and managed therein; or (g) affects the grant of relief from federal taxation on incomes in respect of income taxed or taxable in the United Kingdom. There are other items mentioned in various parts of the act which also belong in this category. Section 153, for example, provides that "no Bill or amendment which affects the coinage or currency of the Federation or the constitution or functions of the Reserve Bank of India shall be introduced into or moved in either Chamber of the Federal Legislature without the previous sanction of the Governor-General in his discretion."

When a bill has been passed by the chambers, the Governor-General may in his discretion (a) assent to it in His Majesty's name, (b) withhold assent, (c) reserve it for the signification of His Majesty's pleasure, or (d) return it to the chambers with a message requesting its reconsideration and suggesting alterations which will make it acceptable. An act assented to by the Governor-General may be disallowed by His Majesty within twelve months, in which case it becomes void on the day when the official notification of the disallowance is published. This should happen very rarely because the Governor-General can always consult the Secretary of State before he acts on a bill that is laid before him or he can reserve the bill for signification of His Majesty's pleasure. It is really a reserve power which will be used only when the Governor-General yields too much to legislative pressure. A bill reserved for the signification of His Majesty's pleasure will not become an act of the federal legislature unless and until, within twelve months, it receives His Majesty's approval.

In addition to his special responsibility for safeguarding the financial stability and credit of the federal government, the Governor-General will have wide financial powers of a more positive character. In respect of every financial year, he will cause to be laid before both chambers an estimate of the receipts and expenditures for that year. Section 33 (3) of the Constitution Act gives a detailed list of the items of expenditure charged upon the revenues. It includes among other things the salary and allowances of the Governor-General and his Ministers, Councilors, and Financial Adviser; the salaries, allowances, and pensions of the judges of the Federal Court; the debt charges of the federation; expenditures incurred by the Governor-General in the discharge of his functions with respect to Reserved Subjects; expenditures incurred in discharge of the functions of the Crown in its relations with Indian States; any sums required to satisfy any judgment, decree, or award of any court or arbitral tribunal; and finally any other expenditure declared by the Constitution Act or any act of the federal legislature to be charged on the revenues. These expenditures are all nonvotable and those affecting the remuneration of the Governor-General and the relations with the Indian States are not subject to discussion. All other estimates of expenditure must be submitted in the form of demands for grants to the Federal Assembly and therefore to the Council of State. But even in this field the control exercised by the chambers is subject to a serious limitation.[21] The Governor-General may restore a demand that has been refused or reduced "if in his opinion the refusal or reduction would affect the due discharge of any of his special responsibilities." A bill or amendment imposing or increasing any tax regulating the borrowing of money or declaring any expenditure to be chargeable on the revenues of the federation can be introduced or moved only on the recommendation of the Governor-General. If it is a bill and not merely an amendment it can be introduced only by the Federal Assembly.

The Governor-General will be able in an emergency to exercise full legislative powers. If at any time when the federal legislature is not in session he is satisfied that circumstances exist which render it necessary for him to take immediate action, he may promulgate such ordinances as the circumstances appear to require. Every such ordinance will be laid before the legislature and will cease to operate at the expiration of six weeks from the re-assembly of the legislature or earlier, if resolutions disapproving it are passed by both chambers. Two courses are open to the Governor-General if he feels that decisive action is necessary to enable him "to discharge his functions in so far as he is by or under this Act required in the

21. A demand rejected by the Assembly will not be submitted to the Council of State unless the Governor-General so decides, but otherwise the functions of the two houses in regard to expenditure are practically the same.

exercise thereof to act in his discretion or to exercise his individual judgment." He may (a) promulgate ordinances which will normally continue in operation for not more than six months, but may be extended for a further period of six months or (b) explain the circumstances in a message to the legislature and then enact as a Governor-General's act the legislation that he deems essential. In the latter case he may act immediately or attach to his message a draft of the bill which he considers necessary and give the legislature a month to decide whether it wishes to coöperate. All of these ordinances and Governor-General's acts have the same force and effect, and are subject to disallowance in the same manner, as an act of the federal legislature.

There are also legislative restrictions designed to prevent discrimination against British imports and British commercial interests in India. The fiscal relations between India and the United Kingdom since 1921 have been based on a Fiscal Convention, the essence of which is that His Majesty's government will not interfere with tariff legislation when the government and legislature of India are in agreement.[22] This has not been satisfactory to either party. The duties on British cloth were reduced while the legislature was not in session. The convention will lapse when the new Constitution goes into effect so the Joint Committee recommended that the Governor-General should have a special responsibility to prevent any action, legislative or administrative, which would subject British goods, imported into India from the United Kingdom, to discriminating or penal treatment. Parliament accepted this recommendation and extended it to cover goods of Burmese origin. As the exact scope of this special responsibility cannot be expressed in statutory language, the committee further recommended that the Governor-General's Instrument of Instructions should give him full and clear guidance. It should be made clear that the Governor-General and the legislature will have the power to develop their own fiscal and economic policy and to negotiate agreements with the United Kingdom or other countries for the securing of mutual tariff conces-

22. For a more detailed discussion of this subject see chap. vi, "Economic and Financial Grievances."

sions, but it will be the duty of the Governor-General to intervene in tariff legislation or in the negotiation of tariff agreements, if, in his opinion "the intention of the policy contemplated is to subject trade between the United Kingdom and India to restrictions conceived, not in the economic interests of India but with the object of injuring the interests of the United Kingdom." It should also be made clear that the special responsibility covers the imposition of prohibitory tariffs or restrictions, even though they apply equally to all countries, if the Governor-General believes that they are conceived with the object of injuring the interests of the United Kingdom.

The provisions relating to other forms of discrimination are more concrete and are embodied in the Constitution Act itself (Sections 111–121). A British subject domiciled in the United Kingdom will be exempt from the operation of any federal or provincial law that (a) imposes any restriction on the right of entry, or (b) imposes directly or indirectly "any disability, liability, restriction or condition in regard to travel, residence, the acquisition, holding, or disposal of property, the holding of public office, or the carrying on of any occupation, trade, business or profession." The right to impose quarantine regulations or to exclude or deport undesirable individuals will not be affected, however, and the privileges themselves may be wholly or partially suspended if the Governor-General of any province in his discretion certifies that it is necessary to prevent a grave menace to the peace or tranquility of any part of India or to combat crimes of violence intended to overthrow the government.

Discrimination in the field of federal or provincial taxation against British subjects domiciled in the United Kingdom or Burma or against companies incorporated by or under the laws of the United Kingdom or Burma is rigidly forbidden, and elaborate provisions are made to prevent discrimination of one kind or another against British investors as opposed to Indians. A company incorporated in the United Kingdom will, when trading in India, be deemed to have complied with the provisions of any Indian law relating to the place of incorporation of a company or the situation of its registered office or the place of birth, race, descent, language, religion, domicile, residence, or duration of residence of its directors, shareholders, officers, agents, or servants; and British subjects domiciled in the United Kingdom who are directors, shareholders, officers, agents, or servants of a company incorporated in India shall also be deemed to have complied with these provisions.

The mercantile marine problem is discussed in another chapter. It is sufficient here to say that Indian companies cannot compete successfully with the old established British lines, that the federal legislature, if it had the power, would undoubtedly restrict coastal traffic to Indian vessels, and finally that the political influence of the British shipping interests is irresistible. The act provides in substance that no ship registered in the United Kingdom shall be subjected to any treatment affecting either the ship itself or her master, officers, crew, passengers, or cargo, which is discriminatory in favor of ships registered in British India. The position of India in this respect will be worse than it is at the present time. A bill like that introduced by Mr. S. N. Haji into the Legislative Assembly in 1928 cannot be entertained by the federal legislature under the new Constitution.

A certain amount of discrimination will be permitted in the payment of subsidies or bounties out of public funds for the purpose of encouraging trade or industry in India, provided it is not *ex post facto* in its operation. The External Capital Committee recommended in 1925 that certain conditions might be attached to grants of this kind and it has been done in a few cases. Broadly speaking, three conditions are usually required: the company must be incorporated in India, it must have a certain proportion of Indians on its Board of Directors, and it must afford reasonable facilities for the training of Indians. These conditions are accepted in the Constitution Act, but a line is drawn between companies which were already engaged, at the date of the act which authorized the grants, in that branch of trade or industry which it is sought to encourage, and companies which engage in it subsequently. The former will receive the grant as a matter of course, but the latter will get it only if they comply with the conditions.

There are a few facts about these privileges which should be specially emphasized. In the first place, they are reciprocal, that is to say, they are to be enjoyed only on the condition that Indians and companies incorporated in India shall receive the same treatment in the United Kingdom. This being the case, a voluntary agreement would be more appropriate than a statutory enactment, but it would be difficult to secure because the advantages of reciprocity are obviously weighted in favor of the British. An Indian steamship company, for example, could never acquire a position in the coastal trade of the United Kingdom comparable to that held by the Peninsular and Oriental Steam Navigation Company and its subsidiaries in the coastal trade of India. The Constitution Act therefore puts the privileges on a statutory basis, although it provides that these sections may be suspended if His Majesty's government and the federal government of India should conclude a convention covering the points at issue and implement it by appropriate legislation. Another interesting fact is that, with the partial exception of Burma, the privileges are restricted to His Majesty's subjects domiciled in the United Kingdom and to companies incorporated in the United Kingdom. This was the subject of acrimonious debate in Parliament, but the government insisted that India should not be compelled to grant privileges to the Dominions or even to the Crown colonies and protectorates.

There are a number of restrictions on the freedom of discussion in the federal legislature. For example, the act forbids any discussion with respect to the conduct of a judge of the Federal Court or a High Court in the discharge of his duties; any discussion of, or the asking of questions about, a matter connected with an Indian State, other than a matter with respect to which the federal legislature has power to make laws for that state, unless the Governor-General in his discretion is satisfied that the matter affects federal interests or affects a British subject, and has given his consent to the matter being discussed or the question being asked; and, save with the consent of the Governor-General, the discussion of, or the asking of questions about (a) any matter connected with the relations between His Majesty or the Governor-General and any foreign state or prince, (b) any action taken in his discretion by the Governor-General in relation to the affairs of a province, or (c) the personal conduct of the ruler of any Indian State or of a member of his family. Matters connected with the tribal areas and the administration of excluded areas also belong in this category, although they may be discussed in relation to the estimates of expenditure. Finally, if the Governor-General certifies that the discussion of any bill introduced or proposed to be introduced in the federal legislature, or of any amendment moved or proposed to be moved, will affect the discharge of his special responsibility for the prevention of any grave menace to the peace or tranquility of India or any part thereof, he may in his discretion direct that no proceedings or no further proceedings shall be taken in relation to the said bill or amendment.

This is a good illustration of the fact that the special responsibilities of the Governor-General are intended to be used in the legislative as well as in the executive field. A list of his special responsibilities has already been given. The legislative aspect of (e), which deals mainly with commercial discrimination, is so important that it fills more than half the space in the Constitution Act devoted to legislative powers.

BIBLIOGRAPHICAL NOTE

THE bibliographies in *The Cambridge History of India* (6 vols., 1922–37) are indispensable. The last two volumes covering the period of European intervention may also be obtained as Volumes IV and V of *The Cambridge History of the British Empire.*

Most of the manuscript sources are deposited in the India Office in London and in the various Record Offices in India, but there are also many documents in the British Museum and the Public Record Office. Students who are interested in the history of the East India Company owe a special debt of gratitude to Sir William Foster for his *Guide to the India Office Records,* 1600–1858 (1919). S. A. Khan's *Sources for the History of British India in the Seventeenth Century* (1926) is also valuable, especially for the documents in the British Museum.

Some of the early material has been published either in whole or in an abridged form. *English Factories in India,* 1618–69, edited by Sir William Foster (13 vols. and a supplementary volume, 1906–28), *Calendar of State Papers, East Indies,* 1513–1634, edited by W. N. Sainsbury (5 vols., 1862–92), and *Court Minutes, etc., of the East India Company,* 1635–79, edited by Miss E. B. Sainsbury (10 vols., 1902–35, in progress) are worthy of special mention. A new series of *English Factories in India,* edited by Sir Charles Fawcett, was begun in 1936. The first volume deals with the Western or Bombay Presidency from 1670 to 1677. Professor H. H. Dodwell and Mr. K. Krishnaswami have also edited and published most of the early records of the Madras Presidency. The eighteenth century has been somewhat neglected, but a tremendous mass of material has been printed in the Parliamentary Papers and other official publications since the beginning of the nineteenth century. The best guides are the *Annual Lists and General Index of the Parliamentary Papers Relating to the East Indies Published during the Years 1801 to 1907, Inclusive* (Parliamentary Papers, 1909, LXIV, 757–1000) and the annual indices to the Parliamentary Papers for the period since

1907. One of the most valuable official publications is the annual *Statement Exhibiting the Moral and Material Progress and Condition of India,* which is usually prepared at the India Office from data furnished by the authorities in India.

James Mill is perhaps the best known among the older historians of India. His *History of British India,* published in three volumes in 1817, attracted wide attention and won him a post in the service of the Company. The best edition is the fifth, with notes and continuation by H. H. Wilson (10 vols., 1858). Robert Orme wrote a *History of the Military Transactions of the British Nation in Indostan* (4th ed., 3 vols., 1803) and made a collection of military documents which is now one of the prize possessions of the India Office. Sir William Hunter is best known as the original editor of *The Imperial Gazetteer* (3d ed., 26 vols., 1908–9), but his *History of British India* (2 vols., 1899–1900) is very good for the period before 1708. There is also valuable material in Mountstuart Elphinstone's *History of India* (1839, 9th ed., 1905), Edward Thornton's *History of the British Empire in India* (6 vols., 1841), John C. Marshman's *History of India from the Earliest Period to the Close of Lord Dalhousie's Administration* (3 vols., 1867), Henry Beveridge's *Comprehensive History of India, Civil, Military and Social* (3 vols., 1867), and Sir Alfred Lyall's *Rise and Expansion of the British Dominion in India* (1894). On the administrative side the outstanding books are John Bruce's *Annals of the East India Company* (3 vols., 1810), Peter Auber's *Analysis of the Constitution of the East India Company* (1826), Sir George Chesney's *Indian Polity: A View of the System of Administration in India* (1868, 3d ed., 1894), Sir John Strachey's *India, Its Character and Progress* (1888, 4th ed. revised by Sir Thomas Holderness, 1911), and Sir Courtenay Ilbert's *Government of India* (1898).

The Cambridge History of India covers the whole field from the earliest times down to the publication of *The Montagu-Chelmsford Report* in 1918. Professor H. H. Dodwell, the editor of the last two volumes, was for several years a member of the Indian Educational Service and Curator of the Madras Record Office and is now Professor of the History and Culture of the British Dominions in Asia, in the University of London. His chief associates were P. E. Roberts, Fellow of Worcester College,

Oxford, and Sir H. Verney Lovett, K.C.S.I., late Reader in Indian History in the University of Oxford. Chapters were also contributed by Sir Richard Burn, C.S.T., C.V.O., Dean Hutton of Winchester, and a number of other specialists. This is the best work on the subject, but it lacks unity, follows too closely the bureaucratic tradition, and is too technical and full of administrative details to interest the general reader. It also neglects the Indian side of the medal to a very large degree and is inadequate in its treatment of economic conditions. *The Cambridge Shorter History of India* (1934) is open to similar criticism, although the modern part, written by Professor Dodwell, is better than the earlier sections. The average reader is likely to be more interested in Sir Valentine Chirol's *India* ("Modern World Series," 1926), or in Edward Thompson and G. T. Garratt's *Rise and Fulfilment of British Rule in India* (1934). He might also read with pleasure and profit W. H. Moreland and A. C. Chatterjee's *Short History of India* (1936), which has some stimulating chapters on the evolution of Indian culture, and A. B. Keith's *Constitutional History of India*, 1600–1935 (1936), which arouses interest in a technical subject without any sacrifice of scholarship.

There is a large and growing literature on the Indian States. The records of the Political Department of the government of India are not generally accessible, but a great deal of material is published in the Parliamentary Papers. The standard edition of the treaties between the states and the British authorities is Sir Charles Aitchison's *Collection of Treaties, Engagements and Sanads Relating to India and Neighbouring Countries* (7 vols., 1862–65; 4th ed., 9 vols., 1909). The first serious attempt to rationalize the doctrine of paramount power was made by Sir Charles Lewis Tupper in a book entitled *Our Indian Protectorate*, published in 1893. His argument was based on feudal principles and was applied to all of the states without regard to size or treaty obligations. The official view is better expressed in Sir William Lee-Warner's *Native States of India*, published in 1910 as a revised edition of *The Protected Princes of India* (1894). He follows Sir Henry Maine in rejecting the Austinian doctrine of sovereignty and treats the states as semi-sovereign bodies, although he admits that the division of powers has never been defined in any statute or collection of rules and implies that "these matters are . . . best left alone as the mysteries of the trade" (p. 2). He also weakens his argument by claiming such extensive power for the Crown that there is very little left for the princes. His work is a masterpiece of erudition, however, and is still regarded as the best treatment of the subject as a whole.

The revival of interest in constitutional reform which began about 1927 has led to the publication of a large number of books dealing with the states and their relations with British India. Mr. K. M. Panikkar's *Introduction to the Study of the Relations of Indian States with the Government of India* (1927) is the best work on the subject by an Indian student. Although it is favorable to the princes, the Standing Committee of the Chamber of Princes decided that a more vigorous statement of their position was needed and Sir Leslie (now Lord Justice) Scott was employed to prepare it. His brief, which was published in 1929, is entitled *The British Crown and the Indian States: An Outline Sketch Drawn up on Behalf of the Standing Committee of the Chamber of Princes*. This is an argument that the rights and privileges of the states are inherent and a plea that treaty obligations should be more rigidly observed. The same ideas are expressed with stronger emotional fervor by A. P. Nicholson in *Scraps of Paper: India's Broken Treaties* (1930). *The Report of the Indian States Committee*, commonly called the Butler Committee (1929), is a statement of the official point of view. It upholds the doctrine of paramount authority without attempting to define it and gives the princes a guarantee that they shall "not be transferred without their own agreement to a relationship with a new government in British India responsible to an Indian legislature." P. L. Chudgar's *Indian Princes under British Protection: A Study of Their Personal Rule, Their Constitutional Position and Their Future* (1929) is a plea that the people of the states should be relieved from the inefficient and autocratic government of their hereditary rulers. Sir Sidney Low's *Indian States and Ruling Princes* (1929), D. K. Sem's *Indian States: Their Status, Rights and Obligations* (1930), G. N. Singh's *Indian States and British India: Their Future Relations* (1930), Sir George MacMunn's *Indian States and Princes* (1936), and N. D. Varadacharia's *Indian State in the Federation* (1937) should also be mentioned. Mr. Varadacharia accepts the Austinian doctrine and argues that the states do not have any sovereign rights because sovereignty is indivisible and unlimited.

Most of the biographies of the British rulers of India were written in a partisan spirit and without access to all of the material that is now available. Although some of the Lives in the "Rulers of India Series" are good, they are too short to permit an adequate treatment of the subject. The two great pioneers have fared better than most of their successors. There may still be a few blemishes on the character of Lord Clive, but Warren Hastings has become the idol of the new generation of Imperial historians. Sir George Forrest's *Life of Lord Clive* (2 vols., 1918) is badly arranged and the copious extracts from the sources are likely to bore the general reader, but it is based on wide research and is full of meat for the specialist. Professor Dodwell's *Dupleix and Clive: The Beginnings of Empire* (1920) is equally erudite and more readable. The rehabilitation of Hastings was begun by Sir James Stephen, *Nuncomar and Impey* (2 vols., 1885) and Sir John Strachey, *Hastings and the Rahilla War* (1892) and was continued in later years by G. W. Hastings, *Vindication of Warren Hastings* (1909), M. E. Monckton-Jones, *Hastings in Bengal,* 1772–74 (1918), Sophia Weitzman, *Warren Hastings and Philip Francis* (1929), and A. M. Davies, *Warren Hastings: Maker of British India* (1935). Miss Monckton-Jones called attention to the tendency of the older historians and biographers to emphasize the dramatic episodes of Hastings' life and to neglect his marvelous work as an administrator. Mr. Davies' book is a survey and a defense of his hero's career based on a careful study of the sources. Some of the material which he uses has been made generally accessible by Sir George Forrest in *Selections from the Letters, Despatches and Other State Papers Preserved in the Foreign Department of the Government of India,* 1772–85 (3 vols., 1890) and *Selections from the State Papers of the Governor-General of India: Warren Hastings* (2 vols., 1910).

There are very few good biographies of the other Governors-General for the period before the Mutiny, but a large part of their correspondence and official papers has been published. See, for example, Charles Ross, *Correspondence of Charles 1st Marquis Cornwallis* (3 vols., 1859), R. R. Pearce, *Memoirs and Correspondence of . . . Richard Marquess Wellesley* (3 vols., 1846), and Montgomery Martin, *Despatches, Minutes and Correspondence of Marquess Wellesley* (5 vols., 1836). P. E. Roberts' *India under Wellesley* (1929) is useful. For Lord Minto, see *Life and Letters of Sir Gilbert Elliott*, 1751–1806 (3 vols., 1874) and *Lord Minto in India* (1880), both edited by his grandniece, the Countess of Minto. There is valuable material for the history of Lord Hastings' administration in his *Private Journal* (2 vols., 1858) and in H. T. Prinsep's *History of the Political and Military Transactions in India during the Administration of the Marquess of Hastings*, 1813–23 (2 vols., 1825). The Governors-General from Hastings to Dalhousie, 1823–48, have been sadly neglected, although there are numerous works dealing with the military history of that period. There is some interesting personal material about Lord Auckland in *Up the Country* (2 vols., 1866) and *Letters from India* (2 vols., 1872) written by his sister, Miss Emily Eden. Lord Colchester's *History of the Indian Administration of Lord Ellenborough* (1874), Sir Algernon Law's *India under Lord Ellenborough* (1926), and Lord Hardinge's *Viscount Hardinge* (1900) should also be mentioned. *The Marquis of Dalhousie's Administration of British India* by Sir Edwin Arnold (2 vols., 1862) has been in large measure superseded by Sir William Lee-Warner's excellent life of the *Marquis of Dalhousie* (2 vols., 1904). *The Private Letters of the Marquess of Dalhousie*, edited by J. G. Baird, was published in 1910.

The post of Governor-General has nearly always been filled, not by promotion, but by sending out an aristocrat or a politician who has won his reputation in England. Owing to his lack of Indian experience, he is sometimes more or less overshadowed by some of his official subordinates. There was a remarkable group of men in the service of the Company during the generation before the Mutiny, none of whom reached the highest post except Lord Lawrence and he was not promoted until after the period was over (1864–69). Most of these men have been the subjects of interesting and valuable biographies. Among the best are the lives of Charles, Lord Metcalfe (2 vols., 1854, revised ed., 1858), Sir John Nicholson (2 vols., 1856) and Sir John Malcolm (2 vols., 1856) by J. W. Kaye; of Mountstuart Elphinstone by Sir H. T. Colebrooke (2 vols., 1884); of Sir Thomas Munro by G. R. Gleig (3 vols., 1830) and John Bradshaw (1906); of Sir Charles

Napier by Sir William Napier (4 vols., 1857) and T. Rice Holmes (1925); of Sir Henry Lawrence by Sir H. B. Edwardes; and of Lord Lawrence by R. Bosworth Smith (2 vols., 1883). F. P. Gibbon, *The Lawrences in the Punjab* (1908) and J. L. Morison, *Lawrence of Lucknow, 1806–1857: The Life of Sir Henry Lawrence* (1934) are also worthy of mention.

INDEX